SINGING the SONGS
of MY ANCESTORS

The Civilization of the American
Indian Series

Helma Swan (1918–2002)

SINGING the SONGS of MY ANCESTORS

THE LIFE AND MUSIC OF HELMA SWAN, MAKAH ELDER

By Linda J. Goodman and Helma Swan

Foreword by Bill Holm

University of Oklahoma Press : Norman

Publication of this book is made possible through the
generosity of Edith Kinney Gaylord.

LIBRARY OF CONGRESS CATALOGING-IN-PUBLICATION DATA

Goodman, Linda, 1943–
    Singin the songs of my ancestors : the life and music of Helma
Swan, Makah elder / by Linda J. Goodman ; foreword by Bill Holm.
        p.   cm.   — (The civilization of the American Indian series ; v. 244)
    Includes bibliographical references and index.

    1. Ward, Helma. 2. Makah Indians—Biography. 3. Makah Indians—
Music. 4. Makah Indians—Social life and customs. I. Title. II. Series.

E99.M19 W317 2002
781.62'979—dc21   20020202070

ISBN 978-0-8061-3451-2 (hardcover)
ISBN 978-0-8061-6868-5 (paper)

Singing the Songs of My Ancestors: The Life and Music of Helma Swan, Makah Elder
is Volume 244 in The Civilization of the American Indian Series.

Frontispiece. Helma Swan (1918–2002) working on a linguistics project at the
Makah Cultural and Research Center, Neah Bay, Wash., Oct. 13, 1998.
Photograph by Linda J. Goodman.

Indian women are the reason we have survived.

SHERMAN ALEXIE
Spokane Indian writer
March 12, 1995

CONTENTS

ILLUSTRATIONS

MAPS

SONG TRANSCRIPTIONS

FOREWORD

By Bill Holm

In 1974, when Linda Goodman first headed out to the Washington Coast to find a source of information on Northwest Coast Indian music for her planned doctoral dissertation, she had no idea that trip would lead to a long and deep personal relationship with a Makah woman whose life story is the subject of this book. The book is about music, but music is more than entertainment in Northwest Coast cultures. It is intimately bound up with family histories and prerogative, with rank and privilege, with family solidarity and inter- and intratribal rivalries. The story of music became a complex and intimate account of Makah life in the twentieth century from the viewpoint of a woman of noble heritage who wanted her knowledge recorded and trusted Linda Goodman to do it.

Helma Swan is the daughter and granddaughter of chiefs. Her story is about chiefly prerogatives and relationships. But it is also about everyday Makah life in a time that saw great prejudice and suppression of Native ways by church and government, the loss of traditions, economic hardship, and cultural disintegration. The fact that Makah culture survived as well as it did is due in no small measure to the persistence and strength of a few strong traditionalists like Helma Swan who lived to see a day when it was no longer disgraceful to be an Indian.

Linda Goodman and Helma Swan became fast friends. They were no longer the ethnomusicologist and the Native informant. Linda's stays in Neah Bay immersed her in everyday life and in the intensity of potlatch preparation. The record she made of Helma Swan's life is an intimate view of a Native woman coping with and adapting to a time of great transition. It's also the story of the survival and the revitalization of Makah culture.

ACKNOWLEDGMENTS

Thanks are due to many individuals and institutions who aided in the completion of this work. The contributions of all who have been involved are gratefully acknowledged. Any inadvertent omissions or inaccuracies lie with the authors.

First and foremost, I would like to thank Helma Swan for so generously sharing her knowledge, understanding, and cultural insights, which, along with her initial request and motivation, were responsible for the development of this book. Her friendship, fine sense of humor, and unflagging enthusiasm made our work time a delight and helped us weather life's inevitable hard times. Her family, also, has been most supportive over the years, especially her three children: Arnie Hunter, Babe (Lina Mae) Hunter Markishtum, and Mike Hunter; and her husband of almost thirty-eight years, Oliver Ward, Jr., who passed away in June 1997. All gave freely of their time and provided invaluable help and information.

Northwest Coast Indian knowledge and support was generously supplied by Lilly Bell Williams,* Queets and Hoh River; Pansy Hudson,* La Push and Hoh River; Ruth Anderson Swan,* Muzzie Claplanhoo,* Meredith Parker,* Tom Parker,* Shine Wilkie,* Nora Barker,* Helen Peterson,* Harry Bowechop,* Jill Markishtum, Ron Markishtum, Jr.,* Marcy Parker, and John McCarty, all from Neah Bay; John Thomas* and Kelly Peters,* Nitinat, B.C. ; Edith Simon* and Odelia David Hunter,* Clayoquot, B.C. ; Peter Webster* and Johnnie Jacobson,* Ahouset, B.C. ; Harry Dick* and daughter Dora Dick Sanvidge, Gold River, B.C. , but living in Oyster River, B.C. in 1982; Jimmy John* and son Norman John, Gold River, B.C. , but living in Nanaimo, B.C. in 1982; Benny Jack, Gold River, B.C. ; Chief Adam Shewish,* Margaret Shewish,* and Ed Shewish,* Port Alberni, B.C.

Assistance was much appreciated from former and present Makah Cultural and Research Center staff: Greig Arnold, Ann Renker, Janine Bowechop, Maria Parker Pascua, Cora Buttram, Melissa Peterson, Yvonne Burkett, Kirk and Debby Wachendorf, Bobby Rose, Theresa Parker, and Keely Parker.

Knowledgeable dialogue and expert guidance came from special teachers, mentors, and friends: Bill Holm, Professor Emeritus, University of Washington; Louis A. Hieb, former Director, Center for Southwest Research, University of New Mexico Library; Charlie* and Libby Peck, formerly of Queets, Washington; Hope Merrin, Santa Fe, New Mexico; Stuart Martz, Santa Fe, New Mexico; and Laura Holt, Museum of New Mexico. Academic, musical, linguistic, and general manuscript assistance was generously provided by Richard Daugherty, Professor Emeritus, Washington State University; B.A. Nugent, former Dean, Washington State

University; Helmuth Naumer,* former New Mexico Officer of Cultural Affairs; Timothy Maxwell, Director, Office of Archaeological Studies, Museum of New Mexico; David P. McAllester, Professor Emeritus, Wesleyan University, Connecticut; Loran Olsen, Professor Emeritus, Washington State University; Matt Davidson, State University of New York, Buffalo; Robin Wright, University of Washington; Kate Duncan, Arizona State University; Albert Seay,* Professor Emeritus, Colorado College; Carlton Gamer, Professor Emeritus, Colorado College; Michael Hoffman, Colorado College; Michael Nowak, Professor Emeritus, Colorado College; Ray Druian, formerly of Chico State University; Richard Keeling, formerly of UCLA; Wes Weir, Professor Emeritus, University of Washington; Ivan Doig, Seattle writer; Susan Libonati-Barnes, University of Washington; and Daisy Levine, formerly of the Museum of New Mexico. Many thanks to Susan Zeni, Carol Erickson, and Mary Jo Janowsky at Colorado College, who typed the tape transcripts.

This project could not have been completed without the help of the following librarians, archivists, curators, and institutions: Maxine Miller, Port Angeles Public Library; Karyl Winn, Gary Lundell, Janet Ness, and Nan Cohen, Manuscripts and University Archives Division, University of Washington Libraries, Seattle; Richard Engeman, University of Washington Special Collections, Seattle; David Piff and Joyce Justice, Sandpoint Federal Archives and Records Center, Seattle; Vince Kueter and Gayle Palmer, Washington State Library, Olympia; Laura Holt and Mara Yarbrough, Laboratory of Anthropology Library, Museum of New Mexico; Johanna Humphrey and Felicia Pickering, Smithsonian Institution, Washington, D.C.; the Provincial Archives of British Columbia, Victoria; and the Jefferson County Historical Society, Port Townsend, Wash.

Help from the following photo librarians, photo archivists, and photographers is also greatly appreciated: Carolyn Marr, Museum of History and Industry Library, Seattle; Elaine Miller, Washington State Historical Society Library, Tacoma; Rod Slemmons, University of Washington; Daisy Njoku, National Anthropological Archives, Smithsonian Institution; Dave Burgevin, Office of Photographic Services, Smithsonian Institution; Kris Kinsey and Nicolette Bromberg, University of Washington Libraries; Kathryn Bridge, British Columbia Archives; Dan Savard, Royal British Columbia Museum; Mardell Lloyd, North Olympic Library System, Port Angeles, Washington; Ed Hosselkus, Port Angeles photographer; John Vavruska, Santa Fe photographer; Ron Mizia, Idaho Falls, Idaho photographer; Pat Smith, Smith Western Post Card Company, Tacoma, Washington.

Funding, grant, and institutional support are gratefully acknowledged from the following: Washington State University Graduate Student Summer Research Travel Grant, 1974; WSU Research Assistantship, 1974–75; a series of Colorado College Humanities Faculty Summer Research Grants, 1970s and 1980s; American Council of Learned Societies Fellowship, 1982–83; and a leave of absence from my position

Acknowledgments

as Ethnohistorian, Office of Archaeological Studies, Museum of New Mexico, 1993–94.

Others who were consulted and willingly contributed their knowledge include: Laila La Due, Branch Chief for Titles and Records, BIA Portland Area Office; Betty Scissons, Title Government Services Office, BIA Portland Area Office; David Buerge, Catholic Historian, Seattle; Chris Taylor, Archivist, Catholic Archdiocese, Seattle; Vera McIver, Volunteer Archivist, Catholic Diocese, Victoria, B.C. ; Father Lacelles, Archivist, Oblate Provincial House, Vancouver, B.C., Father Jack Ryan, St. Francis of Assisi, Tofino, B.C. ; Marina Ochoa, Archivist, Catholic Archdiocese, Santa Fe, New Mexico; Kathy Erickson, Kakawis Christian Family Community Center, Meares Island, British Columbia; and Gene Joseph, Union of British Columbia Indian Chiefs, Vancouver, British Columbia.

Thanks is also due to others in Seattle who have supported the project in various ways over the years: Lorna and Bob Butler; Carolyn Berg; Toni Carmichael and Gary Larson; Arlene Segal; Helen Arrowsmith; Lois Hartzell; Mary Pierce; Paul McCaw; and Paul Karaitis.

A project such as this could never have been completed without the loving support of my family, who read, edited, criticized, offered suggestions, discussed ideas, and generally provided strength and encouraging words when energy or enthusiasm flagged. Heartfelt thanks go to my parents Nelson and Florence* Goodman, brother Michael Goodman, sister Nancy Goodman-Waldman, and to my dearest and most patient husband, Loren Jacobson. All were great sources of inspiration, especially in the later stages, as the work neared completion.

I am most appreciative of the help and support provided by John Drayton, Director; Sarah Nestor, former Managing Editor; Jo Ann Reece, Acquisitions Editor; Shelia L. Buckley; and other staff of the University of Oklahoma Press. Their knowledge, assistance, and guidance have been essential in creating the final version of this work.

Finally, I would like to express my gratitude to the Makah tribe for allowing me to live on the reservation and participate in many activities and events over the years, thus providing an opportunity to learn and come to understand and appreciate many things about the Makah way of life, first-hand. As for Helma Swan, I hope this work captures the essence of many of the stories she has longed to tell, and that it also provides her with a vehicle to continue the teaching which she feels is so central to the survival of her family, her tribe, the music, and a unique way of life.

* Deceased.

MAKAH
PRONUNCIATION
GUIDE

VOWELS

Short		*Long*			*Dipthongs*		
a	as in cut	a· or aa	as in father		ai	as in high
e	as in bet	e· or ee	as in cat		ey	as in ate
i	as in bit	i· or ii	as in beet		—	
o	as in for	o· or oo	as in hello		oy	as in boy
u	as in look	u· or uu	as in moon		uy	as in buoy

CONSONANTS

b, t, k, p, d, s, m, n, w, l, y, h   are pronounced as in English

ts	as in	cats
č or ch	as in	church
š or sh	as in	ship

SIDE SOUNDS

ł   (barred l) is an l sound made by blowing air around
the sides of the tongue

ƛ   (barred lambda) combines the tl sound as in the word "cattle,"
with the ł sound as in "Tlingit"

DEEP SOUNDS

x   a sound made by rasping air through the roof of the mouth,
as in the name "Bach"

x̌   a sound made by rasping air farther back in the throat than is
done for the x.   x̌ is almost a gargling sound

q   is a k sound, but made farther back in the throat than the x̌ sound

ROUNDED SOUND

w   is made by rounding the lips. It can be attached to the
     following consonants: kʷ, qʷ, xʷ, x̌ʷ

GLOTTAL

ʔ   is a glottal stop that precedes a vowel and creates a pause or catch
     in the throat, as in <u>Uh Oh</u>*!*
’   is a glottal mark which is placed adjacent to a consonant, creating a
     "pop-like" sound of that letter. The sound is louder and is made with
     more air and force. The following consonants can be glottalized or
     "popped": ts’ č’ k’ kʷ’ λ’ q’ qʷ’ p’ t’

ACCENT OR STRESS

’   placed over a vowel indicates that this syllable is accented, as in "Makáh"

Source: This pronunciation guide is based on an unpublished work, "Qʷi·qʷi·dič̌čaq, Makah
Alphabet Pronunciation Key," Makah Language Program, Makah Culture and Research
Center, Neah Bay, Washington. No date. Linguist Matt Davidson (personal communication;
October 8, 1998), also advised on this guide.

PART 1

THE
MAKAH
PEOPLE

INTRODUCTION

FIRST ENCOUNTERS

As I guided my beat-up white '59 Chevy through the twists and turns of the only blacktopped road leading through the western part of the Olympic rain forest in Washington State, my mind touched on a thousand different thoughts and images—what incredibly beautiful country! A native of Colorado, I had never seen forests such as these—the profuse growth, thick, rich, soft looking; fallen trees, rotting trees, new trees growing out of dead trunks, the smell of decaying organic material blowing in through the open window. I felt the wonderful dampness of the air, watched the sun suddenly bursting forth and filtering through the hanging moss on hoary dead trees, occasionally sending intense shafts of sunlight piercing through the darkness, creating dazzling bursts of color. The ocean, glimpsed now and then whenever the road came close enough, on this day looked blue and deceptively calm as it lolled in the vaguely warm October sun.

It was fall 1974, and I was on my way from the small Quileute Indian village of Queets to the Makah Indian village[1] of Neah Bay, Washington, to begin a project that would ultimately result in my Ph.D. dissertation in 1978 and, many years later, this book. Much had happened preceding this sunny autumn day when I was finally on my way to a new adventure.

In June 1974 at the urging of Loran Olsen, Professor of Music at Washington State University, I visited Libby and Charlie Peck at their home near Queets, Washington. Charlie, retired from the WSU Extension Service, was a photographer and gardener at the time. His wife, Libby, worked as a reading teacher at the Queets-Clearwater Grade School. Both were well liked, respected, and accepted by the Indian people on the western Washington coast, and Loran Olsen thought I should talk to them, since I was planning a project on Northwest Coast Indian music for my Ph.D. dissertation. There was an almost immediate rapport between the Pecks and myself, and the exchange of thoughts and ideas was comfortable and productive.

They suggested that I talk to Helma Swan Ward,[2] a Makah woman from Neah Bay, who they felt was one of the most knowledgeable people in the area. As the daughter of a chief, she had learned a great deal about the customs, songs, and dances of her family and her people from her father, her grandparents, and other friends and relatives. That June, Libby Peck and I made a trip up the coast to Neah Bay, about one hundred miles north, to visit with Helma and to discuss with her the knowledge she had and the project I wished to undertake.

Helma was warm and hospitable as she greeted us in the living room of her weathered wood house, which sat nondescriptly on Bay View Street, just across the road from the beach, in Neah Bay. As we shared coffee and cake, I explained my project to Helma, told her I was interested in learning about the music of her people, knew she was most knowledgeable about it, and explained that I would like to work with her if she was interested. I emphasized that this would be a joint project, one I hoped she would want to undertake. She told me she needed to think about it and talk with her sisters and the rest of her family before she could make a decision. I understood, said that I was going away for the summer but would contact her when I returned in the fall.

In early September I called Helma and subsequently visited her a number of times while staying with the Pecks near Queets. She was still undecided. She needed more time. She hadn't yet been able to talk to her sisters. Later, she told me that she knew and trusted Libby Peck but had to make up her mind about me. She had to see and talk with me enough to decide if I were reliable and honest and could be trusted with her material.

Finally, during a telephone conversation in mid-October 1974, Helma told me that she'd been looking for a place for me to stay in Neah Bay so she and I could work together. I was very pleased and greatly relieved. Now I knew we could actually begin. At first, we planned to record her family-owned songs and stories and put together her knowledge of Makah traditions and music. This was the project that she wanted us to undertake. Later, I had to change the focus in order to write an acceptable Ph.D. dissertation, but told her we would return to her family history and personal life story, including the music, as soon as possible after the dissertation was finished. In the summer of 1979, we began serious collaboration on her life history—work that has continued sporadically ever since.

Over the years a close friendship has developed between the two of us, and we have shared many professional as well as personal activities and experiences. During the 1970s and 1980s, while teaching ethnomusicology at Colorado College, I brought Helma to Colorado Springs a number of times so she could help teach a course on American Indian music. She became a favorite of the students as well as the Indian community of Colorado Springs. Many looked forward to her visits, which usually included public music and storytelling performances. The Colorado Springs Public Schools also hired her to teach several classes each time she was in town. She looked forward to her Colorado trips as "vacations from the Northwest Coast," which offered her a chance to "dry out her webbed feet," as she described it, referring to the incredible rainfall of the Olympic Peninsula, which averages about one hundred inches per year.

Helma originally asked that this project be undertaken so that all her family's songs and stories would be permanently recorded for posterity, and also so no one else in Neah Bay could try to claim them. As treasured parts of the family's heritage, these privately owned pieces of personal property must be passed solely to the next generation of Swan family descendants. Since Charlie Swan, Helma's father, was descended from two Makah chiefs (Peter Brown and Yelák'ub) and one Canadian chief (Cedakanim or Sitkeenum), there were many stories to tell and much to be preserved. There was also an interesting connection between Charlie Swan, his mother, Ellen Swan, and the white man, James G. Swan, who had worked in Neah Bay for a number of years and was a great friend and supporter of several Makah families. All of this in combination with Helma's strict, traditional Makah education, created a rich body of material on which to draw.

This book is the result of more than twenty years of intermittent collaborative work. Part of the information was collected during my 1974–75 stay in Neah Bay; part during my sabbatical year in 1982–83, with the aid of a generous grant from the American Council of Learned Societies; and a portion during return trips to Neah Bay over many summers, several of which were supported by Colorado College Faculty Research Grants. Some of the information was gathered when Helma came to Colorado Springs; a portion, when I was in Seattle and Helma came to stay with me there. There have been many interruptions, mostly involving jobs and families. My teaching job at Colorado College, which began in 1975, and a move to a new job at the Museum of New Mexico in 1987 created additional delays. Helma has continued to live in Neah Bay, and since 1980 has worked at the Makah Cultural and Research Center, undertaking a variety of linguistic and cultural projects. In 1993–94, a leave of absence from my position as ethnohistorian in the Office of Archaeological Studies at the Museum of New Mexico allowed me to complete the library and archival research, and, together with Helma Swan, to finish a first draft of this manuscript.

PRESENTATION OF LIFE HISTORY
MATERIAL AND RELATED DATA

Helma and I had several goals in the creation of this work. She wanted to tell her story in her own words, validate her family's rights to particular ceremonial property, and at the same time leave a written record about Makah music. I wanted to place her story in an appropriate cultural, historical, and musical context so the general non-Makah reader could envision the larger picture from which one woman's life and traditions emerged. We worked together to accomplish these goals and ended up with a book divided into three parts.

Part 1 presents a number of background topics in this introduction, followed in chapter 1 by a discussion of various elements of Makah culture, history, and music. Part 2, Helma's story, is told in her own words, roughly in chronological order. This is not the way we recorded it. In the taped interviews, we began with one subject, which often led her to another topic, sometimes related, sometimes not. The process became almost "stream of consciousness" at times. Therefore, material from the tapes had to be edited and reorganized before publication. We discussed how best to do this and decided on a presentation that began with her birth and early years (chapters 2 and 3) and then moved through later times and events she considered important (chapters 4–9). Because music was such a central part of her life as well as her father's before her, she felt it essential to include as much of this information as possible (chapters 5–8). Other portions of her story (chapters 4 and 9) do not relate primarily to musical events; rather they show Helma as a Makah woman trying to live in two worlds, and as a person who has faced the same joys and sorrows that have always been a part of the human condition.

Part 3 is devoted entirely to music. Chapter 10 includes discussion, translation, transcription, and analysis of ten songs owned and sung by Helma Swan. Thus, the tone of each part of the book is different, but all parts are intended to be complementary. Together, Helma and I reviewed, discussed, read, and reread the entire body of material presented here. Clearly, we influenced each other throughout.[3]

Most of the archival data and stories of Swan family ancestors, which help validate Helma's claim to songs and other ceremonial property, may be found in Appendix B (following the family genealogical charts in Appendix A). Helma specifically wanted this information included because it ties actual persons to her family history and to the ownership of the songs. These stories (aside from breathing life into some of her relatives who have only been names until now) help her explain who she is, who her ancestors were, her connections to them, and her rights to their songs. She considers the published stories, as well as excerpts from James G. Swan's journals and the compiled documentary evidence, to be essential additions to her own story. Without these written records, she must rely solely on the oral tradition, which no longer provides adequate proof of relationship and ownership in the modern world.

Because the taping of oral interviews for this project has been ongoing for over twenty years, it was inevitable that repetition of some stories and events would occur. It is noteworthy that Helma told the same stories and recalled the same details even though she may have stated them ten or fifteen years apart, so that one version of a story is almost identical to another. This speaks to the effectiveness of the oral tradition and the method of rote learning. It is also an indication of Helma's excellent memory. In order to eliminate repetition, the best parts of each account of the same event have been selected and combined into one version, presented here. Repetition of words or phrases within a particular story does occur as part of Helma's manner of speaking. We felt it important to maintain this element of her storytelling style. The basic English and Makah vocabularies have been kept essentially intact; however, some grammatical editing has been done while trying to retain, as much as possible, the flavor of English in the Makah style.

METHODS USED IN GATHERING THE MATERIAL

Interviews

In early December 1974, Helma Swan Ward and I began a series of tape recorded interviews in Neah Bay. Working either in her living room or in my one-room apartment located on the nearby public school grounds, we soon established good rapport, trust, and respect for each other's knowledge and ideas. At first, we discussed Makah music and customs in general, then we moved to more specific aspects that had affected and shaped Helma's life and the lives of her siblings. All of our interviews were conducted in English; however, since Helma is one of the few remaining speakers of the Makah language, we decided to include Makah terms where appropriate in her narrative.

Flexible interview sessions allowed us to deal with whatever material was relevant at the time. Casual and enjoyable, our discussions sometimes brought back nostalgic memories and at other times raised questions not previously considered. I found that asking leading questions about certain topics offered Helma the option of responding with either long or short answers, which sometimes led to other topics she wished to discuss. While recording, I always took handwritten notes, thus creating a rough outline of the subjects covered on each tape. This method also allowed me the opportunity to write down relevant Makah terms. Since Helma was not comfortable recording or even talking about her life, family, and music when others were present, we made tape recordings only when we were alone. Her immediate family was aware of our project, but even they were seldom present while we were working. Over a thousand typed pages of tape transcripts currently exist. Occasionally Helma asked me to turn off the tape recorder when she was speaking about especially sensitive topics. At times she allowed me to write some of this information in my notes; at other times she did not. I always honored her wishes. None of the material she considers sensitive is included in this book.

I made an effort to corroborate particular kinds of information and stories that Helma told me. Interviews or casual conversations with various elders in Neah Bay, Hoh, Queets, and La Push, Washington, and with elders and tribal historians from a number of tribes along the west coast of Vancouver Island often supported Helma's statements.[4] Because she did not want others to know about this project, I was rarely able to take notes during these conversations and few of them were recorded. I wrote about them in my daily journal, after the fact. Various pieces of information on music, ceremonies, organization of the society, ways of passing on the traditions, family relationships, and so forth, were, however, verified in this fashion. People who knew Charlie Swan, Helma's father, remembered the time he was made a chief; they also stated that they had heard her father sing and had seen Helma, as a child, dance many times at potlatches. They spoke freely of these events and sometimes recalled the specific circumstances. Few of their children knew of these activities and their significance, and, in fact, as the elders shared their knowledge with Helma and me, their descendants heard some of these stories for the first time. All of these old people have passed away since we talked with them in the late 1970s and early 1980s.

Participant-Observation

The participant-observer method of fieldwork involves living and being actively involved in the community, and also observing and writing about one's experiences. While living in Neah Bay in 1974–75, and on numerous return trips, I participated in many Makah activities and kept a daily journal in which I described people I met, events, activities, recording sessions, and so forth. Because I did not want to just take information from Helma and the Makah people, I felt it was also important to give whatever I could in return. Therefore, I sought opportunities to contribute in small ways to the community. As a singer myself, I was asked to provide the entertainment at the Senior Citizens' Christmas Party in Neah Bay in December 1974. This I happily did. I also worked with some of the teachers in the grade school to plan several English and spelling lessons that involved the use of music. A number of times I helped the women in the community with food preparation for potlatch parties and other occasions. Sometimes I served as a driver, taking elders to the clinic, grocery store, post office, or other places they needed to go, or I ran errands for them since they could not drive and their families were often too busy to take them.

Most of my time, however, was spent with Helma. Many absorbing hours passed quickly as she taught me things I needed to know in order to interact properly with people in Neah Bay. From her I learned about Makah life, music, art, and traditions, as well as contemporary culture and activities. I usually assisted her in whatever task she was undertaking. For example, we spent considerable time preparing Makah foods. We gathered mussels, clams, sea urchins, and other edible tidewater creatures, and I learned how the Makah utilize them. Helma taught me the proper way to clean and fillet a salmon and how to prepare a variety of other kinds of fish. In spring and summer we gathered abundant wild berries (salmonberries, blackberries, sallal berries, strawberries, thimbleberries, and others) that grow along the edges of the rain forest, and prepared them in a variety of ways. No matter what the job at hand, Helma always talked and explained how things were done when she was young, how she had learned to do certain tasks, and how things had changed in recent years. She was always teaching, and I was always learning. It was an exciting and wonderful time! In return, I ran errands, did grocery shopping, drove her places she needed to go, cleaned her kitchen, washed dishes, washed clothes, helped her clean house, and did a variety of other tasks. We usually managed to fit in a recording session somewhere during the daily routine. Often, I stayed up late at night writing in my journal about the day's activities and typing transcripts of the tapes we had recorded earlier.[5]

Helma and I made several trips to Canada together in order to talk to people she had known as a child but hadn't seen for many years—people she thought could help us fit together pieces of the Swan family story. These trips were always enjoyable as well as informative: we met new people, Helma renewed old acquaintances, and we spent productive time together in museums and archives searching for family-related materials. Working as partners, Helma and I equally enjoyed the detective aspect of our research.

In the realm of ceremonies, I felt honored when asked by Helma to help her organize and prepare for two major potlatch parties she was giving—one in June 1983, the other in March 1987. Her three children had not yet become seriously interested in helping her maintain the Makah traditions, and she needed a great deal of assistance at those times in order to host successful ceremonies. Therefore she called on me. I left my job, went to Neah Bay each time and worked alongside her, doing whatever she asked in order to prepare for these elaborate ceremonies. There were lists of guests to be created, the community hall to be reserved, the rental fee to be paid, cooks to be hired, menus to be created, food to be ordered and then prepared for about three to four hundred guests. Also, there was a master of ceremonies to be chosen, songs and dances to be selected and practiced, the performance order to be decided, costumes and masks to be refurbished and prepared, thousands of gifts to be bought for general distribution at the end of the ceremony, decisions to be made on gift giving to important chiefs and their families, money and checks to be saved and turned into small cash, which would be given as payment to chiefs and honored visitors for witnessing the events, and on and on. It was all very exhilarating and very exhausting! In the end, each potlatch was a success, and Helma was pleased with the results.

The ceremony held in 1987 appeared to be a turning point for her family. Helma's oldest son, Arnie Hunter, was made a chief, something which came as a surprise to him. From this time on, however, he gradually began to take his responsibilities more seriously, and ever since, Helma has had help and support not only from Arnie but from all of her children and some of her grandchildren whenever she has planned and hosted potlatch parties. Now when I attend them, I still help out as needed, but Helma's children have taken over most of the tasks that I did in 1983 and 1987. This is as it should be. I learned many things as I helped Helma and was pleased to have had the opportunity to do so, but now it is essential that her children learn to organize and run such ceremonies, because they will be the ones to carry them on in the future.

Library Research

In addition to oral interviews with Helma, discussions with Northwest Coast village elders, and participant-observation activities, it was also necessary to explore written records on the Makah, the Nootkan tribes,[6] and Helma Swan's family. Standard published references[7] on the Northwest Coast were examined as well as a variety of specific ethnohistoric materials such as letters, diaries, documents, photos, newspapers, and other writings of early settlers, explorers, adventurers, anthropologists, and missionaries in the Northwest Coast region. Libraries, archives, and museums, located primarily in the Northwest, provided excellent source material.[8]

Three collections proved to be of special value for this project. First, the unpublished, handwritten diaries of James G. Swan,[9] housed in the University of Washington Manuscripts, Special Collections, and Archives Division, provided invaluable information on the Makah tribe in Neah Bay in the latter half of the 1800s. His writings also disclosed lifelong friendships with a number of Makah families and included previously unknown information concerning individuals who were part of the Swan family of Neah Bay.[10] Second, the Museum of History and Industry Library in Seattle holds a fine collection of James G. Swan's letters, some of which expanded on information contained in the diaries. Third, the British Columbia Archives, in Victoria, B.C., houses the Nootka field notes of anthropologist Philip Drucker and also the Newcombe Family Papers, both of which added to the knowledge of several Swan family relatives. These sources helped flesh out scant oral remembrances concerning some Swan family ancestors.

THEORIES OF WOMEN IN SOCIETY
AND GLUCKMAN'S EQUILIBRIUM MODEL

In addition to reviewing the Northwest Coast ethnographic material, it was also clear that theories relating to women's studies were relevant to Helma's life story, and thus some discussion was in order. Anthropological studies of women, their roles, and their power or lack thereof (known more recently as feminist anthropology) initially explored the belief that men were dominant over women in every culture and in every period of history, and that men, their work, and public activities, were more important and of more value than the largely domestic and private activities of women.[11] The placement of higher value on men's roles created a state of unbalance in the society. Accompanying unequal division of labor based on sex was the universal devaluation of women.[12] As thought provoking as these early hypotheses were, it has since become apparent that people in every society do not always value one or several roles over others, nor are women always found in the private domain and men in the public. Such concepts may reflect what is known in anthropology as an "etic" approach—primarily the constructs of outside researchers.

As products of western Euro-American culture, it is possible that some researchers have been conditioned to value certain roles and activities over others and have, perhaps, transferred these concepts to non-western cultures where they may not be appropriate.

Rather, it may be more helpful to look at specific cultures and ask people within those cultures to discuss *their* perceptions of roles, values, and the place of males and females in their societies. A focus on insiders presenting and explaining their first-hand cultural knowledge is known as an "emic" approach. A number of life histories, biographies, and autobiographies of women have utilized this method,[13] and as a result have provided data that constrasts with some of the early views presented above. It is clear that very different concepts and theories can be developed, depending on whether an emic or an etic approach is used.

Recently, a new focus has emerged concerning the roles of women and men in various cultures, one based much more on an "emic" viewpoint, as presented by Laura Klein and Lillian Ackerman in their 1995 book, *Women and Power in Native North America*. The essays in this publication explore the theme of "balanced reciprocity" as a guiding concept for gender relations in eleven American Indian tribes. Balanced reciprocity means that some roles in a society are filled by men, others by women; however, these roles are not necessarily perceived as being superior or inferior by the people themselves. Rather, the roles of each sex are considered necessary for the continuity and well-being of the whole society.[14] Sometimes there is overlap in male and female roles; at other times there is not. The specifics of these roles and how they are valued varies from society to society. The people themselves, however, determine role-appropriateness and value within their group, and their views may be quite different from those of outsiders. In North America, each native culture has established its own guidelines and, ideally, is respectful of the individual and his or her special abilities in particular positions.

This model of balanced reciprocity fits the Makah case, and its essence has been expressed in various ways by Helma Swan as well as other Makah elders over the years. Fiery feminism is largely absent. Instead, people speak calmly of men's roles and women's roles, how some aspects have changed over the years and others have not. In the past, the division of labor established by the society was acceptable and worked fairly smoothly. The goal was for individuals and families to survive so that the society would survive. Superiority or inferiority of either sex was not an issue. Men and women worked separately and together for the good of all. Men held most of the important ceremonial roles, but women held other roles equally as important in the economic and domestic spheres. Women did not feel undervalued or inferior; they were aware that their duties and obligations were different from those of the men, yet still essential. Therefore, in the eyes of the people, a state of "balanced reciprocity" existed.

Over a period of years, however, due to the accumulation of acculturation and modernization pressures, this balance was upset. As explained in more detail in chapter 1, the men began abandoning their ceremonial roles. Concerned that these roles would disappear, the women took them over. They did not move into these positions willingly or joyfully but did so out of a sense of duty and necessity. There were no feelings of finally being equal or superior to the men. There was a sense of sadness that things had changed so much that they (the women) had to accept a different reality and take on new roles if they did not want to see important ceremonial functions die. Family traditions and prestige were at stake here, not male or female dominance. During this time the women continued to perform their other regular societal duties as well.

Max Gluckman's equilibrium model, as it relates to a changing social structure, is worth noting at this point.[15] In essence, Gluckman says that in order to distinguish and delineate change in a society or some of its parts, one must have an assumed starting point, with some idea of how things operated in regard to roles, modes of behavior, purposes, and controlling rules with guiding beliefs and values.[16] All of this is described by the researcher "as if" it were real, "as if" the system were, at some point in time, truly in equilibrium. Actually, such a description is only a framework or device that allows one to handle the "time element" when dealing with change. Since societal structures develop in time and change through time,[17] one must have a place to begin in order to discuss change. Thus, one could, perhaps, assume that elements of the Makah sociopolitical system (including kinship structure interwoven with the system of chiefs) and the music system (including behavioral and song ownership rules as well as specific male and female roles and responsibilities) were roughly in a state of equilibrium in pre-contact and early contact days (see chapter 1). These systems and their individual elements were interdependent and probably functioned most of the time with relatively minor internal changes. Neither the sociopolitical nor the music system could stand alone; each supported and strengthened the other. The same could be said for male and female roles within Makah society, thus adding another dimension to Klein and Ackerman's concept of "balanced reciprocity."

Major changes began to occur after Euro-American contact, however, and especially after governmental and Christian intervention in the 1860s and 1870s. The Makah native political system (controlled by the chiefs) was entirely eliminated. The social (kinship) and music systems suffered a series of changes, yet survived and continued to support each other, though not as easily as in the past. The former close-knit interdependence of the sociopolitical and music systems, however, was gone. Eventually, after a period of turmoil and stress, a new form of equilibrium began to emerge (approximately in the 1960s and 1970s) when the women took control, thus allowing the systems to continue to function and the parts to interact, although in somewhat different ways than previously. This result was achieved largely through the efforts of Helma Swan and several other dedicated Makah women who stepped in when various systems were near collapse and kept them alive. The balanced reciprocity that existed previously in regard to gender roles and duties also underwent some corresponding changes.

In the 1990s, however, another shift began to develop. Some of the younger men became interested and began to learn the former male roles and responsibilities of their ancestors. The older women happily taught and assisted them, then slowly began turning ceremonial functions back to them. There have not been hard feelings, a sense of loss, or a power struggle. Even though not often verbalized, there is a certain order for how things should be in this society, for each sex. Tribal members subconsciously know this order, feel comfortable with it, and say, "This is the way things should be."

So again a somewhat different equilibrium is establishing itself, not exactly like the old, but approximating it—both in regard to social systems and roles appropriate for each sex. According to Gluckman, "If an institution is functioning, balancing forces and redressive mechanisms come into play to restrain the effects of the disturbance in order to preserve or restore, as far as possible, the earlier form."[18] First the women saved the system; now the men are reacquiring their former roles. It appears that a strong attempt is being made to at least partially restore the system to an earlier form. Based on history, one may expect to see more changes and more upsets in the equilibrium, but, as has happened several times before, new players or mechanisms will undoubtedly appear when necessary to allow the system to survive. The system is dynamic and will continue to rebalance itself, no matter how many attacks it must endure. Both women and men are important participants in this ongoing process and it is likely that their roles also will continue to change and rebalance over time. Thus, combining the concept of "balanced reciprocity" as expressed by Klein and Ackerman,[19] with the concept of change, as expressed through Gluckman's version of an equilibrium system, helps explain the Makah circumstances.

Debate over women in the domestic or private domain and men in the public or outside domain is not a significant issue for the Makah. First, domestic roles and activities are not considered unimportant or inferior, and, at least in the past, both men and women took an active part in them. In some families this is still true; in others it is not. In any case, these domestic roles are critical for the maintainence of the family, which is essential for the survival of the culture. Public roles have undergone more far-reaching changes as a result of the influence of government agents, Christian churches, and Euro-American schools in Neah Bay. With modernization (and an increase in the number of roles available) has come an increase in the number of women filling public roles. Women have held, and continue to hold, public positions as Makah tribal council members, tribal judges, realty officers, school teachers, teacher's aides, artists, nurses, secretaries, store clerks, restaurant owners, professional cooks, directors of the senior citizens' center, museum directors, museum curators, and other positions in and around Neah Bay. Almost any public, nonceremonial position available may be filled by either a man or a woman. Basically, among the Makah, the individual is valued for what he or she can contribute to the society. Both male and female roles are necessary to maintain tribal viability. Only in the area of ceremonial roles does there continue to be a strong belief in a sexual division of labor. The women, as well as the men, feel that certain ceremonial roles should still be held by the men. However, tribal members, including Helma Swan, do not feel that this situation creates a role imbalance between the sexes.

DIFFICULTIES IN DISCOVERING SWAN FAMILY RELATIONSHIPS

In the past when potlatching and other ceremonies, as well as the oral tradition, were the primary methods of passing on the history of a Northwest Coast Indian society, tribal intermarriages and family relationships could easily be remembered and recounted. Also, certain individuals known as tribal historians were charged with retaining and reciting countless details. Over time, many families have forgotten much of their specific history and tribal historians have passed away without training replacements. Therefore, in many cases, the oral histories have not been clearly and fully passed on. Indian ancestors, names, and relationships have been forgotten, and lines of descent have become clouded. People still know they are related to one another but don't always know exactly how.

As the oral tradition has begun to fade, other sources such as church records, government records and documents (including census data), have become more important. There are, however, large gaps in this information as well. For example, the first church (Presbyterian) appeared in Neah Bay in 1903.[20] There are no church records before, nor even for many years after this date.[21] Also, many Makah never became members of the Presbyterian or any other church. Thus, for the purposes of this study, church records cannot be used to establish or clarify early Makah lines of descent and family relationships.

The keeping of U.S. Census records for Northwest Coast Indian people began in 1885; few official records of families, individuals, names, and ages exist prior to this time.[22] Dates of birth often constitute educated guesses by the census takers in the early years. Indian names present another challenge. Often the written names are a vague approximation of the actual Indian name. Sometimes the written version of the Indian name changes drastically from year to year because different census takers heard it and wrote it differently. At times no Indian name was given at all. In Northwest Coast societies where Indian names were critical because they were part of the rights and wealth of the chiefs, the inaccurate presentation of these names or their total absence is a major loss. Therefore, it often is difficult, and sometimes impossible, to trace ancestral connections through the documented records. English names were given almost at random; sometimes different brothers within the same family received different English surnames from the census takers. Written records thus can obscure the family relationships. In some cases it is hard to find any rationale for a sudden name change of an individual or a whole family. A particular family might appear with one last name in a series of census reports, and suddenly the following year, the whole family might appear with a different last name. The first names usually (but not always) remained the same. Such incidents create confusion and greatly increase the difficulty of discovering forgotten family relationships. Many of these kinds of situations were encountered during the search for Swan family material. There were numerous marriages, deaths of young wives (in childbirth), remarriages by the young widowers, intermarriages with neighboring tribes, changes of Indian names from youth to adult, sudden appearances or disappearances of Indian or English names, and so forth. Many of the names and relationships were not recorded at all, or were so poorly recorded that it is hard to know who certain individuals really were. Therefore, the stories related in the following section and in Appendix B, which concern Helma Swan's relatives, have some gaps that may always remain. So far, no written documentation has been found that can account for all of the remembered but unnamed family members.[23] Notwithstanding the gaps, it is important to relate what is known of Helma Swan's ancestry, for it is essential to an appreciation of who she is and what she believes. She embodies many of the qualities exhibited by her ancestors regarding support for the people, the culture, and an entire way of life.

A BRIEF INTRODUCTION TO THE THREE CHIEFS AND OTHER SWAN FAMILY RELATIVES

Often filled with mystery, intrigue, battles, and death, ancestral family stories of the Makah frequently revolve around great chiefs of the past. These imposing figures, in addition to being recognized as overseers of the welfare of their people, were renowned as leaders who gave away large quantities of goods while hosting great feasts and ceremonies. Also known as outstanding warriors, they defended their fellow tribesmen, led raids of reprisal when necessary, yet had the wisdom to know when to choose peace.

Helma Swan is descended from three well-known chiefs who fit the above description: Peter Brown (c.1835–1908), also known as How-á-thlub or As-chád-a-bek, considered to be the last chief of the Makahs; Flattery Jack, also called Yelák'ub or Yellow-cum (?–c.1853), a respected and powerful leader from Neah Bay; and

Sitkéenum or Cedakánim (?–1897), an important leader of the Clayoquot Band of the Nootkans from Vancouver Island, British Columbia. All three were great warriors in their younger years; later in life, each determined independently that peace was more productive and allowed for an easier working relationship with the white government officials who controlled their areas.

The lives of these three chiefs are known only from sketchy tales and fragmented descriptions either passed down as part of the oral tradition or recorded by a variety of authors and journalists who were their contemporaries and knew them or their families. James G. Swan was well acquainted with Peter Brown and Sitkéenum, and both appear numerous times in his diaries. Chief Yelák'ub (Flattery Jack) died a few years before Swan arrived in Neah Bay, but since the latter was friendly with two of this popular chief's sons, information about all of them is included in Swan's diaries. Because these chiefs are Helma Swan's ancestors, her family has inherited certain rights and privileges from them or their descendants. Thus, she felt it important to include information about each of them in order to give more depth to the family history, as well as added perspective on her own life and stories. Therefore, excerpts from Swan's diaries as well as descriptions and stories written by other authors have been edited and placed in Appendix B. The same is true for a variety of other relatives who, though perhaps not chiefs, had varying amounts of influence on Helma's life. Where relevant, detailed footnotes provide supporting documentation on family relationships.

Aside from the chiefs, a few words must be said by way of introduction about several other main characters who appear in the text, the appendices, or both. Chief Peter Brown's only surviving son, Chestoke, or Chestoqua, Peterson,[24] eventually the owner of several sealing schooners, was the father of Charlie Swan and the grandfather of Helma Swan. Chief Yelák'ub had two surviving children: Billy Balch, or Willub, the older son, who succeeded his father as chief; and Sikesy or Saxey Balch, the younger son. Sikesy was Charlie Swan's maternal grandfather, and Helma Swan's great-grandfather (see the Swan Family Genealogical Chart in Appendix A). Chestoke Peterson, Billy Balch, and Sikesy Balch were friendly with James G. Swan, who recorded, in his diaries and letters, essentially all that is known about them (see Appendix B).

Ellen Swan, daughter of Sikesy and granddaughter of Chief Yelák'ub, learned to read and write English, was interested in getting an education, and along with several other children became good friends with James G. Swan. She was married "by Indian custom" to Chestoke Peterson,[25] and in 1886 their son, Charlie Swan, was born. Tragically, a year later, Ellen contracted measles and died suddenly.

Charlie Swan, Ellen Swan's son and Helma Swan's father, was raised, after his mother's death, by his maternal great-aunt, Mrs. Weassub, or Hedatokobáitl, a wonderful woman whom Charlie always called "grandmother." She taught him to

Fig. 1. Chief Peter Brown (left) is pictured with Charlie White. Chief Peter was Charlie Swan's grandfather and Jeff Davis was Charlie's cousin. Circa 1900. *Photograph courtesy of Washington State Historical Society, Tacoma (Samuel Morse Photo Collection, neg. #209).*

Fig. 2. Curley (left) and his father, Chief Setakanim, from Clayoquot, British Columbia, circa 1880. This chief was also the father of Frank and Benjamin (Atliu) and the grandfather of Annie Atliu Williams. Many of his chiefly rights and belongings were given to Charlie Swan by Annie at a 1930 potlatch in Clayoquot. *Photograph perhaps by Maynard, courtesy of the Royal British Columbia Museum (neg. #1441).*

Fig. 3. Portrait of three Makah girls, 1880. Left to right, Martha, Fanny David, and Ellen Swan. Ellen, who was thirteen at the time of this photo, was Charlie Swan's mother and Helma Swan's grandmother. On August 27, 1880, James G. Swan, according to his diary, "took these three young ladies to Mr. Stevens and had their pictures taken." The dentalium breastplate worn by each (called *chiti·duk* in Makah) was a sign of wealth, according to Helma, as were their dentalium head bands. *Photograph by B. F. Stevens, courtesy of MSCUA, University of Washington Libraries; neg. #NA 1411.*

Fig. 4. Helma Swan Ward and her mother, Ruth Anderson Swan, in Neah Bay, 1975. *Photograph by Linda J. Goodman.*

Fig. 5. The Swan family sisters (left to right): Dicie, Joy, Helma, Dolores, Bessie, and Bessie's granddaughter Olivia. Neah Bay, Washington, 1993. *Photograph courtesy of Helma Swan.*

Fig. 6. Fred Anderson (Helma's maternal uncle), a fine hunter and fisherman, with his catch of hair seals at Ozette village, circa 1915–1920. The Anderson family was originally from Ozette; later they all moved to Neah Bay. *Photograph courtesy of the North Olympic Library System, Port Angeles (Bert Kellogg Photo Collection, Ind. Port. 0013).*

Fig. 7. Atliu painting one of his newly carved masks. His metal carving tools are laid out on the cloth at his feet; other carvings are propped against the door. He is sitting on a woven cedar bark mat. Circa 1890–1900. *Photograph courtesy of the Museum of History and Industry, Seattle (McCurdy Photo Collection, neg. #1955.970.470.2).*

Fig. 8. Portrait of three Neah Bay residents, circa 1900. Atliu (on left) holding the same carved club shown in fig. 7. He also wears a silver medal of honor presented to him by the Canadian government. His daughter Annie Atliu Williams is seated beside him. Another relative, Shubert Hunter, stands behind them. All three were originally from Clayoquot, British Columbia. *Photo courtesy of Washington State Historical Society, Tacoma (Samuel Morse Photo Collection, neg. #73).*

Fig. 9. Charlie Swan in ceremonial dress, 1948. His wolf headgear and grizzly bear button blanket had formerly belonged to Chief Sitkeenum and were given to him by Annie Williams at the 1930 potlatch where she made him a chief. He made the drum he holds and painted the design of the thunderbird and man on the back of a whale, with two lightning serpents above them. This is an adaptation of the design on the Swan Family Curtain (see fig. 26). *Photograph by Ernest Bertelson; courtesy of MSCUA, University of Washington Libraries (neg. #NA 1642).*

Fig. 10. Makah men singing and performing a masked dance by the beach, Neah Bay, Washington, circa 1920s. Left to right: Jim Hunter; Shubert Hunter; Charlie Swan, wearing mask; Dan Tucker, sitting; Charlie Anderson, holding drum above his head; Larry Irving; and Skyler Colfax. Note salmon barbecuing in right background. *Photograph courtesy of Helma Swan.*

cherish his family as well as culture, traditions, and music—elements that became central in his life and that he later passed on to his own children. Charlie's father played little part in his upbringing.

In 1909, Charlie Swan married Ruth Anderson, daughter of an Ozette chief. Having a Quileute mother, Ruth was fluent in this language as well as Makah; however, she was consistently a woman of few words. As a BIA employee for many years, Charlie Swan, with the assistance of his wife, Ruth, and his daughter, Helma, built a number of houses for BIA personnel, some of which are still in use. Ruth and Charlie worked hard their entire lives to support their large family of thirteen children, only eight of whom survived to adulthood. In 2002, the five remaining daughters are Helma (Hallie) Swan, Dolores (Dallie) Loveland, Bessie Bain, Joyce (Joy) Smythe, and Fernell (Dicie) Koffman. Each has a number of children, grandchildren, and great-grandchildren who continue the family musical traditions.

Little is known about Ruth Anderson Swan's side of the family (see in Appendix A the Anderson Family Genealogical Chart). Her younger brother, Fred Anderson, an expert hunter and fisherman, often supplied the family with fresh meat and fish. An older sister, Annie Phillips, died in 1910 at the age of twenty. Virtually nothing is known about Ruth's mother, Alice Taylor Anderson, other than the fact that she was Quileute from La Push, Washington. Ruth's father, Charlie Anderson, an Ozette chief and a muti-talented individual, significantly influenced Helma, as well as several other grandchildren, whom he taught to be good people, to work hard, and to participate in Makah life and ceremonies.

Two of Chief Sitkeenum's sons, Frank and Benjamin Cedakanim, though technically Canadian, were often visitors and lived for a period of years in Neah Bay. For a time, Frank was married to the daughter of a Neah Bay chief. Benjamin, also known as Atliu, was an excellent carver and some of his works are said to reside in the Smithsonian Institution. His pieces were greatly admired by James G. Swan. It is not known whether or not Chief Sitkeenum's younger son, Curley, traveled to Neah Bay with his father, but Helma Swan recalls that a few times her great-aunt, Annie Cedakanim Williams, brought one of Curley's sons (Ernest) with her when she came from Canada to visit Charlie Swan and family. Sitkeenum's sons were related to Ellen Swan, but the exact family ties were not recorded and have been forgotten. James G. Swan wrote about Frank and Benjamin Cedakanim and, indirectly, their ties to Ellen Swan. (See Appendix B).

One of Benjamin Cedakanim's daughters, Annie Cedakanim Williams, who lived in Canada, was Charlie Swan's aunt and Helma Swan's great-aunt. A highly talented woman, Annie was a fine basketmaker as well as an excellent singer and dancer. She and her husband, Charlie Williams (not the same person as Charlie Swan's second cousin of the same name), spent much time visiting the Swan family in Neah Bay and teaching them the cultural traditions she knew and loved so well.

The two families were very close. During an especially memorable potlatch held in Clayoquot, British Columbia in 1930, Annie passed her chiefly inheritance on to her nephew Charlie Swan (see chapter 8). More detailed information concerning family relatives may be found in the appendices.

THE SIGNIFICANCE OF HELMA'S STORY

Helma's material is unique when considered in light of the three other major published works on the Makah. James G. Swan's ethnographic study, *The Indians of Cape Flattery* (1870), contains cultural information Swan collected over 125 years ago and provides a good comparative baseline for Helma's narrative. Frances Densmore's *Nootka and Quileute Music* (1939) relies in large part on Swan's material for ethnographic background and includes brief descriptive passages relating to the music but is primarily a specialized study emphasizing song structure, transcription, and musical analysis of a number of Makah and Quileute songs that she recorded during the summers of 1923 and 1926. Finally, Elizabeth Colson's *The Makah Indians* (1953) is a study of Makah assimilation and changing cultural conditions in 1941–42 and draws on information gathered from a number of anonymous tribal members. Her main conclusion—that the Makah were not assimilating and disappearing into the surrounding white society at that time—still holds true in the early twenty-first century.

Helma's story, however, is the first presentation of a large body of Makah material from the viewpoint of a knowledgeable tribal elder. Her narrative first and foremost provides a record of life, events, art, music, and ceremony as seen by a woman who has been an astute observer and active participant in Makah culture for the largest part of the twentieth century. As a child, she became the star pupil of a number of the Makah elders of her village as well as the chiefs of several Canadian Westcoast (Nootkan) villages; thus she received a thorough Makah education that went far beyond Indian music. Over the course of her life, she has always loved learning the old customs and traditions of her people and then teaching them to others.

Second, since Helma considers music an extremely powerful force among her people, she feels that both Makahs and non-Makahs need to understand its essence, the complexity of its operation, and how it functions traditionally. In a society where men were the primary figures in the musical life, it is quite unusual to find a woman who has been so deeply involved in music since she was a small child, and one who is an excellent singer as well. Aside from her special musical gifts, she happened to be in the right place at the right time and thus was able to acquire extensive musical knowledge. She feels honored to have this knowledge and desires to share it and leave it as a legacy for her descendants.

Third, it becomes evident that through her story Helma presents a significant and carefully reasoned view of the role of a woman in her society. Generally she feels that women should not disregard the old rules of proper Makah behavior, even in this modern age. Now more than ever she feels the roles of men and women need to be upheld and reaffirmed. However, she also recognizes that the old rules must bend at particular times due to new circumstances created by the outside world. Inflexibility is not a healthy approach to changing times and conditions.

Fourth, Helma's presentation is important not only because she recalls details of unusual and significant events and activities, but also because she has a special gift for bringing them to life and making her audience empathize with the situation at hand. In short, she is an excellent storyteller. Among many vivid recollections, perhaps the most significant is her account of the ceremony where her father, Charlie Swan, was made a chief in the Canadian Westcoast (Nootkan) village of Clayoquot, British Columbia, in 1930. This was a great honor for him and for his family. Helma, at age twelve, was quite impressed with what she saw and heard, and considers this to be one of the most important events in her life.

From another perspective, Helma's story gains significance because she is a member of an important Makah family, one with an especially interesting history. Since families provide the basis of the social and political organization, as well as the ceremonial life, they are central to the functioning of the Makah tribe, and thus the story of one family becomes more meaningful. From her narrative one can see how a family operates, how members interact, and how they survive in good times and bad. Her father, as a descendant of three chiefs, took his family responsibilities seriously and taught his children to do the same.

Finally, the important issue of culture change is subtly present throughout the work. As discussed above, societal and gender role changes have occurred, and rebalancing is in process. Helma's story also provides a glimpse of how one individual and her family have responded to continually changing circumstances in areas such as work, school, church, native ceremonies, music, politics, and social life. Often old and new ways do not fit well together, and the result is discomfort and conflict at various levels. Clearly, Helma and her family have discovered ways to survive the turbulence and change in their lives. They exemplify the difficult and continuing struggle to preserve the best and most important parts of the old Makah traditions while at the same time learning to live within the framework of the dominant white society. Finding a workable balance is the key, and this is the challenge of a lifetime.

MAJOR THEMES IN HELMA'S NARRATIVE

Helma's narrative illustrates several themes that are not specifically named by her but that have reappeared numerous times throughout our interviews over the past twenty years and also appear to a greater or lesser extent in the edited version of her story presented here. Essential to the survival of Makah culture, Helma speaks of these themes or concepts in a variety of contexts.

Initially, as a child, she as well as others learned the concept of "responsibility." Girls and boys were taught appropriate roles and activities, and they were given various tasks at a young age. For example, from the time she was seven or eight years old, Helma had to take care of her younger siblings. She had no choice in this matter; at times she was unhappy about it, but this responsibility was given to her, and she accepted it. While her parents worked hard to support the family, she was expected to help with other household duties as well. Some of these tasks were more enjoyable than others, but Helma was required to do them all. Music, however, was a responsibility on an entirely different level. She was expected to participate and perform, but since she had always loved musical activities, she never considered them a chore and never complained about them.

In the domain of adult responsibility, women's and men's roles were clearly delineated, as were areas in which some overlap was allowed. This was true in work activities, in social and political interactions, and also in music, dance, and ceremony. Women did not feel inferior to men because some of their ceremonial responsibilities were small. There were other parts of life where women's responsibilities were greater, and they felt that it all balanced out in the end.

Another theme focuses on the importance of "structure, order, and discipline" in Makah life. These concepts ultimately ensure the survival of the tribal heritage. When Helma was young, children were raised with strict sets of rules and guidelines. They were taught to sit quietly, to listen and learn from their elders and to watch carefully what was going on around them. This is what she and the other children did. She was taught to respect other people's property as well as her own and to care properly for items received as gifts, purchased, or made—such as the family masks, costumes, and musical instruments. Her father also brought structure and order into his children's lives as he taught them songs, dances, and ceremonies. His discipline was strict, and she and her siblings didn't always like his methods; however, they later realized that they had acquired privileged knowledge from him that they have never forgotten. Helma is aware that the discipline and order with which she grew up are no longer a part of the contemporary lifestyle, and at times this saddens her.

Structure and order were visible on a general societal level as well. In the past, the tightly knit, ranked organization of chiefs gave the society its basis for operation. Ceremonies, music, and dance, based on chiefly ownership and descent, held a central role in the maintenance of this system and thus were carefully controlled. The same was true for the *tupáat*, a ceremonial duty, obligation, or privilege. Each *tupáat* (such as song leader, drummer, messenger, and so forth) was hereditary, was fulfilled by a specific high-ranking individual, and was an essential part of the structure that helped maintain the order of the society (see chapter 8 for more on *tupáats*). As a child, Helma watched people perform their *tupáats* and was taught their importance.

"Maintaining family standing" is another theme that is closely tied to the structure of the society. If one is descended from chiefs, one needs to uphold one's family standing, and this is accomplished by hosting ceremonies (particularly potlatches), performing one's family-owned songs and dances, and giving away gifts and money to witnesses in the accepted manner. One must learn the Makah conduct and practices and then act accordingly. All of this was originally taught to Helma by her father, her grandfather, and her great-aunt from Canada.

Receiving a "proper Makah education" constitutes another important theme in Helma's story, one closely tied to the final theme: "being an active participant" in Makah life. One cannot be a fully contributing member of Makah society if one does not know one's cultural traditions. Helma spoke often and with affection of her father and how much she learned from him as a child. As her primary guide and teacher concerning Makah customs, heritage, and values, he always treated her with respect and dignity, an approach she found most supportive. Charlie Swan also provided her with a positive role model. He was an adult who had learned to survive in a complex non-Indian world while continuing to participate fully in his own deeply cherished Makah culture (see fig. 9). Helma loved accompanying him to the potlatches where, as part of her training, she usually performed with him. Charlie Anderson, Helma's maternal grandfather, was also an important teacher in her life (see fig. 10). He, too, was kind and had great patience when working with his grandchildren. Thus, she learned many of the ceremonial duties and responsibilities of her people from these two male family members. Normally much of the information they taught her was reserved for the oldest son, but because both the oldest and second oldest sons had died at young ages, Helma, the oldest surviving daughter (who, incidentally, had an insatiable curiosity and desire to learn), received this gift of traditional knowledge.

Other important teachers included a number of the old people in Neah Bay who were friends or relatives of her parents; her great-aunt Annie Williams from the Clayoquot tribe in Canada; and several other female friends and relatives from Clayoquot. Thus, over a number of years, Helma was privileged to acquire both female and male knowledge, which gave her a broader understanding of Makah culture as a whole and allowed her, as she matured, to be an active participant. For her, there was no option other than to "participate fully" in this culture that she knew and loved so well. It would have been unthinkable to do otherwise.

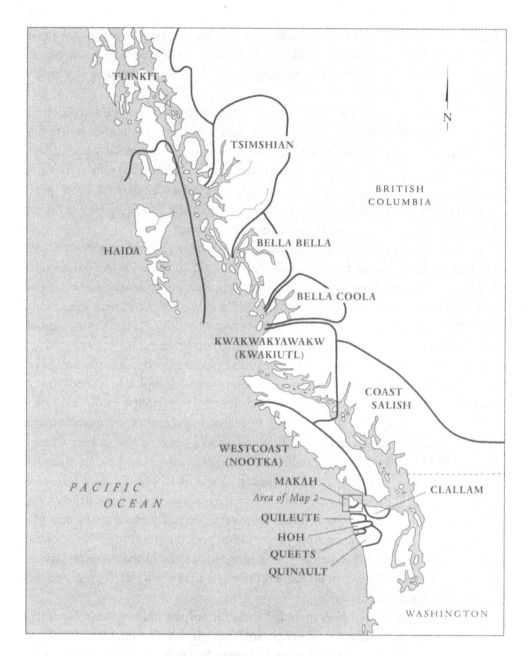

Map 1. Tribes of the Northwest Coast. Adapted from Goodman 1978, fig. 1.

CHAPTER 1

MAKAH CULTURE, HISTORY, AND MUSIC

In a land bathed by fog, mist, and rain, in villages nestled between dense rain forests and storm-lashed ocean shores, tribal peoples of the Northwest Coast have fashioned vibrant, resiliant cultures. Names such as Tlinkit, Haida, Kwakiutl, Nootka, and Salish come to mind (see Map 1), along with images of imposing long houses and elegant totem poles displaying beautifully carved thunderbirds, whales, wolves, and grizzly bears. A portion of this rich heritage was contributed by the Makah Tribe, located on a small reservation south of the Strait of Juan de Fuca on the tip of the wild and windswept Olympic Peninsula in Washington State (see Map 2). Over the centuries, members of this tribe have developed complex sociopolitical and ceremonial systems while maintaining a thriving economy based on fishing, whaling, hunting, and berry gathering.

MAKAH CULTURE AND HISTORY

Tribal Names and Languages

The Makah are the southernmost of a group of approximately twenty tribes included under the general term "Nootka." It is said that this word was introduced in 1778 by Captain Cook, who, after sailing into the area, thought the natives (actually people from the village of Yuquot) were telling him that Nootka was the name of the sound where he was anchored. According to stories told by native elders, the words he heard, *nutkšiʔa* or *nuˑtkaˑʔičim*, meant something like "Go around over there!" to guide the Europeans to a safe haven where they could anchor their ships.[1] Since the time of Captain Cook, the term "Nootka" has become standard and has been expanded to include all the tribes whose cultures, languages, and ways of life are similar: the currently existing Canadian tribes (which number anywhere from

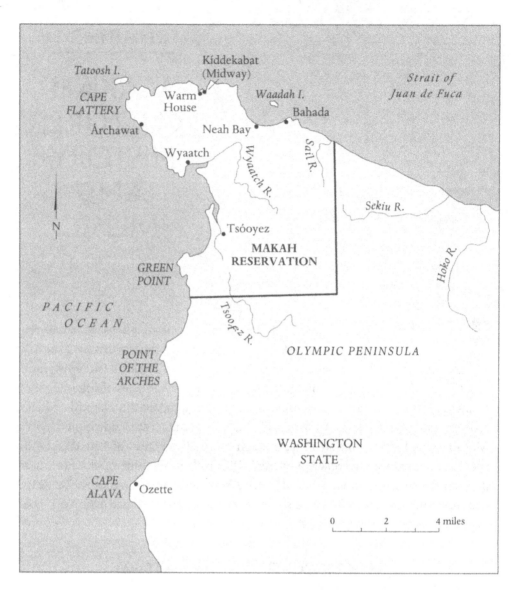

Map 2. The Makah reservation. Adapted from Samuels and Daugherty 1991, fig. 7.

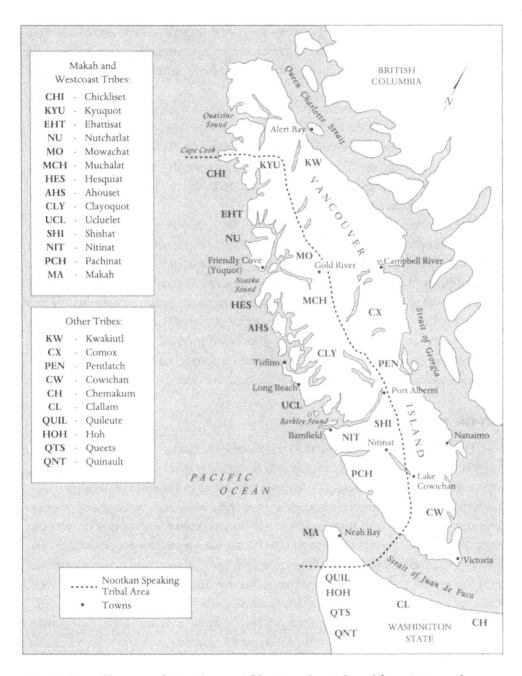

Makah and Westcoast Tribes:

CHI - Chickliset
KYU - Kyuquot
EHT - Ehattisat
NU - Nutchatlat
MO - Mowachat
MCH - Muchalat
HES - Hesquiat
AHS - Ahouset
CLY - Clayoquot
UCL - Ucluelet
SHI - Shishat
NIT - Nitinat
PCH - Pachinat
MA - Makah

Other Tribes:

KW - Kwakiutl
CX - Comox
PEN - Pentlatch
CW - Cowichan
CH - Chemakum
CL - Clallam
QUIL - Quileute
HOH - Hoh
QTS - Queets
QNT - Quinault

----- Nootkan Speaking Tribal Area
• Towns

BRITISH COLUMBIA

Queen Charlotte Strait

Quatsino Sound

Alert Bay

Cape Cook

CHI

KYU

KW

VANCOUVER

EHT

NU

MO

Friendly Cove (Yuquot)

Nootka Sound

Gold River

Campbell River

HES

MCH

CX

AHS

Strait of Georgia

CLY

Tofino

PEN

ISLAND

Long Beach

Port Alberni

UCL

Barkley Sound

Bamfield

SHI

NIT

Nitinat

Nanaimo

PACIFIC OCEAN

PCH

Lake Cowichan

CW

MA

Neah Bay

Strait of Juan de Fuca

Victoria

QUIL

CL

CH

HOH

QTS

WASHINGTON STATE

QNT

Map 3. General location of West Coast neighboring tribes. Adapted from Arima and Dewhrist 1990, Suttles 1987a, Mauger 1991.

fifteen to twenty-two depending on how they are grouped) and one American tribe, the Makah.[2] The Canadian Nootkan tribes, however, no longer like to use the term "Nootka." Rather, they choose to call themselves either "Nuu-cha-nulth" or "Westcoast" (see Map 3).

The Makah prefer to retain the name "Makáh," which evidently was given to them by the Clallam at the time of the signing of the Treaty of Neah Bay in 1855.[3] In the Makah language, the people call themselves $K^widič'če?at$, "People who live on the Rocky Point," or "The Cape People."[4] In everyday speech, however, they continue to refer to themselves as Makah, and to their northern neighbors as Nuu-cha-nulth, Westcoast, or Nootka.

The Nootkan language is subdivided into three closely related dialects: Nootka proper, spoken in the north, from Cape Cook to the eastern shore of Barkley Sound on western Vancouver Island; Nitinat, used by the central groups around Nitinat Lake on Vancouver Island; and Makah, spoken by the Cape Flattery (Makah) people to the south.[5] Nootkan is also related to the Kwakiutl language, spoken by members of this group of tribes (also known as Kʷákʷakyawakʷ, Kʷágiulth, or Kʷákʷala), who live directly north and east of the Westcoast (Nootkan) peoples. Both the Nootkan and Kwakiutl languages are part of the Wakashan language family.[6] The Salishan languages, spoken by Coast Salish tribes to the east, are entirely unrelated.

Location and Environment

The isolated and beautiful Makah reservation contains great contrasts in terrain, vegetation, and wildlife. Large expanses of forest are edged by long sandy beaches or dark rocky shorelines (see fig. 11). Several river drainage systems cut through rough mountainous terrain, then wend their way to the sea through small grassy prairies, swamps, and bogs. Steep, jagged cliffs, many honeycombed with caves, overlook the Strait of Juan de Fuca on the north and the Pacific Ocean on the west. Abundant rainfall, averaging ninety to one hundred inches per year,[7] gives rise to dense, temperate rain forest with lush stands of Western red cedar, Sitka spruce, Western hemlock, Douglas fir, Pacific yew, and Red alder, to name just a few.

Originally established by the Treaty of Neah Bay in 1855, the Makah Reservation presently includes Cape Flattery, the land roughly six miles south and six miles east of it, and two offshore islands.[8] Before the treaty was signed, the tribe claimed a much larger area, extending from either the Lyre River or the Hoko River on the east,[9] to Cape Alava on the south. Presently, Neah Bay is the only surviving Makah village on the reservation. In the past, there were five small permanent winter villages: Baháda, or Bi?íd?a, east of Neah Bay approximately in the area of Baháda or Baada Point; Neeah, in the western section of the present village of Neah Bay (see fig. 12); Wyaatch, at the mouth of the Wyaatch River; Tsooyez, on Tsooyez Beach facing the Pacific Ocean; and Ozette, about fifteen miles down the west coast, at

Cape Alava.[10] Customarily each year many people moved from these villages to three temporary summer villages: Kíddekabat, Tatoosh, and Árchawat—all of which were located closer to good fishing grounds.[11]

Makah Life In the "Old Days" (Pre-1920)

Economic Activities

The two great providers for the Makah were the rain forest and the ocean. Nature was more than generous in this remote corner of the world, and the abundance of foodstuffs allowed the people to create a varied and nutritious diet. Fishing and sea hunting were the two primary male occupations, with land hunting being a distant third. The icy Pacific waters teemed with overwhelming numbers of fish, including halibut, the principal staple, as well as salmon and cod, which were caught almost as frequently. Sturdy cedar canoes allowed the men to brave dangerous seas in order to hunt several species of whales and seals, prized for their meat and oil. Less frequently, hunters entered the woods to kill deer and elk.

Makah women contributed significantly to the food supply as well. Aside from processing most of the meat and fish brought in by the men, they gathered, prepared, and preserved vast quantities of salmonberries, salal berries, blackberries, cranberries, and numerous other berry species which ripened from June through October each year. In addition, they regularly sought a variety of other edible plant foods that grow in the woods on a seasonal basis. At low tide the women collected and prepared a multitude of small sea creatures (clams, mussels, sea urchins, sea anemones, and others), which abound in the rocks and tidal pools at the water's edge.[12]

Aside from food, the rain forest also provided materials necessary for ceremonial activities and for everyday life. Using long cedar trunks, the Makah hollowed and carved canoes essential not only for deep-sea fishing, sealing, and whaling, but also for trading and warfare. The men cut and adzed huge cedar logs and planks in order to build longhouses that were approximately sixty feet long, thirty feet wide, and fifteen feet high.[13] In their daily activities the men used a host of tools as well as hunting and fishing implements constructed of wood, roots, bone, stone, shell, and other local materials. A seemingly endless supply of cedar, spruce, and alder trees provided expert carvers with material to create totem poles, ceremonial masks, rattles, and drums as well as bentwood boxes and a variety of elaborately carved wooden feast dishes and bowls. Cedar bark, peeled from the trees then properly cut and softened, was woven by the women into clothing, baskets, mats, and blankets.[14] Artists and craftsmen alike had time to fashion useful as well as beautiful items for those who wanted and needed them. Both land and sea were generous providers, and the Makah were adept at utilizing the wealth of resources available for their basic food, clothing, shelter, transportation, and ceremonial needs.

Kinship and Sociopolitical Organization

The rich natural environment of the Makah allowed them to develop and maintain an elaborate sociopolitical organization. This hereditary, ranked system included three classes: chiefs and their noble families, commoners, and slaves.[15] Kinship provided the foundation upon which this three-tiered structure was built: the extended family was the basic kinship unit, and each had its own chief. Most commonly the oldest son of a chief succeeded his father. Descent was reckoned bilaterally with a slight patrilineal preference. In other words, a person could inherit privileges from either the mother's or the father's side, depending on which was directly descended from a more important hereditary line. The preferred choice was the father's line, but rank and prestige to be gained were the primary determinants.[16] Direct line of descent within a certain family was the critical factor in determining rank.

Within this system, the chiefs and their nuclear families held the highest rank. A chief, wealthy and powerful, controlled and was responsible for all the possessions, rights, and privileges of his extended family. These prerogatives included important economic resources such as halibut and salmon fishing grounds, shellfish areas, hunting grounds, and berry tracts. Also included were a host of ritual possessions: songs, dances, ceremonies, masks, costumes, family names, titles, and certain art motifs, called crests (stylized representations of supernatural beings such as grizzly bear, raven, whale, and wolf, along with others that had helped this family in the past).[17] Finally, the chief exerted considerable authority over members of his extended family and local community; he planned and managed ceremonies; and he had the final voice in matters of group policy.[18]

Since a chief necessarily had to maintain his rank in a visible manner, he periodically hosted large potlatch ceremonies.[19] Along with the feasting, singing, and dancing that accompanied this event, he publicly passed on some of his hereditary family privileges and displayed portions of his great wealth in the form of family names, crests, house screens, masks, costumes, songs, dances, and other ceremonial possessions. As part of the ceremony, he was obligated to give away vast quantities of goods and money to the assembled multitude who witnessed the proceedings. A chief's continued rank and prestige depended not only on his hereditary birthright but also on how much he gave away at potlatches.[20]

In order to maintain his wealth, it was necessary for a chief to cultivate friendly relations with his kin, no matter how distant. There developed a symbiotic relationship between them. If he supported and protected his relatives properly, then they also helped him. He allowed them to live in his longhouse, use his berry tracts and various fishing areas. They in turn presented him with a small token of the catch or a basket of berries for the privileges he granted them.[21] When preparing for feasts and potlatches, they hunted, fished, and cooked vast quantities of food for his guests. They also made masks and other ceremonial paraphernalia; created new songs if so requested; practiced old songs which the chief wanted performed; and made baskets, blankets, mats, and other assorted gifts that he would give away to those attending and witnessing this display of his wealth and power.[22]

Not only did an outstanding potlatch maintain a chief's rank and increase his prestige, but the spinoff reflected on all the family members who helped him. By being related to him, and participating in his potlatches, their own small amount of prestige was increased.[23]

Below the chiefs in rank were the commoners—more distant relatives of a chief, usually not in his direct bloodline. These were the people who, by and large, maintained a symbiotic relationship with the chief. Under normal circumstances they owned little in the way of prestige items and were not the givers of potlatches and other ceremonies. They were the solid members of the society whose work kept it going.[24]

At the bottom of the ranked system were the slaves, people captured from other tribes in warfare. Slaves had no property rights and owned very little. Considered to be pieces of property, slaves could be bought and sold by chiefs, thus adding to the latters' total wealth. If a chief married one of his slaves, as occasionally happened, he usually lost his position, power, and prestige. The children of this union were also considered to be slaves who could not inherit any of their father's former chiefly possessions.[25]

Warfare

Tribes of the Northwest Coast frequently engaged each other in warfare in the past, and the Makah were no exception. Often men, women, and even children were either killed or taken as slaves in battle. Heads of the dead were sometimes taken so that the bodies could never come to life again and attack the living. The goal of warfare was not primarily the acquisition of booty to add to one's wealth (although this did occur), but rather the avenging of wrongs.[26] Warfare and related activities ended well before 1900.

Music

Songs, most of which were personally owned pieces of property, generally reaffirmed a person's or a family's rank and status in the society. Usually sung by a chorus accompanied by drums and/or rattles, music has been an element essential for maintaining Makah religious, sociopolitical, and ceremonial life. A variety of types of songs were sung for feasts, potlatches, puberty ceremonies, secret society activities, curing ceremonies, whaling, warfare, gambling, and general entertainment. These events could not be held without the appropriate songs, performed in the proper manner.

Religious Activity

Among the Makah, religion was primarily a private and personal affair, based on the "seeking" of a guardian spirit, called a *tumánuwos*.[27] This spirit, a positive source of strength and power, provided aid and supernatural guidance throughout one's lifetime. A *tumánuwos* was sought either by a man or woman during an individual vision quest, which involved going alone into the woods, praying, fasting, bathing in icy pools, and scrubbing the body with evergreen branches. If the seeker was pure and of good heart, then suddenly, without warning, a spirit would appear, either in a dream or a vision, bringing special abilities, possessions, and perhaps supernatural powers to the new owner. Along with occupational skills (fishing, whaling, warfare, curing, and so forth) and special powers, the *tumanuwos* often bestowed new songs, dances, costumes, and masks on a receptive individual.[28]

Medicine and Curing

The treatment of illness, handled by a medicine man or woman, required particular skills, supported and strengthened by the curer's personal *tumanuwos*. Each doctor developed his or her own specific ceremonies and rituals to effect a cure; however, several basic techniques were used by all. The healing of an individual involved the singing of powerful, personally owned medicine songs; the use of a rattle with supernatural powers; the removal of foreign objects from the patient's body; the prescription of various herbal medicines; and most importantly, the aid of particular supernatural powers. The special talents of healers (who were often commoners) allowed them to acquire a certain amount of wealth, prestige, and privilege that otherwise would have been denied them. Often, even though not strictly hereditary, certain families became known for their curing powers.[29]

If an individual doctor was not powerful enough to effect a cure, then several worked together, or else a curing ceremony called a Tsáyak (*Ts'á·yiq*) was performed. The Tsáyak involved the efforts of a doctor, a number of helpers, much ritual singing, and several days of secret ceremonies. It was performed by a secret society of the same name.[30] Both the secret society and the ceremony disappeared sometime in the early 1900s.

Secret Society Activities

Aside from the Tsáyak, a number of other secret societies existed among the Makah in the past; however, few details are known about most of them. The Klúkwali (*λú·kʷali*) was the principal secret society of the Makah, and its major ceremony, also called the Klukwali, or Wolf Ceremony, was an initiation of young people, based on mythological stories involving wolf spirits. During a dramatic reenactment, the initiates were stolen away by wolves and carried into the woods where, for a number of days, they were taught tribal and familial lore. Later, a battle ensued, and the captives were freed by humans who fought to rescue them. Much masked dancing and feasting followed. The ceremony and ritual training served to reaffirm each person's status in the larger society.[31]

The Hámatsa was a secret society ceremony originally thought to have been acquired through marriage with some of the Kʷákʷakyawakʷ people to the north. Called the Cannibal Dance, and based on an old myth, this ceremony focused on a new initiate, who had to be of noble birth. He was carried off for a number of days, during which time he received supernatural power, and returned possessed by a wild cannibal spirit that had to be tamed. A series of dances were required to accomplish this, including some performed by giant bird characters. Only portions of the ceremony were acquired by the Makah, who performed it most often as part of the Klukwali.[32] The Makah Klukwali and Hamatsa disappeared sometime in the early 1900s.

Feasts and Potlatches

With food abundant and readily available, chiefs often hosted tribal feasts in the past. Potlatches—held to reaffirm the rank and wealth of a chief by publicly displaying his family-owned songs, dances, and other privileges—were held less frequently. Potlatch preparation required great amounts of labor and the collection of vast quantities of goods, which would be paid to witnesses (the audience) for validating the ownership of these privileges. Usually included as parts of the former secret society ceremonies, both feasts and potlatches were given for numerous other occasions as well. Either could be held to celebrate individual rites of passage (birth, puberty, marriage, death), distribute surplus food acquired by a chief, celebrate the harvest of the first foods of the season, or acknowledge the receipt of food or special items given as gifts by other chiefs or affinal kin.[33]

Alterations in Makah Life

The foregoing overview briefly depicted Makah life as it existed approximately 75 to 125 years ago. Even during this time a number of customs and traditions had either been lost or altered from what they had been in precontact times. This trend has continued, and over time, incremental changes have become massive. A series of historical events were instrumental in bringing about many of these changes.

European Contacts and Early Changes

Compared to other parts of North America, where exploration began in the 1500s, the Northwest Coast was spared foreign contact and influence until much later. It was not until the 1770s that the first European ships appeared on the horizon of the northern Nootkans. In 1774, the Spanish, under Captain Juan Perez, were probably the earliest to visit and write about the Yuquot at Nootka Sound. Captain James Cook and his English crew were perhaps the second, arriving in 1778.[34] Numerous others followed.[35]

In the Makah area, Captain John Meares and his crew are credited with being the first Europeans to appear, in 1788. However, it was a Spaniard, Manuel Quimper, who, after landing at the place he named Nuñez Gaona (Neah Bay) on August 1, 1790, first claimed it and all the surrounding lands and villages as possessions of Spain.[36] In May 1792, Spanish Lt. Salvador Fidalgo sailed into Nuñez Gaona with orders to build a fortress where all ships sailing in or out could be seen. His crew constructed a fort, and friendly relations were established with the Indians. Even though a good trading relationship developed initially between the Makah and the Spanish, with the latter exchanging copper sheeting for the Indians' furs, fish, and berries, trouble soon followed. A Makah warrior killed a Spanish officer, First Pilot Don Antonio Serantes, who had gone alone on a fishing expedition with some of the Makah. The Spanish retaliated, killing six Makahs in two canoes. Sensing that more trouble would follow, the Spaniards soon received orders to abandon the fort, which they did forthwith.[37] "Spanish Fort," as the Makah called it, eventually fell into ruin, and was never reoccupied. Numerous other Spanish, British, and American ships continued to visit the area and trade with the Makah, but no one again tried to establish a base of operations in Neah Bay for approximately sixty years. Interaction with outsiders, however, set in motion a chain of events that, ever after, affected the lives of the Westcoast tribes and the Makah.

The early Europeans quickly discovered that the Indians not only fished and gathered huge quantities of berries, but that they also hunted sea mammals and were willing to trade sea otter pelts for various European goods. The foreign adventurers were well aware that the Chinese loved this fur and would pay dearly for it. Once the outside world learned that sea otter pelts were available in large numbers on the Northwest Coast, the rush began: many ships sailed into the area to trade with coastal tribes for this desirable item. In exchange the Indians received firearms, iron and copper, wool blankets, and blue trade beads, along with other lesser items. As a result, previously established Indian trade networks expanded, some tools began to be made of iron, there was an increase in ornaments and ceremonial items fashioned from sheets of copper, and blankets and trade beads became important commodities at potlatches.[38]

This early trading period, which lasted from approximately 1790 to 1840 in the Makah area, allowed the tribe to increase its wealth and also strengthened the powers of the chiefs, who were in charge of goods given and received. During this time, the foreigners were not seeking Indian land, trying to proselytize, or change the native way of life. They were principally interested in profits. Thus Indian institutions and belief systems survived the initial contact period largely intact.[39]

The first major negative impact came in the form of diseases that were introduced through European contact. Smallpox, influenza, measles, venereal disease, and others arrived with the first visitors. At various times, epidemics swept through whole villages like wildfire, devastating many Northwest Coast populations, which had no immunity. Sudden major population loss weakened native social and political organizations as did the deaths of many chiefs and their heirs.[40]

By the 1830s the sea otter had been hunted practically to extinction, and much of the coastal trade with European ships had disappeared.[41] Since culturally the native peoples had not been greatly disrupted by the early European traders (aside from the impact of disease), many tribes returned essentially to their former ways of life.

Twenty years later, however, another round of changes was underway. Several new forts and trading posts appeared in the region, making trade goods more easily available to the Nootkan peoples once again. By the mid-1800s, as tribes were better armed with guns, warfare became more lethal. Diseases continued to weaken some groups and eliminate others. In response, the Canadian Nootkans created a number of political confederacies in order to consolidate reduced populations and to protect member tribes from other warring groups.[42] The Makah suffered population losses from several smallpox epidemics that struck in 1801 and 1824–25, a measles epidemic in 1848, and another smallpox epidemic in 1852.[43] However, in spite of population reduction and frequent skirmishes with nearby tribes, the Makah never formed or joined any confederacies.

In their extreme isolation, the Makah were also spared the impact of early white settlers and missionaries. The absence of roads into the area meant that all visitors came and went by boat, and only a few hardy, self-reliant souls ventured to this unknown corner of the world. Apparently the first white man who tried to settle in Neah Bay was Samuel Hancock. He began a short-lived trading venture there in 1850. The Makah, who did not like his intrusion, made life difficult for him, and he soon departed. Two years later, Hancock returned and tried again to establish a trading post. The Indians, however, were still quite hostile to him, and in 1853, after a short stay, he was forced once more to leave.[44] He did not fare any better than Salvador Fidalgo had in 1792. By contrast, the diary of George O. Wilson described pleasant trading interactions with the Makah when the brig *George Emory* dropped anchor in Neah Bay harbor in December 1850.[45]

In 1853 Washington Territory was created by an act of Congress, and an army engineer, Isaac I. Stevens, became governor. One of his first tasks was to sign treaties with each of the Indian tribes in Washington Territory and acquire some of their land for future white settlement. To this end, on January 31, 1855, he signed the Treaty of Neah Bay with a number of the chiefs and subchiefs from all the Makah villages then in existence. This treaty ceded much of the former Makah territory to the U.S. government and in exchange the Makah received a few thousand dollars; a small reservation, approximately six miles square (located on the northwest tip of the Olympic Peninsula); an Indian agent to supervise the tribe; the promise of an agency school; a farming program; a physician; and the promise that the Makah could continue to maintain and utilize their regular fishing, whaling, sealing, and hunting areas.[46]

The Impact of U.S. Government Policies

Following guidelines set forth in the Treaty of 1855, the Neah Bay Indian Agency, established in 1863, became a dominant force in changing the old ways of life. For approximately seventy years (1863–1933) the Makah were under the control of one U.S. Indian agent after another. In essence these men became absolute rulers on the reservation. As one elderly Makah man described the situation to anthropologist Elizabeth Colson, who was working in Neah Bay in the 1940s:

> We weren't allowed to have any of our Indian things because the agents didn't believe in it. I always think of it as though we were just a bunch of wild animals penned in here with the agent who could do anything he liked to us. The agent was just like a king. . . .[47]

The goal of the U.S. government policy that was carried out by the Indian agents was "complete assimilation of the Indians into American society in as short a period as possible."[48] Essentially the Makah lost their rights to retain their old customs if these did not fit with the values of the dominant white culture and the Indian Service at that time.

In order to achieve assimilation, the agents decided that many elements of the old Makah culture had to be eliminated. These included the language; the old household living arrangements (extended family groups living together in longhouses); the sociopolitical organization, with its chiefs, commoners, and slaves; warfare; the ceremonial system with its secret society initiation ceremonies, potlatches, and feasts; native curing methods and ceremonies; subsistence activities; and the native education system where children were taught proper Makah values, beliefs, and behaviors by their parents, grandparents, and elders.[49]

Education was one of the principal methods used to effectively eradicate the old Makah culture. A day school was first established in Neah Bay in 1863. It became a boarding school in 1874 and was returned to a day school in 1896.[50] In the 1930s the school became part of the Clallam County School District and was no longer under the control of the Bureau of Indian Affairs (BIA).[51] For approximately seventy years, however, the BIA school was seen as the primary instrument for "civilizing" the Makah. One of the early teachers stated that his policy was to take Makah children

> entirely out of barbarous surroundings and put them into the midst of a civilized Christian home. . . . The Indian tongue must be put to silence and nothing but English allowed in all social intercourse. Meanwhile, habits of industry

must be cultivated. The girls must be practised in all domestic duty, in cooking, sweeping, scrubbing, sewing, and knitting, and the boys must be practised in gardening and all kinds of useful work. . . . When . . . they learn that in their teacher they have found the best of all friends, it will be easy for him to . . . awaken in their minds moral convictions, knowledge of God, of retribution, and the way of salvation.[52]

The children were also taught basic academic subjects for a portion of each day. In 1875 an educator stated that there would be "such a change in the child's tastes and habits that he will never return to Indian life but will seek new social alliances and a better form of life."[53] There was no recognition by educators or Indian agents that native beliefs and customs might be of importance and value to the Makah people themselves and therefore deserving of support and preservation.

Makah school children were required to attend weekly church services and daily prayers. They could speak only English in school and were strongly urged not to participate in any Indian-related ceremonies or activities. The children were taught to regard their elders as "ignorant and superstitious barbarians whose advice should be ignored."[54] This indoctrination was destructive not only to individuals but to the society and culture as a whole. In spite of the fact that their former lives were ridiculed and made to seem insignificant, the Makah had little desire for and did not readily accept white, "civilized" ways. Generation after generation of Makah children were subjected to these pressures by the school.

Ceremonial life also came under strong attack. In the late 1880s the American government outlawed the potlatch, bone games, and other ceremonial activities. In 1890, the Annual Report of the Commissioner of Indian Affairs stated the following:

All heathenish and barbarous practices I have endeavored to stop and where possible prohibit altogether, such as the "Cloqually [Klukwali] Dance." . . . Potlatching of all kinds . . . has been carried on here without stay or hindrance, and I have had a great deal of trouble in carrying out *the instructions of the Indian Department* in this matter. I have been successful in a measure, so much so, that it is practically stopped on the reservation, though they now give potlatches on an island near Cape Flattery, in the Pacific Ocean [emphasis added].[55]

The giving away of great quantities of goods at potlatches was considered excessive and improper behavior by government officials. Potlatches also strengthened the positions of the chiefs, reinforcing a native social structure that did not fit with the government policy of assimilation, mentioned earlier.[56] In addition, Indian agents strongly disapproved of the singing, betting, and gambling that accompanied bone games; therefore these activities were forbidden.[57]

Another change not orchestrated by government policy yet one that had a major impact on Makah ceremonial life was the introduction of a cash economy. The Indians had always operated under a trade and barter system, with chiefs the primary figures in the transactions. This system was still in operation as late as 1872, according to Neah Bay Indian Agent E. M. Gibson, who stated that "for their principal articles of traffic with the whites, which are oil and furs, they do not receive money, but trade in exchange; so they really have but little money." [58] By 1880, however, this situation had changed, and the Indians were receiving cash:

> The chances for money-making by seal-catching have kept some otherwise inclined to farm from doing so.
>
> The run of fur-seal on the coast . . . this year was greater than for many years past, and attracted many vessels to engage in catching them, which gave employment to all the male Indians of both tribes [Makah and Quileute] . . . . It is estimated that about $20,000 was thus made and distributed among the two tribes. Most of the Indians have a small sum saved up for winter's use. [59]

Another means of acquiring cash was through wage work, which began about 1881:

> The farmer, carpenter, and blacksmith, each with his Indian apprentice, have assiduously given their time to the different duties required of them and been so successful in teaching their appprentices their respective trades, that by order of the Department, I have discharged the white employees and appointed the apprentices to fill the different positions. [60]

With these economic changes, a Makah man no longer had to work to support the wealth and position of his chief; instead, he could work to benefit himself and his own immediate family. These were the results that the government wished to see. Each man began to build his own small power base using the money acquired through wage work. Thus anyone who had money was capable of giving potlatches and acquiring songs, a situation that had never existed before.

By 1894, and probably earlier, there were no longer any chiefs in Neah Bay. It is not known what happened to them. Swan in his diaries states that there was no head chief in 1863, nor was there one in 1878. [61] He does not mention the presence or absence of chiefs in the 1880s or 1890s. Indian Agent W. L. Powell stated, however, in 1894:

> There is no headman, chief, or tyee of these Indians, which is rather a disadvantage to them and, for this reason: There are several who would like to be headmen, but they can not agree. The consequence is that they are divided among themselves. [62]

In the absence of hereditary chiefs, and with most men working, bringing in cash, and saving money, feuds could easily develop among those still claiming descent from chiefs. The fact that the Makah were already divided among themselves in 1894 implies that this is what was happening. Thus the stage was set over one hundred years ago for the difficulties surrounding ownership of chiefly rights and privileges, difficulties that continue today.

During the late 1880s, Makah land status was also being threatened. Traditionally, each chief and his extended family owned certain pieces of land which were used for specific purposes.[63] Under the Dawes Allotment Act of 1887, however, the reservation was surveyed and each individual was allotted a certain portion of land, to be held in trust by the government for twenty-five years. After this time, the individual would be granted outright ownership and would then be free to rent or sell the land as he or she wished. Any extra land not allotted would be sold to white settlers.[64] Thus, conceivably, individuals could have sold off most of the reservation and been left without either land or livelihood. In general, the Dawes Act had a disastrous effect on Indian land and life. Coming as they did from vastly different cultural backgrounds, Indian people could not survive as imagined by the creators of this bill. Many tribes, though not the Makah, lost much of their tribal reservation land as a result of this law.

Years later, with the passage of the Indian Reorganization Act of 1934, the anti-Indian government policies described above were largely reversed, and an attempt was made to rectify some of the earlier injustices.[65] Commissioner of Indian Affairs John Collier and his administration tried, through the provisions of this act, to make amends for the approximately seventy years of cultural abuse and destruction supported by previous government policies and administrations. As part of a series of changes, the allotment policy was ended, and land allotted to individuals was reconverted into tribal trust land that could not be sold to nontribal members.[66] In essence, the Dawes Act of 1887 was reversed, and in this way the Makah reservation was preserved. The Indian Reorganization Act also encouraged tribal self-government, extended financial credit to tribes, began to improve education and medical programs, restored Indian religious freedom, and promoted a revival of Indian culture.[67]

In spite of the new, constructive policies, many of the earlier negative changes had been in place for so long that it was impossible for Indian peoples to return to the old ways. Former Makah living arrangements could not be reestablished, nor could the system of chiefs, the secret societies with their music and ceremonies, or the old style of Indian education and language acquisition. Traditional hunting and fishing techniques had also largely disappeared. Therefore, individuals and families still had to seek other satisfactory ways of merging remnants of their old lives with elements of the new.

Recent Changes: Contemporary Neah Bay

According to 1992 census data, 1,079 enrolled tribal members live on the Makah reservation.[68] Neah Bay, as might be expected, is very different in appearance from what it was one hundred years ago. The former longhouses have all been torn down,[69] and even the single-family frame homes which replaced them have mostly rotted from the damp weather or burned down and not been rebuilt. Either mobile homes or HUD (Housing and Urban Development) houses now fill much of the landscape. The HUD houses, built over the past twenty years, have not survived especially well in the humid environment of the rain forest.

Most families now live in single-family dwellings, and old people sometimes live alone. Housing for a number of senior citizens has recently been constructed in the center of the village across from the Senior Citizens' Center. There is a continual housing shortage in Neah Bay; the supply cannot keep up with the demand. When new HUD houses are built or old ones vacated, families who are at the top of a long waiting list can either rent or buy them.

Though physically still quite isolated on this remote corner of the Olympic Peninsula, the Makah maintain connections with the non-Makah world by means of radio, television, Citizen's Band radios, computers, and cellular telephones. One precarious paved road, Highway 112 built in 1932, connects Neah Bay with the outside world. Before 1932, boats were the only means of transportation.

Located in or near present-day Neah Bay are the Makah Tribal Council offices, Housing Authority, Realty Office, Day Care and Head Start centers, public grade school and high school, a Fisheries Office, Forestry Office, the Makah Cultural and Research Center (museum), the Makah police station and tribal court, and a public health clinic. Eleven churches are also present, along with one large community hall where potlatches, bone games, and other community functions are held. Along Bayview (Front) Street, adjacent to the bay, are several motels, a restaurant, a gas station, the post office, Washburn's General Store (recently rebuilt five or six blocks east of its former location after a devastating fire in 1992), the Senior Citizens' Center, an alcohol treatment center, and a number of sports fishing enterprises.

Many (though not all) of the above offices and activities are run with the help of the Makah Tribal Council. This body, created under the provisions of the Indian Reorganization Act of 1934, replaced the former system of chiefs as the political arm of the tribe. The council controls a variety of Makah enterprises and oversees many activities in the village. Elections are held every December to select one or two of the five council members, who hold their positions for staggered three-year terms.[70] Anyone who is a member of the tribe and at least one-quarter Makah is eligible to run for the council, whether descended from chiefs, commoners, or slaves. Family and factional alignments play an important part in Tribal Council elections and subsequent decisions and job appointments. There appears to be no prejudice against women being members of the council; several have been elected, and one was chosen vice chairman in the past. In 1984, two of the five council members were women. Others have served in 1993, 1996, 1998, and 2001.

The U.S. armed forces have added another dimension to life in Neah Bay. Two small bases have brought a steady stream of outsiders into the area. The Neah Bay

Coast Guard Station has been present at the east end of the village since 1904. The Makah Air Force Base, located about two miles southwest of Neah Bay proper, opened in 1950 and employed approximately 120 men.[71] Due to federal budget cuts, it closed in 1988. Since 1996, the Makah Tribal Council and a number of other tribal agencies have occupied this facility.

Over the years, a number of the non-Indian men stationed in Neah Bay have married Makah women and settled in the community. Consequently, the number of full-blood Makahs living on the reservation has decreased.[72] Marriages with members of other Northwest Coast tribes are still common, however, as was true in the past. Extended families, perhaps less strong than in early contact days, continue to aid each other in child rearing, ceremonial, and political endeavors.

The majority of Makah men have, until recently, supported their families by fishing and logging. Since 1981, however, both of these industries have been on the decline. As a result of new environmental laws, many years of poor logging practices, and changing economic conditions in the United States, the logging industry has been in trouble and, for a period of years during the 1980s, ceased operation entirely in the vicinity of Neah Bay. Due to clear-cutting, the richly forested mountains and hills around Neah Bay are now mostly bare or contain only scraggly growth. In 1984 no Makah men were employed in the logging industry. In 1988 some logging operations moved back into the area, but few Makah men were employed. In 1989 and 1990 a few Makahs worked independently as gypos,[73] but not as actual loggers. As of 1994 less than half a dozen Makah men were working in the logging industry.[74]

Because of severe fishing restrictions imposed by federal and state laws and regulations, only a few Makah men have been able to make an adequate living as fishermen since the 1980s. In 1994 the Makah had 142 fishing boats, most with two men to a boat; however, not all of these men were full-time fishermen and not all could make a living by fishing.[75] One hundred years ago, fishing and sealing provided comfortable livings for many young Makah families.[76] In the early twenty-first century, this is no longer the case. Sealing has long been outlawed to protect various species from extinction, and fishing has been on the decline for many years. In 1994 Makah men were only allowed to fish for salmon for ceremonial use. No commercial salmon fishing occurred at all off the coasts of Washington and Oregon because the salmon runs had dropped dangerously low and extinction was imminent unless drastic steps were taken.[77] Since then, commercial fishing for salmon as well as other species has once again been sanctioned, but government regulations limit the times severely, and the catches are much smaller than before.

Given the recent determination that the gray whale is no longer endangered, the tribe is trying to reinstitute whale hunting, which was halted over seventy years ago. With approval of the International Whaling Commission, the Makah are allowed to hunt up to five gray whales per year for ceremonial and subsistence use.[78] One whale was taken in 2000, and the meat and blubber distributed among all tribal members. Currently the crew is training for future whale hunts.

Over the years, the natural food supply on the reservation has dwindled. Shellfish and other sea life in tidal pools along the shore have declined drastically in the past twenty-five years and no longer provide a steady alternative source of food. The elders speak sadly of these changes. Berries remain plentiful in the woods and some families do gather and preserve them, but such activities are no longer undertaken by the majority of women and children in the community. At present, most people rely on food from the grocery store.

Moving from the sea to the forest, the men hunt deer and elk more frequently now than in the past, because they can no longer confidently rely on fish and sea mammals as their staples. The amount of land hunting attempted depends partially on a family's economic condition. If several family members are employed and can provide adequate support, there is no need to hunt. Otherwise, the men feel an obligation to do so in order to supply their families with meat.

Due to circumstances largely beyond their control, the economic picture for the Makah in Neah Bay today is far from ideal. In the past, tribal members were self-sufficient and most survived comfortably by successfully utilizing the natural environment.[79] Recently, however, nothing has filled the vacuum left by the loss of logging and the reduction in fishing. Therefore, some families have been forced to depend on unemployment compensation, food stamps, and welfare.[80] Most people would rather have jobs; the problem is simply that very few are available either on the reservation or in the surrounding areas. A limited number of people work in tribal government, the fish hatchery, the schools, the museum, Washburn's General Store, the restaurant, the filling station, or in the few BIA positions still existing in Neah Bay.

Some families survive by creating handmade items for sale to tourists and art collectors. Makah artists specialize in woven baskets in a variety of sizes and shapes; miniature totem poles; carved masks; canoe paddles; drums; wall plaques; prints; silver earrings, bracelets, pendants; bead and shell jewelry; and special Makah T-shirts, jackets, and baseball caps. A number of families supplement their incomes by creating art objects; others rely totally on the income from these sales. Even though the items bring good prices, the quantity sold by any one family usually is not enough to do more than allow them to survive. Perhaps a half dozen young Makah men in their thirties and forties are becoming well known in the art world as carvers and jewelers and are on their way toward developing successful careers for themselves.

Living and working off the reservation is not a viable option for most Makah. Many feel strong ties to their land and reservation and do not want to live elsewhere. A number of younger people do move away for a few years in order to go to college or to find a decent job; however, at the first opportunity, most move back. Even though the younger generation often suffers financially by returning to Neah Bay, there are psychological needs that are stronger and that take precedence. The world outside the reservation remains alien.[81] Even with all its problems and the prospect of a lower standard of living, the reservation represents home. Much has changed in the lives of these people over the past one hundred years, yet they maintain a strong sense of group identity, pride in being Makah, and a desire to perpetuate as many aspects of their culture as possible.

A BRIEF OVERVIEW OF MUSIC IN MAKAH LIFE

Makah Songs

Each Makah song owned by an individual or a family is valued for its inherent beauty and also for its ability to reinforce the rank, status, and prestige of its possessor.[82] When performed, a song distinguishes its owner from all other Makahs. A complex system of rules governs both songs and owners—unwritten rules which must be learned and followed in order to honor the songs, preserve the traditions, and also strengthen the position of one's family in the society.

Traditional and Contemporary Song Ownership Practices

Song Ownership in the Past

One hundred twenty-five years ago, songs, like people, were ranked in importance. Chiefs, owners of the most important songs, gave them to their successors—usually their oldest sons or other immediate family members. Occasionally, high ranking songs could be given by a chief to upper class persons who were not family members. In contrast, commoners possessed songs of lesser significance, and slaves were not allowed to own songs.

Upper class men owned most of the songs; however, some could be given to, and owned by, high ranking women. For instance, a chief often gave songs to his daughter on the occasion of her wedding; or, in order to strengthen the bonds between two families, a chief might give a song as a gift to the daughter of another chief. It was understood that these women would later transfer such songs to their sons. If they had no sons, then the songs would be given to a daughter or a niece, who would pass them on to a son or other male relative. Generally, women were considered musical caretakers who eventually transferred their songs to male descendants. (The same is still true today).

Each song transfer, whether to a family member or other upper class person, always occurred at a potlatch hosted by the current song owner. The speaker announced the name of the song to be given, related its ownership history, stated the new owner's name, and then presented the justification for his or her rights to the song. After being sung (so that those present could hear and remember it), the owner publicly relinquished all title to the song and turned it over to the new owner, who then had exclusive ownership rights and full responsibility for its proper use and perpetuation. In a society which utilized the oral tradition, this process eliminated potential confusion over song ownership and reaffirmed the social order. The giving of gifts, *p'ačił*,[83] to the guests who witnessed the transfer, was the final seal of the transaction.

Important hereditary songs (which had to remain within the upper class), were never given casually. Before being considered for song ownership, a person had to demonstrate that he or she was responsible and could be trusted with a new song. After receiving one, the new owner was not at liberty, later, to give it away to just anyone, but was required to consult with the former owner (if that person was still alive), or else with other knowledgeable elders and family members before passing it on. Songs given to non-family members had to be paid for appropriately at a potlatch hosted later in time by the new song owner. By accepting a song, an individual also accepted the obligation to learn and use it properly, which included its periodic performance at potlatches followed by payment to those who served as witnesses. Song ownership and financial responsibility went hand in hand. Therefore, aside from being a trustworthy recipient, one also needed the ability to acquire and distribute wealth. Thus, traditional song ownership was a serious undertaking.

Song Ownership in the Present

The clear cut, well-regulated musical rules briefly described above are not as well known nor fully understood by many younger Makah today. In some areas significant change has occurred, while in others, activities closely resemble those of the past. Songs are still regarded as treasured pieces of personal property, but since the last of the old Makah chiefs died long ago, many of the songs are now owned by their descendants. The situation grows more complicated when one understands that in a number of instances, the chiefs did not choose specific successors to inherit either their positions or their songs before they died. Therefore, the direct lines of descent have often become clouded and, at times, feuds have developed over rightful song ownership.

Makah potlatches, now often called "parties," or "potlatch parties,"[84] continue to include essentially the same elements as in the past: a feast, singing and dancing of family-owned songs, the honoring of special guests, the giving of names, titles, songs, dances, or other privileges to deserving family members, and the giving away of money and gifts to the witnesses. This normally joyful occasion is now sometimes surrounded with tension resulting from song ownership disagreements.[85]

Currently, the activities surrounding a song transfer at a potlatch remain much as they were in the past. The present owner, no longer a chief, but usually the oldest member of the family (either male or female), after a discussion with family members, transfers the song to a son, daughter, grandson, grandaughter, nephew, niece, or to another upper class friend or relative. Preference is still given to the oldest son if he is deserving of the honor. When bestowed on a non-family member, a song must be paid for properly at a potlatch hosted later by the new owner. Song ownership continues to require the expenditure of large amounts of cash. In spite of changes over time, one overriding concept endures: Makah songs must be treated with respect and honor.

Past and Present Occasions for the Performance of Makah Music

Puberty, Courtship, and Marriage

Traditionally, music was a central element in a girl's puberty ceremony, in courtship, and in marriage. Each chief inherited his own specific songs, dances, games, and rituals which were used during these activities; therefore, the ceremonies and music belonging to one chief differed from those belonging to another.[86] By approximately the 1930s, puberty ceremonies, courting, and special native wedding activities had nearly disappeared in Neah Bay. Presently, families do not participate in courting rituals; this is handled individually by the involved couple. A girl's puberty, if noted at all, is celebrated with a feast or potlatch. Family approval is no longer required before a marriage takes place. Today, a wedding potlatch, given separately by each parental family, includes a feast, the performance of inherited songs and dances, the giving of gifts to the bridal couple and their families, and payment in gifts and money to those who witness the event. Other significant changes: songs are seldom given to a new bride on the occasion of her wedding, and male games of strength, formerly quite common, no longer occur.

Religion, Medicine, and Secret Societies

In the past, music played an important part in individual religious activities, especially those involving a guardian spirit or *tumánuwos*. Today, the old, personally-owned *tumánuwos* songs are no longer sung, and rarely, if ever, do men or women go alone into the woods either to seek such power or to acquire new songs. The same situation applies to medicine men or women, their rituals, and their curing songs. Such activities and music are no longer seen as relevant in modern Makah life and much of the esoteric knowledge has been forgotten.

Concerning the secret society ceremonies mentioned earlier—the Klukwali (Wolf Ceremony), Hamatsa (Cannibal Ceremony), and Tsayak (Curing Ceremony) —each had its own types of songs and rituals, most of which were owned by individual chiefs. All of these ceremonies and much of the accompanying music disappeared by the 1920s or '30s. The few individual Klukwali and Hamatsa songs and dances which still exist are performed at contemporary potlatches by descendants of the former chiefly owners.

Potlatch Ceremonies

As previously mentioned, potlatches in the past were occasions where, among other things, the host chief's most important songs and dances were performed. Each chief had his own activities, rituals, and music for the various types of potlatches which he was obligated to hold for his family (principally birth, puberty, naming, marriage, the making of a chief, and memorial). James G. Swan wrote a brief description of a potlatch held in the 1860s, beginning with some of the preparation activities:

> [After all the gifts to be given by the host have been decided upon] . . . . Messengers are then sent to invite the guests. If the party is to be a large one, there will be from fifteen to twenty messengers who go in a body, with painted faces, and sprigs of evergreen in their hair. They enter the lodges with songs, and one of their number announces the intended feast and calls aloud the names of all who are invited. On the set day these assemble at the lodge of the Indian who gives the entertainment, and after much feasting, singing, dancing, and masquerade performance, which sometimes lasts several days, the articles are distributed. The blankets are displayed on poles, or cords stretched across the lodge for the purpose, and all the other articles are placed so as to be seen by the assembled guests, who are seated at one end of the lodge opposite the goods. The herald, after making a speech, extolling the great liberality of the donor, strikes the board with his stick, and calls a name; thereupon an attendant takes the intended present and deposits it in front of the person who is to receive it, where it remains till all are served. Then a song is sung, a dance performed, and the party retire.[87]

An initial procession into the host's lodge was usually a part of the proceedings. In some cases the women might enter, singing and performing a social dance (Group Dance); at other times men and women together might perform either a social dance or a more serious dance.[88] In 1878 James G. Swan attended a potlatch given by one of the Makah chiefs for his children. In his diary he described the procession which preceded the dances:

> . . . . First a procession headed by Russian Jim, naked, except for a short pair of drawers, and with a barbed seal spear thrust through the skin in each side of his waist, another Indian leading him by a string fastened to the seal spear. Johnny's father with skewers through both arms and the calves of both legs. Kichusam and Haiusub and Sessaluk's wives, each with her arms and legs cut and bleeding freely, and several young men with . . . masks on following behind jumping and howling.

THE MAKAH PEOPLE

After this procession had passed around the fire a few times they retired and then the dancing commenced, in which all joined. Some of the dances and costumes were very picturesque and the whole performance was an agreeable pastime. . . . [89]

Many of the processions and dances at an event such as this were highly dramatic, and the description of the spear through the waist, skewers through arms and legs, and blood freely flowing may well have been carefully arranged and staged for dramatic effect rather than being the real thing. Potlatches held today in Neah Bay normally do not have the same dramatic impact as those held over one hundred years ago.

The frequency and elaborateness of contemporary potlatches seem to fluctuate with economic times in the United States. In the 1980s there was a steady decline in the number of jobs and also in the number of potlatches given in Neah Bay. When economic times improved, as they did in the 1990s, more potlatches were given. Those hosted in the 1990s usually involved a tremendous financial commitment, averaging $4000 to $15,000 per ceremony.[90] Help from the extended family is usually required to make such an event successful.

Potlatch parties, now lasting approximately eight to twenty hours instead of several days or even weeks, still include a feast and a number of different kinds of activities, songs, and dances. Generally, there is less variety than in the past, and a much reduced body of songs on which to draw. The reductions are largely the result of U. S. government policies in effect between the 1880s and the 1930s, during which time the ceremonies were outlawed and a great many of the songs, dances, speeches, and other ritual activities banned and subsequently lost.[91] Potlatches still mark important points in the life of an individual even though perhaps fewer events are celebrated than formerly (primarily birth, birthday, marriage, or memorial). Each family now owns just a small number of "important" songs, called Family-Owned Dance songs, which they perform over and over again at the parties. The ceremony, however, still serves as a mechanism by which families proclaim and maintain status and prestige in a highly visible and public manner.

In March 1987, more than one hundred years after James G. Swan attended Makah potlatches, this author kept a journal while helping Helma Swan Ward gather materials and put together a potlatch party for her oldest son, Arnie Hunter. The following excerpts from that journal provide an interesting comparison with Swan's earlier potlatch descriptions, and also with those of Helma, who speaks of her 1983 potlatch in chapter 7.

To set the scene, several weeks before the potlatch, Helma's youngest son, Mike Hunter, designed and mailed an attractive party invitation to the guests. He had drawn a human face mask on the front, and the message inside read: "You are cordially invited to attend a *Wahbit* party given by Arnie Hunter. Neah Bay Community Hall, March 28, 1987, 1:00 P.M."

March 28, 1987: . . . . This *Wahbit (Wá·bit),* "extra food" potlatch was given because Pansy Hudson, the grandmother of the chief from Hoh River, had given a large quantity of food to Arnie Hunter. She gave him 30 pounds of elk meat, many pounds of smelts, 30 pounds of potatoes, 3 bags of apples, 3 bags of oranges and 3 bags of onions. It was Arnie's responsibility to give a potlatch and feed his own tribe this food, add much more to it, invite the Quileutes and Hohs, and feed them all a wonderful meal. He had to pay Pansy back several times over. This is the proper way the situation should be handled. Several of the guests, when they rose to speak during the party, commented on this. "This is the way such a party should be given and such a gift should be repaid," they said. "No one should go hungry. There should always be plenty of food." And there was. It was a fine party.

Preparation for the Party

March 25, 1987: . . . When I arrived at Helma's house today, most of the rooms were full of gifts for Saturday's Wahbit potlatch. . . .

March 26, 1987: . . . In the evening, Helma and I went over to the Senior Citizens' Center to use the kitchen and start baking. Used Betty Crocker Yellow Cake Mix: 4 packages for each layer of a 2 layer cake—cooked in giant rectangular pans. . . . Earlier in the evening we had organized the gifts, put tags and labels on all the blankets and put a name on each blanket. Made a list of all the people who were to get blankets. Helma is giving gifts to each of the families in Neah Bay who give potlatches, whether or not they are descended from chiefs. . . .

March 27, 1987: Helma asked me to stay at her house [today] and give out the various jobs she had assigned to different family members. She and Arnie went to Port Angeles [70 miles away] to get vegetables, more blankets, and more gifts. . . . Her youngest son, Mike, was working and her husband, Wimpy, went fishing, so neither of them helped us during the day. Her daughter, Babe, came over and did a number of tasks. . . . I made a huge boiled cake, as Helma requested. . . . After he got off work, Mike and a friend went to dig clams for clam chowder for tomorrow. . . .

In the evening we packed up things that needed to go to the [community] hall, and went over there. Some of Helma's female relatives were there and others came in as the evening progressed. Bessie and Dallie, her sisters, were there, and a number of their daughters and some of Katherine's children and grandchildren. Babe and her daughter, Rhonda, and her kids were there. [Nieces] Alice Radke and Juanita Carron, and others. . . . After greeting each other and chewing the fat a bit, the work began. We set up and covered long tables to feed approximately 300 people . . . then the whole crew began peeling 180 pounds of potatoes. . . . It took us about 1 and ¾ hours to do all those potatoes. Once they were completed we began on the carrots [for the stew]. They went faster than the potatoes. . . . Arnie Hunter was there for a good part of the time, talking to all of us, making little jokes, giving moral support, and overseeing the operation. Everything was going well, and he was pleased. . . . After completing the carrots, everyone sat around drinking coffee and eating bread rolls which had been baked for tomorrow. . . . There was lots of gossip and jokes and laughter. . . . When we got home, Mike had brought in a huge pail of butter clams, steamers, and cockles. Helma decided to open and clean the butters and have them ready for the chowder for tomorrow. . . . She left the steamers and cockles in fresh water, to be cooked in the morning. . . .

The Potlatch

March 28, 1987: This was the day of Helma and Arnie's Wahbit Party in Neah Bay and we worked all morning getting ready for it. . . . Helma's cooks had arrived at the hall and all the female relatives too, so the tables got set, the food got cooked and decorations put up—crepe paper across ceiling and daffodils on the tables. Everything looked lovely. We raced home at 12:45 P.M. to get dressed for the party which was to start at 1 P.M. . . . Mike had gathered all the costumes, masks, and dance gear and had them in several boxes ready to go. He loaded everything into the car for us. He and Wimpy stayed behind to get dressed and to bring over all the gifts.

Helma and I then went over about 1:30 P.M. and the hall was full. Everyone was sitting patiently at the long tables, waiting. . . . All the guests were at the two long tables on the west side of the hall. The Makah were at the tables on the east side, generally sitting in family groups, except for the senior citizens who sat as a group at one table on the far east side.

The Makahs sang their Dinner songs to begin the festivities. Ed Claplanhoo [the Master of Ceremonies] announced that this was a Wahbit Party, not often held in Neah Bay anymore, and that Helma Ward and Arnie Hunter were giving it. Helma's female relatives were serving the meal while the songs were being sung. Then the Quileutes got up and sang a very long Dinner song. When this was finished, the people could finally start eating. The food was excellent! Joan Carol was the primary cook. There was elk stew, fresh smelts, kippered salmon, cole slaw, mashed potatoes, green beans, bread rolls, buckskin bread, canned fruit, the layer cake, the boiled cake, coffee, and juice.

When everyone had finished, the women cleared the tables and took "Wahbit"—"extra food," home to eat later. The men folded and moved all the tables and swept the floor where the dancing would shortly take place. Everyone pulled their chairs back against the walls. The Swan family all sat together at the south end of the hall.

The five guests of honor included Helma's three children: Arnie, Babe, and Mike Hunter; Sarah Woodruff, from Quileute, the oldest living member from Helma's mother's side of the family; and Joy Swan Smythe, Helma's younger sister. They sat out in front of the crowd on the south side of the hall (see fig. 13). Ed Claplanhoo, the Master of Ceremonies, announced the opening event, called the Love Circle, where a Group Dance song was sung while everyone in the audience who wished to do so, got up and marched [or danced] around the room in a counterclockwise circle, greeted the guests of honor, gave them a dollar, and shook their hands.

Then Ed announced the visitors from the South—Hoh, Queets, and Taholah. They had the first turn singing and dancing. Each family present sang one of their songs, some with the help of Dave Fourlines [a white man who had lived among the Quileutes for many years], and then . . . gave away to the hosts, to the honored guests, and to other important people present. When they were finished, the Makahs took their turn. . . . Quite a few Makah families sang and danced one or two Family-Owned Dance songs [mostly Wolf Dances, Hamatsa Dances, Grizzly Bear Dances, or Eagle Dances] using the appropriate costumes, and then each family gave away.

Helma had some of her relatives pass coffee and pop around, then rolls and cake, later on, clam chowder, then apples and oranges, later yet, tuna fish sandwiches. She had something going around almost every hour so people didn't get hungry while sitting there all that time. All of the singing, dancing, and giving away continued over many hours.

. . . Next, Andy Callicum, the Chief of Nootka at Gold River on Vancouver Island, B.C., stood and sang a long chant . . . followed by another of his family's songs. . . . When he finished, he spoke to the audience in English. He spoke of the power he received from the people who were attending this event. He thanked everyone for their generosity. He spoke of the dignity and pride of Arnie Hunter's family.

Finally it was the Swan family's turn. Helma Ward made a speech . . . in which she spoke of Indian beliefs. "Indians pray every day, not just on Sunday," she said. Her father had always told her, "Be yourself. Don't be anybody else! Be yourself! You will always be an Indian. You will never be anything else, so don't try to be." "This is what my father told me," she said. "Now I'm trying to bring my three children up the same way."

Then she called upon all her Swan family relatives who stood and came to the center of the room. There followed a major naming event (see fig. 14). Helma spoke each person's Indian name, and told the audience they were the witnesses and heard all these names and who they belonged to. She said that no one from other families was entitled to use them. Mike Hunter got a new name, Dashúk, meaning "Strong," which belonged to Charlie Anderson's grandfather, who had been a whaler. [Charlie Anderson was Mike's great grandfather.] Several of the cousins got new names as well. The entire audience witnessed this.

[When the naming was completed] Helma sang [one or two songs] for each of her sisters in turn, and then each of them gave away. She sang two Grizzly Bear songs, her father's Hamatsa song, a Fan Dance song, and finally she sang the Changing Mask Dance Song which Arnie has danced for many years and which he danced again that night. He used the full face masks which represent

Fig. 11. Hobuck Beach on the Pacific Ocean side of the Makah Reservation, 1994. Vast expanses of open beach are ringed by thick coniferous vegetation. *Photograph by Linda J. Goodman.*

Fig. 12. Panoramic view of the Neah Bay shoreline with numerous houses and canoes, circa 1905. *Photograph courtesy of MSCUA, University of Washington Libraries (neg. # NA1277).*

Fig. 13. Guests of honor at Swan family potlatch, Neah Bay, Washington, March 28, 1987. Left to right: Mike Hunter, Babe Hunter Markishtum, Arnie Hunter (Helma's three children); Sarah Woodruff (Quilleute relative [now deceased] from Helma's mother's family); and Joy Smythe (Helma's younger sister). *Photograph by Linda J. Goodman.*

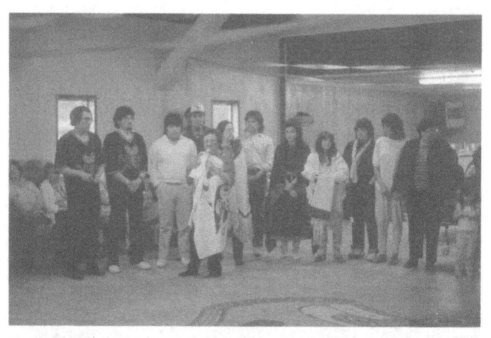

Fig. 14. Helma speaking and giving Indian names to some of the Swan family members. Left to right: Arnie Hunter, Mike Hunter, Ron Markishtum Jr., Brian Kaufmann, Karen LaChester, John LaChester, Lois Smythe, Billy Jo Balch, Regina Baines, Simone Radke, Alice Radke. Swan family potlatch, Neah Bay, Washington, March 28, 1987. *Photograph by Linda J. Goodman.*

Fig. 15. The first of two photos depicting a portion of the Changing Mask Dance performed at a potlatch given by Helma Swan Ward in Neah Bay, March 28, 1987. At the beginning of the dance, Arnie Hunter (Helma's oldest son) wears the inherited, double-headed raven button blanket, has a black band painted across his face, and dances without a mask. (Note that background dancers are wearing painted dance capes instead of the usual black dance capes.) *Photograph by Linda J. Goodman.*

Fig. 16. During the final portion of the Changing Mask Dance, Arnie Hunter, still wearing the double-headed raven button blanket, dons the "Mask with the Open and Closing Eyes." March 28, 1987. *Photograph by Linda J. Goodman.*

Fig. 17. Making Arnie Hunter a chief. Arnie is holding his newly acquired copper—one symbol of his chiefship. Andy Callicum, from Gold River, British Columbia, is singing and Helma Swan Ward is drumming. Swan family potlatch, Neah Bay, Washington, March 28, 1987. *Photograph by Linda J. Goodman.*

the four changing seasons, and then the fifth mask which opens and closes its eyes, allowing the chief to see all his people and guard and protect them (see figs. 15, 16). Following the performance of this dance, Arnie and Helma, [as hosts] began giving away [huge quantities of gifts], beginning with the Quileutes and Queets and Hoh people. Some of the men sang short victory songs upon receiving their gifts. After gifts had been given to all the visitors, Helma and Arnie gave away to all the Makah who always appear at the parties. Each family got a blanket and some money. . . .

When the gift-giving was completed, Andy Callicum came forward and sang another set of songs. . . . followed by a long speech announcing that he was making Arnie Hunter a chief. First they took out a copper[92] and announced that it belonged in this family and was worth $75,000. The copper was made for them by Dave Fourlines and is called "X'á·qʷa·" in Makah (see fig. 17). It provides the strongest protection a family can have. Then he took the copper and held it in front of him and was followed by Helma and Arnie. They began a counterclockwise circuit of the room, making small counterclockwise circles at each corner of the room. Then Andy announced, "Chief Arnie—this is the time he is being made a chief." He thanked everyone for coming and honoring him and paying their respects and witnessing this important event. . . . Andy also talked about the importance of being a chief and the responsibilities that go with it. This is very serious, he said, and not to be taken lightly. Andy is an eloquent speaker. A number of people listened attentively, but many were talking and didn't hear him at all. . . .

Helma then thanked everyone present for listening to the names and the songs and giving her the opportunity to get them all straightened out [their ownership]. She named the others who had coppers—who were chiefs and were entitled to have them. . . .

After everyone had been properly thanked, it was time for the games to be played. . . . They played four games. . . . Everyone enjoyed them and almost everyone stayed to watch. When these were ended, the potlatch party was at an end. People gathered up their belongings and their kids and began to leave. . . . about 10 P.M.

[After the party, Andy Callicum came over to Helma's house and he talked to us while we were feeding him again.] He said that he hoped that the people listened to him and heard what he had to say about the importance of remembering who they were and maintaining their traditions and keeping the family ownership and descent straight. It was very important that they not claim things that were not rightfully theirs. Arnie Hunter had the rights to the chiefship, to the songs, dances, and names, and therefore, he, Andy, was officially turning them over to him (Arnie), and his mother (Helma) would no longer be caretaker.

Thus it is clear that many potlatch elements present more than one hundred years ago can still be seen in Makah potlatches performed in the late twentieth and early twenty-first centuries.

Entertainment Activities

A number of different kinds of Makah entertainment songs existed in the past, several of which were typically performed at potlatches. Some were family-owned, others were not, but none were closely connected with status and power, as were most other kinds of songs. Two particular types of entertainment songs, *T'abáa* songs and Group Dance songs, often provided a break from the more serious parts of potlatch ceremonies. T'Abáa songs, family-owned social songs, were not considered important for upholding status and prestige, but were sung for fun at potlatches. No dances accompanied them. Today, T'abáa songs continue to be performed occasionally at potlatches, but are more often heard at small family gatherings or at special dinners held at the Senior Citizens' Center in Neah Bay. Group Dance songs allowed all tribal members attending a potlatch, no matter what their rank, the opportunity to dance and take part in a musical performance. Whether the specific Group Dance songs were family-owned or not, everyone who wished to do so, was free to participate. Although sometimes performed at potlatches today, Group Dance songs are most commonly seen during Makah Day.

Makah Day, established in 1926, first celebrated tribal members' new legal status (granted in 1924) as American citizens.[93] Occurring each year on the third weekend in August, festivities now include a series of races, games, Indian dances, and a salmon feast (see fig. 22). It is a time greatly anticipated by the children, who always dance, and by the elders, who have an opportunity to teach them about Makah music and culture during the rehearsals which precede the performances.

From the past came another enjoyable form of entertainment—the bone game. Usually held on Makah Day, as well as at other times, this popular adult gambling game includes many well-loved songs. Always played by two teams, the side hiding the bones [in the clenched fists of two players] sings its songs as loudly as possible, with great strength and conviction, in order to bring winning power and to keep the other side from correctly guessing where the bones are hidden. The songs are not connected with political power or prestige and most are not individually owned.

Songs in several other lighter veins included lullabies sung to infants and story songs sung to children. The latter were integral parts of stories relating incidents in the lives of various strange and wonderful mythological creatures. Children loved both the stories and the songs. Lullabies are rarely used today; story songs are heard only occasionally when elders sing and tell them to the young.

Even though the types and quantity of music have decreased over the years, a number of traditional songs (including primarily Family-Owned Dance songs, Group Dance songs, T'abáa songs, Dinner songs, and Bone Game songs) have survived and are still loved, learned, and performed by the Makah.

Changes in Musical and Ceremonial Roles

Clearly, many elements of Makah music have changed over time, largely as a result of white influence and a host of government policies, several of which were described earlier. Also impacted have been the musical and ceremonial roles of Makah men and women. The late 1950s saw the passing of the last of a group of elderly men who had sung, danced, and run the ceremonial life of the tribe since their youth. Even before the deaths of these elders, however, many of the younger Makah men had lost interest in acquiring their knowledge. Busy at day jobs and often the objects of ridicule and derision from non-Indian co-workers, young males no longer perceived native ceremonies as good and valuable parts of their culture. Thus most had not spent necessary time with their elders practicing songs and dances and learning the traditions. The resulting change was striking. The younger men stopped planning and hosting potlatches. Fewer and fewer filled standard male ceremonial roles such as speech makers, song leaders, singers, drummers, and so forth. Ultimately, they could no longer teach these male ceremonial roles and duties to their descendants.

Enter the women. A few who had been well-trained as children and young adults retained this knowledge even though they had not used most of it previously. They were determined not to let the traditions and ceremonies lapse. Acquiring roles formerly held by men, they slowly began guiding their tribe back to some of the ancient, cherished cultural practices. A small group of older women assumed ceremonial responsibilities they had never held before and in this way were able to perpetuate the potlatches. They became potlatch planners, hosts, speech makers, song leaders, singers, drummers, and occasionally, lead dancers. During the 1960s, '70s, and '80s, mothers, grandmothers, and other female relatives also began teaching songs, dances, and proper ceremonial behavior to the children.

Now, in the early twenty-first century, these children have become adults, and many of them continue to value the cultural traditions they were taught. Several of the younger and middle-aged men, with guidance from the older women, are again assuming their former roles and duties in Makah musical and ceremonial life. However, it is unclear whether the young women who learned from and assisted their mothers and grandmothers in the recent past will be content to return to the ceremonial sidelines. Thus, the entire musical and ceremonial situation currently is in flux. Because cultural interest has been rekindled, however, there is a strong likelihood that the Makah heritage, sustained and transmitted by the older women, will become more deeply ingrained, once again.

PART 2

HELMA'S
STORY

CHAPTER 2

THE EARLY YEARS: LIFE WITH MY PARENTS AND GRANDPARENTS

MY ARRIVAL

Oh, yes, it was snowing when I was born! My mother used to tell me, "You were born with the snow. It was *snowing* when you were born!" That was unusual because it doesn't snow that time of the year. Every once in a great while it will, but it's not common. It rains all the time; it doesn't snow.[1] My birthday is January 31, and the year was 1918. My mother said Mrs. Kalappa, the Indian doctor, delivered me. She delivered most of my mom's babies, and later on she delivered two of mine. After I was born they put in eyedrops. Dr. Woods, the white doctor on the reservation, made out the record because the government has to have some kind of a record. That's all my mom ever told me, and I wasn't curious enough to ask—I guess because she was always having babies, and I was always kept busy helping her.

She did say that I never learned to crawl. She said, "Well, you would *never, ever* crawl, not like the other babies. You were just different. Whenever you needed anything, you rolled after it. You just rolled!"

Before that, though, when I was just a little baby, my mom used to pack me on her back. When you pack the babies on your back, you have both hands free to do whatever you want to do. That way she wouldn't have to look after me. She was a hardworking woman, always doing men's work. So this is the way she would take care of me—tie me on her back.

My mom was mostly working with my dad. He started teaching her early, because ever since I could remember she was a carpenter, a bricklayer, she used to shingle houses, and eventually she went into plumbing. He did all these same jobs, working for the Bureau of Indian Affairs in Neah Bay, and she worked right along with him. She worked for many years and didn't get any money for it.[2]

Since my mom was working, my grandmother, Alice Holden, took care of me most of the time when I was little. She was married to my grandfather, Charlie Anderson, for a long time, but they separated and got a divorce when I was very small. Then she married Gilbert Holden, and I can't remember her being other than Alice Holden. She used to come over to our house early in the morning and stay there all day until late at night. Her husband had cattle out at Tsooyez beach, so he'd be out there most of the time. That's why my grandma used to come over to our house, I think.

RIDING THE HORSES TO GREEN POINT

Right beyond Tsooyez beach is a place called Green Point. We still own that land, but there's no house there now. My grandfather, Charlie Anderson, used to live there, on the hill. When we were young children, we'd have to go up there on horses right after school. You couldn't get a wagon up there; there was only a horse trail. In the spring my mother used to go out there to plow up his fields. He had his own garden up there. I suppose my dad could have taken care of us then, but he was working, so it was easier for us to be with mom.

Right after school on Friday, we went to the barn (my dad had a good-sized barn in Neah Bay), and we'd have to bridle the horses ourselves and saddle them and then ride up there to Green Point. We'd leave Neah Bay on Friday evening. You could hear all those owls hooting, and *it was just scary,* and I hated it![3] It was scary because of the owls. You heard them hooting. Sometimes they'd fly right by you, and when they did, they smelled so terrible! I can remember I was so little, and I would be crying. My sister [Katherine] would run away and my brother [Conrad] would go ahead, and I'd be the last one. We had three orange horses. I've never seen any more like them. They were all orange, and they had black manes. One we called Fritzie, the next one we called Candy, and the oldest one was Mutt. They used to give me Mutt because he was old and stiff. Maybe they were afraid I'd fall down, being the younger one. So, I couldn't get old Mutt to run as fast, and they'd be way ahead of me, and I'd be sitting on that horse crying, "Wait for me! Wait for me!" And those old hoot owls would be going like mad. I just hated going up there in the spring and then coming home. It was like pulling teeth for me when we started back home to Neah Bay from my grandpa's place on Sunday. We had to go across the beach because there was no road out there, and we'd have to wait for the tide to go out. In the spring and in the fall the low tides are still late in the evening, not in the daytime like they are in the summer. We had to start back on Sunday because of school the next day. Sometimes my mother would stay with her father at Green Point until the next day, so we went back alone.

SPRING PLANTING

My mom needed our help in the spring when she planted a garden for her dad at Green Point. First she'd plow, and then she'd harrow the earth and get it all smooth. Us kids had to take up all the grass and throw it to one side of the garden. When she put the lines on the ground, then sometimes we'd be out there helping her plant the seeds. If it was potato time, we'd have to be putting the potatoes in and then hoeing them closed, putting them under. We weeded too; put them in buckets and dumped them against the fence. I guess that's why we went—to work with my mother; but mostly they worked by themselves, just my grandfather and my mother.

Every once in a while they'd move the garden. If they didn't move it, they'd plant in a different direction. Maybe one year the garden goes north and south, and the next year it might go east and west. They would never keep it in one place all the time.[4]

My grandfather used to grow what we call Ozette potatoes, or finger potatoes. They grow long, and they're just full of eyes—all kinds of eyes. Some people call them Indian potatoes, but we call them Ozette potatoes. He used to have a whole patch of them. He'd get them all grown and just put them away—seed potatoes in one bin and eating potatoes in another bin. Mostly they boiled them, or they'd bake them. That's the only way you could eat them because there were so many eyes in them. He had a whole mess of those, plus he used to like those little red potatoes, too, and planted them mostly for baking.

He also grew parsnips, turnips, peas, carrots, rutabagas, beets, radishes, onion sets, cabbage, lettuce, and occasionally beans. He used to say that beans were white man's food. Cucumbers wouldn't grow; tomatoes wouldn't grow: it was too cold. He just grew a little bit of lettuce off and on because it would never get round in this part of the country. Evidently the climate isn't right, and the leaves would be very loose. So mom just planted the leafy kind, and we had salads out of that. It wasn't very enjoyable, so she never planted too much of it.

My grandpa dearly loved turnips and rutabagas and parsnips. They'd grow just so big, and then he'd slice them up and sit there and tell stories, eating and crunching on them. In the wintertime my grandpa would feed us a lot of raw vegetables. He'd slice up some rutabagas and turnips, and then he'd bring out the seal oil. We never had any of them without dipping them in seal oil. He'd slice 'em; we'd dip 'em and eat 'em. So, we had snacks just like anybody else. We used to have a lot of fun out there.

He had a good way to store those vegetables, too. He'd keep them in a little shed next to the barn, where it was cool. He used to take the cabbage and just pull them up by the roots and hang them up. Then he used to line a box with fir-tex (a kind of pressed board) and put all the carrots in there. They used to keep all winter. The same with the beets, parsnips, turnips, rutabagas. He always made a separate box for each one of them, so we knew where to get them. We used to let the potatoes sit outside for a day or two and dry them out, then bring them in the house and give them a real good drying out, and then put them in the same kind of boxes. We used to plant a *lot* of potatoes of all kinds: purple potatoes, finger potatoes, red potatoes, and regular potatoes, too. Our family was never in need.

Aside from my grandpa's garden, we also planted at my mom's place in Neah Bay. We lived down at the west end of town—what the Indians used to call Díia. Her parents didn't help her, so we had to. My dad used to help too, in the evening. Mostly what we had was a potato patch. The potatoes would be big enough, and nice on the inside, but I think because it was kind of rocky at Díia, they would be lumpy on the outside. The Indians used to say, "That looks like 'itch.'" When you got "itch" it was little sore spots all over. I don't know whether it's because it's rocky down there or whether it was the clam shells or what. There's an awful lot of clam shells and mussel shells around there, scattered all over the place.

Not only did we have to help my mom and my grandfather with their gardens, but we used to have to help my grandmother Alice Holden, too. Here the potatoes grew well—the skins were just fine. No "itch." I think that's why my mom wanted to plant all her vegetables over at her father's place at Green Point and at her mother's place on the east end of town here—because of how the potatoes grew.[5] So, we used to have most of our vegetable patch with either my grandfather or my grandmother, and only a small one at our own house.

Now, nobody ever has a garden. The last one who used to have a garden was Bertha Smith. She died about twelve or thirteen years back, and she hadn't gardened for four or five years—she was getting pretty old.[6] She even used to grow pumpkins. Come October, she'd make pumpkin pies for the kids and give out pumpkin pies. She was the last one I knew that had a garden.

LIFE WITH MY GRANDFATHER

From the very early times I can remember living with my grandfather over at Green Point in the summers. He used to wake us up at four o'clock in the morning. Every morning—four o'clock! He'd say, "The birds are singing, and they're telling you to get up. Get up, get up, get up. It's four o'clock now. You're not going to sleep your life away!" So, we'd just *drag* ourselves out of bed, and he'd have everything cooked. His wife never cooked. He did. He used to say, "You sleep your life away, it isn't good for you." He told us that the air was better in the morning than it would be in the later part of the day. Everything's been still all night, nothing's been stirring, so the air is very fresh in the morning. Then in the afternoon everybody starts breathing and everybody is walking around. Therefore, it isn't really healthy for a person later in the day. You have all the fresh air in the morning. So he would tell us it's healthy for us to wake up early.

By five o'clock we'd be on the beach picking up shells, looking around. At that time the shells were plentiful. It might sound kind of boring to kids nowadays, but it was sort of peaceful and quiet. You were way out by yourself, and there weren't that many people there.

When we were with my grandpa, we had something to do all the time. We never had time to get bored. Sometimes we helped him get bark—cedar bark—for making baskets. We walked a long ways for it out to the cape area, but we got it. He used to find it and peel it off the trees; then we'd sit there and peel the outer bark off of the inner bark.[7] After it was cleaned, he'd bundle all the pieces up and tie them on his back, and we'd go back down.

Every minute of the day we had something to do with my grandfather. Sometimes we'd be gardening with him; we weeded and we hoed. At times blue jays used to raid the garden; they'd eat the seeds before they started to germinate, so sometimes my grandpa would give us a chance to get out there and use a gun and shoot at them. Most of the time we'd just scare them away, that was all. Just one time I hit one. He told me to take the smallest gun this time, and they were all watching out the window. I went, and I did get the smallest gun, but I got the wrong one. The one I got was shorter than a twenty-two, but he wanted me to take the twenty-two. I didn't understand what he meant, cause I didn't understand the difference between guns. He said, "Get the smallest one," so I got the shortest one that was there. It must have been a little bit bigger than a twenty-two (he later said that I got the twenty-five–twenty). So, I just squatted down, and I aimed, and I hit the blue jay. They were watching me from the window, and, oh! They just about died laughing, cause the blue jay went over, and I went over too! They never did let me live that down for a long time. They said, "Oh, you're a good shot, but when the blue jay went over, you went over, too!" It was quite a sight, I guess, cause I got up off the ground and looked at the window and saw them all laughing at me. It wasn't the bird that bothered me, it was the idea that I went over. I was really embarassed. I never did try that again. That was the only time I handled a gun.

In the late summer when it was time for my grandfather to pitch hay, we had to stay inside the barn and stack the hay evenly—see that it got safely up about four to six feet high. He'd give us rock salt to throw all around the hay, then we'd stack more up to the same height, and then throw some more rock salt on the hay as a salt lick for the horse. He just had one horse, so the barn wasn't too big.

Some days at Green Point we didn't have other jobs to do, so my grandpa had us on the beach by five o'clock, and we'd stay there until noon. We'd go home for lunch unless we were going too far away, and then we'd carry lunch with us. Then we'd go back home later. We'd be all worn out by the time we got back—going up and down those hills. He probably knew what he was doing—just wearing us out—and by the time seven o'clock came, we were ready for bed. Oh! Were we ready for bed! We'd eat supper about five o'clock, then we'd just lay around, and he'd start talking, telling stories about things that had gone on a long time ago. Then it was time for bed.

SUMMERS AT MIDWAY—FISHING AND SMOKING FISH

In my younger days we were down at Midway some summers with my grandfather and step-grandmother. In Indian this place is called ƛaƛakiš x̌ú·wis, "Two Rocks Standing," because there are two of them, like two people standing there. My grandpa used to spend his time there in the summertime because he used to fish a lot. While the plants in his garden at Green Point were maturing, we'd move out to Midway. It's about six or seven miles, by water, around Cape Flattery to Green Point beach, ta·qʷáʔat. We would live at Midway with my grandpa so he could go fishing while his garden was growing. Every once in a while we would all come back to Green Point to weed the garden.[8]

My grandfather Anderson fished from a canoe. Nobody ever used a motor boat. There was no such thing then, in those days. We used to have big waves come in here to Neah Bay before the breakwater was put in, and they had to paddle through all those waves. So, rather than start from Neah Bay early in the morning, he used to start from Midway. It was easier to go from there. That's why we lived there in the summertime. Also, it was much closer to Tatoosh and other good fishing areas. He used to catch ling cod, bass, kelp fish, and once in a while he'd get halibut, but he never did go salmon fishing that much; it was mostly white fish. Then he would have my step-grandmother dry that.

When he came home with bass, ling cod, or small chick halibuts, then we'd have to help his wife, Katy Anderson, get them ready for curing and smoking. First we took them down to the beach and washed them off real good in the salt water, then we brought them up and put them on a bed of kelp so they wouldn't get sandy. We used to have to bring all that kelp up on the beach.

Katy Anderson used to like to sit on the sand while she cut the fish, so she had a board that she worked on. My real grandmother, Alice Holden, wasn't much for sitting; she was always standing, and she used to have a table to work on. But Katy always sat down anywhere. She was one that wouldn't stand up and do anything; she would always sit. She was a real heavy-set woman.

So we'd help her. We'd go down and put the kelp on the beach and make it thick enough so the sand wouldn't get to the fish that were already washed. Then we'd set them there so she could just reach for them and start cutting. We never washed them after she cut them. I got curious and asked her about this once, "How come we have to get those fish so clean?" She said, "Because we don't wash them afterwards. If we wash the meat in fresh water afterwards, when you dry them they get stiff as a board." That's why we used to have to clean them real good before we brought them up there to be cut. This way they are easier to chew. The fish always had slime on them. We used to scrape all the slime off before we brought them up there. She'd cut them up early in the morning. Then we used to be the runners for her; we'd take them and hang them on the cedar poles over the fire right on the beach. They would drip a little during the day and get enough smoke on them so that by the evening we could move 'em to the smokehouse. Since there were seagulls around, we had to stay there and watch the fish all day. We'd stay there while she went up to make a dinner and bring it down, or else she cooked dinner down there and we'd always eat on the beach, outside.

My grandpa had a little smokehouse, qʷišóˑwas, where they'd smoke the fish. It was maybe nine by twelve or twelve by twelve, just one small room. They had a fire right in the center of the building. They made grates, very much like grates in the oven, except these were all cedar, and they'd hang the fish on them, and then the grates were hung up in the center of the house. When they built the smokehouse, they didn't use two by fours, they used regular round trees for the studding and everything. And then they put shakes on the outsides. They never bought any material from anywhere. They just went out and got small trees, and those were what they used for their two by fours; they were round, and they'd chip them. The outside and the top were all shakes, and some of them had an extra little roof, just off from the big roof where the smoke could escape. This was so the fish wouldn't get so terribly smoky.

In the evening, we'd carry the cedar poles with the fish up to the smokehouse. We got them all back up there and got them all put up and then started the fire. You had to build the fire after you put them up, because otherwise you'd get all smothered in smoke! We'd build a very small fire, just enough for a little smoke. We left the fish up there about four or five days and then brought them into the house. I guess that was why they called us smelly Indians.

When there was enough smoke on there [on the fish], what they did was take them out of the smokehouse and pile them on top of each other on a grate above the kitchen stove. Of course, the fish didn't dry all the way through until they were up inside there, but then you don't want too much smoke on them anyway; otherwise, they get bitter. So they'd smoke them for four or five days, bring them in the house and put them over the cookstove, and this is where they would finish drying. We could smell that fish all through the house! Then when they were dry we wrapped 'em up and put 'em away. We never put them where it was damp, either; we kept them where it was dry. We used to keep them in the kitchen, pile them in boxes, put them in sacks, and leave them in the kitchen where it was warm all the time.

To cook them, if they're really dry, you have to soak them a day ahead of time. And then you boil them. And then sometimes . . . this was the way I liked them, if it's salmon or halibut, you wet them under the faucet first—get them all wet. Then you take and put the fish on an open fire and just toast it. That's *real* good! Then you fold it up, fold the fish, then you hit it on both sides. This takes off the char-burn. Then you pinch it in little pieces and set it on a plate, and you eat it that way. Oh, that's *good!*

Sometimes when my step-grandmother, Katy Anderson, was cutting up the fish, she would send us down the beach to gather food for our lunch. We gathered limpets—little black-shelled limpets, x̣á·čqʷa·l, and then another kind that were smaller, sidú?u·. Sometimes we'd get littleneck clams, and she'd boil them up. So we'd just sit there on the beach and have steamed clams and then the broth. She used to keep great big horse clam shells all cleaned and washed, and we'd dip them in the broth and just drink right out of the clam shell. We liked doing that.

MY GRANDPA'S HOUSE AT MIDWAY

My older sister Katherine, myself, and the one next younger than me, Dolores, also used to have a lot of fun when we spent our summers at Midway with my grand-father and his wife. He had a house there—he made it all himself out of driftwood. There was always driftwood coming in: boats were always getting in wrecks, so he just picked up the lumber off the beach and built a house with it. Then he used small cedar to fill in where he had to fill in. The lumber was good that drifted in, and that way he and the others didn't have to go out and cut the trees. But they did make their own shingles, however. They made flat, long shakes, and they were nice.

We used to like to stay there in that house because they had homemade bunk beds which we really enjoyed. We thought that was something really great! We never had seen a bunk bed in our lives! My grandfather made the bunk beds, two of them, and one was built right into its own nook in the wall. That was really some-thing great. They slept on the bottom one, which was wide, and one of us would sleep on the top. We really looked forward to that! Later on he built another room; then they had the privacy of their own room and us kids had all four bunks. We used to always fight for the top bunk every time. Sometimes we'd bring our friends, and we got the use of the bunk beds. Kids used to like to come out with us cause they never saw bunk beds either. We really enjoyed it!

BEACHCOMBING WITH MY GRANDPA

We did fun things most of the time with my grandpa. When he thought maybe we were getting bored, he'd say, "Well, let's go up to the next beach, let you kids look for shells for a while." The three of us girls walked up there—say about a mile and a half over the hill from Midway. It was a little trail. He used to say, "You guys walk. I'll row over there." So, he'd row over there, and then we'd be looking for shells. At that time there were all kinds of shells on the beach; now you hardly find them anymore. We used to pick up those empty sea egg shells, kʷ'ičká·piž [sea urchins], whole bunches of them. They'd be nice big ones, all white. We used to pick a whole bunch of those. Then there were those limpet shells with the sharp top on them, q'u q'u·dá·bats . . . and all different kinds of limpets. We'd put them in a sack and bring them home. We'd play on the beach with them.

We used to pick up glass balls on the beach, too.[9] At that time there weren't many people coming in here, and we found ever so many glass balls. We used to bring a sack down with us, and we'd come back with about a fifty-pound sack full of glass balls in all kinds of odd shapes that you don't find nowadays. There'd be some shaped like a rolling pin, almost. They were about two and a half inches round in the center, and then they looked like you stretched them, and they had a little knob on each end. We found a bunch of those. Some of them came in a kind of pinkish, purplish color. Some of them were green and some real light green; others were just white. Some were blue, dark blue, and amber color. Every once in a while we used to find a real dark purple one, but you never see anything like that come in now. We'd dump all these in his smokehouse. Pretty soon he had to build another smokehouse. I wonder what happened to them. . . . They probably sold them.

Every once in a while he'd take us down to the beach and we'd pick these little things that look like wheat. They look just exactly like wheat. They grow like a little seed, just like wheat, except that they're green.[10] And he'd say, "Well, you kids probably want candy by now, and I can't go down and get you any candy, so let's go get some from the water." We'd go down there. They're green, and they grow about three to four feet high in low tide pools. When the tide was lowest, he would take us down there. I think this was in the summer. It was just a little ways west from Midway—just around the point. We'd go with him in his canoe because the tide pools were deep and we couldn't walk in them. We'd break the tops off these plants and get a little sack full. We'd eat them while we were down there, and they're sweet! They're *really* sweet! A little salt from the salt water was on them, but it didn't matter. We'd break the tops off them and eat them while we were picking them, and then we'd bring some of them home, only as much as we needed; he'd never let us take too much.

TOYS WE PLAYED WITH ON THE BEACH

Aside from eating the Indian candy, we used to play with some of the objects that washed up on the beach. The bones from the head of a fish . . . they looked like a little horse. They stand up, and they've got two little things that come down on the side, and we used to think that they looked like a horse, so we'd play with those on the beach after they'd wash up. We'd take them and wash them and get them all dried up, and then we'd play with them. We'd have great times with those. All the kids used to do that; I wasn't the only one. And these backbones from the seal—we used to play with those a lot, too. They'd wash up on the beach, and they'd be nice and white.

In Neah Bay they had all kinds of canoes on the beach. Kids would play either in the canoe, outside it, or around it. This way the kids used to keep busy, but you don't see canoes on the beach anymore. Sometimes they had small canoes with no sharp ends on each end—these were called salmon canoes. Sometimes when the men would come in from fishing, they'd turn their salmon canoes upside down and leave them that way. Then the kids would cover a canoe, put sand all on it, and it'd be dark under there. Then the kids used to get under there and play and have just a great time! You could hear them playing around. Nowadays the kids will run in every direction, but then there really were no problems. They just amused themselves with canoes, or with kelp cars. We made cars out of kelp—they were just little ones, about eight to ten inches. We played with them on the beach, had lots of fun with them, too.

STORYTELLING AT MY GRANDPA'S HOUSE

When we were living with my grandparents at Green Point, we used to hear lots of Indian stories. They'd tell stories every evening. It might have been the same ones over every now and then, but they were just as interesting as could be, even though you heard them over and over—like the stories of old Kwaatie and Ishkus, and then the Snot Boy,[11] they called him, and stories about whales. We listened to them all the time and never got tired of them.

There were a number of people who lived scattered in the area around Green Point who came over and told stories. My grandfather used to invite them by using different kinds of signals. Some families lived down below the Tsooyez River, and he was on the hill (Green Point). The people on the east side of them could see his light up on the hill. There'd be so many flashes—he'd cover the window. And for the people up the river on the southwestern side, he used to use a certain number of rings on a triangle. That triangle iron rang so loud they could hear it clear up the river. He'd always watch which way the wind was blowing—then that sound would carry up the river. Sometimes he'd have to use it maybe two or three times, waiting for the wind to carry. And this is the way he used to invite them. Then they would all come up about an hour later, carrying their lanterns. Everybody would be there, and then they'd sit down and tell stories. He'd feed them first, give them a good feed, then he'd roll out a mat, a cattail mat; my step-grandmother had her mats all ready to roll on the floor before anyone came. Some of these mats were made about four feet wide and others about one and a half feet wide. Every one of the guests had one of these mats. They'd take off their shoes at the door and leave them there. Then they'd roll the mats out, and everybody would sit down on them. The short mats they'd leave rolled up for pillows. Then they'd all lay down, and they'd say, "Now, you tell a story." They'd start telling stories, counterclockwise. And they'd just lay around there and listen and listen. Each one had the same story, yet it came out a little different—each one of them giving their version of the stories their parents had told them. We just listened. They would sit on the floor or the men would lay on the floor, and it wasn't like nowadays. You wouldn't catch Mr. and Mrs. laying on the floor against somebody else's Mr. and Mrs. They'd just lay there and tell stories.

My friend and cousin, Ramona Colby, would always be there with me. She was Lance Kalappa's granddaughter, and she was about the same age as I was. We were with my grandfather. We never laid by my grandmother. We always used to fight for my grandfather. Ramona had her own grandpa there, but we would always fight for my grandpa. So, he'd say, "Well, you get on one side and she'll get on the other side." Then we'd lay there and listen to the stories. There wasn't much for us to do other than just play together in the daytime outside. But during the evenings we really enjoyed ourselves. We were taught to be quiet. The Indian kids in those days weren't rowdy like they are now. They were taught to be quiet, so they had manners. We were taught never to run around, never to make noise during the time they were telling stories. There was really no noise at all, even though there were more kids every once in a while. We never had to go to the bathroom, either. We just stayed right there until it was all over with.

My step-grandmother, Katy Anderson, was a *beautiful* storyteller, and she would sit up and tell stories sometimes. She was *our* storyteller. You could sit and listen to her anytime. However, she wouldn't tell stories during the daylight. She used to say, "I can't tell stories unless it's dark." She was quite a storyteller. We used to love to listen to her because she could really put expression in it! It seems like we really had a nice time. Now I bet any of the kids would give anything to be able to understand Indian and listen to them, because sometimes there's hardly any meaning to the stories when you have to bring them out in English. It's hard. Sometimes the story loses all its meaning.

When they were through telling stories, of course, we'd have something to eat. And then they'd just lay right where they were and go to sleep. And there was nobody messing around with anybody else's wife. They all seemed to behave themselves.

The storytelling would go on like that for maybe two or three nights. They'd each bring something, maybe dried fish, fresh fish, or whatever they had. Then the next day they'd all get up and go down the beach or something, because they wouldn't be around the house. They'd take their lunch with them, and they'd be back in the evening again. Those that were close would go home and then come back. But those that had to paddle down from the river, some of them didn't go home. Then they'd all be back in the evening to continue with the storytelling. Some of those stories were really, really good. But then, as part of it, after I thought back about it—thought back on those years—there was always a moral to the story. More or less, they were telling us how to live our lives.

FORBIDDEN BONE GAMES AND INDIAN DANCES

I can remember when they started having their bone games and Indian dances at Tsooyez at Tom Holden's big house. At that time the government didn't think it was right for us to have bone games. It was considered gambling. So, that was the reason they forbade us to have bone games. I don't really know why they didn't want us to Indian dance. So the Makah started having their bone games and Indian dances at Tsooyez. My step-grandfather, Gilbert Holden, had a nice big house just before you cross the river, just by a little road that goes to the left. He was married to my grandmother, Alice Holden. They'd have bone games usually at his son Tom Holden's house, which was nearby, or sometimes they'd have them at Gilbert's.[12]

Since the bone game was outlawed, our people must have had lookouts, probably men on horses. That's the only thing I could think of, because I was little and could never go out to see. But anyway you could hear them come running in, hear the horses coming. And so they would come running in and say, "Well, the policemen are on their way! The policemen are on their way!" So they knew when the policemen were coming. And then they'd disband. They'd all scatter. The ones with their babies would just run, some of them would go to my grandmother's—make believe they'd been sleeping for hours. If they were close enough to go home, they'd go home. Sometimes they'd get into their canoes and start paddling up the river, because not too far was Shubert Hunter's, Bill Tyler's, and Hays Wheeler's places. Some would stay with my grandmother or her stepson-in-law. Then they'd blow all the lights out, because they had kerosene lamps. And different people would stay there with my grandma. If they were related, they'd be staying there. There wouldn't be too many left, anyway. Some would wait in the woods until they decided "Well, the cop's gone," and they'd all come back again. Of course, that used to spoil the bone game, but once in a while they'd start all over again. Then there were times that they'd just quit.

So, I saw all that excitement every so often, because the government wouldn't let the Indians have bone games. They weren't allowed. I must have been about seven years old then, when this was going on. I remember my dad just picking me up and throwing me on his back, saying, "Hold on," and then he just ran up the trail to my step-grandpa's. Mom strapped the baby on her back and ran in front of him. I just barely, vaguely, remember all the excitement, and my eyes would get *big*, you know, watching everybody run around and all the lights being blown out.

The government knew what was going on, but their policemen weren't fast enough, so. . . . When the government started watching pretty close is when the people had to start going to Tatoosh Island to dance—have Indian dances, potlatches, and bone games. The Makah would all get in canoes and go to Tatoosh

Island, for a celebration of any kind. The government found this out, but they couldn't get anybody to go over there. That was out of limits for them, so they couldn't go.[13] I can't remember why it was off limits, but this is what they said.

We went out to Tatoosh Island, *hupáčakt*, or *čá·di·*,[14] in sealing canoes. That was our only transportation; there wasn't any road in to Neah Bay then, either. Each family had its own sealing canoe and would load it up with groceries and dried fish. This was the first time that I remembered the old-time celebrations. I imagine I was around eight or nine or so. The only thing I could remember was being afraid of the waves when we landed on Tatoosh Island and hanging on to the canoe to get into the harbor there. The waves were always *big!* It's *never* calm. You have to count how many waves are going up and down to get in. I remember being afraid because they have to count waves to get in there. In fact, one time I heard them, when we were all in line trying to get ashore there. They said, "One canoe tipped over!" And then they had to pick them up. They said, "Another canoe tipped over!" And after that I was so afraid! I just remember two tipped over.

They'd stay out there at Tatoosh for about a week for celebrations—dance and sing, dance and sing. Men fished for halibut for the celebration. This is the way we were all fed there; we brought our own food. Each family fed themselves. My grandfather had an old *ba?ás*[15] there where we used to stay. We lived there the whole week long. The rest of them would stay with relatives that had longhouses there, too. They traveled with feather beds; they didn't have mattresses in those days. They caught ducks and saved the feathers and the down until they had enough to make a feather bed. Finally, in 1926 the government set us free, and they decided, well, we're going to have Makah Day now.[16] Now we can bone game and have our Indian dances right on the reservation here. We didn't have to go out to Tatoosh anymore.

TALKING INDIAN

When I was with my grandparents, I had to talk all in Indian; that was the only way I could talk to them. It was nothing to me. I could just go ahead and rattle it off and get across what I wanted to get across, but now I'm forgetting a lot of that. We used to have to talk Indian because my grandparents never talked that much English. My grandfather did, but my grandmother didn't because she was part Quileute from La Push, so that made the difference. She learned to talk Makah, so I didn't speak that much English at home. I had to talk Indian because my grandparents were all there. Starting from my father's grandmother, I had to talk Indian.

It must have been my grandparents who were teaching me most, in those days. I listened to the older people—listened to them and took care of them, too. Since they had lived their lives, they told us little stories. By talking and telling us little stories, was the way they had. By telling stories about birds—birds and bees—it was through either animals or birds. Then you began to understand and know what they were talking about. Then as you grew a little older, you began to look at these things and you'd see, "Well, this is what they were telling me about."

My father spent time talking to me, too. I had to know things, how they came about and why, and Mom knew that Dad was always telling me things. My father taught us his ways, where my mother never taught us much of her ways.[17] My father chose the Canadian side, and he taught me all of that. The other kids in the family wouldn't listen much, but I'd sit and listen more than they did and ask more questions than they did. Of course it made a big difference, too, that I had to go with my dad wherever he went in Canada. We went to all these potlatches across there, went when people asked us.

I had to learn by myself by listening to my father and to other people. I guess this was why I did a lot of listening. Like I say, little pitchers have big ears. So, . . . maybe purposely, I'm not so sure, they used to sit and talk. In my young days the women used to get together a lot more than they do nowadays. They don't get together *at all* nowadays. But they used to get together every time their husbands were out working. The ladies would go out themselves and get what they call slippers, *ts'iˑdax̌tup,* China slippers. These were little black chitons. Or, they'd go out together, pick berries, and we had to go along with them wherever they went. Or if they weren't picking berries, or getting China slippers, they'd be getting Indian rhubarb or sprouts. And always there were women—no men, no boys—just women. And this is when they would have their women-talk. Of course, we were all there, just little girls. So we listened to them. The women were talking "girl-talk," you might say. This is where I learned all mine. It was easy to pick up, because they explained in detail. One might be younger, just turning into a woman, and they'd say, "I had to do this. I had to do that." It wasn't hard for them to talk, because these were all women. Like they used to go in bunches, eight, nine at a time, and all get their baskets and put 'em on their backs. They made little baskets for us to carry. So we'd go out to the beach and get China slippers or even clams. It was just women—just women and little girls. But you don't see that anymore.

When I was twelve, I was still just a little kid, a real little kid. I used to sit at my grandma Alice Holden's feet and listen to her singing these songs for little babies—lullabies. She would always hold my brother Emil in her arms and sing to him and sing to him. She didn't *make* me sit there and listen; I just did. I sat there and listened to her and played around. Maybe we liked the song or something, I don't know. But we used to play around my grandmother's feet, round and round, when she was sitting there, rocking my brother and singing to him. And I know sometimes she would pray. She wasn't a Makah, anyway, so she'd pray in Quileute. I would sit very quietly and listen to her, even though I didn't know what she was saying. Then sometimes I'd look up at her and say, "I wonder what you're saying; I *really* wonder what you're saying," because she'd never talk Makah; she always talked Quileute. I never understood anything she said. My mother and grandmother never taught me Quileute. My mother understood. My grandmother would talk Quileute to her, and she'd answer in Makah. She'd talk to my mother when she wanted to tell her something that she didn't want us to know about. Then she'd talk to her in Quileute. I never got to learn that, and I regret it.

GRANDFATHER ANDERSON, THE BASKET MAKER

My grandfather Charlie Anderson was the one that taught me how to make baskets. My own grandmother never taught me, my mom had no time for me, so he did. Mom made baskets. When she was pregnant, she'd have to be still. So then she'd sit down and make baskets. When I'd ask her for help, she'd say, "I have no time to teach you. I got to get this basket done because we need some things at the store, so I can't teach you." But my grandfather heard her one day, and he said, "I'll help you." And he did. He taught me how to make baskets. In the wintertime, when it was too rough and stormy to be out at sea, he used to stay home, finish his nets, and then make baskets. In those days they just bought the rope and made their own nets. Now they buy them, but then they used to have to make them. In the winter, when he was through with the nets, that's when he would start making baskets. He'd be still long enough to make a few dollars on baskets.

It was him and my uncle Freddie Anderson and my granduncle Elliot Anderson that used to make the real fine baskets. Real fine baskets! I don't think I've ever seen my mom make fine baskets. My grandma, a little bit. But it was too much work for them, I guess. So they didn't make the fine baskets. I never saw any of the other men do it. But those three used to. So, when I wanted to learn, my grandpa helped me; he showed me how.[18]

GRANDUNCLE ELLIOT ANDERSON,
THE LAST FULL-BLOOD OZETTE INDIAN

My granduncle Elliot Anderson, the last living full-blood Ozette Indian, used to make real fine baskets. That's what he spent the winter doing. He had white friends, trading people, that he used to exchange with—he'd make a bunch of baskets, and he'd send them down to California. They'd either send him Navajo rugs, or they'd send trade beads. That's how I got these trade beads—was through him.

A lot of people thought he was dumb because he was deaf—he couldn't hear. But he was very good at reading lips, so we never had to talk loud to him. He'd watch our lips and understand what we were saying. I never did find out why he was deaf. When I was growing up, I knew he was deaf, but he wasn't crazy or anything; he was normal in every other way. He could talk all right, but he was real soft-spoken; he wasn't loud. He lived up here at the end of the ball field. A lot of people didn't think too much of him, but he was smarter than most of them, because he repaired telephone lines.

He used to work on the telephone lines between here and Tatoosh. Those lines went from here in Neah Bay across Cape Flattery to the bluff at the edge of the water, and from there right across to the island.[19] At that time we had wind-up telephones—long, short; or short, short, long. So, he'd repair the telephone lines and the light lines running up to Tatoosh. He'd walk—there were no roads, just little trails—and this was what he used to do. But he had the whole run of that line all the time. Sometimes he used to leave in the night if somebody'd come call him, or the policeman used to come get him, and he'd say, "Well, Tatoosh's line is down, so you have to go." Uncle Elliot had a trail that was all luminous in the night, so he could find his way out there. For the longest time he used to pick up rotten alder trees and line his trail with these, so it would be kind of luminous. He said they had to be real rotten before they would be like that, and he spent a lot of time picking up things like that. It was pretty dark out there at night when it was raining. The reason he wasn't afraid was because he was deaf. Nobody else wanted that job. No one else would take it.

Now, they have roads that go all the way up there. And I think everything's cables. Everything's cable now. You don't have to worry about whether the line falls down or not. They've got modern telephones, now.

SEAL HUNTING IN THE CAVES

My granduncle Elliot also was an excellent seal hunter. He would go hunting for the harbor seal, *k'a·š č'uʔu·,*—he's spotted gray. He'd take those, and he'd skin them and dry them. He liked to go seal hunting, and because he was deaf, he could swim right into the caves where the seals were and always come home with one. He never came home empty-handed. He said the caves were crooked; they weren't straight-up like I was led to believe—that they were like a regular cave and open. He said they're sideways. He'd swim in there, and he knew just where to find the seals and when they were in there. Then he'd club one on the head and throw it in the canoe.

He started telling me one day about taking Paul Parker with him into one of those caves. Paul was partially hard-of-hearing, but he wasn't deaf. Paul used to hunt a lot, too, but he never, ever went into the caves. Never! He would get seals when they were swimming out on the rocks, or near the mouth of the river. He was a pretty good hunter anyway, in his own fashion. But my granduncle used to hunt right *in* the caves, where you could just go in among them, club them on the head, tow them out, and put 'em in the canoe. He went to the back of the cave and would club one back there, because if they heard the noise they'd stampede like cattle and he could get run over. They were pretty heavy because of that blubber. They could have killed him when they headed for the mouth of the cave. It was so much easier for him that way. Being deaf, he could swim right into the caves, not realizing that there was an awful lot of noise in there that couldn't be stood by a normal ear.

So, this one time, the two of them got out of the canoe and tied it to a rock there, somehow. Then they swam into the cave and my grand uncle said that he could see Paul's eyes just grow big, and he shook his head, and he motioned to my granduncle with his hands. Then he shook his head again, and he swam out. My granduncle knew that he meant the cave was too noisy for a person who could hear—too noisy with the waves and the roar of the ocean. So Paul swam out, and he wouldn't dare go back in there. My uncle Elliot brought one seal out, then he brought two out—one for him and one for Paul's family. Real nice, big seals. My uncle got in the canoe and started laughing and said, "What did you come back out for?" Paul explained to him, "I can hear and you can't. Even though I'm partly deaf, the noise in the cave was just roaring so bad it was scary, and I couldn't stay in there. It was just too frightening. I had to go back to the canoe again; I just wouldn't go in there." But since my granduncle was deaf, that was how he used to get his seals.

He told me about one time when he said he was so afraid. He didn't know what was going on. He took off his clothes and swam into this cave. Then, inside, there were the brand new little seals that had their heads cut off—just their heads. They were laying there just flipping. And there were some of the big ones that were like that, too. He couldn't figure out whatever did this to them. He didn't know what to think. He said he just grabbed one that was still alive, and then he took off. Since he didn't know what did this to them, he chose his own, hit it as fast as he could, and then away he went. He had one of those Indian-made clubs—special big ones of his own that he used. He left there in a hurry. He was afraid of what he would meet there. He made it out of there without meeting whatever it was that was doing this to them. He says they were little baby seals and some of the bigger ones. Their heads were just chopped off and hanging by a little bit, just flipping there and just bleeding away. He never did find out. Years later he went back, but he never did see anything like that again.

He never did write a song about it. But there'd be times when he had to go from here to Tatoosh Island to fix the lines, or else he'd go around Tsooyez and then come back through Hole-in-the-Wall. Then there would be houses there that he'd use for stopovers. He'd sit there and make a fire and rest. He was telling me about a tea kettle that he put on to make some coffee or tea once. He said, "Well, I'm deaf, I can't hear, but I could listen to it as plain as you could hear me talking. That thing was just a-singing away. The tea kettle was singing! And this is what it was singing." He sat there and he started singing. The song was really pretty. I was sorry there was no way I could get it down. He came home with lots of songs like that. It seemed like he never ever got scared, going out there like that. Then, he'd just sit there and sing, and I'd listen. I can't recall any of those songs. I wish I could, though, because when I'd listen to them, they'd be pretty.

My granduncle Elliot was also a cobbler. He used to re-sole shoes for people. Even though he was deaf, still he had compassion for people with big families. He'd buy sheets of leather, and then he'd let them take them home if they couldn't afford to pay for it. They'd say, "Can we pay later?" He'd say, "Sure, go ahead, take it." He'd never try to collect from them, and they'd never bring any back. He could afford to do that because he was alone. I think he was married twice, but his wives died.[20] He had one child, who died just after birth. So he was really alone. Off and on he used to move in with us. Then again he'd go back to his own house, and then later on he'd move back in with us. When he moved out and decided to stay out altogether, he took my younger sister Bessie with him, and he brought her up. She was pretty little at that time. He'd bring her to his house, and then he'd take her back to our house the next day, just back and forth. He didn't take her altogether. He took her every so often, whenever he felt like it or when she wanted to go with him. Bessie really liked him. He spoiled her by giving her all the things she wanted. In this way he wasn't alone all the time.[21]

BURIAL GROUNDS

When I was only about eleven or twelve, my granduncle Elliot Anderson brought me to the last burial grounds up here at the Cape Flattery area. He said, "I'm going to show you something that you've never seen before, and I want you to remember this for the rest of your life, because you'll never see anything like it again." I was with my younger sister Dolores; she was little then. So, he took us—he used to pack her on his back—he took us over there, up the cape area there . . .and way, way up . . . in the highest tree . . . was tied a canoe. And he said, "This area used to be our burial grounds, so don't ever hang around here when you are older and start getting around. Because you will, eventually; you kids will start walking in the woods." At that time they used to do a lot of that—go here, go there—just walk from beach to beach.

We shouldn't walk in the burial grounds because they were supposed to be sacred. And then, they believed if you accidentally fell and you fell on one of those things—that meant it's your time to go. There was quite a bit of superstition with that stuff. They used to say, "Oh, they'll pull you underground." But, what they meant was, "They'll pull you in the ground and then at the same time they'll take your shadow, or your spirit, *quʔáyčʼid*, away from you." We're supposed to understand that that means we are just going to pass away. This was their way of telling us.

So, we went over and looked at the burial grounds, and he kicked up some of the bones and put them back by the tree, close to the tree. He said, "Well, we're not supposed to disturb them, but they should be together." So he put them all together under different trees. He said, "That's something you'll never see anymore; times are changing, and changing fast. We never bury our dead anymore." And there were crows, you know, and ravens up there. We watched for a while, and then we left.

I really didn't know what to think of all this. I just kept thinking of the people and wondered how they got them up there. They're people, and yet they got them all the way up in those tall trees. But I never did ask him cause he was deaf. He could read lips, but I never bothered to ask. I just kept thinking to myself, "I wonder how they got them up there? How did they get such a heavy canoe up there and put the person in there—way up there?" Of course, I was kind of afraid too—I didn't want to stumble over one that had fallen from the trees.[22]

One time when I was about twelve, we were at Clayoquot[23] when they were preparing to make my dad a chief. My parents were busy, so I just played around on the beach with some of the kids. It was kind of hard for me to play with some of the kids because they all talked Indian. And at the time I wasn't very familiar with their language; it was different from ours, so I was sort of mostly by myself or with Michael Brown's daughter. Her name was Ida, and we wandered over toward the west end of the village there. This was the first time I saw how they buried their Indians over there. We buried ours on the top of the tallest trees that we could find, and in Clayoquot they buried theirs in boxes, sort of in a sitting-up position with their knees way up to their chest almost. And their burial boxes were about three feet long and about four feet high, depending on the size of the person. They were all made out of cedar, and they had Indian designs that were carved real nice. And you could see those that had been busted open, how they sat them up inside—and all their beads, and all their goodies—and nobody bothered them. There were some nice boxes there that were still closed yet. But some of them were busted open. Then I got afraid when I saw some of the skeletons sitting up in the boxes there, so we turned around and went back.

We were *never* allowed to go to funerals. That wasn't the place for little children, so I really don't know what funerals were like a long time ago. We never had nice caskets for people when they died because we had no way to get them in here—there was no road. I used to watch my dad build them, though. He'd make nice boxes, line the bottom with blankets, and then he used to put outing flannel on the outside of them to make them white. I used to watch him, but he never liked us to watch him. We used to go upstairs and look out the window. We didn't know what was going on, but we were very curious.

The first one I saw for a burial service was my brother. His name was Conrad, and he was older than I was. We were allowed to visit him before he died, but he was too delirious to know anybody. I think he had tuberculosis. I'm not sure because they never would tell us, but he just got thinner and thinner and thinner, and then he died. At that time we didn't know exactly what tuberculosis was, either. He just wasted away and died when he was about fourteen or fifteen. I must have been about eight or nine.[24]

They believed in keeping his body in the house for five days, and each member of the family—aunts, uncles, cousins—took turns sitting with the casket. They'd sit around, people would come in and out of the house, they'd stay for an hour or two and then leave again. They did that every day. Then after that was over, instead of bringing him through the door, they brought the body out through the window—never, never through the door. They believed that he'd be restless and want to keep coming home, and sort of haunt the house. I can remember them lowering him down through the window. He had the upstairs room—when anybody came to visit him before he died, they had to go upstairs. I guess we were watching too hard when they took the casket out, so my mom got mad and sent us to my grandma's house. We had to stay there—we couldn't be at home anymore until it was over.

After my brother died, my mother gave away all her dishes and whatever valuables she had—gave some to each person who came in. She gave until we were just about down to nothing. In Canada, they wait for a year and then they have a give-away party, but over here they used to give away everything right then, during those five days. When somebody came in, my family would just pile them up with dishes or whatever they thought was pretty nice—just give it to them.

Then after that we had to start all over again, buying new things. But the habit was that we never ate at home for a whole month after that. We were invited to different homes three times a day. However, my mom never took us around with them. She used to feed us first, then just she and Dad would go. Or else we'd go to my grandmother's and eat there, or to my grandfather's. But my parents never stayed home to eat for the whole month—people would invite them out. We used to do that for any family that was in bereavement. I can remember we had to feed quite a few, too, the same way. But now, this has all changed.

The bereaved family now has to invite the whole village for one meal. First they have the funeral service, and right after the service the family feeds the two or three hundred, or however many there are. It never used to be like that. The bereaved people used to be invited.

STORIES ABOUT MY GREAT-GRANDMOTHER

I must have been about four or five years old when my father's grandmother died.[25] I don't remember her name. We just used to call her *Aab*, "Grandmother." What she looked like, I can't remember. Sort of vaguely I remember her as being very gray headed.

Being brought up all Indian, *Aab* never would sleep on a bed; she never sat on a chair. She always sat cross-legged, even as old as she was, just on the floor of where we used to live. "She just refused a bed altogether," my dad used to say. Sometimes she'd sit on the feather bed which was in the corner of the living room where she always slept. She had a real nice thick feather bed, and I'd just flop out on there and sit and talk to her. So, she'd just fluff up her feather bed and either sit on that or sit on cattail mats on the floor. She was very clean, though. She always had clean seagull wings that she used to sweep with and dust everything with. She never used a broom. She swept up her corner with the seagull wing. I remember that. She'd sweep under the feather bed and plump it up every day. And when one feather wore out, she'd get a new one.

In those days we had no toothbrushes, either. We didn't know what a toothbrush was, but my great-grandmother always kept seagull feathers, and she'd pull those apart to clean our teeth. She'd get the shorter part of the feather, where it was a little bit stiffer, and she'd clean our teeth with that. I never kept it up after the white man brought us the toothbrush.

I can remember when we were kids—the three of us—my older sister, Katherine, my brother, Conrad, and I (I was the smallest one at that time)—I can remember my great-grandmother feeding us. If I got hungry, maybe I'd go get a piece of dried fish—those are strips from the edge of the fish, you know—this was our in-between snack. The old people were always afraid that we were going to get choked or something, so she would say, "Wait a minute! Wait a minute!" and she'd go into the kitchen and get her feather and start scrubbing her mouth. She would start scrubbing her teeth and then rinsing her mouth out. She'd spit the water out, and then she'd rinse her mouth out, and spit it out again. Then she'd say, "šuʔ," "I'm ready now!" in Indian. And she'd take my fish and chew it up. She'd sit there and just chew on it until it was really soft. Then she'd take it out of her mouth and give it to me! And I'd sit there, and I'd really enjoy it. She'd chew it all up for me.[26] This is the thing that I remember about her. Every time we'd eat fish, she'd do the same thing—wash her mouth out, chew it up for us, and then give it to us. But all the old people were like that. I wasn't the only one that was treated like that.[27] They'd make sure we never choked on dried fish. It didn't seem unusual to me because all the old people were that way with their grandchildren.

If I had an orange, she'd peel it for me and take off all the membranes, and then she'd give it to me. I guess she did sort of spoil us, in a roundabout way. And apples, she'd slice the top off an apple and get a teaspoon and scrape and scrape it. She wouldn't let me have a solid piece. This time she wouldn't chew it for us, but she'd use a spoon and scrape it and give it to us. She'd see to it that it was real fine, then spoon it into my mouth. I can remember I'd just run and jump on her feather bed, and then I'd start talking Indian to her and telling her, "I want to eat my apple," and then she'd say, "Go get a spoon." I'd go and get a spoon. She'd be sitting there; she'd peel half of it and start scraping, and put it in my mouth. It would end up like baby food when she'd give it to me. And I really enjoyed it. In those days that was perfectly acceptable. She really took care of us.

USE OF BLACK ROCKS

If my great-grandmother wasn't around, there was another way we could get the fish soft. We had some of those great big, black shiny rocks in the house, and they were clean all the time. If my great-grandmother wasn't home and we wanted some dried fish, we'd just take a piece and put it on one of these rocks and pound it with another rock. Then we'd sit there and chew it. Everybody used to pound the fish with these rocks. The fish was dry, so in order to get it soft, they pounded it.

They used these black rocks for quite a few other things, too. I used to watch Young Doctor [a Makah carver] when he would make totem poles. He would rub those rocks on there, and the cedar, or whatever wood it was, would get shiny. They called those rocks ƛ'ačá·pł. All the old women had them, too. Some of them were shaped like an egg, they'd just fit in their hands, and the women would use them when they were making baskets. They'd pound on each part of the basket so the weaving would look even. They'd start with the bottom, work the bottom of the basket, then pound on it to make it look even, then they'd rub the rock over it so the basket would get shiny, too. My mother used to keep hers in her basket-weaving box. They always had a box where they put their basket-weaving, and that's were my mother used to keep her black rock, and my grandma did, too. And then Fanny Parker used to hang around our place, and my grandfather's second wife, Katy, she had one, and I remember when they'd all get together in the summer and go down the beach just to shoot the breeze. The ladies would bring their basket-weaving and go down on the beach and sit around and talk, and they'd bring those black rocks down with them, too.

ACTIVITIES OF MY GREAT-GRANDMOTHER

My great-grandmother was always busy, either making baskets or cutting fish or drying fish. Sometimes when she'd be tired of staying inside, she'd go out back where we had a big shed, and she'd build a fire in there. She would pack[28] the cedar mat and spread it out and sit by the fire and make her baskets. All the old people seemed to have that habit. They'd build a little fire, sit around there, and make their baskets.

Sometimes she'd sit by herself, and then other times she'd go visit Gallic Cheeka's mother. These two old ladies would go back and forth. There was a shed in the back of Cheeka's house where they put their wood, so Gallic's mother would always build her fire in there and just sit and make baskets too. And my great-grandmother would go across the way and spend the day with her. I remember I'd run in and out of there because her door was open all day long. I used to listen to them; they'd be talking, and they'd just sit around the fire. I imagine they used to reminisce about the old days. It wasn't all that comfortable in there, but that's what they liked, so they'd sit around in there. And then this old lady, Jongie Claplanhoo's mother, lived next door to us, and she'd pass by with her tea kettle or pot, and the three of them would sit around the fire. And old man Coballi sometimes used to join them. His wife, who was from Clayoquot, had died and my father used to take care of him, when he needed help. Maybe some other old fellow'd come in, and they'd sit and talk for a while and then leave. But they all seemed to have that habit. They'd build a little fire, sit around there, and make their baskets.

Aab always did things for us. My dad, instead of telling us that she was going to baby-sit us when he and Mom would leave, he'd say, "You stay home and take care of your grandma." He'd tell *us* to take care of *her*, but now I can see that she was babysitting us, not us her. My dad always took care of her, and he never let her want for anything. She took care of him when he was growing up, so afterwards he was good to her. She must have liked us because she took good care of us, too.

Sometimes she even made toys for us to play with. In the dusk of the evening the bats used to fly around. Maybe because there weren't as many houses then— the bats just used to go! They just kept flying back and forth in front of the houses. As kids we used to go out there and use my grandfather's spears or rounded off poles for devil-fishing. We'd stand out there and wait for those bats to come out, and then we'd hit them. Of course, we didn't know some of them could be rabie bats. Funny, at that time they never told us to watch out for bats, or they're going to get in your hair. They did after we started growing a little bit more, though. So, we'd get out there and use those sticks and as they came along—hit them. And sometimes we'd get three or four of them. One day my great-grandmother said, "Well, bring them in, bring them in. I'll fix them for you, and then you can play with them." We picked them up and brought them in to her, and you know, she skinned the bats and gave them back to us to play with. She didn't mind cleaning them. She gutted them, took the head off, cleaned it, took the tail off. She skinned them so nicely, and the backs had a little furry stuff on them. She gave us just the wings and the back with the furry stuff, and we'd play with them. The bats were little; they couldn't have been any more than six inches across. We'd play with those things because they were furry looking. It's funny we weren't scared of them. Now I'm scared of bats; I don't know why we ever played with them. Now I couldn't do it.

My older sister, Katherine, never seemed to like my great-grandmother. I don't know why. I could remember my mom telling a story about her. Evidently my great-grandmother didn't say much, never talked too much, but just used to sit there and watch you, like she was mean or something. But I remember I put up with her, and I never had any trouble with her. However, my mother used to say Katherine didn't like her too well. One day my sister got hungry, so she crawled up on top of the kitchen stove where all the fish is stored to keep it dry. They leave the fish there to dry completely. And my great-grandmother must have been sitting there in the house because she just watched my sister crawl up there, watched every move she made. It bothered Katherine that this great-grandmother of ours would just sit there and watch her and not say anything. It made her mad, so when she came down, she took this dry fish and folded it. It had been butterflied, so she folded it, and she went up to my great-grandmother, and she had this fish flipping in front of her face, and she hollered, "IT'S ALIVE! IT'S ALIVE!" Then she turned and ran away. Apparently my great-grandmother hadn't said anything, just watched and stared at her.

Maybe she *was* quiet, but the rest of us smaller ones, like myself, my uncle Freddie's two boys who were about the same age, we never had any problems with her. Every once in a while Virginia Holden's daughter would come over to play with me, and Evelyn Peterson, too, and we'd sit around and talk to her. Maybe she'd be making something, and we'd sit there and watch her . . . maybe bread or whatever. Sometimes she would chew dried fish for us. Then the kids would sit there and talk to her. Everybody talked Indian. We had no problems with her just sitting there and staring at us. So, I have good memories of her.

INTERACTIONS WITH FRIENDS AND RELATIVES

Every so often my family used to go over and eat with Ed and Susie Weberhard when I was little. They were friends with my family, and he was just like a grandfather to me; I spent a lot of time over there. I guess we had gone over there to eat one day, and I, as a little child, would always watch him eat. He always ate with his eyes closed. And he talked with his eyes closed while he was eating. He never ate a meal where he didn't close his eyes and sit there and chew. I don't know whether he was concentrating on what he was eating, but this was a habit of his. My mom told me that we were eating there one day and that I started talking to him in Indian and I asked him, "Why do you always close your eyes when you eat?" And my mom was just punching me. And I looked at her, and I said, "Well, he always eats with his eyes closed; he never opens them." Then Susie, his wife, started laughing, and she said, "He does, doesn't he? He always closes his eyes. Well, I never noticed it. Just out of habit, I guess." And Ed said, "Oh, I *like* to eat this way. I can't eat unless I have my eyes closed." My mom told me that as little as I was, I looked at him, and I said, "Well, I'm going to give you a name. I'm going to call you *Tapláa.*" That means "eyes closed." So that's what I gave him. I gave him a name, and he was just kind of tickled about it. And every time I went over there I'd say, "Well, hello, *Tapláa.* How are you? It's a nice day, *Tapláa.*" He got used to that name, *Tapláa.* I was the only one that called him that. I'd go in and out of there a lot, just like if they were my grandparents.

After I got a little older, I can remember we always had a houseful of people. I can never remember when my mother and dad were ever at the table by themselves.

By this time my great-grandmother had died. But all the other people were there—my grandpa and stepgrandmother, my grandmother and stepgrandfather, and their friends: Annie Long Tom, Susie Weberhard, Mrs. Phillip Ladder, Mrs. Jefferson Davis (who later became Mrs. Washington Irving), Fanny Colfax, and Fanny Parker. More or less they were my grandmother's friends. They stayed with us all the time. They'd get up in the morning, and they'd come over, just to be there. And then Randolph Parker and Jack LaChester used to come around, and once in a while, Dan Tucker. My uncle was there every day, too—my mother's brother, Freddie Anderson. My granduncle Elliot Anderson lived with us off and on, too.

So, there was always a crowd at our table. My dad never seemed to tire of all this company. He was working for the government then, and he never seemed to think we didn't have enough money. Everybody kind of brought something to help out, too. Freddie Anderson was a good fisherman, as was my grandfather, and they would always bring fish. Then my grandmother and her husband, Alice and Gilbert Holden, would come over. He raised cows, so he would kill one a year and salt the meat. There was no other way to preserve anything except by salting, so he'd salt it, and when we got tired of fish, he'd bring over a bunch of salted meat. And my mother raised chickens, had her own eggs, so when we got tired of fish or meat we'd have chicken and dumplings or chicken stew. Never fried chicken. Then, my uncle Freddie used to get the boots and the slippers and the sea eggs and stuff like that from off the rocks at low tide. So actually we weren't really in need because of all of them.

So that's the way we got along, and it seemed like most of these people were always at our house. I never questioned it at all, as to "How come we're living like this?" or anything—that's just the way it was. Now that I think about it, the people that are divorced today won't even be under the same roof at the same time. My grandfather was married to my grandmother, and they separated, and then they married a brother and a sister, and they were all under our roof at the same time. There was no squabbling: they'd talk and laugh and tell stories. They still got along with each other just fine.

CHAPTER 3

THE EARLY YEARS: CHILDHOOD ACTIVITIES AND DUTIES

CHILDREN'S CHORES

I used to like being with my grandfather. In fact, I liked it better staying with him than I did with my grandmother. We had a lot of time to play, pick up shells, and things like that. Not with my grandmother, though. Seemed like we were just never out of work when we were with her. She used to make us pick berries when we were with her in the summer. Then she'd always make us watch her when she was canning. We'd have to wash the fruit for her; but then after that, it was all up to her. We had to do other things for her, too. She was a clean woman; always busy keeping things clean. There were times we had to clean the house and do the dishes for her, times we had to help her wash. Maybe we didn't do everything right, so some of the things she did herself. We didn't have to do any of these things with my grandfather.

BERRY PICKING AND BABY-SITTING

It was like this all the time that I was little, that I can remember. In the summer-time we'd be with my mother and my grandmother a lot. We didn't get our fruit like people do now—go to the store—we couldn't. So, in June we had to go out salmonberry picking with them, and we had to help them. They'd can salmon-berries, *qákwey,* and then after that was over we'd pick red huckleberries, *hisi·ʔa·d,* and black huckleberries, *x̌ux̌ú·yaqƛ,* in July or August. They'd pull the branches over their baskets and then hit the branches with their hands, and the berries would fall into the baskets. Lots of leaves fell in too, so we had to pour them out on a blanket and take handfuls and let them drop slowly so the wind would blow the leaves away and we'd be left with only the berries. They'd get about fifty or sixty quarts. Then they'd can them—put them up in jars.

Salal berries, *k'akyí·tsapiẋ*, ripened in August. We had burden baskets, *qaʔá·wats*, that we brought with us when we picked these berries. And since my grandmother was faster, she'd go out picking. We'd have to sit in the clearing with our shawls on the ground and baby-sit. We watched the babies there and the younger kids. And we weren't just sitting there doing nothing, either. We'd have to be cleaning these salal berries, picking them off the stem—they kind of grow on a vine.

We'd bring our lunch, and along about noontime the ladies would all come back there, and they wouldn't be just sitting there eating, either. They'd be cleaning off the vines while they were eating. So we used to get most of the cleaning done while we were out there. Then all we had to do was wash them off when we got home. We wouldn't have to be picking all the berries off the stems.

When we got home, my grandmother would wash them and mash them with a wooden masher and form them about eight inches square and an inch thick, and then dry them. She'd put them on cedar slats which she put above the stove to dry. Then she'd put them away for the winter. In the wintertime she'd pull them apart and soak them overnight in water, and they'd taste just like fresh salal berries. She'd never mix anything else in there. They really tasted like fresh salal berries.

Blackberry season came next, in September. We picked blackberries, *qaqá·waš-k'uk*, and then my grandma used to make jelly, or sometimes she'd just can them. I never used to see my mother make jelly or jam.

Late September was about the time the cranberries would come out, and then we'd have to go cranberry, *p'áp'ʔés*,[1] picking. We'd cross the Tsooyez River—somebody would have a canoe in there, and we'd just paddle straight across. Then you'd be walking south and all of a sudden you'd see a clearing where it was really marshy, nothing but marsh. You walk in that marsh, and you'll come to a cranberry field there.[2] It's just open, with maybe a tree here, now and then. We wore boots into those marshes. We all had rubber boots that went over our knees 'cause we were on our knees most of the time, picking. And then we wore what I thought used to be real cute: the brush from the cranberries is hard on your hands, so my grandmother used to take our old black socks and make them into sock gloves (we all wore black socks, then). My mother would start saving our socks when they had holes, but she never did darn. My grandma would cut them up the heels, and she'd sew them so they'd fit in between each finger—so that your hands don't get scratched too bad when you're in the cranberry marsh. After we put them on, then they'd pin them up close to our shoulders. And then they did the same thing for themselves. The only thing that got scratched up was the ends of your fingers. She left little holes on the ends of the fingers. But she'd sew them in between so your fingers would fit through there like a glove. And we all wore those when we picked cranberries.

The mothers and grandmothers kept us pretty close. We had to do our share of picking but had to baby-sit at the same time. I remember going to the cranberry marsh with one of my mom's babies strapped on my back and another one attached on one side of me, and I would pick with one hand. My mother used both her hands and didn't have any babies with her; I had them. It only stands to reason that she was bigger than me and she could pick faster than me, so I baby-sat out there and picked what I could pick. I took care of the kids so it wouldn't keep her from being slowed down, because that was our only means of having fruit in the wintertime. The women wanted to get as much as possible, which they did. They'd get about fifty or sixty quarts of salmonberries during the summer, and then about the same with the red huckle and black huckle and the cranberries. They put them up in glass jars and canned them. Sometimes my grandma would make fresh pies with the cranberries. Oh, they were good! Now you don't see any of that.

Then there were the elderberries, *tsíkyey*. I only tasted them once—they were so bitter! They come in clusters, like grapes, but they're very small and red. Sometimes my grandma would just leave them that way, and sometimes she'd take them apart to store them. What she'd do is peel an alder tree and make that bark into a cone shape and leave the top so you could push it over. Then she'd sew up the side with whatever she had. She'd put those berries in there and then close the top flap. Then she'd just put it into the creek at the back of her house and leave it there all winter long. When she'd take them out of the water, they used to look really fresh. That's the way they used to save their elderberries, but us kids never did like them because they tasted bitter.

CHILD BABY-SITTING ACTIVITIES

When we were picking berries wasn't the only time I had to baby-sit. Ever since I could remember, I took care of my younger brothers and sisters. My mother was plowing one time, and I had to stay home from school that day—I must have been about eight. I didn't get too much schooling because my mother was always working and needed someone to baby-sit. I ended up being the oldest one 'cause my sister Katherine got married so she wouldn't have to work and take care of kids. She said she was tired of taking care of us. But, oh! I *never* had a chance to say I was tired of it! It seems like I did it from the beginning.

Well, my mother was plowing up at that place where my grandfather's wife lived. And my mother said, "You're going to stay home today. You're not going to go to school cause I've got to go plow grandpa's field." And I said okay. I didn't care. So she was plowing that afternoon, and before she left she said, "You be sure and keep the baby quiet, and keep the baby dry." So I did. And then the baby started crying—this was my sister Dolores, who is six years younger than me. At that time babies never wore fancy clothes, just an undershirt, diaper, and something to wrap them up in when they're sleeping. So she started crying, and she kept crying after I cleaned her up. The babies were tied down straight, you know. You pinned them up by the shoulder, you pinned them around the stomach, and you pinned them down by their feet. I did that to her, and I wanted her to go to sleep. But she cried and she cried and she cried, and I couldn't stop her in any way! I took her out of the cradle, and I said, "Go to sleep . . . go to sleep . . ." and then I started crying and crying; I was so young myself. I couldn't stop her crying, so I picked her up and ran and took her down to my mother, and I was just crying great big tears, and I said, "Mama, I can't stop her crying, I don't know what's the matter with her." So, Mom undid the plow and stopped the horses. She came over and she sat down, and my step-grandmother knew there was something wrong, so she came out and sat down and asked what was the matter with the baby. My mother said, "I don't know," and she started taking her apart. And do you know, I had the safety pin clear through her shoulder! My mom was so mad at me! She said, "What are you doing to her! You never pay attention to what you're doing!" I just cried. I didn't say anything because I was afraid I'd get swatted across the face. My dad and granddad taught me never to talk back.

Ever since I could remember, it seems like I was always taking care of kids. When I was pretty young, my mother's mother used to come over and baby-sit us. When she'd come, she'd say to me, "Well, you have to stay with me again today. You're not going to go out because you have to be my legs; you have to be my feet. I don't run that fast. The kids are all home, so if they run away, you're going to go get them. If I need anything, you're going to walk after it. I'm here just to watch, and you're going to be my legs, and you're going to be my feet. You'll be with me so that none of the kids will get into trouble." So, I was always running after kids, bringing them back, taking care of them.

I even used to have a baby tied on my back sometimes when I was playing around. My grandmother used to tie one on me. She would make a triangle out of the shawl, fold it so it was on the bias, then cross it over my shoulders and under my arms and tie a knot under the baby's bottom. This way the baby would hang on my back, and my arm would be free so that I could play around.

I had to carry one on my back almost all the time when I was working. In the spring I had to get up early in the morning with my mom. She would tie one baby on my back, and I'd be holding the hands of two others, and I still had to weed the garden with her. While she did the hoeing, I did the weeding. I made the toddlers play on each side of me, and if one took off, I'd have to go and bring him back. The "baby-est" one I had to carry on my back all the time. Mom would only take the baby off my back when I got all wet in the back. Then it was time to take it off and change the baby. But I can remember going around with the baby on my back and pulling weeds and putting them in a bucket and then throwing them over the side of the fence, while my mom just went around hoeing the weeds out of there.

One time I got so mad I said, "Why do I *always* have to take care of them?" My mom wouldn't explain. My grandmother was the one. She said, "Sit down. I'm going to tell you why. Your mother is bigger than you, and she can work faster than you can. If she had to depend on you to do all this work, it would never get done." Seems it was always left to my grandmother to tell me these things. Maybe that's why I didn't get rebellious with my mother, because my grandmother used to tell me. They never told us in a harsh way either. They always told us real nicely. And that was enough explanation for me. I must have been about eight years old when I was doing all of this; I know I wasn't very old.

MORE ABOUT BABIES AND MY BROTHERS AND SISTERS

Another one of my responsibilities was to bathe the babies. We had #3 galvanized tubs, and that's what I used to bathe them in. Nowadays people bathe them in their sinks, but we never did put them in our sink. Never! We did have sinks, but they were for dishes. They were not for babies. So we used to use a galvanized tub #3. I would bathe them about every day because a baby messes every day and has to be bathed.

My mom nursed her babies all the way through. I used to have to run looking for my mom when it was feeding time. *I looked for her.* She didn't look for me. But I always knew where she was. I brought the baby over for a feeding and then left again. Babies were most generally weaned between ten months and a year. Feeding them was not my responsibility. When my mother got home from work, she cleaned herself up and got ready, and the babies were always fed right from the table when they were old enough. She used to take a fork and mash everything up. We were never fortunate enough to have baby food like they do now, so she just mashed everything up. When they fed us a long time ago, like I said, my father's grandmother used to chew the food for us and then put it in our mouths. That was the way they took care of us. By the time my younger brothers and sisters came along, they weren't doing this anymore. Mom just mashed it up for them. Once they could eat regular food, we didn't have to look for Mom. We just fed them right from the table.

And at that time we had . . . I guess you'd call it an Indian cradle. They had a rope across the corner of the room, and it was double. We threw a blanket over the ropes, an olive drab blanket, and then put a pillow in there. How that blanket didn't fall through the ropes I really don't know. It stayed together, somehow. Then when they'd get sleepy or if I wanted them to go to sleep, I'd put the baby in there, put a string on it, and pull on it—you know, rock the baby. We used to tie the babies up when we put them in the cradle. Their arms were tied down to their sides, and their legs were all tied together tight. They did this just to keep them still, to keep them from rolling, because we had them in that cradle in the corner of the room. They were probably tied up like that so they wouldn't fall out. But the kids learned to sleep really good that way. They never woke up. Then we would pull on that rope there and just swing them. . . . They would just swing. I used to take care of my brothers and sisters in this way, and my mom took care of me this way when I was a baby.

My mom used to have her babies about twelve months apart, most generally. But she had quite a few miscarriages, because she was doing all that hard work along with my dad. One time we asked her how many children she would have had if they all had lived. Fifteen, she told us. She had miscarriages at three months, four months, and up to seven months. We just figured that since she was working, maybe there was too much heavy lifting for her and maybe this is why she lost quite a few. Several children died when they were quite young. So now there's just eight of us: Katherine [deceased], myself (now the oldest living member of the family), Dolores (Dallie), Emil [deceased], Bessie, Joyce (Joy), Levi [deceased], and Fernell (Dicie). The last four are quite a bit younger than me [see the Swan Family Genealogical Chart in Appendix A].

WASHING CLOTHES IN THE CREEK

I also helped with the clothes washing when I was little. We used to have to go to the creek with my grandma when it was time for her to wash. This was my mother's mother, Alice Holden. My mom used to send me down there on weekends to help her tote her clothes. We'd pack them in pillowcases for her, from her house which was about six blocks away. Maybe I'd make two or three loads, and my grandmother would pack what was left. She used to have them all separated already—the lights in one and the darks in another pillowslip. Then she'd say, "All right, soak these first, and be sure to have them down below in the creek there." We always put our whites up above, then the colored, and then the dark clothes. That's the way they taught us how to soak them in the creek.

At that time we had no washing machines. We had to use big flat boards in the creek. And then we used to have to rub the soap on the board, and then after that, bunch the clothes together. We had a club we used to keep hitting them with. Then we'd rinse them off in the creek, and us kids would take turns twisting them to get the water out. It would take two of us, but we'd get it done. We never, ever had tattletale gray wash. Today the experts say, "Your clothes aren't going to get clean if you don't use warm water." But I don't think any of the Indians here ever had tattle-tale gray sheets, unless somebody didn't take care of them. They were just as white as can be, and we never used Purex. Never! There were no clotheslines, so we'd just hang them up on the bushes to dry. We'd have to start early in the morning so they'd be dry by afternoon. That's the way we used to wash clothes and dry them in the summer a long time ago.

And always the men cleaned the creek out. They used to go over there and rake it and clean it so there wouldn't be any green moss or whatever that green stuff is in there. They'd clean it at least twice a year, I guess. We didn't use the creek in the wintertime; we did the laundry at home, inside, in #2 galvanized tubs, or sometimes in the little canoes. My dad had a small canoe, and we'd pour water and put soap in that. Then we'd just get in there and stomp on them. Us kids would stomp on them to help wash them. We thought that was really fun! It wasn't a chore, it was fun.

Ever since I could remember, we had running water in our house. My dad was a plumber, so we always had hot and cold running water. I don't think the whole village did, though. Some had pumps in their houses. My grandparents used to have a well pump in their house, and we used to fight to help pump their water.

CARING FOR THE ELDERS

When I was little, aside from taking care of my younger brothers and sisters, I also helped out with some of the old people. Ed and Susie Weberhard lived very close to us. He was just like a grandfather to me, and I went in and out of their house all day long. I had to help take care of him just before he died—that was when I was about ten. His wife was busy taking care of him, so I went down there to see whether they needed anything, because she couldn't go anywhere—she didn't leave him. And if she left him, my mother used to relieve her so she could go visiting or something. Most generally I didn't go to the store for them, but if they needed something and if Mom had it, I'd bring it down to them. Like, if they needed potatoes, I used to bring them to her. And if she needed anything cooked, if she couldn't do it, well then I'd take it up to my mom and have her cook it, and then I'd bring it back to Susie. As I grew older, after he died, then I was old enough to do the cooking; then I'd do the cooking for her and bring it down to her. She went on living for a year or two after him. I'd sweep up her house, wash her dishes for her, clean it all up, and fix her beds. This was the sort of duty we felt we had to do, because that's the way my parents brought us up.

Then I did the same thing for Charlie Coballi and Annie Long Tom, too. She was a full-blooded Clayoquot Indian. She was a widow ever since I could remember; I never did see her husband, Mr. Long Tom. She lived just across the creek from us, so that it was a short run for me to go over and see if she needed anything. My father asked me to take care of Annie Long Tom and Charlie Coballi; my mom asked me to take care of Ed and Susie Weberhard because Susie was half Quileute, as was Mom. Charlie Coballi lived right next door almost, and he was Makah. I never saw his wife, either; he was a widower when I knew him. In those days I had to get up in the morning earlier than usual, before I went to school, and run to Coballi's to see if he needed anything or if he had breakfast. I always had to see that he had breakfast, because he was blind. Charlie Coballi was blind. Because of this,

I spent more of my time cleaning up his place, fixing his bed, keeping his clothes clean. My mother used to make me take his clothes down to the creek, wash them, hang them, and then bring them back up to him.

I took care of all these people until they died. I liked them and enjoyed being with them. Sometimes they'd tell me stories and tell me about things from long time ago—fiction as well as true stories. So it was something that I really enjoyed, and I didn't mind helping them at all.

MEMORIES OF NEAH BAY IN THE 1920s AND 1930s

Neah Bay was quite a bit different in those days when I was little and was helping those old people. There weren't so many houses in the back like there are now. All the houses were close to the front—near the water (see fig. 18). Of course, we just had a sandy street then. We didn't have the blacktop road like we do now—it was all sand then. And some of the older people that I really didn't know too well lived on the beach. They had little, little houses down there which I can vaguely remember. They were old-looking houses—no paint, no nothing—made out of wide boards.

In those days there were always lots of canoes on the beach, too, not far from those houses (see fig. 12). The men'd pull all the canoes up on the beach there. Each canoe had its own sail; they'd just put the sail up and sail out or sail home, and that way they wouldn't have to row all the time and get so tired out. Sometimes when the men went out in their canoes, it'd be raining, so when they got close to home they'd roll up their sails and put them away. Then when they got home, after the rain ended, they'd set their sails up, open them up, right there on the beach, and then you could see all those designs from one end of the beach to the other. What a sight that was! Some of them would have halibuts painted on—the halibut spirit, or the salmon, the seal, the whale, whatever—just different kinds of fish and sea mammals. When I think of it, it's too bad we never got any picture taken of it. There's no sails anymore, no canoes; everybody's got motorboats.

We only had one photographer here that I remember. His name was Dan Quadessa. He used to print on tintypes. The picture turned out blue, and yet it brought out the picture anyway. Some of them were tintypes, and some came on brown postcards. You don't see any of that kind of printing anymore.

When I was a kid, they always had a hall in Neah Bay where we had our dances—just a big, long, empty hall with a wood floor. All the longhouses were already gone. The first hall that I remember was called Star Hall. When the Star Hall was sold to the Apostolic Church, Jim Hunter, my husband Wimpy's grandfather, built one on his lot. They called that one Hunter's Hall. We paid five dollars a night to use it for parties. That was a lot of money, then. In 1975 we had to pay twenty dollars to rent the Makah Community Hall. In 1994 we paid fifty dollars, but got thirty dollars back if we left the hall clean when we were done.

When I was a child, we lived near the west end of the village, at what they called Spanish Fort.[3] That's where my great-grandmother's property was, and she ended up giving it to my dad because she lived with us till she died. That's the first and only place we ever lived when I was young. The house I grew up in was a two-story wood house, built by my dad. Densmore has a picture of it in her book.[4] They finally knocked that one down, burned the boards on the beach, and then built a new one in the same place. They bought two houses from Metheny and Bacon,[5] and Dad joined them together so we'd have four bedrooms for the whole family. All of us girls were married and gone by then, so this house was smaller. Just my mom and dad and the two boys, Emil and Levi, lived there. Others of us stayed there for a while and then left. My niece Alice Johnson lived there for a while, and so did I, with my kids, and my other sisters came sometimes. That house is gone now, too; someone tore it down after my dad died. We were in Tacoma going to school when that happened.

My dad built a lot of houses in Neah Bay besides ours, but all the others were for the BIA (see fig. 19). He built a nice house for Dr. Verhalen, who was a real good doctor and lived on the hill right at the edge of the bluff, above the BIA offices. I think there were about twelve of those houses that my dad built for the BIA workers. Eventually the government moved out of here and gave up most of its workers. The land became the property of Crown Zellerbach Logging Company. So Crown bought most of the houses on top of the hill, too. Crown has moved most of them off the reservation now, to Vista Drive, about six miles east of here in that housing area for their workers.

STORIES ABOUT BOATS

Everything our people used for building had to come in on a big boat, unless they were making houses out of driftwood. There was a big boat they called the *Utopia* that used to come in here. I was too little, I guess, to even remember it, but I do remember the *Comanche,* after the *Utopia* quit coming. There was no road in here then, so we had to get in and out by boat. Everybody'd get so excited when they'd hear the *Comanche* blow its whistle around the corner there by the Coast Guard station. The boat only came in once a week, and everybody'd run out to the dock to see what was happening.[6] Even if people were sitting down eating, if you heard that boat whistle coming around the corner, boy, you got your coat and ran, to be sure you were there before anybody else, so you could be in the front line to watch who came down the gangplank. "Let's see who's going to come off today! Let's see who went to town last week. Let's see who had enough money to go and stay in town for a whole week!" At that time we weren't getting all the money that's coming in now. It was all you could do to save one or two dollars a month. If you went to town on Tuesday, you'd have to try like the dickens to find another way back, because you couldn't come back on the *Comanche* until the next Tuesday. So that was a big day for us—to run out to the dock and see who went to town, who came back, who had enough money, and all that.

I remember one time, I must have been about eight or nine years old, and Washburn's store was on the west end of town. I'm standing in there—you know how the candy counter was then; they had little windows on each one of them, different kinds of candies inside—and I was standing there with my nickel. A nickel was pretty good money then, and I was pounding on that window case. I was pounding on that glass window where the candy was, waiting for someone to come and wait on me. Harry Washburn was in the back, in the office, but he must never have heard me. It must have been in the evening, and I heard that boat whistle blow away—it was coming around the corner, and, oh dear! I started pounding louder. And he still didn't hear me! He just took off! He locked the store door and just took off, and there I stood, crying, because I knew there was nobody in there . . . nobody in there, and I didn't know how to open that latch! And I was standing there, big tears rolling down, and I'd try the door every once in a while, and I said, "I want to go out to the dock, too, but how do you open this thing?" And I couldn't get out of there. Everybody passed by, and I was standing there with my hand pressed against the window, and people were passing by and nobody paid attention to me. Finally, Roger Colfax passed by. He saw me standing there, just a-crying, and he came running up on the porch, and he said, "Turn that little thing up there." I looked around, and I pushed everything I could, and he said, "Turn it. Turn it!" I did, and I finally got out of there. I could have had a pocket full of candy or something, but I didn't. I don't think I'll *ever* forget being locked in like that.

We liked being around boats. We'd go out to the dock for entertainment when we were kids. We used to stand on the dock and ask the fishermen, "Can we take care of your skiff?" Sometimes we'd run into a grouchy one, and he'd tell us to go home or something. But there'd be some nice ones, and they'd say, "All right, all right, you can take it, but be sure you don't give it to anyone else, though. And keep it until I get back." Sometimes he'd be gone three hours, four hours, maybe half the day. And we'd be out there just rowing, you know. We'd just play and ride the waves. We liked to go out and ride the waves. There wasn't any breakwater then, and the waves were big. And then when we wanted to go ashore, we'd count waves, and on the seventh one, then you go ashore. You sit out there in the skiff until you see the biggest one coming, and you wait for it. So from that biggest one we'd have to count seven. Then when we counted seven, we'd just row like mad and come in; I'd pull the skiff up on the beach and run up and tell my mom I was hungry, or if I needed to go to the bathroom I'd run up there. Then after I was ready, I'd pull the skiff back out into the water again and row to the dock and check to see if the fisherman had come back. If he hadn't, well then I'd stay right close around the dock in the skiff and watch for him. I guess we learned how to take those chances with the waves and paddle the little skiffs. Our parents didn't seem to mind. None of us ever drowned; we just learned how to live with the ocean.

And then sometimes our parents used to make spears for us, and we'd go out, and if it was pretty calm, we'd use the skiffs to get flounders. They used to be here in the bay before they built the breakwater. We'd go out and fish for flounders with a spear. We spent a lot of time doing that, and then we'd wash the boat out when we were through, and bring it back out again. We'd bring the fish to the old people; they used to eat it. They'd fillet it or just cut it up and boil it. They used to really enjoy it. They'd say, "Well, next time bring me some more." So we spent our time doing that, too, when we were kids, if I wasn't out with my grandfather. That's what we used to do for entertainment. We'd hurry back to the dock in the skiff and hold it there until the fisherman got in, and throw him his rope. Sometimes he'd be nice enough, and he'd say, "Well, here's a quarter." Or, "Here's a dime." Actually we didn't ask for the skiffs because we wanted to be paid. That was just a means for us to have fun.

INDIAN FOODS: SHARING AND PREPARING—
MEN'S AND WOMEN'S JOBS

There used to be three, four, maybe five bachelors who'd fish for the older people—for the women who didn't have husbands who could fish, or women whose husbands were too old to go out anymore. The women used to watch for these bachelors to come back with fish. They'd pull their canoes up on the beach and holler, "Fish! Come and get it!" (qeʔíˑks).[7] Then the ladies would run down to the beach and pick up what they wanted. They never were greedy people in those days. They'd just take as much as they figured they needed, and away they'd go again. Nobody ever took too much. There was always enough for the next person who came down.

And it was the same with sea eggs, too, you know. If somebody got hungry for sea eggs [sea urchins], kʷ'ičkáˑpix̌, they'd tell these bachelors, and off they'd go. They'd tell each other, and pretty soon they'd all go. They'd almost never go alone, because if anything happened then they'd be able to help each other. Usually they'd go in twos. My uncle Freddie Anderson was the only one that used to go alone. He used to like to fish a lot, so he wouldn't wait for anybody, he'd just go. These bachelors would go out and get a canoe load, maybe two canoe loads of sea eggs. They'd come back in, and they'd holler, and if there were kids down there they'd say, "Go on, tell so-and-so that we got sea eggs," and then one lady would tell her neighbors and so on all the way down, and pretty soon everybody was down there on the beach. They'd never bring those sea eggs up off the beach; they always ate them on the beach where they could just throw the shells back in the water again. They always ate them raw; they never cooked them. I never could eat them. . . . I tried. . . . They leave a sweet taste in your mouth. My mom kept telling me, "Don't keep it in your mouth, just swallow it!" and I wouldn't. I used to just sit there and suck on it until I'd be sicker than all get-out. The longer you keep it in your mouth, the slimier it gets. That's why she said, "Don't keep it in your mouth, swallow it!" So, I never could eat sea eggs. My kids like them, though.

The old people liked sea roses, too. Sea roses [sea anemones], *k'idi·ł tubáts*, are green, and they stick on the rocks, and they open up like flowers. To fix these my mom used to use a grater, scraping all the green off of there, and then when they're clean they're just little. She'd put a branch from a salmonberry bush right through them, like a skewer, and then boil them. This way they're easy to lift out. They're kind of like gristle when they're all cooked. You don't dare overcook them because they get yucky. If you don't overcook them, they're supposed to be good. I learned to eat them now and then, but I'm not really crazy about them. They're just kind of gristly-like. They say these are real good for rheumatism. They say the same about sea eggs, too.

Most of the time it seemed like our diet was just boiled fish or dried fish. We had fried fish, but not very often; mostly boiled fish, dried fish, baked fish. We mostly ate kelp fish, ling cod, halibut, salmon, and snapper.[8]

Women didn't do the fishing; the men did.[9] Women weren't allowed to go whaling and seal hunting, either. They were supposed to stay home and do the drying; and they did most of the skinning for the men, too, after they went out seal hunting. The men would bring in the seals. Most generally they hated to throw the meat away because that was something for us to eat. If they had an especially good day and had an overload, then they would do that—skin them and just throw the meat away—so they could stay out in their canoes a few days longer. They hated to throw the meat away, and this only happened if they had an overload; most generally they would bring the seals home. They sold the skins for about three dollars apiece, then.

Seals weren't so big that they would last a long time. The seal looks big, but when you strip him of his blubber and his fur, there's not much left. So, two, three, four of them aren't going to last long. The first one they might have eaten fresh, but I never did like fresh seal meat. I can't even explain what it tastes like. . . . There's so much blood in there that it all boils to the top. . . . Then when you bite into it . . . I can't even explain it. It was too fishy and has an altogether different taste. When it's dried, at least half-dried, it has a nice smokey taste. They used to cut them in little strips to dry them. That was another thing my grandmother used to do—show me how to cut 'em. She'd give me a little piece and show me how to cut it. And even the ribs—we wouldn't throw them away. We'd cut between them on one side and then the other side, until they hung in strips. And the better parts we'd just kind of strip the same way, first one side and then the other, until it's sort of like a long string, *čidi·qakt*, (seal ribs in strips). Then you hang it over one of those racks in the smokehouse for about three or four days. It gets black and shiny and doesn't look very good, but the meat is just right then—not too tough or too dry. When seal meat gets too dry, it gets very tough. That's why they never dried them too long.

If we had too much seal meat, we always shared; we never had it long enough to put it away. It always went to different houses. We'd share it with our relatives, whichever ones came over, and if other people happened to come to visit, we'd give them some before they went home. My mom always gave it to them. They came over when they knew she'd be home, and she would always give it away. It was her house, and out of respect to her, the hunter let her give it away. Sometimes my dad or my granduncle or my grandmother had friends that they wanted to give some to, so they told my mom and she gave them some.

Since my granduncle Elliot Anderson kept us in seals, it was really no effort to have seal oil all the time, too. My mother used to render the fat, and we used to sit and watch her. It was something I never had to do with her. My grandmother used to help her. First they'd skin the seal. My granduncle would save the skins and tan them too. (He'd use them for a back throw on a couch or chair, or else put them on a bedroom floor.) Then after they skinned the seal they'd trim the blubber off. My mother would rinse it off because there's blood on the blubber. Then she would put it in a great big copper kettle, about a fifteen-gallon pot, and boil it for about four to five minutes, until it's firm. When you first cut the blubber off the meat, it's kind of squishy, squashy, spongy. So, she'd put it in the water and boil it for a few minutes till it's real firm so you can get your knife through it. Next she'd cut the blubber in strips, six- to eight-inch-wide strips, and hang 'em over the fish-drying racks. They'd hang overnight in order to let the water drip out of them. If she didn't let the water run out, then it would pop and splash when she'd render the oil. The next day she'd cut the strips into six- to eight-inch squares. Then she'd cut each square into little strips; that way the oil renders out faster than if she put a whole square in. She'd just put a certain amount in there, because if she put all of it in there together, it just wouldn't render out very good. It might make it too dark—it might kind of burn the fat, instead of rendering it real nice. So she'd do it a little bit at a time, and there'd be little crackley strips left. She'd bring those in, and they used to eat them with the fish and potatoes, instead of dipping in oil like they usually did. I didn't eat those crackley strips because they were too greasy. They never forced us to eat anything we didn't want to eat. We'd taste it, but to me it was always too greasy, so I wouldn't eat it. I did dip in the seal oil, though. I like the seal oil. It's different from those greasy strips. Those strips were just too rich, and I couldn't eat them.

My mom used to have three or four of those light bluish-greenish glass bottles—they were five-gallon bottles with real skinny necks, and they had basket-weaving on the outside. She'd take that rendered oil and pour it in those big glass bottles and store them out in the smokehouse, in a corner where it was cool. The oil would last a whole year if it was kept cool. Then we'd just pour out a little bit at a time, into a quart fruit jar, and bring it in. Once it's brought into the warm, it starts to get bitter, so they'd only bring in little bits at a time.

A few times I heard the men talk about whales—whaling. They'd gather on the beach, and since there really was not a lot for them to do around here, they'd sit on a log and talk. Maybe somebody would drop by and say, "Well, let's go down the beach," and they'd go down there. Other guys walking by would just naturally join them. Pretty soon maybe there'd be eight or ten of them, and us kids used to go and play around there because my grandpa used to go down the beach, too, and sit around, or my uncle. Of course, my granduncle couldn't do it since he couldn't hear. He could read lips, but he'd prefer not to sit there and have to stare everybody in the face. So my grandfather or my uncle used to go down there, and they'd sit around, and you could hear them talk about every little thing. Sometimes I heard them talk about whales. I never saw any of the whales that came on the beach because I was just too young. I was born too late to see something like that. My mother said she saw two of them come in, but I never saw any. So, I'd sit and listen to them talk about when the whale came ashore, when they towed the whale in, and the first piece that they cut off. That was the fin. After this was cut off, the one who owned the fin would take it. My great-grandfather used to get the fin like that when he killed the whale.[10] Then they would start from the middle of the whale and work out. There were different people. . . . They used to call them all by Indian names, and each of them would get about a foot clear around the whale. Everyone that wanted one got a portion. Maybe some of them didn't want the whole thing, so they would get just as much as they wanted.

The only whale meat I ever ate was canned. My dad's aunt, Annie Williams from Canada, used to have it canned over at Caldonia, and every time she came down from Canada she'd bring us two cases of it. It tasted like corned beef. We didn't holler. We ate it. It was almost a wine-colored meat. My mom made hash out of it, or we'd just eat it in sandwiches. We didn't complain. We just thought it was a funny corned beef until we heard them say that this was canned whale meat. But by then we'd already been eating it. It was already good to us, so we didn't complain. I enjoyed it.

The women used to make something else that really smelled terrible, called "stink eggs," or á·čpab. About in June, when the salmonberries were still sprouting new branches and the king salmon have loose eggs that are not in clumps, the women used to get together and make this caviar-like stuff. A long time ago table salt used to come in ten-pound sacks. They'd save all the empty sacks, and they'd fill them with salmon eggs. This was the time those salmon spawned, so they would take those eggs and make caviar out of them. They'd put the eggs in these sacks and then sew them up. Then they'd put flour on the outside so that the salmon eggs wouldn't dry out. They'd keep putting flour on them until it dried real good, and then they'd put the sacks up in the smokehouse and just leave them there. As it aged, it kind of smelled like limburger cheese. . . . It used to really stink! They'd break salmonberry sprouts and use them to scoop out the caviar and eat it.

In May when the salmonberry bushes are just beginning to sprout, we used to have to go with the ladies when they went to pick sprouts. They'd bring gloves or use double thicknesses of towel and then break the branches off the bushes, about one and a half feet long. They'd get together—the old ladies—and they'd split up into three groups. One group would be down on the beach early in the morning, like about five or six o'clock. They'd build a fire as big as they could, a long, oblong fire—they'd put rocks in there and keep this fire going. In the meantime the other two groups would go sprout picking. The women would come in with bunches of sprouts. They'd pack one bunch and cook the other bunch, because they had to share with the women who were taking care of the fire. They timed themselves and got down there about the time the fire was ready. Then they'd pull the rocks and the fire to one side, line the hole with kelp and then sacks, put the cleaned sprouts in there, put the rocks back on top, and wait. Sometimes they'd put clams or fish at one end and cover them, too. They kept them separate so the flavors wouldn't mix. Mmmmm, were they good when they were all done! The sprouts came out kind of a tan color, and the taste reminded me of asparagus. I really liked that stuff when it was cooked. We called it *t'ič'ú·p* (cooked under the sand). Then they sat there and ate those. Sometimes the husbands would come down and eat, or the women would just tie the cooked sprouts up in three or four different places and pack them home for their husbands.

Sometimes when they'd be doing this, they'd also make bread on the beach at the same time. They'd make buckskin bread. They called it that because when they were done baking it, it looked about like buckskin. They'd roll it out flat, about two feet long and as wide as they wanted it. They'd make about six or eight of those. Instead of putting them in a pan, they'd put them on newspaper. They'd dust the newspaper with flour, put the dough in between pieces of paper, put them under the sand, and cover them back up. They'd leave those breads for about forty-five minutes, take them out, and dust the sand off. No sand or no nothing on there! That was *really* good! There's nothing like eating bread made in the sand! We don't do it anymore; even my mom didn't do it in her later years. They'd wrap it in the news-paper before they baked it. It seemed like the paper would burn, but it didn't. The bread would be nice and golden brown.

Of course, sometimes we also cooked clams or salmon down on the beach along with the bread. The clams were put under the sand; the salmon was boned and but-terflied and put between upright sticks and barbecued above the flames. We still fix the salmon this way sometimes. This is the Indian way—the best way to fix salmon!

CHAPTER 4

GROWING UP

BECOMING A WOMAN

During the years I was growing up, getting a little older, my grandparents used to talk about what it was like in their day, how a girl became a woman. When a girl reached puberty, around twelve or thirteen, they hid her away for a whole month. They wouldn't let anybody see her; she could not be seen by any man at all. Only her grandmother could see her. They put her on a sort of loft on a bed that was high up in the longhouse, and they waited on her hand and foot. This is the way it had to be because they wanted her to be pure. When she became a woman, she had to be pure. Otherwise, if she wasn't, she was a disgrace to the tribe; very much of a disgrace. And to her family too. As far as I know, this is what was proper for girls from upper-class families; I haven't heard too much about what they did for lower-class girls.

So the girl would be hidden away, and then when she started having her period, they kept her clean. They bathed her every day. Apparently she had ten girls who would wait on her hand and foot. From the way it sounded, these girls were mostly slave girls, and they would take her down to the creek and bathe her every day. They would keep her clean and keep her changed. There had to be one adult woman who went with them. When they went down there with her, they were always singing. Singing and singing. Nobody ever said what kind of songs they sang, but I would imagine that their songs might have been some T'abáa songs and some lullabies, because they were still such young children. At that time, eleven- and twelve-year-olds were still really children; not like nowadays—they've almost got their own kids when they're eleven and twelve. In those days twelve was just considered a little kid, a real little kid, and this was still true when I was twelve. In the days of my grandparents, the women had to talk to the young girl every day. They probably talked about what she had to do in her life, how she was going to go through these periods for the rest of her life, how this brings her into the age of puberty where now she will be able to have children, and then they probably talked to her about sex. They had some older women that used to be able to talk real good.

After she got through that month, it was publicly told that now this girl was at the age of puberty. She was a woman. She was of marriageable age. Her father would have a big potlatch party for her, and when they did the inviting, they'd tell everyone right away that this was a "coming out party," a womanhood party for this certain girl. They called it a *q'its'e·yit*. To them a long time ago, it was sacred; it meant something important; it wasn't treated lightly. It was really important to the girl and to her family.

By the time I reached this age, it had all changed. The girls weren't hidden away anymore, and no one in Neah Bay gave parties for them. People were more or less getting modern; not living like they used to. I never even heard of them hiding the girls away on this side [the American side] when I was little; nothing like this was done for me when I reached puberty. The only womanhood party I ever saw was the one that Francis Frank and Annie Williams gave for my cousin Clothilda Frank up at Clayoquot in 1930. They continued that custom longer up there [in Canada] than they did down here, but they haven't done it up there for a long time either.

Today, "coming into womanhood" doesn't mean very much. These younger ones will call it a "blood party," and it's not anything sacred to them anymore. It's just a big joke to them. They'll tease their children and say, "Hey, let's announce your blood party." Then the girl gets real embarrassed and says, "Oh, no! You're not telling anybody I'm having my period." This is not something that a girl should be teased about. This was something very important to them a long time ago; not something to joke about. Things have changed so drastically since those days, even since I've grown up. If my dad or my grandfather knew what was going on now, they'd just be turning in their graves. Nothing is sacred anymore.

Today, if they want to give a girl a womanhood party, they call it a birthday party or a naming party, and it's no different than any other birthday or naming party.

Actually, I didn't know what coming into womanhood was all about when it happened to me. That's something they never talked about over here. I knew of the puberty party, but I had no idea exactly what it was until I was older, much older. My mother never talked about it; my grandmother never talked about it. They talked about blood parties, but I didn't understand what a blood party was all about.

After the fact, my mom started to tell me what I had to do. She told me this would completely change my life. Now I was a young lady, and I was not to play around rough like a little girl anymore. I had to start acting like a woman. At first, I didn't know what to think of it. They hadn't prepared me for it like they should have. Later on, though, I felt better about it. From the time I found out that my girlfriends were just the same as me, then this part of my life wasn't a problem for me anymore.

TEENAGE CHORES

During my teenage years I was busy a lot helping my folks. What I did most was help my mom by taking care of the younger kids and baby-sitting them all the time. I didn't go to school after I was about fourteen so I could stay home with the kids. I also did most of the cleaning, the housekeeping, the clothes washing, the cooking, and I had to teach my sisters to dance. My dad made the little ones learn to dance; especially when they'd get into mischief and were being noisy, he'd say, "Everybody put on your shawls." And they would do as he asked and start dancing. If they were wrong, he'd stop in the middle of the song and say to me, "Now you show them what they have to do." My sister Dolores and I used to get mad, because we'd have to show the little kids how to dance. I felt like I didn't really want to do this, but I had no choice.

Since there were no boys old enough to help out in our family, my sisters and myself had to do all the boys' chores. Since we didn't have any garbage dump at that time, my duty was to go down the beach every day and dump the garbage. That was a job that the boys in other families did. Cutting wood and splitting wood were other jobs we had to do, since the boys were too small. Even when my two young brothers got older, my mom pampered them. They didn't have to do these chores. She'd let them be and get us to do those chores instead. If the boys didn't do something she asked, she wouldn't always get after them as much as she got after us. We had a big air-tight, wood-burning stove in those days, and we needed a lot of wood to keep it going. So, us girls did all the cutting and splitting of the wood. If the blocks were too big, then my dad would quarter them for us, and we did the rest—making kitchen wood and splitting them small and making kindling. My mom used to get up before my dad in the morning and make the fire and make breakfast, so we always had to have kindlings ready at all times for her to use. Sometimes if my granduncle Elliot was staying with us and there was cedar around, we'd watch him make shavings to use in starting the fire. He'd set them down so that they'd be there for my mother when she woke up in the morning. We used to have a lot of fir wood around in those days too. We were able to cut drift logs on the beach, without the government or Crown Zellerbach saying we couldn't. We used to be able to get logs six feet through, so we burned an awful lot of good fir wood in those years.[1]

There were times when I used to feel resentful about all the work I had to do; I wasn't too happy about it. Now I think differently about it, though. I say to myself, "Well, gee whiz, we didn't have things at that time like we have now. Why should I have felt like that? It was one of those things that had to be." We had things to do then, where nowadays I realize that the kids are so different; they're having gangs and things like that in order to find something to do. Then I think sometimes, "Well, we were fortunate to have parents who made us do things that had to be done to make their life easier." When I think about it, I was kind of glad every so often that I could make things easier for my mom, because she tried to make things easier for my dad. Then again, I can think back to the good times I've had and how different they were. We used to have a real lot of good times.

HAYING AND HORSES

When summertime came, it was exciting for us kids, real exciting! That was the time we helped the guys that had the big, big barns in Neah Bay.[2] All the land out at the prairie, along the Wyaatch River, used to be fenced so that they could grow hay for all the horses that were around here. They don't do that [grow hay] anymore. Some of the kids that didn't have any horses to take care of, they'd start looking for a job helping with the haying, piling hay. They really never got paid; they'd work for free just for a ride out to the country and a ride back. All us kids from Neah Bay used to have to get out there and hay during the summer. We used to have a real good time haying. My dad had to watch the weather, whenever it got good and the hay was ready, like in the middle of July, August, and for about a month's time, we'd get to help him. We had this place out there they used to call the Government Field,[3] out on what we call the Prairie.[4] We had so many acres there where we could grow hay, then cut it, put it on the wagons, bring it in the barn. And then my dad had a place of his own, toward the east of the Government Field, where we did the rest of our haying. My mom had eight cows, he had five horses, which had to be fed. It took thirty acres of hay to fill my dad's barn each year.

At that time all the Indians used to take care of their horses and grow hay for them every year, but they don't anymore. No one looks after their horses and takes care of them now. That's why, until a few years ago, they roamed everywhere in town, eating garbage and anything else they could find. Now people try to keep them out of town, so we see fewer horses than a few years ago. Our job used to be to bathe the horses once a week and then comb them down after we bathed them in the evening. We used to use warm water and then rinse them off with cool water, then dry them off, put a blanket on them. No one does that anymore. Nobody knows what a horse blanket is now. We used to have to take care of their "frogs," too—what we called frogs underneath their feet. These were soft places on the bottoms of their hooves where gravel could get caught. We had to check them every day to see that they didn't get gravel caught there. We watched their hooves, and the minute the nails grew too long and started cracking, then we'd have to start cutting their nails down. If one cracked and we weren't watching, my dad would really have a fit at us, cause then he'd have to make a horseshoe to fit it. He was a blacksmith too, so he'd make us get out there and nail those horseshoes on them, too. He'd say, "You have to watch. You have to watch and listen." Cause the minute they got loose, we'd have to take the horseshoes off and trim their hoofs again. So we'd watch, and we'd do that.

I used to be the only one in our family that would go with my dad when it was hay cutting time. My oldest sister was married, and the younger ones were too little, so just he and I would do the mowing. I used to make up our lunch and go out there with him. When it was noontime, I'd spread out the lunch and serve it to him and just sit out there and be with my dad. The only free time I got was when I went with my dad in the summertime to help him with the haying. That was the only time I felt like I was really free. Most of the rest of my teenage time I had to take care of my mother's kids while she worked with my dad. Once in a while he'd let me run the hayrake while he'd sit and wait; then he'd take his turn and run it.

After the hay was dry, the kids would all come out to help—a bunch up here, a bunch up there on the Prairie, in different wagons. Just my dad and I would work in our area. When it was time to turn the hay, if it was too thick, then I was the only one with him turning the hay over. When it was time to put it in piles, I was there helping him again. There were lots of people all doing their haying out there at the same time: Jim Hunter, Charlie Smith, Edwin Hayte, Shubert Hunter, Horace Claplanhoo, Frank Smith—they all had horses and raised hay. The teenage boys would be hired out to different ones to help them when they were haying. Boys whose parents didn't have any horses were willing to be hired so that they could borrow a horse every now and then to ride, whenever they felt like it. They'd work just for that; that was their payment. They [the men] didn't have to pay them; all they had to do was feed them.

The teenagers would start lumping the hay, putting it in piles, just so they could get a ride out to the country. When it was time to bring a wagonload of hay back into town to be emptied, us kids would stay out there on the Prairie a lot of the time and take off our clothes and jump in the water and go swimming. We never had swimming suits, we used to just bring extra clothes or wear them out there and bring another set to change into afterward. Then we'd go in swimming in the Wyaatch River until he [Dad] got back. Sometimes we'd all swim together, but if the boys didn't bring extra clothes they'd go up around the bend of the river to a place we now call Second Bridge, and they'd swim there, naked. And they were good about it; they stayed there and swam until they were ready to come back. They never tried to sneak up on the girls like they would nowadays. We used to be way down by Red Creek, close to where the Air Force base is now. Then when we'd see the wagons coming back, we'd get dressed and go up and start loading hay again. There were times when my dad wouldn't let me stay out there; however, I didn't rebel against him when he said no. I did enjoy it when he'd let me stay out there and swim with the kids, though. After we came back from swimming, we'd be all nice and fresh and full of vim and vigor. Then we'd start working hard again, pitching the hay.

Sometimes, if we didn't feel like swimming while we were out there, we'd go salmonberry or huckleberry picking instead, and eat the berries right off the bushes. We'd go in a bunch, and nobody strayed away or ever got lost. It was more woody then. The logging hadn't come in, so the woods were really nice and clean, not like they are now—full of slash. Now you can't walk through the woods like you could in those days. We had buckskin bread with us and maybe dried fish for lunch, and then we'd end by going out and picking the berries and eating them right off the bushes. We didn't bring any back with us. Come evening, after a day of haying and swimming or berry picking, we'd all come back into town on one load of hay. That was really fun for us in those days.

We didn't bale the hay, just put it up bulk in a huge lump. My dad would put a rope from the front to the back and tie it onto the wagon. Then we'd ride back on it. The road wasn't like it is now. There were a lot of ruts in it then, and the wagon just used to pitch back and forth. One time when we were coming home, my friends Muzzy and Ramona were on top of the hay there with me. My dad told us to hang onto the rope up there. So we were going and just a-swaying back and forth as we ran from one rut into another. The wagon kept swaying over to the side, and I kept telling Ramona, "Hang onto the rope! Hang onto the rope!" She was just being a real nonsense girl all that day, just sitting there, talking and playing and singing every now and then. Suddenly the wagon took a great big dip, and in that dip was a mud puddle. And over she went! Over into the mudhole! Ooohhh! We just laughed and laughed. She was *all* muddy! My dad was so mad at her, he said, "I told you to hold onto the rope!" We just didn't think it was that serious; we laughed and laughed. Things like that were a lot of fun. Now the kids don't know what that kind of fun is anymore.

Those days were so good for me! I didn't have to have any of my mom's babies with me then. It was playing time for me because I could have my girlfriends there with me. Course I wasn't the only one that had to baby-sit. Other girls had to lug their younger brothers and sisters with them, too. It was hard to be the oldest! You got out of a lot of work if you were the youngest. But I sure did enjoy those days when I didn't have to be in the house with the kids, when I could be outside, when I could work with my dad, and when I could go swimming with my friends.

WORKING WITH MY DAD

I got to work with my dad a few other times, too. When my mom was pregnant and had to stay home, then I used to get sent with my dad. I went out with him when he was building houses for the BIA. I was there to sweep up the sawdust as he worked, keep things cleaned up while he went on ahead and built the house. My dad had another duty, too, which was to go to the doctor's house and do things like split his kindlings, make his kitchen wood. So, when Dad would be mowing the doctor's lawn or something, then I'd be there splitting kindlings and cutting kitchen wood. The kitchen stove had to be kept going all day in order to have hot water in the hot water tank. So that's why I used to have to be up there to cut wood for them. I did this for Dr. Verhalen. He was a real good doctor. Dad built the house he lived in, which was at the end of BIA hill point. Dad built about eight or nine houses for the BIA on top of the hill, and about ten or twelve of them down below. Later on, most of them became the property of Crown Zellerbach Logging Company.

I enjoyed working with my dad more than staying home with Mom, because somehow or another Mom and I didn't get along so well. She never showed any affection. I don't think she was very affectionate really. We just simply grew up without that. But I got a lot from my grandfather; not much from my grandmother, though; she wasn't much to show her affection, either. My dad gave us a lot, however. So I guess whatever I lacked from Mom, I got from my grandfather and from my dad. Wherever my dad went, I went along with him. I went to all the Indian dances with him; this helped break the monotony of working around home— staying there all the time and taking care of all the kids. So, my dad would take me across to Canada with him, even when there was nothing going on, even if we just went to Esquimalt, to Victoria there, he'd take me along. I ended up spending a lot of time with my dad, more time than I did with my mom.

Mom used to give me orders all the time, and I just never could get close to her. It seemed like Mom always used to get after us, holler at us and make us do whatever she wanted us to do; she just kept riding us all the time. But when we had to do things for our grandparents, they didn't have to ride us, they just asked us nicely. I used to do things for my dad without his having to holler. Oh, every once in a while he did, but not as much as my mom. It seemed like he and my grandfather were the real bosses in our family. They were the ones to show us what to do, tell us what not to do, and talk to us day by day, whenever it was possible. I don't know about the other kids, but I felt closer to my dad than to my mom. She did show a little more affection to the youngest ones—Joy, Fernell, and Levi—but she just never showed very much to the rest of us.

I never really saw my parents being affectionate to each other either. But I had a feeling that they did care for each other. I could tell just by the tone of my dad's voice. Every once in a while my dad used to call my mom "Dear." He had a pet name for her, too. Her name was Ruth, but he always called her "Lou." When he'd be talking to her, I knew that he did love her. I could hear it; they really didn't have to show it. Every now and then I'd hear her talk to him that way, too, but not as much as he did to her.

SCHOOL IN NEAH BAY

There were a lot of times when I wasn't around the house, though, because I had to go to school. The first place I went to school was here in Neah Bay at the Day School. They didn't allow the Indian kids to go to school with the white kids up at the Coast Guard station, so the Indians had their own school down here, and they called it the Day School.[5] I went to school four years there; it was where the

Presbyterian Church is now. They had a bell that rang every morning, and that meant for us to go to school then. They let us off for lunch; everybody had to go home for lunch. We had an hour. Then we had to be back in school by one and stay there until four. All the kids walked to school. There were no such things as cars here, and I don't think they allowed them to ride horses to school. Mrs. DePoe taught grades one to four, and her husband, grades five to seven. They burned sulphur on the stove every morning, and we'd be coughing like mad. They thought we were dirty and they'd catch diseases from us if they didn't do this.

One good thing about Mrs. DePoe and her husband—they had something special going on for us kids every month. We were constantly busy doing something. They had plays for the kids once a month, like January they had some kind of winter play, and February they'd have some sort of play for Valentine's Day. She always managed to find something to put on. I remember one month in spring they put up a curtain with little holes in it. A face went in each hole, and they had drawn flowers around each. Then the kids would talk, and they made believe the flowers were talking to each other. This was fun. She was nice, but he wasn't. He used to tell us that none of us would ever reach high school, let alone college. He was from Depoe Bay, Oregon, and she was from Geary, Oklahoma. They met at Indian boarding school.

I remember a few things about the clothes we wore to school in those days, especially the shoes. When we were little, we never wore shoes. Our parents didn't mind if we didn't have any; it saved them from having to look for them. Then when we got bigger, we started wearing shoes. I was about six, I think, when I started wearing shoes—when I first had to go to school. We had button shoes then, and I used to feel smart because I was able to carry around hooks [to button up the shoes], like everybody else. Patent leather, button shoes . . . oh, my! I really liked them! I didn't get to wear them after I was about eight or nine years old, though. Evidently we were too rough for those kind of shoes; we must have crawled around a lot or something because the toes of our shoes used to wear out. About that time, Dad said, "I'm going to buy you boys' shoes. You aren't going to wear girls' shoes no more." The front of the boys' shoes used to be brass, lovely brass-toed shoes. So, he bought me a pair. Oh, was I *ever* proud of that pair of shoes! I'd pull my sleeve down and just shine that brass every time it got dirty! It never bothered me one bit to be wearing boys' brass-toed shoes. I wasn't the only one that used to wear them; there were other girls who wore them, too.

I can also remember when they bought us those hickory-striped, bibbed overall pants. They used to say we had dresses on all the time, but I can remember when we started wearing overalls—I was about eight or nine. Most of the time I did have dresses on, though. We wore them about midlength until I was fourteen or so. After that we wore them not too far above the ankle, with bobby sox and girls' shoes. We had to wear dresses to school.

So, I went to school in Neah Bay through the fourth grade. However, I begged and I begged to be able to go to boarding school in Tulalip. One of my girlfriends, Lillian Tucker, went there; her mother let her go there. My mother didn't want me to go, but I begged and I begged for two whole weeks. My dad kind of sided with me. He said, "Well, let her go. Let her go." And finally, after I finished the fourth grade, they let me go.[6]

TULALIP BOARDING SCHOOL

The Tulalip Indian Boarding School was in Everett, Washington, on the Tulalip Indian Reservation. It's right on the water, like Neah Bay, and that's why I never minded going there. I got lonesome the first three months I was there, however, and I came home. But then after I went back the next year, I didn't get lonesome anymore, and it was a lot easier to stay there. I was there for about two and a half years. There were kids from a lot of the Northwest tribes there: from Lummi, La Conner, Darrington, Tulalip, Marysville, and Neah Bay. There were 150 girls and 150 boys; it wasn't a very big school. We always spoke English at school. Nobody spoke Indian. Since we were from so many different tribes, there was no reason to talk Makah.

We got along fine with the teachers. We didn't give them any guff or anything; most of us were pretty good most of the time. We didn't dare answer our teachers back in any way. They always had a ruler handy; they used to hit our hands with that. "Hold out your hand!" they'd say. Then the matron used to have a leather strap. It was a wide one, and she was allowed to go ahead and whip us if she wanted.

If we were bad, we also got demerits. We had to work one hour for one demerit, so we were very careful not to get a demerit. We didn't want to have any extra hours of work to do.

When I was in sixth grade I got myself in trouble, though. I used to really enjoy painting Indian pictures with watercolors. I did a lot of them. I really liked Miss Mitchell, my teacher, too. She let me go ahead and paint and put my pictures all up, until she reached a point where she got tired of me doing this, and she said, "I'm only going to tell you *one* time. You can't sit and draw all day. You've got to do some studying, too." She did just tell me once, and I didn't listen to her. I just kept painting. At the end of the year I flunked sixth grade, and I really felt bad. She said, "I told you I was going to tell you just once that you had to study." Boy, the next year, I didn't behave like that anymore. Mr. Goldstein was my teacher, and I didn't give him any problems! I only drew when it was time to draw. And I passed. I didn't like being in the same grade with the fifth graders that next year. All those that I went to school with were in the seventh grade. That was horrible! I never experienced anything like that before. All the kids I'd been in the same grade with were way up there, and I was way down there.

We were always busy working at school, too. We had a matron, an assistant matron, a dining room matron, and a cook. Then we had student company officers for the A, B, C, D, and E companies. They had to be in high school to be officers. We had five companies, I think. They called F Company the lazy company, and everybody used to make fun of them. Each big kid had two little ones to get completely ready each morning on time. There were real problems if they were bed wetters. We had to clean them up, get them dressed, change their bedding, take care of their dirty clothes—a lot of hard work. We had to work very hard to get them in line on time every morning to go to breakfast or to go to school, because if we were late getting in line we ended up in this F Company, the lazy company. Each one of our companies had an officer, and we had to march to school, march to the dining room, march everywhere. This kind of training, I think, helped us a lot. We had to have a schedule and do it like clockwork.

We got up at five every day, and weekends too. We had to make our beds and see to it that everything was straightened up. We didn't have bedspreads, but we had two sheets, so we had to fold the top one over halfway and then fold it under so that everything was straight. And we had to stand our thin pillows up on the end of the bed. Then they came and tested; they'd flip a quarter on the bed to see if it would bounce.

We'd all go to school in the morning and then do our work in the afternoon. Or we'd switch off and work in the morning and then go to school in the afternoon. I didn't seem to mind this schedule at all. Some of us went to the sewing room to patch up clothes, darn socks, sew up the girls' ripped school dresses and the boys' coveralls, or what have you. Then there were a bunch that spent an hour in what we called DS, which was Domestic Science. Now they call it Home Ec. Even the names of things change. We'd divide into about four groups. Some of us would be cooks, some waitresses, teacher's helpers, and some would be customers or tasters. Then they'd cook for each other and then trade off, different ones cook, waitress, and eat. This is the way we learned to cook and to sew. One month we'd learn cooking; the next, sewing. It switched back and forth.

The first semester we were issued our school dresses, then later on we made another set ourselves. Our everyday clothes were hickory dresses, no shape, just a hole here and the sleeves cut down. That's why, when a lot of people came over, they'd think it was a reform school. If we were lucky, we had belts of our own. I remember I kept begging my dad for a belt, so he sent me one. He found a horse-hair belt that was real "dingey"—it was really good and I liked it! It was a pretty one, had all kinds of designs sewed up on it. That was one nice thing he sent me there, and I had it all through school. I don't even know what happened to it now.

Our Sunday-go-to-meeting clothes were navy blue pleated skirts made out of serge. We had to make them ourselves, know how to measure them out so the pleats will come in even, and then sew all the pleats down. We had middy blouses and red sweaters with shawl collars that the government supplied, too. We had black stockings and black round-toed shoes which we wore only on Sunday.

All our dirty clothes were thrown into the laundry room and went to the laundry together. We each had a number, and this is how we kept track of our clothes; there was a little check sewed in the back with a number on it. There was a girl taking care of the checkroom to check out our clothes. If our dirty clothes didn't go in, we never had clean ones. So we had to see that they were all sent in.

Then they had a plant there that the boys had to take care of. Some of them were cobblers. When our shoes wore out, they were sent down there. They were all numbered on the tongue of the shoe, so we could keep track of them. The boys did their own farming, also. They took care of the cows and made their own garden —planted tomatoes, cucumbers, potatoes—all the things that were a necessity in the dining room.

We also were assigned to details to help with the work in the kitchen. We only had half an hour to eat, then about half an hour to get the dishes washed, get the tables cleaned, sweep the floor, get the tables reset again, and then leave.

There was no sleeping in on Saturday or Sunday, either. We had to go salute the flag on Saturday morning and then do our exercises. We had a cement court in the backyard, and this is where we did our exercises first thing Saturday morning. Then we were allowed to go on a four-mile hike—four miles one way and then back. That took up most of the day.

On Sunday we went to church. We had to. We were made to go to church. We had a Presbyterian minister. I didn't mind the church services at this time because the Protestant churches didn't bar us from having our Indian dances; not like the Pentacostals. The Protestants didn't say, "You can't do this, you can't do that." There was no reason for them to bar me from anything like that. And anyway we didn't do any singing and dancing as long as we were up there. Not until we got home. They didn't tell us that we shouldn't do it when we came home.

I did get to play in the forty-piece all-girls' harmonica band while I was there. I practiced until I learned how to do it, and then played with them. It was fun. The only thing I regretted was that they never taught us to read music.

I learned a lot of things there at Tulalip. Actually this caused me some problems when I came home. As part of our table manners at school they taught us to say, "Please pass such and such" and, "Don't touch it, pass the whole thing." When I came home, I can remember I said, "Please pass some bread." And instead of passing it to me, somebody *gave* me one. I said, "I don't *want* it, you *touched* it!" And everybody at the table just pounced on me. "Hah! You think you're too good now!" That was what they had taught us at school, and that was what I was used to. I had to break out of that every time I came home.

Being at boarding school created other kinds of problems, too. We were just a little bit smarter than those kids that stayed in Neah Bay. We knew how to do more things because we had our work details to do. So that created problems when we got here because we knew how to sew, how to cook, and how to serve. We were taught which way to serve from, and which way to take away from. That's what they taught us in our domestic science.

My mom cooked a certain way at home, and one thing we never had was scrambled eggs. They were just fried, poached, or boiled. No scrambled eggs; that was too much problem. Everybody had something to do, so they didn't have any time for that. So, every so often, when I was home from school, I'd make myself scrambled eggs or eggs a la gratin. That's just creamed eggs with a little white sauce mixed up in it, put over toast. Everybody sat there and said, "Now! What's that?!" I used to create little things like that when I got home. And then one of the girls would say to me, "Think you're smart, huh?!" Times like these were difficult.

While I was at Tulalip, once every other week we got to go to a little gas station which had candy and stuff. We went for a walk about three miles up and back. We got to spend our money any way we felt like spending it. Everybody, naturally, just bought candy bars.

We had to send home for our money. We couldn't write for money very often, either. They read every letter that went out; they read every letter that came in, too. So, mail call, we'd all get in a line. Then they'd holler out our names. I was lucky to get two dollars a month from my dad. I was one of the poor ones. Course he didn't realize and he didn't know, but if he had known, he probably would have sent me five dollars a month. I didn't ask for more. I just got my two dollars a month.

The little ones, like in first, second, or third grade were only allowed a quarter each time we went to the store. Then from fourth on up, we got issued fifty cents. When we were in the sixth grade, we got a dollar. Unless we were going to town. Once in a great while, they'd let us get in a truck and take us to Everett. They'd take us to the dime store. Then, maybe the most we ever got was five dollars. But other than that, if we spent our money faster than we should have, then we didn't get to go to town. I think I only went once. I drew all the two dollars and went to town with it. The rest of the time I would get only fifty cents to go up to the gas station and back. But I didn't complain. It used to be enough for me. Only that once did I go to Everett.

It was kind of dangerous to go to Everett because we had some sticky-fingered girls, too. That's another thing that made me scared. They went to the dime store and stole little bits of this and little bits of that. They got picked up, and they got in trouble for it. They had to pay back what they took, and they couldn't go to dances or shows. I never ever wanted to get in trouble. I felt like I was just too far away from home and no mom and no dad around to help me out.

I liked going to school at Tulalip. I really enjoyed being there. That was partly because I didn't have to take care of all my mom's kids while I was there. In fact, a lot of us were crying when the school closed down. We didn't want it to close. The government decided they were too short on money and they couldn't afford to keep it open. So they closed it down.[7] And I knew that if I wanted to go to boarding school at Chemawa (in Oregon), my mother wouldn't let me, and sure enough I was correct. Two girls died up there. They came home in a coffin. After that, our parents always said, "Well, if you go to Oregon, you'll just come back in a box." So most of the mothers didn't want their children to go there.

RETURN TO NEAH BAY

After Tulalip closed down, I came back home again and went to the Day School in Neah Bay. I was in seventh grade then.[8] They had six grades in one room, so it was really hard to concentrate. I listened to one class after the other, and I was expected to study while the other class was in session. I didn't really like school here. I wasn't an exceptionally bright person. And, I don't know, it could have been I was so tired out from working all the time, taking care of all the kids, that I just felt like I was lazy every time I went to school—like I was tired. I never felt like studying when I was home. When I was in boarding school, it was different because we knew we were far away from home and that we had to study. We had study hour every Monday and Wednesday night, too. There was just no getting away from it there. In Neah Bay, I only went to school for a few months more, like September to January. Then my mother needed me at home, so I just quit going to school. I never went back again. Mom worked just like a man right along with Dad, so I was needed at home to take care of the kids while she went out to work with him.

I didn't really feel bad about leaving school. I didn't know many of the kids down there anyway, so that made it easier to leave. I'd been away from them for the last two and a half years, and I didn't really get along with them too good. So it didn't make much difference to me. The kids here kind of have an attitude like, "Well, you were gone, this is my reservation now. You're not good enough to be back." The kids won't accept you and keep picking on you all the time. It makes you feel real bad. So it didn't bother me to leave school and stay home.

GIRLFRIENDS IN NEAH BAY

I did have some nice girlfriends, though, and we did things together whenever we could. Minnie Butler was a friend of mine, and she lived with my family when I was in grade school. She later died of TB. Ramona Colby was probably my best friend. We spent a lot of time together. She was also my cousin. When we were little, we listened to the adults tell stories at my grandfather Anderson's house. When we were older, we'd help with the haying in the summer and go swimming with some of my other friends, Muzzie and Laura Wheeler, and Evelyn Peterson, another one of my cousins. We played together, sometimes went to potlatches and

July Fourth celebrations together, and sometimes went to dances together. Laverne Ulmer was the girl I sang with when we wanted to get into the dances in Tacoma for free, or when we went on the bus with the baseball team or went to hear the jazz band. I did have some good times with my friends during my teenage years when I didn't have to work for my mother or be in school.

OLYMPIC LOOP QUEEN CONTEST

One of the good times I had was when I was the runner-up for the Olympic Loop Queen. They had the Olympic Loop Highway opening when the road was completed from Port Angeles around through Hoh and Queets and Kalaloch on down to Hoquiam and Aberdeen and back around. This was in the early 1930s, but I can't remember just when. I must have been about thirteen or fourteen then. The contest took place in Kalaloch. I think they called this Kalaloch Day, too, besides the Olympic Loop opening. The reason we went there was to do some of the Indian singing and dancing. We danced most of the afternoon and then again in the night. I didn't even know they were going to have this contest. My dad said, "Go ahead," so I entered. I borrowed my mother's khaki costume. I never really had one of my own, so I had to borrow hers. She made hers out of old army discards, shirts and stuff, so it was all khaki. Then she had a headband made out of dentaliums and trade beads. That was the only thing that was really nice, was that headband. The dress was Indian style, but I didn't even wear a dance cape. I just went in the dress. But it must have done the trick anyway because I was the runner-up.

I'd never seen a beauty contest before, and I thought it was kind of funny because there were some real old ladies that couldn't even walk that entered, too.[9] They had all their baskets in the front of them. Maybe they thought they'd win if they had their baskets in the front of them, but there were a lot of baskets out there (see fig. 20). There were only five young ones: Adele Martin, Mary Black, Pearl Cultee, Catherine Eastman, and myself. We were more like eighteen or nineteen. Nina Bright and her sister Rebecca were there; Ida Taylor, who was in her late thirties, was there, too. Pearl Cultee took first, and I took second place. We each won some money; I got twenty dollars. That was pretty good money in those days. Then they took our pictures, too (see fig. 21). After that I went back to the dancing, and my mom and dad wanted me to stay close around them, so that's what I did.[10]

EXPERIENCES IN SEATTLE

I don't remember exactly how old I was, but when I was somewhere between fourteen and sixteen, I spent some time in Seattle. My older sister's husband came and asked my mom if I could go to Seattle and baby-sit, because my sister was pregnant again. She had three kids then. And my mom said, "Sure. Take her." And I said,

Fig. 18. Neah Bay houses, circa 1910. Newer pitched-roof, frame wood houses coexist with the older, Native-style shed-roof houses. Canoes are pulled up on the beach in front of family dwellings. *Photograph by Asahel Curtis; courtesy of Washington State Historical Society, Tacoma (neg. #20172).*

Fig. 19. Two houses built in the 1930s by Charlie Swan. Located on Government Hill, near the site of the old Makah village of Baháda, these houses were still in use in 1983 when this photo was taken. *Photograph by Linda J. Goodman.*

Fig. 20. Indian beauty contest, Kalaloch, Washington. When Highway 101 (the Olympic Loop Highway) was completed in August 1931, part of the celebration included this Indian beauty contest. A carved welcome figure stands behind the seated contestants. Left to right: Nina Bright (La Push), Rebecca Cole (La Push), Violet Black (La Push), Catherine Obi (Queets), Helma Swan (Neah Bay), Nellie Sam (Queets), Nellie Williams (La Push), Pearl Cultee (Taholah), Mary Black (La Push), Adele Martin (Queets), and, standing, Ida Taylor (La Push). *Photograph courtesy of the North Olympic Library System, Port Angeles (Bert Kellogg Photo Collection, Ind. Port. 0014).*

Fig. 21. Kalaloch beauty contest winners, at opening ceremonies for Olympic Loop Highway 101, August 26–27, 1931. Helma Swan (left), runner-up, and Pearl Cultee, Olympic Loop Queen, with unidentified white officials. *Photograph courtesy of the North Olympic Library System, Port Angeles (Bert Kellogg Photo Collection, Ind. Port. 0027).*

Fig. 22. Makah Day singers performing for the Group Dances, August 25, 1984, in Neah Bay. The principal singers, seated left to right: Helen Peterson, Ruth Claplanhoo, Helma Swan Ward, Muzzie Claplanhoo, Meredith Parker, Maria Parker Pascua, Vida Thomas, Mary Green, Ham Green, Alice Parker Arnold, Mary Lou Denny. *Photograph by Linda J. Goodman.*

"I don't want to go." And my mom got mad at me . . . and she told me I better go, cause my sister needed me. So, I went. I figured I had no choice. I stayed with my sister and her kids in Seattle for two weeks, and I worked pretty hard all that time.

After I finished taking care of her, I went down to the employment agency in Seattle, and I looked for a job. I just kind of luckily ended up with one woman who said she was sick and needed a maid right away.

Well, when I got there, I got put to work right away. The baby was in the maid's room, and he was in the playpen, and he had messed *all over* that playpen. He was just a complete mess, and she didn't want to clean him. So I had to end up doing that. From that time on I was working there. The next day, she got well and left, and her two little boys were my boys all the time I worked there—for about six months. Her husband was the president of the Fifth Avenue New World Life Insurance Company.

I did the cooking, and it was kind of easy because they had a menu there, week by week. So all I did was go by the menu, cook whatever was there. I had to make breakfast for her husband in the morning and send him off. And the rest of the day was all my day—me and the two little boys. One was about two years old and the other one was one.

She gave a party a couple of times, and this is where I learned how to make hors d'oeuvres, with another Japanese girl they brought in. So I worked with this girl at the parties.

This job wasn't that different from working at home, really, except that I got paid twenty dollars a month. I got my room and board and twenty dollars a month. Soon, there was just altogether too much work there for me. It was just like being home: take care of kids, take care of kids, fix the beds, wash every day, do all the cooking, and on and on. It was just too much for twenty dollars a month. I think I probably didn't enjoy it cause there wasn't that much money in it. It might have been better if I'd gotten maybe thirty-five dollars a month. Finally, I decided I had enough of the city, and I came home.

FIRST MARRIAGE

When I was only about sixteen, I got married for the first time. I did it because I really wanted to get away from home. I got tired of working. My older sister, Katherine, had gotten married because she didn't want to baby-sit, and I felt like I was being taken advantage of, having to baby-sit all the time. Since I was the oldest one left at home, I had to do it whether I wanted to or not. So I was really ready to get away from home, not have to be there and not have to be bossed around so much. But much to my surprise, after I got married, I discovered that married life wasn't exactly what I thought I wanted.[11] No one told me what my marriage duties would be. My mom, my dad, my grandparents—no one talked to me about marriage. After

I thought about it, I really didn't know the man, except to know him from being around Neah Bay and know that everybody thought he was such a big catch. Then when I really did begin to know him, I just found that I didn't like him and that I didn't want to stay with him.

But before I knew all this, we were given some nice parties. They gave two parties for me when I got married. The Neah Bay party was first, and the La Push party, by his Quileute relatives, was second. There was about a week between the two parties, so they were pretty close together. We didn't invite the Canadians then, just the Queets, Hohs, Quileutes, Taholahs, and Neah Bays—five tribes. We had it in the wintertime, and the boat, *Moqúinna,* only ran once a month, so it was hard to have the Canadians come over. And besides, my dad wasn't making too much money, so he figured that he couldn't really afford to ask them all to come over. My grandaunt Annie Williams, from Clayoquot, did come for it, though. She was still alive then.

My dad gave a big potlatch party for us over at Young Doctor's hall. Star Hall was already going to shreds, and they didn't try to fix it, so Young Doctor's was the biggest, and we used that. There was a nice feed and then entertainment. We played these games—one was Annie's *tupáat,* and the other was my dad's *tupáat.*[12] Annie's was a feather game. She wore a band on her head which had a long stick attached, and a feather on the string on the end of the stick. The men try to catch the feather. She just stood there in one spot and kept moving her head in order to keep the men from catching it. She was really good at it. But then, finally, she let my husband-to-be catch the feather to let everybody know that he and I were going to get marrried. There was a song that went with this, but I don't know it anymore. When they got through with that game, they started the whale games. We had two of them, and they were my dad's *tupáats.* My dad made the wooden whales they used, and the spears.[13]

When they finished these games, which they did only for weddings, then they danced and gave away. Annie did the dancing and giving away for our family. She did this because she was still alive and wanted to take over, and being that she was older than my father, she had the right to do that if she wanted. My dad sang for her, and she danced. She wore the grizzly bear headdress that looks like a helmet with a beak on the front and ermine skin down the back, and she danced the two Grizzly Bear songs that Captain Jack gave to my dad and me. She really liked these songs and used to dance them all the time when my dad was around. And was she ever good at it! Oh, she was nice to watch![14] That headdress had all the down put loose in the top of it, and when she nodded her head, turned her head this way and that, those down feathers would just go in all directions—fly out and land gently all over the floor. My dad sang while she danced to both "Wo hey" and "Hu ya."[15]

I didn't get to dance at all. As one of the honored guests, I was just supposed to sit there, not get up at all. So that's what I did. And I can remember the dress I had on—a long dress, with cape sleeves. It was a navy blue print with little red flowers, little teeny flowers. I enjoyed that party, had a good time there. I was happy my dad gave it for me, but that was all. I didn't know what I was getting into. We received lots of gifts and money. I don't even remember how much money we got, but we got quite a bit. It was like three or four hundred dollars, and at that time, that was quite a bit of money. It isn't like now where you get seven, eight hundred dollars. Then we got mounds and mounds of blankets as well as other things. All the blankets were store-bought, none were handmade. My mother and dad gave us twenty or twenty-five dollars and a blanket, and Annie gave us the same. My mother gave us a full set of dishes, service for twelve. She gave us a silverware set as well. I don't have any of those things left now.

I didn't have to do anything to help get ready for this party. I think this was because I was an honored guest. Really it should have been my husband's family that gave this party, but since his father was all by himself (his wife died a long time before), and he wasn't a wealthy man, my dad gave it instead. He did all the arranging; Annie told him what to do and helped him out. My mother helped, too. They probably hired some of the other women about her age to help with the cooking. They would have been paid for their help; they weren't relatives.

About a week later, my husband's uncle from La Push had a party for us there—a nice big party, too. I don't even remember what happened there; I just remember that it happened. All I recall is that he gave us the house and the lot that he owned, and he wanted us to come live there.

Actually, I had such a funny feeling at the party my dad gave for us. I didn't know whether I was happy or miserable, or what. All I thought of was getting away from home because I was tired of working. For the life of me I don't know why I married him; I did not enjoy married life.

I decided I didn't want to stay married 'cause I really didn't like him. I just stayed with him for four months, and then I left him. Actually, I'd come and stay for the day at his father's house where we were living, but then I'd go home to my parents' house in the evenings; I wouldn't stay. My husband and I sort of got in a fight about that, and this went on for about four months. My dad said, "Well, what in the world did you ever do something like that for?" And I said, "I don't know." It was just something I thought I should do, and then afterward I decided I didn't like it. It wasn't quite four months when I told my husband I didn't want to stay with him. So I left and went home. It wasn't what I'd really call a marriage. I got a divorce.

I moved back home, and my parents did start treating me differently than they had before. It seemed like they were more respectful of my feelings. They thought more about it, and instead of *telling* me what I had to do, they started *asking* me if I would do this or that. It wasn't like I *had* to. I liked that better, and I stayed there and was happy. I never thought about my first husband anymore. It was like he didn't even exist for me. I don't think I ever loved him. I haven't any idea whether he loved me or not. This was a bad experience for me, and afterwards I just put it completely out of my mind. I was happy again until after I got married the second time.

CHAPTER 5

CHILDHOOD REMEMBRANCES OF CEREMONIES

TRIPS AND ACTIVITIES CONNECTED WITH WEDDINGS

In the 1920s, I was lucky enough to get to go to Canada with Jim Hunter when he was asking for Odelia David's hand in marriage. She was from Clayoquot. He was from that same tribe but living in Neah Bay, and he knew her. I think he made three or four trips asking for her hand in marriage—in Indian fashion. He had to take the most prominent people with him and all the people that sing their songs. He chose who he wanted and had to pay all their expenses over there and back. He had to keep doing this until her family said yes, or if they didn't want him, then they'd say no. So this is what he had to go through to get the lady that he married, Mrs. Hunter. My dad and I made every trip with him when he went.[1] My mom came with us a couple of times, because she wanted to see what this was like.

When we got there, the group of people gathered and went to her father, Philip David's house, and stood there and sang and talked and asked for her hand in marriage. Jim Hunter had some speakers with him, and they did the talking. I got to go over on the boat with them, but I couldn't attend this ceremony where they asked for her hand. Kids weren't allowed to be there.

Jim Hunter had to bring blankets and dishes for gifts each time. These were given to her family. At the wedding potlatch her family gives all this away. Jim ended up giving a big potlatch back in Neah Bay when they finally got married.

During the time that they have the wedding potlatch, they used to play certain games; each family had its own inherited games. In our family we have this Feather Game that they play. It belonged to Annie Williams; it was her *tupáat*, and she gave it to my dad. I've seen this done when I was little, and then Annie danced it at my own wedding.[2] They start the song, and she gets out there and dances, and the men will try to catch the feather. The man that asked for the girl's hand—she finally lets him catch it. If the girl didn't want him, and her family didn't accept him, there wouldn't be any potlatch, and there wouldn't be any game. After he was accepted and he caught the feather, then came the time when they would get married.

Jim Hunter owned a Feather Game different from ours, which has been passed down in his family. For this game the women got in a line and had their shawls pinned on backwards, and they all danced in line, just swaying, singing a song. These were all women this time, no men. One woman started out hiding the feather. She passed behind the line of women, touching each one, so the others wouldn't know who she gave the feather to. This went like "button, button, who's got the button." Everybody in the crowd took turns guessing where the feather was. They'd sing all the time; they had a regular Indian song for it, but I don't know what it was. We've been looking for that song. Mrs. Hunter knew it, but she never could remember it. I saw them do this Feather Game three or four times when I was little, and it was a lot of fun, even if you were just sitting there watching. Of course, little kids weren't allowed to get in on it, just the adults, so I only watched. It was just a guessing game, not a gambling game, and it was a lot of fun.[3]

We had a game that my dad carved that they played after the wedding. It consisted of a whale, about a foot and a half long, and he had it sliding up and down on a piece of board. They had a spear, and on the top of the whale was a hole just underneath the fin, and you were lucky to get that spear in there—in the blowhole. That was the game. Anybody could take part in it, both men and women if they wanted to, and those that didn't want to just sat around and watched. This was strictly for fun, and it belonged just to our family; it was one of our *tupáats*. My dad made another whale, afterward, but this time instead of moving up and down on the board, it went across the room, pulled by a string. On the side was a little hole where you were supposed to try to spear it.

CEREMONIES FOR ADULTS ONLY

When I was young, there were many ceremonies that we weren't able to go to—they made us stay home. "No such thing for little kids," they'd say. Those ceremonies must have been important, though, since kids couldn't go. I know they'd come home and talk and say, "They're going to have a Tsáyak tonight; are you going to go?" Or, "It's going to be a Secret Order of the Ravens; are you going to go?" But they never mentioned anything else other than that, except one time Mrs. Colfax said, "Do you want to see what they used to do?" She showed us: she had little tattoos all up and down her legs and her arms. I would ask what happened, and she'd say this was what they did in the Secret Order of the Ravens. That's all I ever heard. The older ladies used to wear long sleeves, and every so often they'd roll them up when they were cutting fish, and I could see those tattoos. My grandmother had them on her legs and her arms. In the old days, they said that the men used to be tattooed more than the women. However, this had already changed when I was young. My grandfather wasn't tattooed, but my grandmother and some of the other women in the Secret Order of the Ravens still had tattoos when I was little.

I used to ask my dad about the secret ceremonies. I'd keep after him and after him, and he'd say, "What do you think 'secret' means?" Now they don't have them anymore. They had a Wolf society and a Bear society and a Hamatsa society,[4] and we were never allowed to go to those either. I just don't know what happened in those societies. They were secret, and we were never told. They had societies for thunderbird and eagle but not for deer, elk, loon, sandhill crane, salmon, or halibut. Not for whale either. They had whale dances, but no society.[5] Each whaler was supposed to go and pray by himself and not get caught by anybody else when imitating the whale, chanting, praying, bathing, and keeping clean for a certain length of time. Then he would be able to be a good hunter and to receive songs.

Sometimes the Makah would have what we call ƛaʔiiƚ. That's something that children were not supposed to go to. This is only for adults—they sort of get under power [go into a trance]—and they sing and sing and sing, and just get carried away with their songs. Each person will be singing about a half hour or forty-five minutes, so it takes quite awhile until they all have a turn. They stand there, and they swing their hands from side to side and keep on singing. It was done in the old Star Hall in Neah Bay. Children weren't allowed; they don't want them in there because they don't want to be interrupted. It's not that they don't want them, but they figure this isn't a place for children.

Towards the end, at the time when I was growing up, they weren't so strict here, so I got to see some of this ƛaʔiiƚ. My grandmother Alice Holden and her sister Marion Ward used to do that a lot and then my uncle Freddie Anderson did too. They sang one song right after another and just kept it up and kept it up until it was trancelike. And they just kept on. Nothing really happens to them, they just keep on going. Like, for instance, the Canadians from Nanaimo down to Esquimalt on Vancouver Island [Salish tribes], they have what they call "Black Face Dance,"[6] and it's sort of similar to ƛaʔiiƚ, but we don't do like they do. We don't paint our faces black, and we don't dress all in black. We didn't wear any costumes at all for it, and we never had those human-hair hats that they wear. Ours is similar in that we get under power like they do. The only thing is they sound like they're in pain, and we don't sound like we're in pain. In ours they just got to where they wouldn't stop singing. But the Canadians make an awful noise like they're hurting somewhere— they just groan and moan and groan. We don't do that here. We just stand in one place and swing both hands, but they go dancing around, all over the floor.

When I first saw the ƛaʔiiƚ, I sat there and it bothered me so bad! I don't remember how old I was, but I was young. My grandma started singing and she got that way, she got under power. I sat there and cried all the way through. I guess this is why they didn't let children go. I cried and I cried right along with her until my mother couldn't stand it anymore. Finally she said to me, "Go get a glass of water and give Grandma a glass of water." So, I went over and gave her a glass of water, and she quit. She came out of it. I didn't feel like going to any of them again, after that, but sometimes I used to have to go. That's how come I saw my uncle Fred Anderson get that way too. They'd start singing songs, then they'd push him out on the floor, and they'd say, "Well, we want to hear Fred Anderson sing." So he'd start in singing this song which says, "I'm a doctor, and my spirit power comes from the squirrel." He just repeated that over and over. It's supposed to be a fun song, and he'd be smiling for a while. These are the only kinds of songs that I've seen that they'd smile with—these fun songs—otherwise they'd have a straight face, once they got under power. Then it was serious! It was connected in some way with personal power. They would never dare to smile, and I think that's another reason why they didn't want kids in there—it was something that they really meant; it was serious. If a person smiled when he wasn't supposed to, they'd just take their fingers and pull his mouth apart until it ripped! So you didn't smile. You didn't dare do anything like that, or they'd just come over and rip your mouth. When I was a child, they didn't do that anymore. About that time they began easing up on everything and losing some of our traditions. But I used to hear my dad talking about when they'd go to places like that, and no one could smile. I remember when I was little that there were some ceremonies that my mother and dad used to go to, and they just absolutely refused to take us because of the kind of event it was.

TUMÁNUWOS STORIES

There were some other things that certain people weren't supposed to talk about. My folks always believe that if you see anything like a special power, it's yours alone. It's yours to talk to. You don't share it with anybody! Nobody must see this, just you! And you hide it before you come home, and you never tell anybody where you put it, because that's your *tumánuwos,* personal spirit power. Yours alone! If you don't know how to handle it, it just takes you away with it. This is what happened to my brothers.

When we were kids we used to play out in the woods, and this apparently was what my brother Conrad was doing—playing around on the edge of the beach. Where he saw it was at Scow Creek, that little stream there, going toward Kitla Point. And it was on a bush—on one of the bushes there. It was a tiny gold baby, and it was crying. He saw it, and he picked it up. He held it in his bare hand; he didn't wrap it in anything. This is what he wasn't supposed to do. Later they told us, "When you take this little baby, you can hold it in your hand, you can talk to it, but don't touch the flesh, always wrap it in something." It has special gifts. It will talk to you and say, "Take my leg. This is for whale hunting. Take my other leg. It's for seal hunting. Take my right arm or my left arm"—maybe that's to be a fisherman. You'll never come home empty-handed. Or, "Take my head—this is so that you will see—be able to see everything."

But my brother didn't know what it was for. My folks never told him anything before then, so he picked it up, and he brought it home, and by the time he got there, it was gone. It was gone! He didn't know what happened to it. It probably just vanished because he handled it, and he didn't know what to do with it. When he got home he was going to show my parents. And he looked for it, and he told my mother about it, but he couldn't find it. This worried her.

Afterwards he got sick, and then he died. He didn't live very long. He died very slowly. My mom told us to visit him. So, we went upstairs and we visited him. And he was telling us, "I found this little gold baby up the creek, here." He named where he found it. And he wasn't supposed to do this. He said, "It's crying now, can you hear it?" I mean, this bothered us. And every one of us that visited him, he'd say the same thing. He held it in his hand, like this. We couldn't see it, but he could. And he could hear it.

This would have been his *tumánuwos*. But it just took him. They always used to tell us that it'll take you with it if you don't know how to handle it. And then after this all happened, then is when my dad started telling us about all of these things. And then my grandparents joined in, and they did the same thing.

They told us that we might see a little, teeny whale, just like he saw the baby. But it has gifts, just like the baby. And if you see it, then you've got to grab it, properly. And you have to be very careful of the eagle, because the eagle has very sharp eyes and is watching out for things like that. If the eagle gets it, then it will take away what you should have. Then again, you would probably end up getting sick and dying.

My grandparents also told us, "When you're in the woods, if you see a right hand coming out of the ground, it will want to shake hands with you, but you have to look at what hand it is, first. It may be the left hand, it may be the right hand; and it's only out of the ground as far as the elbow. You want to watch it because you don't want to shake hands with the left hand. The left hand is bad. This only brings bad things. If you learn to do bad things, then you're in trouble all the rest of your life. The right hand brings good things. You can shake hands with the right hand. If you see the left hand, don't shake hands. Back up and ask your great-grandparents for a stick, because they'll give it to you. Then hold your hand out—don't worry, you'll get it. And then when you get your stick, hit that left hand until it's gone." They said it will turn into suds.

And then, years later, my brother Emil found this black, shiny rock. And it was bouncing up and down in the creek, and he did the same thing. That black, shiny rock had special power. You can become an Indian doctor or ask it for whatever you want to be. He could have been a famous hunter—that was what he used to do. He could leave home anytime he wanted to and just go—just think and go. And then he'd always find a deer. He never came home empty-handed. And he got his power from that rock.

Emil was doing just like my other brother was. He was playing around where the new Díia housing area is. The creek ran from that direction down toward the village. They had a little dam that used to be there . . . and he was probably playing around it. You're not supposed to tell where you found it, but this was his problem—he told where he saw it. He came home, and he told Mom. He said, "I was playing around up there. And that black rock you got like you make baskets with?" And Mom said, "You mean the x̣'ačá·pɫ [the black rock]?" And he said, "Yah. There's one up there; it's floating." He said, "You believe they can float? I was over there; I was playing with it; and I kept pushing it down, and it kept coming back up." And Mom said, "You better get up there and hide that—hide that rock! so that *nobody else* will see it but you!" This is what he did. He ran back, and it was still there, bobbing up and down when he got there. So he hid it.

But he probably shouldn't have told my mom, because he didn't live a full life. And he ended out drinking a lot. Something must have been bothering him. Mom probably told him what to do about this rock because she didn't want anything happening to him, but it still did anyway. But she never told my dad about it. Otherwise if she had, I think he would have gone over and looked for an Indian doctor to help him.

Nothing like this ever happened to me. I guess I was always afraid because I listened too hard to the stories my dad and my grandparents told. I never ventured away from my grandparents. Not that much. Or, wherever I went in the woods or on the beach, I tried to stay on the horse so that . . . I didn't want to see anything like that cause it was scary to me.

ATTENDING CEREMONIES
AND PERFORMING WITH MY DAD

I really liked going to parties. My dad would come to me and say, "I want you to come to this party [potlatch] because so-and-so asked you to dance background." So I was with my father all the time, going to every one of the parties because I had to dance for him. My father had no boys to dance for him. (My brother Conrad died when he was about fourteen, and Emil was too young—he was twelve years younger than me.) Therefore, I always danced for my dad everywhere we went—I danced "background" for him. If it wasn't with the wolf headgear, it was with a black shawl, standing there like any woman—doing the background. Only the men were the main dancers.

I can remember one party we went to when I was about eleven or twelve years old. We were invited to Taholah, to a smokehouse party. This was a real smokehouse, and it belonged to old man Pope. We went over in Jim Hunter's truck. He was the mailman, and he had to have a truck, and it was a big one. In those days there weren't many people with cars. We all piled in—all the singers that he could get in. We just about brought everything but the kitchen sink with us, so you know how big of a truck he had. My mother brought pillows, blankets, and featherbeds.

Everybody had featherbeds then, not mattresses. We had two featherbeds on every bed then, I think. My mother brought one, my grandmother brought one, my grandfather brought theirs, and we sat on those going down in the truck. They used these when they put us to bed down there in Taholah.

Usually a longhouse is stalled off, like a barn, for each family. But this one in Taholah wasn't like that. It was a smokehouse,[7] and that's something different. It had something like a step there—kind of like a shelf three to four feet wide. That's where we put our bedding. Everybody put their featherbeds up there, and all the mothers made up their beds. That smokehouse was big enough for three fires—great big fires; that's where they danced and did all the singing, around all three of those fires. Then when it came to eight o'clock at night, we were put to bed up on that shelf, while they sat down below. We stayed in our beds, too. Well, I kind of stayed up—I watched everything that went on. You'd be surprised how many kids go right to sleep like that. That night they all went to sleep; I think I was the only one up. After a while it got kind of boring, and I finally went to sleep, too. The parents were more strict then. You never saw a child running around at a party—never! Every child sat still; even it if was a baby, it learned how to be still when it was awake. No noise whatever. But nowadays the kids just run wild at parties. People say, "Well, you're just like a wild Indian," but in those days you never saw an Indian wild like that when you were at a party. They kept still.

As far as I can remember, my dad never gave any parties (potlatches) for me when I was little. It seemed like I was born at the wrong time. I never had a birthday party, but it didn't seem to matter to me because whenever we went across to Canada and they had a party there, I was with my dad and danced for him most of the time. Whenever they'd give money to my dad, they'd just automatically give to me, too, because I did all his dancing for him. So I always got money whenever my dad got money, and it didn't matter that I never had a party.

My dad did give birthday parties for my sisters when they were kids. These were give-away parties, but they weren't on a big scale, like they are now. They were little ones. My folks just invited down the main people—the singers and the give-away-ers—that's all they used to do then. The party for the baby's first birthday is bigger. This is to show off the child, let everyone know that the baby was born and that it's in good condition, and they're happy because the baby made it to the first year.

Mostly they gave wedding parties and coming out parties. However, at the time I began to grow into womanhood, it was all over, so I never had a coming-out party. They didn't have them over here anymore. In Canada they still did, because I attended one for my cousin Clothilda Frank in Clayoquot in 1930. They used to give a "blood" or "coming-out" party [potlatch] when a girl was growing into woman-hood. They showed her off to the whole tribe when they gave her a coming-out party. At Clothilda Frank's party, which lasted two weeks, everyone would gather in the morning if there were enough people there, and if there weren't enough then they wouldn't gather until the evening. They'd all get together and sing. They'd sing all different types of songs; some of them were just plain singing—what we call *t'abáa*, more or less just for fun. Then they also sang some of the more serious, inherited family songs. Of course there was a lot of feasting, too. My dad had to bring enough food with us to supply the first big meal for all the guests. His aunt Annie Williams from Clayoquot asked him to do this, and so of course he did.

THE NEAH BAY BEE CLUB

The ladies in Neah Bay had what they called a Bee Club. They got together to eat and for entertainment. There weren't any regular meetings; they just got together whenever they felt like it. The women would meet on the beach and eat sea urchins, steamed mussels, and salmonberry sprouts. Sometimes they brought bags of salmon eggs and cut them in slices. I used to come with my mom, and I'd eat the sprouts or China slippers; I just couldn't eat those sea eggs [sea urchins] though. While all this was going on, they sang songs or told stories. They'd tell really funny stories on each other, and we had a good time listening. Lizzie Claplanhoo was the Queen Bee, and she made sure that no bad incidents happened to create hard feelings between any of the women. She was good at that. There was some kind of understanding that no men were to be around when the Bee Club was meeting. If men came over, the women would pinch them until they went home. Lizzie, as Queen Bee, would start pinching the man, and all the other ladies would come over and do it too. Soon, no men came around when the ladies were having a get-together.

MAKAH DAY REMEMBRANCES

In 1926 I remember we had our first Makah Day, and we've had one every year since then. At that time the Indians danced on the beach on the west end of the town, where there was a platform. Now the Senior Citizens' Center is right near where it used to be. Before that we used to have our dances on Tatoosh Island because the government outlawed it here. They didn't want us to dance or bone game. I don't know why the government did this except that we used money, nickels and dimes, for betting in the bone game and the government didn't like gambling. Anyway, in 1926 the government set us free, and we decided we were going to have Makah Day now, in order to celebrate.[8]

We invited all of Vancouver Island to come across and celebrate with us. I remember the Canadians coming. They would come in their own boats, regular fishing boats they bought across there. The Canadian government supplies them with their money, too, and they have some nice fishing boats. They would come in those and tow their sealing canoes behind them. They'd all stop in a line out in the bay. They would line up and tie their boats together and make a straight row. They wouldn't get off until everyone was there—all the nineteen tribes from Canada.[9] Then they'd anchor and untie their sealing canoes. They'd all get in their canoes and wait in them. They wouldn't move until the Makahs were all on the beach.

Then the Makahs would start beating their drums and begin singing. This was the beginning of Makah Day. We would be singing loud—it was beautiful because we had all those male voices like we don't have now. The Canadians, with all their blankets and other things, would get in their sealing canoes while the Makahs were singing. When we finished, the Canadians were already in a line out there in their sealing canoes, and then they would start paddling and come ashore. They would begin singing while they were coming ashore. When they finished, then the Makahs would sing again. They'd sing two songs, and we'd sing two songs, and by that time they would all be near the shore. Then the Makahs would pull their sealing canoes in on rollers. Little round logs were placed under each canoe, and it was then pushed and pulled onto the beach. When all the canoes were in, then the welcoming was over. The Canadians would gather their things out of the canoes and would know who they were going to stay with, so they would scatter all over the village to stay with their relatives.

One year my father and Fred Hunter got together and made a great big thunderbird that must have been about twelve feet high. They put it on a barge and set it out in the water. The bird's head could turn. My dad was a carpenter so he was able to do something like that. He stayed inside the bird and kept the head turning while the Canadians came in. When the Makahs started singing, the thunderbird started making noise like a regular bird, and the head would turn. The people thought it was really something. After everyone was ashore they pulled the bird back onto the sand again. I don't know what happened to that bird. I saw it, because I watched them make it. That was a real nice Makah Day.

The Canadians took part in the morning, and then it was Makahs all the rest of the day. There were all kinds of races. First there were sealing canoe[10] races. They never had what we have now—the eleven-man canoe race. It was always a sealing canoe race, but it's similar except that our old-time canoes were wider, not like they have now—they're long and narrow. My grandfather Anderson had a real good sealing canoe that he made, and he won the race every year with this canoe. Made the Canadians mad, too. Then, they used their regular canoes that they went seal hunting in; they were wide, and they held six men. My uncle also had a sealing canoe and he was captain of his own canoe. The owner was always the captain.

Then they also raced the smaller canoes that they used for fishing out here.[11] They were small and were built with no bows, except one side was just a little higher than the other. They would use these for a one- or two-man canoe race. Young boys or the owners of the canoe would race these little canoes. People from all different tribes used to bring their little canoes down for this race. The Canadians would all bring theirs down behind their boats; anywhere from seven to eleven of the nineteen tribes would come. Some people paddled from La Push, and the Taholahs used to come too. So we had the Taholahs, the Quileutes, and a number of tribes from Canada. We had quite a large turnout, more than they do now. Now there's just a few that are canoe racing. The Elwha and Jamestown tribes never took part. They were always "saved people"—Christians—ever since I could remember. They never believed in Indian dancing or bone gaming; it went against the Christian religion, so they never took part. But the others all came.

They had capsize canoe races, too. They used the little fishing canoes for this. They had to paddle out a certain distance from shore, capsize the canoe, then turn it back over and rock it like a cradle to get most of the water out of it, get back in it again, and paddle back to shore. They quit doing this many years ago—maybe when I was about twelve.

Then they had the women's canoe race. They had six women in a sealing canoe. My mother used to be the captain in her father's canoe. It was always the fastest, and so she always picked it to be in the race. She picked her crew, and then she would be one of the paddlers. The captain had to know how to run the boat well. They had to have an experienced paddler at the front and at the back because they each had to paddle different directions when they were turning the canoe. They had to know what they were doing. They raced from the west end, down to where the Coast Guard station is now, had to turn the canoe and come back to the starting point.

We had other kinds of races for Makah Day, too. They had horse races, starting from the west end of town, down on the beach, and they'd run all the way up to the Coast Guard station on the east end, and then come back. I don't know how many miles they made it, but they'd go up there and back and up there and back again.

The men had foot races all the way from the west end down to the Coast Guard Station. That's a couple of miles up there and back. It seems like they had more fun then than we do now because they had more men to take part in sports then. They trained in those days, and they don't seem to bother to do that now. I remember when they said they were going to have this famous runner from Canada. I think he was from Port Alberni, and they called him Tatóotch. I don't know his English name. The boys from here got interested then, so they trained to beat him, but I don't remember them ever beating him.

Then they had tug-of-war. They had a men's tug-of-war and a women's tug-of-war. This was on the beach. They still do it today. One time they had a kids' tug-of-war, but usually they don't. They have foot races, three-legged races, sack races for the kids, and watermelon eating and pie eating contests.

There was Indian singing and dancing during the day, too (see fig. 22). They danced mostly group dances, with the men coming out first, and then everybody dancing what they call the *łaqáta·tx̌* Dance, Plains Indian Dance.[12] This was a dance they got from trading with the Plains Indians. There were other group dances that they could do for Makah Day: Women's Deer Dance, Pentl'achee Dance,[13] Bow and Arrow Dance, Men's Deer Dance, Elk Dance, Snipe Dance, Sailor Dance, Horse Dance, Fan Dance, Ghost Dance, and many others.

In the afternoon there was a baseball game, and we had to play against Taholah or Quileute, Clallam, Forks, or Port Angeles, because the Canadians didn't have a team at that time. We always had a real good ball team here, and they won most of the time. If there was enough daylight after the game was over, then they'd start dancing again. They had put in quite a day by nighttime.

In the evening when it got dark, they had the bone game. They built three fires on the beach, and these games lasted all night long. Sometimes just one game lasted all night.

That was how they organized their Makah Day a long time ago.

NON-INDIAN DANCES

There was one kind of dance I had to go to that I didn't like so much when I was little. The younger people had dances—white-man-style dances—for entertainment. Here, they did more modern dances like fox trots and waltzes. Mothers and fathers wouldn't let their daughters go out and stay out late all by themselves in those days. The older girls had to take the younger kids with them. So, I was the next younger one, about ten or eleven years old, and I had to start going to dances whether I liked it or not, with my oldest sister, Katherine. I had to tail her along to see that she got home by midnight. And that used to make her mad. My dad used to really beat her when she didn't get home on time. And later on, when I was older, then my younger sister would have to follow me to the dance and chaperone. But I always got home on time—I didn't want to get any beatings.

At the age of ten or eleven I hated those dances. . . . Like a little kid, you know, you just get bored with those dances cause you're not old enough to enjoy something like that. I suppose the parents figured the teenagers had to have protection some way or another, in order to run for help or something, so I always had to go with her, and kids from other families had to do the same. When I think about it, it was funny how at that time us kids, when we'd go, we'd sit still; we'd never think to go in a corner and play by ourselves. We sat still, just so far apart, and watched our older brothers and sisters. Us littler ones would sit there quietly, look at each other, smile, and that's all. We'd never run around. They really didn't have any chaperones, except for all us little kids sitting there. And boy, would we ever get tired.

Then when I got a little bit bigger, I would see some of the young married couples there with their babies. Their kids would be laying on top of the benches sleeping, and the little, teeny ones would be laying underneath, sleeping. They'd bring pillows and blankets and put them to sleep under there, and then some of the kids used to have to sit and watch the little teeny ones. Some of the young married adults wanted to come to these dances and so that's what they did with their kids. These dances took place at the old Star Hall in Neah Bay.

Sometimes, at the same time, the adults would be having a party at Young Doctor's Hall. My grandmother and parents would be there, maybe singing Indian songs or something like that, and I'd have to be baby-sitting my older sister at that dance! I didn't like that at all!

Young Doctor[14] had a great big hall, and on one side he and his family built a home. All of Young Doctor's Indian things were hanging on the west side of that hall, like the great big thunderbirds, the totem poles, and all the other things that he carved. Then they'd have their own parties in there when they felt like getting together. They'd invite the people over there, and we'd have good times. Later on, Young Doctor turned his hall into a roller-skating rink and finally a show hall, where they showed movies, and an old German named Rudy took over.[15] Finally, they tore it down—that must have been about fifty years ago.

CHAPTER 6

MUSIC IN MY LIFE

THE IMPORTANCE OF SONG

A song, *dukú·*, is something that's very important to my people. If you own a song, it means you are an important person: it tells everybody where you're from, who your parents were, who your grandparents and great-grandparents were. In the old days a song used to mean something more than this, but we were never really told much about those other meanings. Anyhow, in those days only the chiefs owned songs. Now, since the chiefs are all gone, their families own their songs. We're having a lot of trouble with this now. Everybody's fighting for a song so they can get in there and be an important person; but many people don't know anymore who the songs or the names really belong to. They're just guessing at them—at the songs and names—and saying they have rights to them, when they really don't. That makes a lot of them fight, because they say, "Well, that belongs to me," and the other person says, "Well, that belongs to me," and then the third party comes in and says, "Well, that belongs to me!" They really don't know their family history or where they come from, yet they want to make chiefs out of their boys.

A song is like a name. It's a hereditary thing and is greatly treasured. Most songs stay within the family: the chief passes them on to his oldest son; maybe he'll give a few to his daughters when they get married, but most go to his son who will be the next chief. If a chief is friendly with another person, likes them a lot, he will sometimes *give* that person a song to own forever, or else give him (or her) the right to *use* a song—this is only a loan. When he or she passes away, the song goes back to the original owner. But that person [who receives the loaned song] must be a chief or from a chief's family. A song can't be given to a commoner. No way! It has to be given by one chief to another chief or a member of a chief's family. It's a great honor to get a song as a gift from another chief. That was something quite special. To me it is something great, because I can't compose an Indian song and never will be able to, like some of the people did a long time ago. As long as potlatches continue, that song will get more important because it's older and older and older and has more history attached to it. Especially today, we don't see any of the kids composing Indian songs. So, to me it's very important to have these songs given by the old chiefs, because when I sing one, somebody will say, "I remember that song. She got it from Chief Edward Joe in 1930. It was a gift from a chief!" And it is important to me to know that I was well enough thought of to be given a song like that.

Songs that are given within the family: father to son or daughter, or to grandson or granddaughter—these songs don't have to be paid for, but all other songs do. If it was something inherited, then you weren't responsible for paying for it. But if you are given a song by someone else, you are obligated to pay for it. There's really no *money* value you can put on a song, but there *is* a big value on it; it's something *very* important to us. It's something very big. When you pay for a song, you give whatever you can afford, but in 1975 you never paid less than one hundred dollars, because that's how important a song was. In 1995, you pay anywhere between three hundred and five hundred dollars for a song, depending on how important a song it is. You give as much as you can spare for a song because it's a great honor to receive one. Songs are always given at a potlatch so everyone can witness that it was given to you, and then you always pay for it at another potlatch that you give yourself. Everyone must witness that you have paid for the song that was given to you. Then you can use that song whenever you want.

LEARNING SONGS FROM MY DAD

My dad was the one who taught me most about these things. He taught me about the value of a song, why a song is important, and how to give or receive a song. I remember how my dad loved his songs, how much they meant to him, and how he taught me and my brothers and sisters. When my dad wanted us (as children) to learn, he'd sing, *dudú·k,* every day, every day. There were only a very few times that I could remember when he didn't sit down and sing. He would have to be sick not to sing a little bit. He'd go to work in the morning, come back in the evening, change his clothes, and lay down in the living room. My mother was never early with her supper because she always worked with him, so she'd be getting supper ready, and he'd most generally lay down. And he'd hammer on the wall, with his fist—that was mostly his way to keep the beat. He'd lay on the couch or on a little cot we had there, and he'd start singing. He'd close his eyes, and he'd just sing and sing and sing and sing. He'd sing one song after the other. I'll bet you that dad of mine could go through a whole month of singing a dozen, two dozen songs every day and not sing the same one twice. If he felt like it, he'd sing the same one over, but mostly he always sang different ones.

He knew we were learning them because we had to sit and listen. Every single day! He'd say to us, "Now sit down and listen, because you have to know these songs sometime in the future. Maybe you'll wish you had listened to them. So I want you to sit down and listen to them now. Then you'll know them and be able to sing them." Actually when I started out, I wasn't very interested—I just didn't care for any of this. I used to think, "Well, what do I want with this? I don't want to do anything like that!" I was getting a little educated then, and I didn't want to listen to my dad. But he'd sing those songs, and I would sit and listen. Every day he did that. Every day he'd sing different songs, and he'd make me sit and listen—just me. He wanted all the rest of them to listen, too, but they'd say, "We heard those songs too many times; we don't want to listen!" And away they'd go. But I would have to sit there and listen. It seemed like from the time I was little, I had to listen to my dad whether I wanted to or not. I guess because my brothers were so much younger than me, he really didn't try to get them all that interested, like he made me. I especially remember one song that he sang that belonged to Billy Mason from Taholah. I really used to listen closely to this one because I thought it was *just beautiful!* It's what we call a *t'abáa* song, the kind of song they'd sing just for fun, or it could be a love song, or a song for when you're lonesome. I really liked Billy Mason's *t'abáa* song!

None of us kids ever *sang* Indian songs; my dad didn't ask us to, but he made us sit and listen to them many times. Sometimes he'd say, "It's quiet time. It's quiet time." Then we'd have to sit down, and if we didn't have anything to do my grandpa would say, "Oh, sit down and make a basket." Then he'd start teaching us while my dad was singing, so we'd be doing something while we were sitting there listening.

HOW WE LEARNED TO DANCE

Even though my dad never taught us to sing, he taught us all how to dance, *hú·tuk.* It wasn't at any special time; he used to make us practice anytime, as long as he wasn't doing anything else. Often in the evenings if he was home, or if he felt like it on Saturday or Sunday, then we'd all have to practice. He'd start singing, and then he'd say, "Okay, girls, get out there and let me watch you dance." And then we'd have to get out there and start dancing. We most generally had a pretty good-sized living room, so we could dance there. He would start in, and my mother would go about her cooking while he'd sort of watch us to see if we were doing okay. He kept us going like that all the time, so this way we couldn't forget. He just kept after us whenever he felt like it; he'd say, "Okay, girls, it's time to get out there," and then we'd go.

We never seemed to mind it, just got used to it, I guess. Nowadays if you asked the kids like that, they'd be ashamed; they wouldn't want to go. They'd be backward. But when he told us, we'd run around and get our blankets or shawls or anything we could get ahold of that we'd just put on. We weren't particular, as long as we had something over us.[1]

The only time we got particular was when it was party [potlatch] time. Then we'd race around and look for our costumes and good dance capes. My dad made us all make our own costumes. I think this is the way that he made us appreciate what we had. And believe me, we took care of them. Then when those costumes started going to pot, we'd talk to my dad, and he'd say, "Okay, girls, it's time to make another one." And then we'd make another one, and we were sort of proud of them.

Nowadays the Tribal Council sends for things, and then the teachers help the children make their costumes, or else somebody comes in and makes their costumes for them, and then the next year they don't have them anymore. They throw them away. Those kids know they don't have to make them themselves; somebody will make them for them, or somebody will give them one, so nowadays it just seems they don't care for anything they've got. However, when we used to make our own, we used to feel really proud of them, like we accomplished something; but that's not true anymore.

When my dad would make us practice dancing, sometimes he'd take his drum down and play it while he sang for us. If he wasn't satisfied with what we were doing, we'd have to go through it more than once, and even if we were standing there and didn't feel like dancing, he'd make us dance until we felt like dancing! We couldn't quit until we danced it just the way he wanted us to. If he didn't like the way we were stepping or the way it looked, he'd just go over the song again.

Then we'd have to know just exactly where the extra beat comes in, where it changes. We knew that our steps were going to be different for those few beats, and then they changed back again afterwards. Just before that extra beat came in, he'd say, "All right, it's coming—when you say such and such" [a certain word in the song text]. You'll hear one word, and then as soon as you recognize that one word, you know that your steps are going to get different, and from then on you count how many steps, because there aren't that many beats in there for it to be that hard. So we learned to count how many steps we had to take before the beat changed back. When we'd start in on a new song, he'd say, "Now, sit and listen; you're not dancing, you're going to sit and listen to this song until you're tired of it. Then you'll know just exactly where the beat comes in and where it changes." So, this was how he taught us to dance, and this is how I try to teach my family now.

One time when I was about twelve years old, Captain Jack, a chief from Nootka, gave me a song at a potlatch—it was the "Wo he," Grizzly Bear song (see chap. 10, song 4). My dad learned it, and then he taught it to me. He sang it over and over and over. There were times when I didn't even want to listen, but I learned that song. My aunt Annie Williams, from Canada, taught me the dance that went with it. She and Effie Frank and Effie's parents, Yašxen Jack and his wife, taught me that dance. They taught me the main part, which you do out in the center of the hall.

MUSIC IN THE LIVES OF MY GRANDPARENTS

All my grandparents used to either sing or dance, and when I was little I watched them a lot. My grandfather Charlie Anderson had quite a few songs and dances from the Ozette tribe, so he took part in potlatches. He used to like to sing, and he danced too (see fig. 10). My grandmother Alice Anderson Holden used to take part in ƛaʔiiɬ and Tsáyak ceremonies, and also doings in the Shaker Church.[2] I never did see her dance in group dances at potlatches or anything like that. But she sang lots of Shaker songs.

She would take us to church lots of times, and we'd have to sit there and keep still, listen to them pray and sing. I learned some of their songs this way from going to Sunday morning services with her, and then again, evening services. I remember being deaf from listening to those bells all evening long, three to four hours. Sometimes the little kids would be put to sleep under the benches so they wouldn't get stepped on. They'd be covered with a blanket and would sleep all night long. She could shake as much as she liked, and the kids wouldn't even see it. It'd be *hot* in there, everybody dancing and singing. Then I'd be so *cold* walking home after church. It was late, and we'd be so sleepy going home and *cold!* We didn't have flashlights then, so they'd put a handle on the bottom of a coffee can and use a candle in there and light our way home with that.

Then I remember my grandma used to sing when she was putting my baby brother Emil to sleep. I used to sit down by her and just listen. She'd be sitting there with him in her arms, and she'd be putting him to sleep, and she'd be shaking and praying and singing over him. She always did this in Quileute, never Makah, and I think that's what fascinated me. I'd sit on the floor and watch her and listen to her.[3]

Then there was my stepgrandma, Katy Anderson—she was a big, fat lady, and she could really dance the Fan Dance. They made fans out of tail feathers, and each dancer carried two: one in each hand. Sometimes the men would get a little bit fancy; they'd turn their feathers upside down and shake them, and it began to look like fun when you watched those older men doing it. But then there were two old ladies who were really good at it, too. They could really shake their back ends. You'd think they were doing a Hawaiian dance, they'd get so carried away. This was Katy Anderson and Mrs. Charlie Smith, called Dasé·ƛub, in Indian. Once in a while Susie Weberhard would also get in there and be every bit as goofy. Those three ladies could really dance! They were sure fun to watch. When they got carried away, everybody else would just sit down and start watching.

There was always music around our house. My grandparents, my granduncle Elliot, and especially my dad were always singing, dancing, practicing, or having singing sessions.

SINGING SESSIONS

The Makah used to have singing sessions long ago, but they don't anymore. They always used to get together and sing; they never seemed to get tired of it. This is the reason they remembered the songs and never ever forgot. They were doing it all the time, and when they felt like they wanted to get together, they'd get together and sing—just plain sing. And that's when us kids had to come, and we sat and kept still—nobody moved. Everybody got along real good because they had song sessions almost every week. Sometimes my dad used to have them two or three nights a week. Sometimes at our house, sometimes at other people's houses.

They always had them at night, like about 6:30 or 7:00 P.M., because the men were working during the day. They'd sit around and sing, and then to break it up, maybe they'd tell stories about a long time ago, or the funny things they did. . . . It wasn't dull, by any means. Each one had something to tell. Then they'd say, "Well, let's stop and sing again." And they'd start in singing. If there was a song they didn't know so well, they'd sing it over and over and over, until they all knew it good. This is why they could sing together real good in those days. And then maybe somebody else would pipe up and say, "Let's learn mine too, while we're at it." So this way it didn't get tiresome singing the same song over and over again. The song leader got to know the song, so he could just beat with his feather because he memorized every one of them. My dad was one of those leaders. This is what they did in those singing sessions to break it up into a variety, so it wouldn't be dull.

They'd finish maybe between 9:30 and 10:00 at night and then serve food. It wasn't anything elaborate. It was just something that they could get full on and go home and be comfortable. They had these nice big crackers, a long time ago; nowadays they're smaller [pilot bread]. They'd give you crackers and butter and tea or coffee; something just to curb your appetite. Or if they wanted to go all out, they'd make Indian dumplings—boiled bread. They're made out of flour, like bread, but there's no leavening in it. And if you wanted to make it extra special, you put raisins in it. They're rolled out little, in the shape of an egg and then boiled up. Then they'd add the sugar later. We call that *q'íniq'ču*, "Indian dumplings." I make it maybe once a year. It's good. If they didn't want to make that, they'd just make fried bread and give you coffee or tea with it, or buckskin bread,[4] all depending on how the cook felt. Buckskin bread is rolled and baked in the oven. Instead of putting it in a pan, my mom and my grandma would dust a newspaper with flour, roll the dough out flat, put it on the paper and push it in the oven. Funny how the newspaper never caught fire, but it didn't. Maybe cause it was a wood fire. When the bread is done, it's all brown and nice and looks like buckskin. It didn't stick on the paper because they dusted it with flour.

At that time nobody had a lot of chairs in their houses. So they'd put down two-by-twelve boards around the room for people to sit on when they came for a singing session. Then they'd have another similar plank in the front of you on blocks of wood so you could spread newspaper on that board, and that's where you ate. Everybody did it like this.

LEARNING NEW SONGS RECEIVED AS GIFTS

When we'd be given a song by a Canadian chief, we had song sessions in order to learn that song. I can remember when Dad first got those songs that his Canadian aunt, Annie, gave him, he had to invite the Canadians down here and keep them under his roof. While they were here he was under obligation to call the heads of the tribe, the singers, and the drummers and have them over to his house every night for a week to practice and learn those songs. If some of his relatives wanted to take the tension off him a little bit, maybe they'd say, "We'll have the song session at our house tonight." My dad had to feed his guests three times a day every day, so that's why the relatives took their turn and helped out. Then if ever they got some songs and had to host their guests for a week, they knew my dad would help them out in return. Every night they'd sing those new songs as well as a bunch of others. After we learned the songs, then our Canadian teachers went home.

Today when a song is given to me, after I learn it, I have to sit and counsel with my family and say, "Well, when can we have this party to pay for the song?" Then when we make up our minds, we have to call the heads of the tribe together again, along with our singers and dancers, and I have to tell them what I'm going to do. We'd sit there and sing the song and see how well we all know it. If we didn't know it well enough, we'd sing it a few more weeks. Then I'd tell them that I've got a certain time set aside, a certain day that I want to call the Canadians back over, and that I'm going to invite other people besides just the family that gave me the song. I tell my tribe we're going to have what we call *hahá·wakts'ub*. This means that I'm inviting other people to come and sit at the feet of those from whom I am learning [about the new song], and these others are going to eat with us. They are going to sit and eat with the people who are giving me the song, and the group will include someone who knows how to talk in the proper Indian way. This group that I am feeding are going to be the witnesses to take this information back home and tell the people there what happened here.

Then when I'm ready, I invite the family that's giving me the song, and I also send out an invitation to the rest of their tribe and tell them to come across to a potlatch. This is where I'll pay for my song. All the people that come are obligated to tell the rest that such and such a person gave me this song. They will hear it sung, too. So, they're the witnesses and will tell the other eighteen tribes back in Canada that this chief gave me this song.

WORLD WAR II AND CHANGES IN MAKAH MUSICAL LIFE

Even though we still have parties to pay for songs we've been given, we quit having singing sessions in the late 1930s. It was before World War II; everybody just quit. At that time we had what they call blackouts. Everybody was quiet. Everybody was afraid, a little bit. They were expecting the Russians or the Japanese to land on our coast. Our windows were all blocked up, and everybody was made to stay home. I remember being afraid all the time because they told us to expect anything to happen at any time. At that time we had an electric light bulb hanging down in the middle of each room, so we had to have a dark cloth over our windows in the evenings; no light ever shining through. Everything was in total darkness outside. You couldn't see anything out there. You had to stay right at home. And all we had was a radio. That was turned down very, very low. I mean, you had to listen, in case something happened.

My dad couldn't sing in the evenings anymore at that time. Instead he would always sing at noontime, lunchtime. And there were no more singing sessions ever again. The parties stopped too, but then after the war actually started they did have parties. Whenever an enlisted son or daughter had a furlough and came home, their family gave a big party for them. They went all out because they didn't know if they'd ever see them again. After the war ended and all through the '40s we were still having the servicemen coming home, and we did a lot of singing for them at parties. Everybody had a party for their son or daughter when they came home.

Then the "warm-up parties" started after World War II. This is where we prepared for the parties. At a warm-up you get together and sing the songs you're going to use at the actual party. Each one who's planning to come sings his or her song. Then the host knows who he can count on, because at a warm-up party everybody will show up, and they work out the order in which each one of them will sing. When we practice, we each *start* our own songs, but then everybody joins in and sings them. These warm-up parties are a *lot* different than the singing sessions we had before. For the warm-up you only spend one evening about a week or a few days before the party. You don't spend two or three evenings every week, like they did for the singing sessions. The family that's going to have the party hosts the warm-up, and has to pay for the meal for all who attend. So a warm-up isn't anything at all like the song sessions they used to have before the war.

The song leaders always had to be at the singing sessions, then later on they were always at the warm-ups, because they had to lead the songs at the parties. My dad was one of the song leaders. He had a feather fan which he used to signal the chorus of singers and also the dancers. Then in his other hand he had a shell rattle. About a dozen scallop shells were all hooked together on a round piece of wire, and he would shake that.

WOODEN BOXES, CEREMONIAL GEAR, AND POWER OF THE MASKS

Since my dad was a carpenter, he made a nice box in which he kept all his ceremonial gear. I don't know what kind of boards he made it out of, but it must have been about four feet by three feet. . . . It was kind of big so the whistles would fit in there. He put a handle on it so he could carry it when we went to parties. He fit all the whistles in there that went with the masks our family owned. He lined the bottom where the masks were, so they wouldn't break. The whistles were on one side, and the masks on the other. Then the button blanket and feather fan fit on top, to keep the masks from rattling around. My dad worked it out so the masks were laying down when the suitcase was open, but when it was closed and upright, they were looking sideways. The case always sat upright so those masks would face north. He also had a silver nose piece and other little trinkets that he kept in a small corner of the case. They all just fit in there perfect so there'd be no rattle and no busting of anything. Since most of my family either sang or danced, we were all familiar with the gear my dad kept in that box.

My brother Emil, who was eight years younger than me, never went to any of the parties, however, and never danced with my dad's gear. Most of the time he was home alone. One night when we were out of the house, he just laid there in his room—he was probably reading—and all of a sudden he heard a noise, like you're clicking your teeth. He got up, looked around, went into my mom's room, didn't find anything, so he went back, laid down again, thought nothing more about it. Pretty soon he heard it again! So he stayed in the kitchen. He made a pot of tea and sat at the table, and then he heard it again. He started drinking tea—he was kind of a tea bug. He heard it again, so he looked over real slow, and then he knew where the sound was coming from. He went back to his bedroom and stayed there. When he closed his bedroom door, he heard those teeth clicking again, but this time he heard the whistles blowing, too. And he never said anything for a while: he just kept quiet—never told mom or dad anything—until the second time it happened. Then he finally told my mom.

My mom told my dad, so my dad sat us all at the table, and he sat my brother there, too, and he said, "Now those things don't know you, that's why they're making a lot of noise like that." My dad said to Emil, "You're the oldest boy, you should be using them—you should learn how to sing and to dance. You're supposed to be the one to take after me—do the things that I'm doing now and take my place, because I don't have too long. I don't know whether I'll be gone today, tomorrow— you never know. You should be the one to take over what I'm doing in this line of Indian dancing, Indian tradition. You're the oldest boy. You're supposed to be learning all these things, but you never listen to me. So this is why this is happening to you—these masks don't know you anymore!" "Instead of you [Emil] doing it," he pointed at me and said, "Helma's doing it. Do you ever hear her telling me that she's hearing those masks the way they're carrying on, and the whistles? She doesn't say anything because she's familiar with them and they're familiar with her. They don't know you because you aren't trying to walk in my footsteps." That's what my dad told him. Then he said, "They don't bother your brother Levi, because he's used them, too. Now they know him."

He explained it to the rest of the younger ones, and they said, "Well, that never happened to us." My dad told them, "Well, you children are learning to dance. You haven't danced with these things on, but you have danced while someone else was wearing them. The masks are familiar with you because you have danced background for the masks and have been dancing with them constantly. But Emil has never stepped foot in there. Neither has the oldest daughter."

My oldest sister, Katherine, wasn't there at that time; she didn't hear any of this. She never did stay around too much after she got married and then divorced and then left. So, nobody said anything about it anymore. About a year or two later, Katherine was at home—she was all by herself. My brother was gone somewhere—he may have gone visiting to my grandmother's place out at Tsooyez. Katherine was home alone that day—all of us had gone out. And then she heard the same thing. She was staying in the smaller bedroom, just below my brother's, and these masks were still in their box in the same place in the hall next to the kitchen. She heard them, and she got scared. She waited a little while before she found out what they were. Well, by that time then, she heard the whistles blowing, plus hearing the chatter of the teeth. And she ran out of there. She didn't do like my brother did—he heard them twice before he told my mother about it. But she only heard them that one time and then ran out of there. And my dad told her the same thing that he told the boy. He said, "You shouldn't have run out of there." When the Indians talk like that they say, 'You lose your shadow'; in other words, those things just take your shadow away from you—your life isn't going to be very long. My brother and sister didn't live very long. They died, both of them, about five years later. They had a lot of problems. Neither of them did what my dad told them. They just wouldn't. It made my dad real unhappy that they were like this, but there was nothing much he could do.

My grandaunt Annie Williams also had several wooden boxes that she'd bring with her every time she came down from Clayoquot in Canada. Her boxes were all painted green. She'd never open them, and she'd never leave them either. She'd just bring them here and then take them when she went home. I don't know how she ever managed all of them. I wouldn't know how to travel like that. We were kids then, and we didn't know what was in those boxes. We asked my dad once, and he said he didn't know either. He said, "Don't ask her, either. Don't pester her. Leave her alone. If she wants to tell you, she'll tell you. Even I don't know what she has in there." So we never did ask. We just let it go. But we'd *look* at that box and say to each other, "I wonder what's in that box?!"

Finally, after all those years of her bringing them back and forth, we found out what was in them. When I was twelve years old and Annie had that party for my dad in Canada,[5] she just pulled out all those boxes and gave them to my dad. In the boxes were all the masks and the curtain she was giving to my dad. She hauled them all out at that party. She gave some of them to him then, and the rest, she said, "I'll give you after I die." But we never did get any more after she died. Problems developed with some of our relatives up there after she died, and I cannot talk about this, except to say we never got the rest of the masks. However, they [the original masks] knew what was happening and responded properly.[6] They no longer exist.

My dad never knew any of the details of what happened to the masks. He wasn't alive when I found it out. My dad had been real close to my aunt Annie. After she died, he stopped going across to Canada. I think he felt bad because of the way things had gone. Our relatives up there didn't contact my dad when Annie was sick. She got sicker and sicker, and finally it was Hyacinth (Hyson) David from up there that called my dad. That's how he found out she was so sick. By the time he got up there, she was gone. I don't think my dad ever quite got over that.

After Annie died, we just stayed on the American side. Dad didn't feel like going back to Canada anymore. But he did continue to sing and dance over here. He kept that up because the songs and customs were Annie's to begin with, and she gave them to him, so he wanted to keep them up (see fig. 9). This is what she would have wanted him to do. Then we went to parties [potlatches] in this area—Quileute, Taholah, Neah Bay. . . . We never went back to the Canadian side again. Never! My dad never did get in touch with any of our relatives across there from that time on.

VISITS BETWEEN CANADIAN AND AMERICAN RELATIVES

When I was little and Annie was alive, I remember going back and forth to Canada all the time with my dad. Annie used to call him (by letter or by telegram), so we'd all go across there and come back. Go across and come back. He always made it a point to keep in touch with her. Then sometimes she would come over here and stay for three months. She'd bring her husband, Charlie, and they'd stay here with us. Sometimes she'd bring Ernest Curley, and they'd stay for six months. It just seemed like they were family, and we didn't feel like we were put out by them or anything. She was really nice. She was sort of like a grandmother to me, except she was a grandmother who wasn't here very often. My mom never let her do anything, so she just sat and made baskets all the time. She was there just like my grandmother. She'd bring her basket material and sit there and make baskets (see fig. 23). That's just the way she was. And her husband would sit and do nothing. He'd get up, go walk around, come back. . . . Eventually he started making masks, and he taught my dad how to make masks. Then he enjoyed himself a lot. Charlie Williams made changing masks and wolf headgears. He was very good at this and taught my dad well.

There were times we used to go across there [to Canada] and stay for about a month. My dad would leave us there. He was working and couldn't stay. He'd come back alone and work in Neah Bay for a week and then return to Clayoquot. Then he'd leave and come back again. Whenever he was with us, Annie kept talking to him, teaching him things.

He and I would go across to parties all the time during those years. My dad was a song leader and he sang and I did all his dancing for him. Whenever my dad got money, I got money too, cause I was right there with him all the time.[7] In a sense I was considered an adult by the people instead of a child, because I was at those parties with him and danced for him most of the time.

DANCING "BACKGROUND"

I danced background[8] for him, most often with a black shawl, standing there like any woman, doing background, what we call *hu·ɫsáts'i?i*. That means, "dancing in the back." Only the women do it. When I was little, each family had their own women do their background for them, not like they do now—everybody goes out there for background. This way you don't know whose family it is that's dancing, cause they're all mixed up. They never used to allow that a long time ago.

Sometimes the head of the family will come over and ask you to *hu·ɫsáts'i?i*, and it's just a natural understanding that you're only dancing for that person cause he doesn't have his family there or he doesn't have enough to dance with just his family. Then when you're through, he pays you in front of the people, and he thanks you for dancing. That way the people will know you are not one of the family—that he asked you. If you've got four, five, six girls—that's enough to dance background. One or two usually isn't enough to make that semicircle that they dance in.

I remember one time when we were in Canada when I was little, I sat in a longhouse and watched the ladies practice doing background all at the same time. They were all in black shawls, and they did it until it was perfect. The lady who led the background carried a stick and when she'd lift her stick, that meant they were coming to the change in the beat. You had to listen carefully. She taught groups of twenty-five women at a time. Each had to get out there and do it alone while she sang the song. She'd call them out of line if they weren't doing it right, and go over that section till they did it right. Then they'd go back in the line. If it still wasn't right, she'd call them out again. They had to pay attention and learn it correctly; they had no choice.

Chief Edward Joe's wife was a good dancer. All of them were so good! They were lined up according to size—the tallest ones were where the singers were standing, down to the littlest—going from the southeast to the southwest—clockwise. The Canadians did it this way. They marched in and out with the short ones first, going clockwise. In Neah Bay they come in counterclockwise.

Now they don't teach the girls how to do the background. No one teaches them. They don't want anyone to teach them, so the older people don't offer. The boys do still get instruction in how to do the lead dance, but not as much as they used to in the past.

Then there's another kind of background that I danced for my dad's Mask-Changing Dance. He danced the lead[9] and used the human-type face masks, and I'd be background and use one of the wolf headgears. There's supposed to be two wolves—sometimes my sister Dolores would be the other wolf; sometimes I'd be the only one. These wolves were always supposed to be there, and they were a different kind of background for my dad. I can't remember any special word for that. Then there are also the group of women doing *hu·ɬsáts'i?i* in a semicircle behind us. The two wolves are not part of that group and have their own way to dance. Because my younger brothers were too little, my father had no boys to do the wolf parts of the dance, so he had me and my sister do it and use the wolf headgears.

DANCING TO SOME OF OUR FAMILY-OWNED SONGS

Then we also had several actual Wolf Dance songs, where there was just one wolf, supposed to be danced by a man who was the lead dancer. Ordinarily it was not allowed for a woman to dance the wolf. I got to do the wolf because my dad didn't have any boys old enough.

When you dance this wolf, you dance with your hands on your hips—you make a half-circle circuit (counterclockwise), squat, and hop for the extra beats. Sometimes there is an extra beat in there. Maybe two to five extra beats. You just dance regular for the other beats. When you're dancing you think like a wolf—look down, sideways, back—and think of the actions of a wolf. You wear a black cape or a painted cape and the wolf headgear. (All our family's designs on the dance capes are the same. We don't use other people's designs, only those that have been passed down to us.)

There was one Wolf Dance song that I really liked a lot. If I felt like I wanted to dance and I didn't have to dance for my dad, I used to tell my mother, because this song was on her side of the family, not on my dad's side. This song was supposed to belong to three people: my mother, Ruth Swan; Matilda McCarty; and Katy Hunter. These three were able to use it and didn't argue about it, didn't quarrel about it. They were all three related somehow, though I don't know how. It was given to the three of them, and they all had to share it. This is the "Yaqʷáyats'i·k Song," which starts out, "Huu Huu Hu Huu." (see song 7, chap. 10).

Katy was always at the parties long ago, but she never took part, so she really didn't care who used it. She didn't want to give money away; she said only crazy people give money away. I used to tell my mother that I wanted to dance that "Yaqʷáyats'i·k," Wolf Dance Song, and she'd say, "Well, you wait until Matilda and Jerry McCarty sing. If Jerry uses his own song, then you can do this one, but if

Matilda wants to sing it, you'll have to do another one." My mother didn't want Matilda to think that we were trying to take over this song. So she told her that she made me wait until she found out whether they were going to use it, and if she, Matilda, wanted to use it first, then she should go ahead, because they could always find me another song. My dad had a lot of songs so there really was not any question about that, but Mom always wanted to be very fair with Matilda. There was no squabble there; they'd always talk it out. Or else, if they didn't talk about it, I'd be the one waiting it out, and it didn't matter to me one way or the other. If I wanted to use it bad enough, I waited.

I really liked that song, and when I danced it, I sometimes wore a wolf headgear. Since my mom never had any, I used my dad's. This was okay for me to do because they were married. If they weren't, it wouldn't have been proper. I also wore my dad's dance cape. My parents always kept their family songs separate. Hers were hers, and his were his. Out of respect, my dad wouldn't sing one of my mom's songs unless she asked him to.

Mostly, Jack LaChester sang this "Yaqʷáyats'i·k," Wolf Dance Song, for me; my dad really didn't. I don't know why. Maybe my mom didn't ask him to sing it. Anyhow, I usually asked Jack LaChester to sing it for me, and he would. I always thought this song of my mom's was pretty, so I used it. I really enjoyed dancing it. I always felt like smiling when I danced it, but I wasn't allowed to, because this was a serious dance. We never could smile for any dance.

The Thunderbird Dance was another one that belonged to the Swan family, and they kept telling us the story about it as we kept dancing it year after year. My sister Dolores (who is six years younger than me) and I were the only ones old enough to get in on this dance. My dad and his aunt Annie always told me that this dance was during the mating season of Thunderbird.

Thunderbird is very important, according to our legend. Long ago the people watched how Thunderbird made advances to his mate, and this is how the dance began to be. It doesn't have any song—of course they're usually just screeching at each other when they mate like that. When you dance it, you're supposed to dance a boy and a girl or a man and a woman. You never do both girls or both women. It's supposed to be a man and a woman because it's Thunderbird mating with his wife. The thunderbirds only have one egg a year. That's the way it was told to us.

I used to dance it with one of the Makah boys sometimes, and if they couldn't, I'd just dance it by myself. They let me do it this way because they wanted to watch the Thunderbird Dance. When you're dancing the thunderbird, you come in with your wings spread—one up and one down. You just keep going, switch every now and then, and then you turn in each corner, more or less in each direction,[10] and then keep on going. You make three rounds, then you come back and stop. When you stop, you're flapping—your arms are going up and down in front of you like a bird with its wings in motion. You sink down into a squatting postion, then you come up slowly to the right. You sink down again, and then you come up to the left with your arms bent at the elbows and the knuckles of your hands meeting at about the level of your chin. You sink down a third time, and when you come up, then you whistle—like a thunderbird—kind of a screeching sound, shrill, whistlelike. Then you shake your head, jump and spread your wings again, and then go around to the place where you exit. This is supposed to look like a bird in flight. The whistle used by the thunderbird is made out of small cedar pieces, and it fits in your mouth. The drum is doing just a straight, fast beat [a fast tremolo] called *t'i·tsqeyaX*, but your motions are behind the beat. It's just graceful; it isn't fast. All you're doing is sliding your foot a little at a time. You shuffle your feet, you don't take separate steps. But the drumbeat is very fast.

Usually I wore a plain black shawl and a thunderbird headgear. There was no other special costume—no wing feathers or anything. There are feathers on top of the headgear, however. There's only small design differences between the headgears for the male and for the female thunderbird.

We also had an Eagle Dance, with two dancers, which was similar, only you don't make like you're flapping your wings in front of you. Your arms are held out straight, switching back and forth (one arm up and the other down). The dancers do more turning than in the Thunderbird. For the Eagle, they turn in the four corners, but also in the middle—between each corner—and it's a little bit faster motion than the Thunderbird. The two dancers are looking at each other when they're dancing the Thunderbird, but with the Eagle, you don't do that. The Eagle Dance is not a mating dance. We do wear a headgear, however; but the eagle is a little bit different from the thunderbird headgear. The eagle beak is more curved, but the thunderbird has more marks on his face. The eagles do screech at each other with a whistle—the same one we use for the thunderbird.

The Eagle Dance came from my mom's side, the Thunderbird from my dad's. Your family from generations back had to be a member of these clans in order to use the headgears and the songs and dances.[11] My mom always said we were Eagle and Wolf on her side; my dad said we were Thunderbird, Grizzly Bear, Raven, and Wolf on his side. My grandaunt Annie gave my dad these things which came from her father, Chief Sitkeenum.[12] We have some from Chief Peter Brown but gave most of those up to another branch of the family because we were taking Chief Sitkeenum's things.

We have several Grizzly Bear songs that I like. A long time ago, my dad used to dance to a Makah Grizzly Bear song called "Hú ya" (see chap. 10, song 6) which came from his Neah Bay side of the family, from his grandfather whose name was Yelák'ub. Then, Captain Jack, the Nootka chief from Gold River, B.C., gave my dad and me each a Grizzly Bear song. They are two songs that go together. "Wó hey" is the one he gave me (chap. 10, song 4), and "Hó yeh" (chap. 10, song 5) is the one he gave to my dad. Anytime we do a dance, there are always two that go together. If there aren't two, there will be chanting first and then chanting in between. Anyway, I used to dance to those two Grizzly Bear songs. Grizzly Bear head motions are like what a bear would do, different from what a wolf would do. Annie taught me how to do this—she was really good. I would imitate her. Captain Jack watched and told Annie what I was doing wrong. Annie then told me and helped me correct my steps.

After I got my Grizzly Bear song and my dad had paid for it, Mike Brown made the headgear for me. He lived in Oopídzit on Clayoquot Island in Canada. They said he was one of my relatives, and he was a real good carver. The headgear he made was like a cap or a helmet, called X̣'á·x̣sa·t', and it has a beak on both sides, the front and the back—like a bird. Then there were sticks on the top to hold in the duck down feathers. When I danced and moved my head, the down scattered. I was not much more than about thirteen when I danced it like that. My dad sang for me. This was a dance that women usually danced. It's different at Alert Bay [a Kwakiutl village], where it's mixed, and more men dance it. I danced that dance as long as my father could sing it for me. That was the only way I could dance, was if he sang for me. When he died in 1958, there was no one to sing it for me, and I stopped dancing it. Then, later on, I had to learn to sing it all by myself, just by thinking about it.

The Changing Mask Dance was the most important one my dad owned. I'm now taking care of it for my son Arnie. [In a 1987 potlatch Helma gave it to Arnie.] This dance represents the "four seasons." The lead dancer changes his mask four times because every season has a different face to it. This is what the dance represents—the changing of seasons. The last mask, the fifth mask, opens and closes its eyes because it is watching over the whole tribe. We had the original masks that were handed down from Chief Sitkeenum. Now they are in the Royal British Columbia Museum in Victoria. We still use the two button blankets she gave us that night. Also, some whistles and a twenty foot by thirty foot curtain were given to us at the same time, and they go with the song and the five masks. Annie Williams gave all these things to my dad.

THE FAMILY CURTAIN

The curtain gives the family history and the family name. On the right side of our curtain[13] there's a round, sort of half circle that's in different colors and looks like a rainbow, with a sea serpent head at either end[14] (see fig. 26). This was Chief Sitkeenum's wife and Annie's mother. Her name was Suwáyukx'otl. I was supposed to get that name, but my dad gave it to my older sister, Katherine, instead. On the inside of the circle, below the rainbow, was my aunt Annie's name, Xwinxwánimo, in the center of the curtain. That's the name I was given, Xwinxwánimo. After Katherine died, my mother gave the name Suwáyukx'otl to my daughter, Lina Mae (Babe) Markishtum. Now she has that name on the curtain. At a party on October 4, 1975, I gave my name, Xwinxwánimo, to my oldest granddaughter, Rhonda Markishtum, so that's no longer my name. The "Wó hey" Grizzly Bear song goes with the grizzly bear on one side of the curtain and with the name Suwáyukx'otl, so I'll probably be giving that song to my daughter in the near future, too.

On the other side of the curtain is a thunderbird above a man who is on a whale. The thunderbird is Sitkeenum, and the man, painted very much like the mask, is Atliú, Chief Sitkeenum's son. Now my oldest son, Arnie Hunter, has been given the name Yelák'ub, because that was my father's name when Annie gave him all of Sitkeenum's things. He didn't change his name to either Sitkeenum or Atliú. So my boy has the name Yelák'ub, but he is in the direct line to get the song, the curtain, the masks, and the whistles, just like my father did.[15]

On March 28, 1987, I had a potlatch party in Neah Bay, and I gave these things to him. I stated that he will carry on what my father had carried on. I'm just a woman, and I can't do it. In other words, a woman isn't that high in our heritage, like a boy ordinarily is. So a woman can only be a caretaker of these things until she passes them on to the next male who is in line for them.

Way over on the right side of the curtain is a totem pole which represented the names of the clans. Atliú was a carver, so that's why that pole is in there. Way on the left side of the curtain is a long totem pole with what looks like a snake going up it. This represents Shubert Hunter, who was from the Clayoquot Tribe and was also a cousin of Annie's.[16] So, she decided when they painted this curtain that she was going to put him on there also. There is a bear on top of that pole, because Shubert is also from the bear clan. Annie presented him with one of these curtains and gave him permission to use it. He didn't own it, but he could use it because he was on part of it. He and his wife only used it now and then; but then later, after his oldest boy died, he felt so bad that he never ever used that curtain again. From what I heard, Shubert gave his brother, Jim Hunter, permission to use the curtain. I don't think anybody's ever told Jim and his family about this curtain being our family history and our background. It belonged to us, and they just had the right to use it; they never owned it. When Jim died, his wife took this curtain and all the rest of the things that he had and sold them to different collectors. We've been chasing them down and finding an occasional piece here and there.

Anyway, the curtain goes with the Changing Mask Dance Song (see song 10, chap. 10), the five masks, and the whistles, all of which Annie Williams gave to my dad at the potlatch in Clayoquot in 1930. Francis Frank's family, across in Canada, are just as close relatives to Annie as we are, so they can use the same songs that we are using, and they have their own masks and family curtain[17] (see fig. 27). Each family is supposed to consult with the other if they want to give this dance to anyone other than a son or daughter.

When we'd do a complete performance of the Changing Mask Dance, we'd use our whistles as background for starting it. There are all different kinds of whistles, and they're always played in pairs: a big one and a little one, like there are two grizzly bears—one has a higher and the other a lower sound. Then there are screech owls, wolves, loons, and sandhill cranes. Some you have to soak the night before, and others you have to fill half full of water to get the sound right. Each one is shaped a little different, and of course the size is different.

OUR FAMILY DANCE CAPES

Ordinarily, whenever anyone was going to sing, dance, and give away, he or she would wear some kind of cape, *hiti·d*. My dad and his good friend Jim Hunter each had similar painted dance capes which were given to them by their Canadian relatives. The designs are about the same, but the colors are different in certain places, and that's how you can tell that they belong to two different families. Parts of some designs were green on my dad's cape, and they were blue on Jim's cape. The women usually wore plain black shawls or capes when they danced.

My dad also had two button blankets [dance capes], which he got from Annie Williams. These had belonged to her father, Benjamin Cedakanim, or Atliú, who had received them from a Kwakiutl chief up north. I really don't know how or when Atliú got them. But she gave them to my dad at the potlatch in 1930, and he used them a lot. The Makah don't usually have button blankets, so we feel very lucky to have two in our family. One has a grizzly bear on the back, and the other has a double-headed raven. My sisters and I have made a number of copies for our family members, who use them all the time when they are dancing.

My dad taught us that if we were going to dance, we were *always* to bring our own things; we were *never* to borrow anybody else's costumes. That was hammered into us so many times. "If you don't have one and you want to dance, borrow from your brother, borrow from your sister, because these things belong to you and to nobody else." The Makah people believe that each thing that you own has its own spirit in it, and that spirit is familiar with you and nobody else. If that costume belongs to you, it has your own *tumánuwos* (spirit power) in it, and this costume begins to know you. Therefore, if you borrow somebody else's, it's not going to do you any good. In fact, it will do your body worse because there's going to be something happen to you—because it isn't yours, it isn't your *tumánuwos* in there, it's somebody else's. So we don't dare ever ask anybody to borrow anything. Whenever I go to a party, I bring my own things, or else I don't use any; I still never borrow anybody else's. Also, you're not supposed to loan your things to somebody else, either. If you do this, then the spirit begins to familiarize itself with that other person, so you aren't

Fig. 23. Annie Atliu, wearing a cedar bark rain shawl and spruce root rain hat, is beginning a cedar bark basket, 1904. Granddaughter of Chief Cedakanim and daughter of Atliu, she was known as an outstanding basket maker. Annie, who inherited the chiefly belongings of her father and grandfather, transferred them to her nephew, Charlie Swan, at a Clayoquot potlatch in 1930. *Photo courtesy of the Royal British Columbia Museum (Newcombe Collection, neg. #548).*

Fig. 24. Three of the five Changing Mask Dance masks, belonging to Charlie Swan. These are said to be the originals given to him by Annie Atliu Williams at the Clayoquot potlatch in 1930 where she made him a chief. The lower two, representing two of the four seasons, are danced before the upper mask, the Mask with the Open and Closing Eyes, which is the final one used in the dance sequence. Because these masks were deteriorating, Helma asked Steve Brown (carver, artist, and former curator, Seattle Art Museum) to make her a copy of this set of masks so the Swan family could continue to dance with them. She then sold the originals in this photo to the Royal British Columbia Museum in Victoria in the late 1980s so they could be preserved. *Photographed in Neah Bay, 1984, by Linda J. Goodman.*

Fig. 25. Charlie Swan posing in his wolf headgear and wearing his double-headed raven button blanket. In the center, placed above his grizzly bear button blanket are his grizzly bear headgear, one of the Changing Mask Dance masks, and a thunderbird headgear. At the base of the grizzly bear blanket are three other original masks belonging to the Changing Mask Dance. On the far left may be seen a small portion of his painted dance cape. All of these items were officially given to Charlie by his aunt Annie Atliu Williams when she made him a chief at a 1930 potlatch in Clayoquot, British Columbia. *From a postcard published by Ellis, 9132, no date; courtesy of Helma Swan.*

Fig. 26. The Swan Family Curtain, originally belonging to Chief Cedakanim, was officially given by his granddaughter Annie Atliu Williams to Charlie Swan during the 1930 potlatch when she made him a chief. On the curtain, note the three totem poles at left, center, and right. Two poles frame the thunderbird, man, and whale on the left, and two frame the grizzly bear head above the double lightning serpents, wolf, thunderbird, and circular rainbow on the right. Photograph by Frances Densmore, Neah Bay, Washington, 1923. *Photo courtesy of the National Anthropological Archives, Smithsonian Institution (Opps-Neg. #84–17963).*

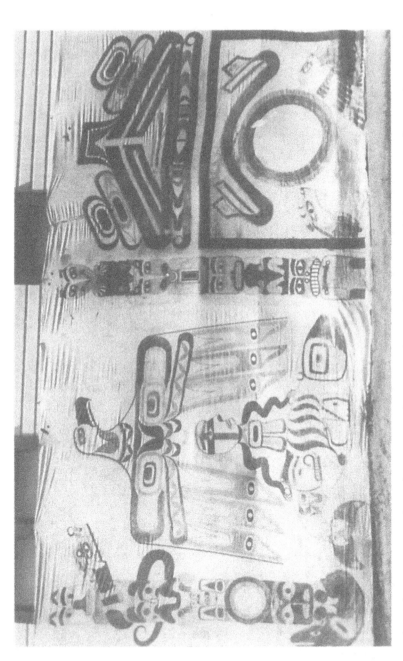

Fig. 27. The Frank Family Curtain is similar to the Swan Family Curtain (shown in fig. 26), but includes a number of minor changes in design elements. Oral tradition states that both curtains came originally from Chief Cedakanim and that each family has the right to use its own version of this curtain. Note especially the differences in the depiction of the totem pole on the left side of each curtain and the body of the whale. The totem pole on the right side of the Frank Family Curtain was not photographed. Otherwise, even though interior designs differ somewhat, the central characters are the same: thunderbird, man, and whale on the left, and more stylized grizzly bear head above the double lightning serpents, wolf, thunderbird, and rainbow on the right. *Photograph by Sister M. Loretta of Christie Indian School, no date [but prior to 1983]; courtesy of the Royal British Columbia Museum (Neg. #PN 4678).*

Fig. 28. The Swan family painted dance cape officially given by Annie Williams to Charlie Swan at the 1930 potlatch where she made him a chief. The central character is a grizzly bear. Other symbols include hands, bird feathers, and whale tails. On either side are representations of the lightning serpent. *Photographed in 1984 by Linda J. Goodman.*

going to have it anymore; that other person can take over after a while. So, I never loan out any of my shawls. One young woman was pretty mad at me one time because I wouldn't loan her my shawl. I told her it's mine, and I don't want to loan it out to anybody, because it belongs to me. She just thought I was being stingy, but that wasn't it at all. My belief is my belief. Later on I made a shawl and gave it to her. By that she should understand I don't want her borrowing my things.

DANCING THE CHANGING MASK DANCE

At the beginning of a party, the curtain is opened out so you can see the whole design on it; it's on a wire strung in the hall, and it's pulled open across the wire. While it's like this, the whole family puts on their costumes behind the curtain. You never get dressed in the open; you're always behind the curtain. While we're getting dressed, we have certain people blow the whistles—only men. They don't allow women to blow them at all—I don't know why. It's supposed to be something that a man does, not something that a woman does. My dad always handed them out to the same ones every time: Henry St. Clair, Jack LaChester, Alec Green, Luggie (Ralph) LaChester, Fred Anderson, Charlie Anderson—those were the ones that would blow the whistles. They each had to imitate the sound of that animal.

Then when we're ready we all march out, in any order, in front of the curtain and stand to the right of the curtain. The singers are already out there, and my dad was out there with them because he was the song leader and had the feather fan in his right hand and a scallop shell rattle in the left.[18] He goes around and starts what we call, *húx̌ix̌*, which means "holler." The singers and the rest of us that are standing there have to holler, "Huuuuuii, Huuuuu." When we say that, the whistling stops. They put all the whistles away then, and everybody hollers. Then my dad, as song leader, would walk around in the middle of the singers, going back and forth, saying, "Huuuuuuii." After he finishes, well, everybody hollers, "Huuuuuu." That means there's a big dancer coming that we have to pay attention to. Then everybody gets still. They're watching. An important character is coming.

Then my dad starts singing the song. Before he starts, all the women doing background get in a U-shaped formation. The main dancer is hidden from the audience. Then he comes out, makes a counterclockwise spin and begins his dance. On his face is a wide black painted band which goes across his eyes and to the hairline on each side. He wears a big black dance cape (usually one of our two button blankets) which hides the masks he's carrying. Part of the time he dances without a mask on, and part of the time he will duck his head into his cape and come up wearing a mask (figs. 15 and 16).

While he's waiting to come out the first time, he gets his mask all ready. There's a certain way to hold the mask so he can take it and put it on his face without getting mixed up. He has to hold it upside down, and then when he's ready, he brings it up and puts it in place. It doesn't have any rope around it. It has a little piece of hemlock root that's wound up and strung on the inside there, and he bites on that and holds it on with his teeth. Then when he goes to take it off, he bends over into his cape, grabs it from underneath the chin, and back to the way he had it. He puts it on his hip. Both hands are on his hips, and the cape covers the whole thing, so no one notices that he's got the masks under there. Then he'll duck behind a small group of people and exchange one mask for another, come back out, and continue dancing at the appropriate time. Meanwhile the two wolves are going back and forth behind him all the time he's dancing, and the women in black shawls are doing *hu·ɬsáts'i?i,* "background," in a semicircle.

My son Arnie, when he dances this, has to go behind the people and change masks every other time, the same as my dad would do. My dad taught him that way. He carries one mask hidden on each side. There's five masks total that he has to use. If it's done right, no one sees him exchange masks. My dad used to look real nice doing that dance, because he was short. My brother Levi learned to do the same thing—he was little, too; he was five foot two like I am. He did it just as gracefully as my dad did. Because they were short, they could squat really low, and they could really spin! My Canadian relative, Francis Frank, was short, and he looked very good doing the same thing. But Arnie's tall. He's way up there, and I've noticed it makes quite a difference. When tall people dance it, they are just too high up there. It looks different with a tall dancer. But still, in all, Arnie does pretty well.

After the dancer finishes dancing with the open and close mask [the eyes open and close], he leaves the floor, the wolves leave, the song ends, and then all the background dancers march back behind the curtain.[19]

Since I am the caretaker of this song, I can use the Changing Mask Dance any time I want, and my son Arnie can dance to it. Most of the time now we don't have the two wolf dancers that go with it. When my dad used to dance it, my sister Dolores and I danced the wolf parts. Many times, if she wasn't there, I just danced the wolf backup alone. Now, I have to sing. Sometimes my sisters, their children, or my grandsons, Ron Markishtum, Jr., and his brother Daryl, will do the wolf backup, but not very often. Most of the time it's just Arnie doing the main dance and me singing for him. No one blows the whistles anymore, either.[20]

CHAPTER 7

MORE MUSICAL STORIES

TIMES I DANCED THE LEAD
IN THE CHANGING MASK DANCE

Twice when I was young I had to dance the lead part of the Changing Mask Dance for my dad. The first time was at a party for David Hudson, one of the Quileute chiefs. My dad was sick and had no one to do the dance for him, and this was considered a very important party. He asked me to dance for him, and I said, "No, I don't think I better. In the first place it isn't proper for a woman to dance it." Before this, the only way I could dance was to do the background for him with the wolf headdress on. Women were not allowed to touch the masks at all, otherwise. This is a man's job and isn't anything a woman should do. I didn't really want to do that dance—I'd never danced his part before. Phillip David and his wife [Clayoquot elders] were there, so my dad turned around and asked them if they thought it was proper for me to dance. Philip David said I'd have to dance because this was an important party and an important man. So, he came up to me and told me that I should do it because my father couldn't dance. And so I danced the Changing Mask Dance that day. I knew how to do it. I'd watched him enough, but I'd never done it before in my life! He thought I could do it. My dad said, "You've watched me enough; you've got to do it." I said, "I've never practiced, though." He said, "Well, you've watched me enough times. Try it anyway." So I did.

I felt sort of funny being a girl and doing that Changing Mask Dance. I don't think I really enjoyed it. I just kind of felt funny, but yet I was honored to go ahead and do it. Then, afterward, Philip David made me feel really good, because he patted me on the back, and he said, "You done really good. You done really good!" I felt honored to have his consent to do it and then his praise afterward. He was from the place where the masks come from, and he knew the rules over there at Clayoquot. Had it been only my dad who asked me, I probably would have said no. My dad also told me I did good and thanked me for dancing for him afterward.

I think the other time I did this dance was about a year later, over at La Push.

It might have been for Harry Hobucket's party, but I'm not so sure. He was one of the prominent men there. Anyhow, my dad wasn't feeling good again, so he asked me to do it. That time I didn't balk because I'd already done it one time. So my dad just used the feather and led the song; he let the others sing. And I danced. Again I felt kind of honored to be asked to do it. I must have been about fourteen or fifteen then, and those were the only two times I ever danced with those masks.

Every time, after we did the Changing Mask Dance or any of the others that my family owned, we always gave away. It had to be this way. We had shown something that belonged to us and that was very special to us, and then we had to pay important people in the audience for witnessing that we owned it and that we performed it.

PROPER SONG OWNER ETIQUETTE AT A PARTY

When the chorus is singing one of my songs at a party, it's proper for me to stand by the drummer. The audience automatically knows that that song is mine as long as I stand beside the drummer. I am not allowed to do the background dancing, and since I'm a woman, I can't normally do the lead dancing either. I have to hire somebody, some male, to do it for me, and then I have to pay him for dancing for me. I could have my father or brother do it for me if either of them wanted to, and then I wouldn't have to pay them. When my father was alive and the chorus sang one of his songs, he always was the song leader for his own songs. If he wanted to do his own lead dancing, somebody else would have to get up and announce that this was Charlie Swan dancing his such-and-such dance. He couldn't announce it himself. Sometimes, for the Changing Mask Dance, he'd be standing there with his cape on, and he'd start the song. Then at the proper time he'd let Henry St. Clair or Alec Green take over as song leader, and my dad would get out there and dance the main dance.

A man who owned a song could be the lead dancer if he wanted. If he wasn't a dancer, then he at least had to make an appearance and stand there right with the drummer. If he is able to sing, then he'll sing, but if he can't (and there's people that just can't sing), then he'll stand there and drum. If it was his song, he'd want to be there, at least standing by the drummer.

The men owned most of the songs, but the women also had some really nice ones that were their own. It was considered proper in the old days for a woman to be given a song if she came from a chief's family. Mostly they owned love songs and lullabies, but they owned some potlatch songs, too. Women were not allowed to lead songs—they had to "ride in the same canoe" with a relative if they went to a potlatch. Or, if a woman owned a song that she wanted performed, she could ask one of the song leaders to lead it for her.

After I grew older, there was this one woman, Mrs. Peterson, Minnie Peterson,

HELMA'S STORY

who used to lead her own songs. It must have been somewhere around 1930 when she started doing that, using her own feather and leading her songs. The other women simply would not do it. I don't know why she did it; maybe she just had more nerve than any of the other women. Nobody ever said anything to her about it; they just let it be. They didn't seem to object to it, but they all knew that it wasn't proper. There were no other women that did it after her, because all the others had husbands that sang at the parties. So the women wouldn't do it.

Ever since I can remember, the men did all the leading. The women just sang with them. Or if they didn't sing, they danced backup. It seemed like at that time a lot of the older women did more dancing. But anymore, it seems like it's the women now that are singing, because there's no men that are interested. Very few of them are singing now.[1] I don't know why, whether they're just not interested, or whether they're too ashamed to do it. Because I remember when I was young, I was too ashamed to sing. I didn't mind dancing, as long as my dad was there, but I was too ashamed to sing. My dad died without ever knowing that I could sing. I never sang while he was alive.

Nora Barker was really the first woman who sang her own songs. Minnie Peterson led her songs with the feather, but she didn't actually do the lead singing of them. Nora took care of old lady Lizzie Claplanhoo for many years before she died, and Lizzie taught her a lot. After all the old men died, there were a number of years with hardly any parties. Occasionally Hal George, from La Push, came up to Neah Bay and led the songs, but not very often though, because he didn't really know them. Seemed like about 1960 there weren't any parties for a while. Finally, Nora Barker became song leader for the whole village for a number of years, until she died in 1979. Right now no one person is song leader, but usually somebody from each family leads their own songs.[2]

None of the other young people sang in the 1940s and '50s, either. It was just all the old men. But the younger ones all danced. There was no problem with that. They all danced, even the younger boys, even those that were way younger than myself. The old men taught them dancing, but they didn't teach them to sing.

Always in the past it was supposed to be the man who would get up there and do the actual giving away after the singing and dancing is finished. My dad used to do his own. My mother never had to. Sometimes he'd say to her, "Well, this is your turn now, you can give away tonight." And then he'd use my mother's songs which came from my grandfather Anderson. Then afterwards he'd do the giving away for her. But it's just changed recently where the women do everything. It's not supposed to be this way, but recently none of the men have been interested enough, or do not know how to talk Indian. They don't learn how, they don't try. They used to lead the singing, do the main dancing, make the announcements, do the talking in Indian and giving away—they gave away for their wives, mothers, and sisters. But it's not that way anymore. It's the women that do most of this now. We don't have enough men that will get up there and do the speaking. Greig Arnold, Spencer McCarty, or Joe McGimpsey [three Makah men in their thirties and forties] will do this if they are present. As the years go by they learn more, and they are coming more often.

When we women do the giving away now, it's always understood that we're doing it for one of our male relatives. I used to help my late husband a lot of the times. I'd sing one of his songs at a potlatch and he'd dance. Everyone knew it wasn't my song, that it belonged to Wimpy. I was allowed to give away with him if I wanted to, because I was his wife. But legally, that wasn't my song. It was his. Even after his death, I don't own his songs. But I'll always own my father's songs, or my mother's songs. But with a husband's songs, I only *used* them and could ride in the same canoe with him when he was giving away. I did his giving away for him because I was his wife. It was understood that I was handling his money and giving away in his name, for him.

Sometimes I do the same thing for my son Arnie. I'll sing for him, and he'll dance—one of the Swan family's songs. Then Arnie gives me the money, and I give it away in his name. I'm considered the respected mother, and out of respect he asks me to handle it for him.

HOW I STARTED TO SING MY FAMILY-OWNED SONGS

I've been doing all these things for quite a while now, but I never did anything but dance while my dad was alive. When he died in 1958, there was no one to sing for me anymore. The other song leaders were pretty old, and they all died within a few years of my dad. Finally, after quite a few years had passed, I just made up my mind that I *had* to sing. I had to learn all by myself—just by thinking about those songs. I realized that I knew many of my dad's songs, but I never did try to sing them. And then the more I thought about it, I had to go looking for a drum.[3] Wimpy and I had just started going to parties again when I first heard that this white man, Charlie Peck, made drums. I asked Granny Williams, from Quileute, I said, "Where'd you get your drum?" And she said, "Well, I got that from Charlie Peck. Maybe he'll make one for you if you ask him." So I did. I got brave. Usually I won't do anything like that, but I was kind of desperate, and I wanted a drum so bad, so I asked my husband to go with me. He said, "Okay, let's go."

We went down to see the Pecks where they lived near Queets, and I asked Charlie if he would make me a drum. I said, "I'll buy it; I'll pay you anything you want for it." And he said, "No, I don't want to go selling Indian stuff like that." And then he said, "I can't make you a drum unless you sing. Do you sing?" I said, "No." And I didn't sing then. He said, "When you learn how to sing, then I'll make you a drum."

And you know, I never danced anymore. All I've been doing is singing. I always laugh now and say, "Well, Mr. Peck put a hex on me." I couldn't dance anymore after that. I had to do the singing.

He gave me the drum and wouldn't take any money for it, so I had to give him in Indian fashion what I thought it was worth. My youngest son, Mike, must have been about thirteen or fourteen at the time, and he made his first mask—a long, narrow one, and it was just a little lopsided, but he was so proud of it. And Mike said to me, "Why don't you give him this one." So, I said, "Okay, if you insist." He said, "Yes, I'd like you to give it." And Mike was so proud of that mask he made. He really wanted me to give it to them. Now he makes nicer ones. He has become an excellent carver. So, I gave his first carving to Mr. and Mrs. Peck. And then, at the following party, I didn't think that was enough, so I gave them a carved thunderbird, too, which Wimpy made with Mike's help.

HOW I GOT SOME OF OUR SONGS BACK

I've been singing ever since that time (about 1971). Some songs I don't know, but I get around to them anyway. When I first got started singing, my dad came to me two or three times in my dreams. I would get really stuck, trying to remember a song, and it'd bother me for quite a while. I had to sit and concentrate like everything for about three to four days—"What can I do about this, what can I do about that?" Then, he'd finally come to me in my dream and tell me. He came to my rescue by coming back and singing me one or two songs that I was very curious about and that I wanted to know things about. Then after that my memory would start working.

But then sometimes he'd bring me another song or two, as well. He'd say, "This belongs to so-and-so, this belongs to so- and-so." And a lot of times I didn't know who they were—I never heard of them. He always gave me an Indian name: he'd say, "This belongs to so-and-so, and he wants you to sing it, but don't forget to say whose song it was. He wants to be remembered." This is what my dad used to say in my dreams.

I can never ever remember names, Indian names, especially when I didn't know the person, so I never sang what he told me to sing. At that time I wasn't that interested in those other people's songs, so I didn't mark them down and I didn't sing them. All I was interested in was my dad's songs: "I want this song back; I want that song back." He hasn't come to me for many years now, but if it did happen again, I would get up and write down what he told me—then I could remember it. There's a lot of other songs: the Cat Woman, the Frog Dance, the Big Man—that are just lost. There were about three or four Hamatsa dances that I know he used to do that I can't remember. He hasn't come back to give me those. I haven't concentrated like that for a long time. I hope he'll come back if I do that again. It just amazed me when that happened. I just couldn't think of those things I wanted to know, and I kept thinking, "What am I going to do?" I kept thinking, "Oh, I wished I'd listened to my dad more, I wished I'd paid more attention!" And then he came! In Indian he used to call me *he·tá·x̌*, "daughter." "Well, daughter," he said to me in my dream, "I came back to tell you what you wanted to know, and here's your song."

So, I was very lucky to get my songs back, and I've been singing them a long time now. Then I had to start getting my husband's songs back for him. When I married Wimpy, he didn't know any of his songs. Odelia Hunter, his grandmother, came from Seattle, where she lived for many years, to sing for us at our wedding. They didn't have all of their family songs then, either, and it wasn't until about eight or ten years after I was married to him that I started looking for their family songs. I found some of them, and they finally got them back. Every time they had a party here, I'd listen to all the songs that were sung. And then sometimes I'd remember the Hunter songs. Then one time some of our senior citizens went to Washington, D.C., and they came back with some recordings. One of them on the recording was Wimpy's grandfather's song, and they hadn't been able to catch up with it until then. I think I picked up two of his songs from those recordings that night.

Then Wimpy started getting interested. His grandfather Jim Hunter also had a very important Grizzly Bear Dance song, too, that you perform only during a wedding ceremony, an engagement party, or a birthday party. It isn't used for anything else and is only for his immediate family. Odelia, his stepgrandmother, had sold all the masks, the curtain, everything. So they really had nothing to start out with when Wimpy got interested. He wanted to find out about the Bear Dance, which we did. He made some masks and began getting some of his things back. I bought a coverall pattern, and out of that, I ended up making him a bear suit. He helped make the bear head. We got this fur-like material, and I sewed it up. Then he was able to use the new bear costume and mask and dance his old inherited Grizzly Bear Dance at some of his sisters' children's weddings. It was quite a lot of work to get all these things back, but we gradually did it.

TEACHING MY CHILDREN

With my own family's things, I have the big job of teaching them to my children and then turning it all over to them. Arnie, my oldest boy, used to listen to my dad a lot when he was still alive. Arnie listened when my dad talked to us and told us how to be and how not to be. When my mother was still alive and here with us in Neah Bay, he'd talk to her about things he wanted to know. Now, he talks to me. It seems to come natural to him, I guess, because he talks just like my dad used to talk when we were making plans for a party. When he was young, we lived with my mom and dad, off and on, so I imagine he must have learned a lot from them. My dad taught him to dance the Changing Mask Dance, which he likes to dance.

My daughter Babe [Lina Mae] is a few years younger than Arnie, and I don't think she sat down and listened too much to my dad. Neither of them learned to talk Indian, but somehow Arnie seems to have learned more than Babe. The summer of 1973 was the first time I sat Babe down and told her what she should tell her children. I've spent time talking to her and taped some of the songs for her. But she does know the songs, I have to give her credit for that. She'll say, "Tape this for me, tape that for me." I'm going to do some new taping for her. She always danced with the group on Makah Day ever since she was little, so she got to know the songs that way.

When I was a kid my dad used to make us sit down and listen to him, and sometimes I used to be kind of bitter about it. I'd think to myself, "Well! Why should I sit down there and listen to all that stuff? I already listened to it before." And then, maybe I had other things on my mind at that time, and I didn't want to listen, and I had things to do. So I decided to talk to my children and in a roundabout way make them ask about a few things, and then I'd start telling them. Otherwise, if I didn't do that, I know they'd feel like I did when I was young. So, I just made up my mind I'm just going to make them ask me a question. And I'd carry on the conversation to where they'd have to ask the question. Then I'd sit down and say, "Well, do you have anything to do? Do you have to go anywhere right now?" If they said no, then they'd have to sit down and listen to what I had to tell them about the question they asked. Sometimes when Babe and I came home together for lunch or for coffee, she'd bring up a topic: "Why did so-and-so do this or do that? I thought they weren't supposed to do this at that time." Then we would start our conversation. I felt like I didn't want to approach her unless she asked me a question, but when she did, then I'd start telling her how they used to do things.

I've talked to my youngest boy, Mike, quite a few times. He was born the year my dad died, so I've had to teach him whatever he's learned. I've been trying to do for him what my dad did for Arnie. Mike hasn't been going to too many parties, so I've had to sit him down more than either of the other two children and talk to him.

He used to be a real good dancer, and he liked to dance. I taught him how. When he was ten years old, we were living in Tacoma—Wimpy was in school there—but we came home to Neah Bay for one month of summer vacation. Mike practiced the Group Dances with the other kids for Makah Day that summer. He never missed a day of practice. Each day when he showed up to dance, his name got put down on the list. Afterwards, those kids that never missed a day of Indian dancing, well, they got paid for it. He didn't know he was going to get paid; he wasn't expecting any pay at all. We left Neah Bay and returned to Tacoma, and one day he got a letter in the mail with a twenty-dollar check in it. He was the proudest kid you ever saw. He brought it to school and showed all the kids. "This is the first check I ever, ever got," he said. He was really proud of it.

That was the only time that Nora Barker ever complimented me on one of my kids dancing like that. She said, "You can really tell that he comes from the Swan family. He really knows how to dance! And he knew immediately how to dance," she said. "He's a real good dancer!" He was dancing the Whale and Wolf Dance that time, and I took his picture, [now lost]. It's been many years now since he's danced.

All three of my children have had training as dancers, but none of them have ever sung. Right now, Arnie is the only one who still dances. He's the one who learned most from my father, and he inherited all of my father's things. My father's name was Yelák'ub, and that's the name that I gave Arnie. Along with this name he received all of Chief Sitkeenum's things, because those were given by Annie to my dad.[4]

Mike also wanted the name "Yelák'ub," but he can't have it because that name has to go to the oldest son, as long as he is responsible and does justice to the name. So at first, Mike thought he would take the name "Atliu," the name of Sitkeenum's son, who was a carver. Later, Mike decided he didn't want a name from the Canadian side of the family but would rather have one from the American side. Therefore, I gave him the name "Dashúk," at a party I gave in Neah Bay in 1987. "Dashúk" means "Strong" in Makah, and this was the name of Mike's great-great-great-grandfather from the Anderson side of the family. Dashúk was a whaler. This part of the family was from Ozette. Along with that name he will inherit the Anderson family songs and things. He's making a copy of the Anderson family curtain, himself. Most of the Anderson names have already been given to other relatives in the Anderson line, but the chiefly belongings will go to him because he is the oldest male in that line.

We were always supposed to talk to our children and teach them their family history. All the older relatives are supposed to help with this so the young ones really know where they come from. Our younger generation in Neah Bay knows very little now. All they know is what they hear from one person, and everything just gets mixed up that way, because a lot of the ones who are telling them now were not told very much when they were young. Many of the older people who are telling them now never went to potlatch parties when they were young, never attended Indian doings. Some of them were drinking, some lived away from the reservation for many years, some married white men or women and didn't care about Indian customs, some joined the Christian church and were taught to stay away from Indian ceremonies. Now when some of those people get old, they suddenly want to become Indian again and to teach their children and grandchildren, but they weren't around very much during all those years to learn very much, so they don't really know very much to teach them. There are some people around who did take part, and do know, but not very many. So, everything's getting pretty mixed up now.

SWAN FAMILY SONG OWNERSHIP

Various people from Neah Bay have tried to claim my father's songs at different times, and they are not related to my father's mother at all. It is through her line, from Chief Sitkeenum to Annie Williams to my father, Charlie Swan, that we are entitled to certain songs. Those songs do not come from Chief Peter Brown and his son, Chestoke Peterson, who are my father's father's relatives. My dad always used to say, "Don't fight for anything, because it will take care of itself later, when the time is right." There's not much you can do anyway, but you *can* have a party and have this explained, where the song came from. That's the only way you can fight for it; you have your *own* party and have somebody come and witness for you. Never do this at someone else's party. It sets a bad example to fight over songs at somebody else's party.

I think what we have to do now is get the old Canadian chiefs and historians to come down and ask them to please straighten out this song ownership business. They'd have to get up and tell how these songs were given, why they were given, and how they should be taken care of. I remember Nora Barker, our old song leader, used to say, "These songs are family songs. So let's all use them. Let's not fight, let's all have the right to use them." But this just can't be. It's just not our Indian way that we should use each other's songs whenever we want. My father's songs are my father's songs, and they're not for her to use because she's not from my father's family. We don't even claim ownership of the songs of our in-laws. They're not part of our family; we don't own their things, and they don't own ours. My late husband Wimpy's songs belonged to him and now belong to his mother's family, not to me. In the same way, his family will never own any of the Swan family songs. Wimpy and I had no children together, so there is no one who could inherit both my family songs and his family songs.

HOW I PROPERLY RECEIVED AND PAID FOR A NEW SONG—1981 AND 1983 POTLATCHES

Prominent people still do give songs to each other sometimes. In 1981, someone was having a potlatch party in Neah Bay—I think it might have been Champ McCarty, but I'm not so sure—and at that party Kelly Peters, an elder from Nitinat, B.C., got up and said we were related and that he wanted to give me a song. I was rather surprised because we've never been on that much of a friendly basis, but my dad always taught me "Don't say no. You can't say no when someone wants to give you a song." He taught me what to do whenever anything like that happened. So I did what I was supposed to do that night when he gave me the song. Kelly Peters got up and sang this song at the party, and then he announced that he was giving it to me. Then I stood up and had Ed Claplanhoo come and interpret for me. I called up Mr. and Mrs. Atleo from Ahouset, and Minerva Claplanhoo and two of her daughters from Neah Bay, and had them come and stand and witness. Ed interpreted for me and said that I accepted that song and that I would take care of it and that I'd let them know when I would have the party later on. (They all knew I meant the potlatch party where I would pay Kelly for giving me his song.) Then I paid them each a dollar apiece for witnessing that Kelly Peters sang that song, gave it to me, and that I accepted it.

The song he gave me is a Wolf Dance song. It's one I don't know yet, so I'm going to have to learn it. I'll learn it from a tape. I knew that when I was ready, I would have a party to pay for my song. At the time when I accepted the song, my grandson Daryl Markishtum was just going into the service, and I thought that it would be a good time to have a party for him, when he came home on leave. Then I'd pay for my song during the party I'd give when he was home from the service, and at the same time I'd give him the name "Dashúk," from my great-great-grandfather on the Anderson side. But it ended up that he only had a four-day pass for that time, so he just came home and went back. I couldn't have the party, and I never gave him the name "Dashúk." Instead, later, I gave him another name, "Willub."

So, I decided to have this party on June 18, 1983. Daryl couldn't be there, so I had it as a birthday party for my son Arnie instead. I invited Kelly Peters and all the Nitinats, and I paid him for giving me his song. I wanted to invite all the tribes from farther up north, but I'd have had to pay each of them twenty dollars while I'm there inviting them, and then twenty dollars after they get here, and then their expenses to come across and go back again. I just couldn't afford that at that time. So I just asked the Nitinats, cause that's where Kelly Peters was from, and then I invited a few people that live in Victoria. Then they in turn can just tell the rest of their people what happened. This wasn't really the proper way to do it, but I just felt that that was about all I could afford. I wouldn't feel right either if I invited them all, like I wanted to do, and then didn't give them as much as I felt I should. But I did invite the Queets and Hohs and of course the Makahs. I could just pay them for witnessing, I didn't have to pay their travel expenses.

It took quite a while to prepare everything and get everything organized in order to put on that party. I had to counsel with my family, with my four sisters. We talked and decided what dances we would each do. Joy and Dicie and their daughters decided to do the Grizzly Bear dances, Arnie would do the Changing Mask Dance, Dolores and her daughter would do their Wolf Dance, I would sing and drum for them. I had to ask Ed Claplanhoo to be my announcer.

Mike didn't get to finish the copy of our family curtain that he'd been painting, so I couldn't use it. Mike's friend Billy Cunningham did a design for the invitations, which I had printed and sent out. Then, for almost a year before, I had been buying lots of glasses, mugs, blankets, shawls, clothes baskets, dish pans, and added the things you brought to give away as gifts.[5] So, gradually it all came together, but there's always a lot of work to do to get ready for a party. The gifts I give away have to be pretty good stuff; it can't be something that a person won't care for.

Fig. 29. Small thunderbird headgear carved in 1988 by Mike Hunter, Helma's youngest son. *Photograph by Linda J. Goodman.*

Fig. 30. Oliver Ward, Jr., (Wimpy) wearing a bear costume made by wife, Helma, performs his family's Grizzly Bear Dance at a potlatch in Neah Bay, circa 1975. *Photograph courtesy of Helma Swan.*

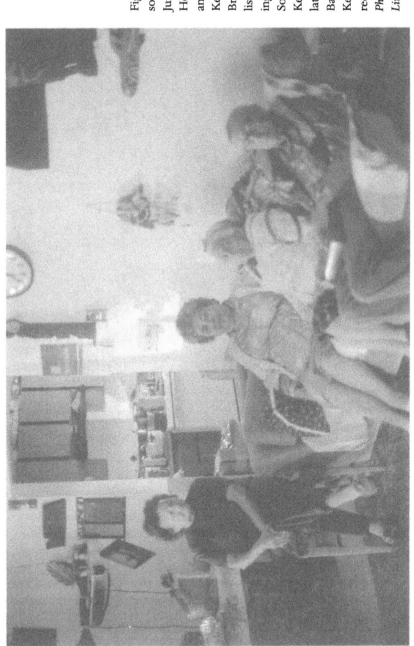

Fig. 31. Learning a new song at Helma's house, June 19, 1983. Left to right: Helma Swan, Ethyl Sport and her parents, Effie and Kelly Peters, from Nitinat, British Columbia. All are listening to a tape recording of the Wolf Dance Song given officially by Kelly to Helma at a potlatch she hosted in Neah Bay on the previous day. Kelly holds the tape recorder on his knees. *Photograph by Linda J. Goodman.*

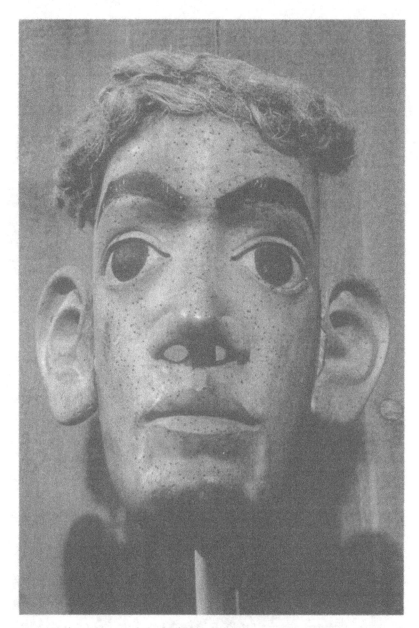

Fig. 32. "White Man Mask," which formerly belonged to Chief Cedakanim of Clayoquot, was given by his granddaughter, Annie Atliu Williams, to Charlie Swan at the potlatch in 1930 when she made him a chief. (The mask is now at home in the Denver Art Museum, and Helma checks on this mask whenever she is in Denver.) The intervening history and transfer from private family to museum is unknown. (Bill Holm [personal communication 1998] stated that this mask belonged at one time to David Storie of Kirkland, Washington, who later sold it to the Denver Art Museum). *Photographed in 1980 by Robin Wright; courtesy of the Denver Art Museum (1966.323).*

I had a lot of decisions to make about money and gifts. I had to decide how much I was going to pay Kelly Peters for the song he gave me, and then put aside that much. Depending on the kind of song, I would normally pay anywhere from two hundred to five hundred dollars, plus a lot of gifts. If it's a *very* special song, I might pay more than this. Then, I have to give the men blankets, each wife a shawl. I have to give something like this to his whole family. Also, I have to pay his family's expenses for coming across. Then, all the other heads—I have to give them five dollars for witnessing and then telling the other tribes what they saw. I have to pay one dollar apiece plus lots of gifts to everyone else who witnesses. So, all in all it costs a lot to put on a potlatch to pay for a new song properly. But this is the correct way to do it.

I got two people, Wayne and Queen Ward, lined up to do the cooking for me. I paid him fifty dollars and a blanket as head cook, and she got forty dollars and gifts for being his main assistant. The menu included braised beef, mashed potatoes, baked beans, salad, canned fruit, bread, coffee, juice, and dessert. Since the fishing was good, Wimpy caught enough silver salmon, and Arnie kippered them, and we served them with the meal. We served somewhere around 350 people. Then later in the evening I had to arrange to serve sandwiches because people get hungry sitting there so long. The party started about 2:00 P.M. and ended about 10:15 P.M. So everyone ate a big meal at 2:00 P.M. and then a small one about 7:00 P.M., when I had egg salad sandwiches and clam chowder served. The cooks made these in advance. Then I also had watermelon and lots of coffee.

Before we started the first meal, it was up to me to lead two Dinner songs that my dad got from Annie (see song 2, chapter 10 for one of these songs). The reason the Makah have these Dinner songs is mostly to thank the people who are giving the party, because everyone knows that it takes so much time to prepare a great big feast; it isn't easy. They realize it's hard to get started and that you have to know whether you've done the right thing or the wrong thing. So we sing these songs in order to give thanks to the people who are working putting this party together, and of course our people believe in God, too, so this is our way of also thanking the creator for what's being prepared and what was given to them in the way of worldly goods and food.

After the meal was finished, the Quileutes sang and danced and gave away; then the Makah did the same, followed by the Nitinats. Kelly Peters, from Nitinat, sang the Wolf Dance song he was giving me, and then it was announced that I was paying him for it, and that now that song was mine to sing whenever I wanted. By doing all this publicly, it was official that I legitimately owned that song and had paid for it properly. All the audience witnessed this. Since I was hosting this party, our family performed and gave away last. We sang and danced a lot of songs, since my sisters Dallie, Bessie, Joy, and Dicie and some of their kids were there and wanted to give away, too. We all gave away a great many gifts and lots of money to special guests and witnesses and to the audience in general. We ended out singing a few *T'abáa* songs, just for fun, before everyone went home.

DUTIES OF SONG LEADERS

A number of different people led their family's songs at our 1983 potlatch. We've seen a lot of changes in this area, too, since I was young. The song leaders used to have more to do and used to be more important in the days when my dad was alive. Because they sang so much then, the song leaders knew every song, memorized every one of them. They led all the singing at the potlatches, and they also cued the dancers.

One song leader would start the song; this would usually have been either Jack LaChester or Alec Green. Every once in a while my dad would start his own song, but most generally Jack or Alec would start the song. When you start singing, you sing the first verse alone. You don't use a drum until after you finish the first verse. Then you start drumming, sing the same thing again with the chorus this time.

When my dad would start the song, he'd sing the first verse through once, then the chorus would all sing the same thing again. Then he would holler the word *q'abá·tšʔaⅩ'*, and that means "Sing the part with the Indian words!" Then he'll holler out those words, and right after he finishes, he uses his feather fan to signal the chorus of singers. He sends his feather forward (straight out in front of him), and then they start singing the words he just finished hollering. He uses that feather to keep time. When the drumming starts, that's when the dancer begins to go. He spins counterclockwise, first, and then goes out. Sometimes there's two song leaders working together. One will start the song and do the drumming, and another one will lead with the feather. At that time there were only three people in town who would use the feathers: Jim Hunter, my dad, and Jongie Claplanhoo. Then once in a while, Jongie's sister Minnie Peterson used to do that too. There were several who could start the singing: Jack LaChester and Alec Green, as I already mentioned; Francis Green, Alec's father; Dick Williams; Henry St. Clair; and now and then, Henry's father, Young Doctor; and my own dad. These were the song leaders at the time I was growing up. Jack and Alec were the ones who started most of the songs, though. At that time, there were about four or five of them that had really *big, booming* voices. They could just carry it a mile if they had to. Those were real, real good voices then—those big, booming bass voices! I wish we had had recorders then. . . . Now the voices are getting higher and higher, instead of lower, like the bass voices that the older people had when I was little. In those days, anyone could ask that group of men to sing for them because they knew all the songs.

It is a chore to start the song. The one who starts it usually sings it twice. Then he starts to get tired because it sort of takes your breath away when you're singing. So then the other song leader has to catch it. So, if Jack had started the song, he'd sing for a while, and then maybe he'd call out, *"Súʔap,"* which means "You take the song." This means that he's tired now and that my dad or one of the other song leaders has to catch the rest of the song and carry on using his feather, leading the chorus, and cuing the dancers until the song is finished. It takes an awful lot out of you when you start a song. You really need a backup singer to finish singing the song for you. That's what I don't have today. There's nobody to back up for me. So I have to sing the song all the way through by myself, and it's hard.

Back in the days when my father was a song leader, they had a whole bunch of singers that sang in the chorus. They had my grandfather, my grandmother, Mr. and Mrs. Skyler Colfax, old man Francis Green, the two Hunters and their wives, Alec Green and his wife, Mr. and Mrs. Jerry McCarty, Mr. and Mrs. Henry St. Clair, Mrs. and Mrs. Young Doctor, and just almost everyone sang then, or someone from every family. At that time there would be twenty or thirty singers in the chorus, and they knew everybody's songs. They were allowed to sing those songs as long as the owner was there. They sang for the owner.

By about 1975, things had really changed. Nobody used the feather any more. All the old singers were gone, and Nora Barker was the main song leader. She used her drum after she started the song, but no one used the feathers. At that time there were only about eight singers: Isabel Ides, Ruth Claplanhoo, Meredith Parker, Nora Barker, myself, Ethyl Claplanhoo, Walter Green, and Ham Green. That was about the size of the singers then.

Today, some of those people have died, and the group is much different. The young ones don't have the Makah tongue; they don't know the language but are trying to sing it. It comes out sounding very different.

GROUP DANCES PERFORMED AT PARTIES IN THE 1920s

Back in the 1920s when I used to go to the parties with my dad, these ceremonies used to be a little different than they are now. The regular people who didn't have songs—they were just the spectators. They'd all come into the hall first and get seated. Some of the commoners used to dance, though, too. We had the Group Dance[6] that included everybody—anybody who wanted to dance. So those that wanted to dance would come into the hall and bring their own dishes for the feast, set them down at the place where they wanted to sit, then sit down for a little while and wait for everybody else to come. Then they'd all get up and leave, but they'd leave their stuff where they were going to sit later. Then away they'd go and gather at somebody's house that was closest to wherever the party was. They had to bring all their dance gear and leave it at the house there. They got ready to do the Group Dances, and there were a lot of them to choose from: the Fan Dance, Spear Dance, Horse Dance, Sailor Dance, Paddle Dance, Plains Dance, and a lot more.

When the dancers were ready, they'd go together in a bunch over to the hall, and they'd be talking with their relatives and friends. Half of the singers were already in the hall, and they knew what dances were going to be done in what order. When the dancers got to the hall, they'd pound on the door, and you'd hear them; then after they made a lot of noise on the door they'd all holler "Huuuii" two or three times and hit the side of the building. Everybody would just holler. Then the door would open, and the man with the shell rattle would come in first, followed by the other half of the singers. All would stop in one spot and yell, "Huuuii," and then the singers would start singing, and the dancers would come in one at a time. They would file in, one after the other, spaced just so far apart, until everybody was in, and then the door would close.[7] Then they'd begin doing their Group Dances.

Group Dance Costumes

When I was little, the only time I saw them wear costumes was when the group danced the Sailor Dance. It was kind of cute. They all had white fans, and they'd come in dancing with their hands behind their backs. They wore white middy blouses—the ladies wore short-sleeved ones and the men long-sleeved shirts. They all had sailor hats, and the ladies wore black skirts, and the men wore black pants. Then they all had the white fans. That's the only costume I ever saw anybody wear for the Group Dance. The ladies used to wear black shawls, *li·šal,* but other than that they just didn't wear costumes for any of those group dances, except that tree limb one.

When they would dance what we now call the Plains Indian Dance or War Dance,[8] they used tree limbs and made a skirt out of them. They'd just go off into the woods and pick hemlock limbs and make skirts out of them, fix them, and tie them together. That's why they had to bring them to someone else's house. Of course, they'd make a fresh one every time they danced, when they were going to do that type of dancing. Then they'd make a headband out of the same thing, with little limbs sticking out in the front. And when they went to that house to get dressed, that's what they had to put on and tie on, and then they'd come into the hall wearing them. They'd do this for the entrance dance. I've never seen them do that anymore since I was pretty little.[9]

Now they all wear red and black costumes when they do Group Dances. After the government turned us loose and we had our first Makah Day in 1926, then we started wearing costumes. We never did before. From that time on, the Makah colors began to be black and red. They wore red Indian dresses with black fringes. This was different, however, from the family dances, where the lead dancers always wore the proper costumes and masks or headgears that went with the dance, and the backup always wore dance shawls.

After the group dancers were all through, then they would just disband. They'd take off everything they had and sit down where they were to begin with. Then they'd sit and watch the family dances that came next—the main part of the party.

And then when the whole party ended, everyone would bring their gear to their own homes and have it ready for the next party.

THE CORRECT ORDER FOR SINGING AND GIVING AWAY IN NEAH BAY

There used to be a correct order for Neah Bay families to sing and give away at parties. Minnie Peterson figured she should be first because she was married to Chestoke Peterson, Chief Peter Brown's son. When Chestoke disappeared or died, Minnie took over in his place. Then after her was her brother Jongie Claplanhoo—he came second. Then Jim Hunter was made a chief before my dad, so he came third. He was made a chief in Clayoquot, the same as my dad, except earlier. And then my dad was made a chief across there, so he came fourth. Jerry McCarty, the Wyaatch chief, came fifth. We could have fought for another position, a higher up position, I guess, but my dad was like he was. He never liked arguments, so he just stayed where he was [in the ranking of the chiefly families]. My dad would always tell us, "Just wait for them" (meaning those who came before us); he'd tell us, "Just wait for them, don't try to make any fuss. Just come in where you're supposed to come in." So we always did. Then the rest of the people (the others in the village) could do what they wanted to do, whoever came next. But always these five people came first. And there was never, never any argument. They knew where to come in when it was their turn.

Today it still stands the same as it used to be a long time ago, except now there's other people crowding in. How it should run now, is that Helen Peterson, Chestoke and Minnie Peterson's last living child, always goes first. Then next is Wilbur Claplanhoo, Jongie Claplanhoo's son. Then comes Wimpy (Oliver Ward, Jr.), since he's Jim Hunter's oldest grandson. Fourth comes me or my son Arnie, who carry on in my father Charlie Swan's place. Now and then Hildred McCarty Ides will sing one of her father Jerry McCarty's songs fifth. Then after that, it remains open for anyone else who wants to, to sing and give away, but it should always be these five first.[10]

SOME RECENT CHANGES SEEN AT THE PARTIES

A number of things have changed at the parties now. When I was young and going to potlatches with my father, everybody joined in the singing or the dancing, or at least having the good feelings that go along with it. But nowadays, if someone comes to a party and they don't care for the person who's giving it or who's singing at that time, they're just going to sit, and they're not going to get up and join in. Before, you joined in no matter what your feelings were, but it's gotten so different now that a lot of them won't get up and dance at all. One time we came in to a party late, and they were already singing. I had a blanket over my arm, so I just put it on, and I stood there and started dancing, and so my cousin Meredith Parker saw me, and she came over and danced with me. That's the way things should be and always were in the past, but now you find so much hard feeling—everybody's scared of somebody else beating them out. You don't want to feel like that, because if you've got a song, nobody's going to be able to beat you out of your own song. It's your own song, you can't be scared! But anymore, they all feel like that. Over the last number of years, they've been giving away songs that belong to other people, so no wonder everyone's scared.

Then there's another thing that's started happening pretty recently. Some of the white wives of Indian men are starting to dance at the parties here and in Canada. They don't really have a right to dance because they aren't Makah, but then I was surprised one time to hear some of these young Makah kids saying they were mad because a white person was standing out there doing an Indian dance when she wasn't even an Indian. Then some of the Canadians came across—this was in about 1974—and they just laughed about the white wives dancing. Then in 1975, we went across to a party over there, and one of those families has a daughter-in-law blonder than those in Neah Bay. She had a headband on and was dancing, too. I just had to chuckle about this because they thought it was outrageous for us to have this white woman dancing, and then we go over there about a year later, and they have their daughter-in-law dancing, and she's blonder than anyone here. Nobody says anything about it. They just let her do it. I don't have anything to say about it because times are changing. I don't know. . . .

PERFORMING NON-INDIAN MUSIC

I used to take part in performing white music when I was a young person. When I was at the Tulalip Boarding School, we had a forty-piece harmonica band. I learned how to play the harmonica, and I was in it. All the kids that played in it were girls; there weren't any boys. There was this girl named Blanche Bob, from La Conner, and she knew how to play the harmonica. For a while she had us over every evening, learning how to blow on them, where to put our fingers—we practiced until we got our part right. Pretty soon we got to know how to blow in it, so we only practiced once a week. Then after a while, we didn't have to practice because we had it down pretty good.

The harmonica band had to be over at the school whenever there was something going on there. One of the company officers[11] used to march us up to the school building where we had all our programs. We got all lined up in the auditorium, and when it was time for the companies to start marching in, then we'd start playing. Then those kids would be just a-trudging along, until they got to their seats. So it was kind of fun. When it was dance time, we had to furnish all the music, too.

I never got to dance. None of us did. Nobody seemed to mind it. We just went on ahead, enjoyed it just like the rest of them. I played the alto part; then there was also the bass and the melody. So we did pretty good.

None of us learned to read music. We didn't have to learn. I was kind of regretting that we didn't have to, either, because I really didn't know anything about it. But they never taught us.

Then there were a couple of years in there, when I was about seventeen to nineteen, when I did a lot of singing of non-Indian songs. My friend Lavern Ulmer and I used to go over to the hop fields near Tacoma just for entertainment. A lot of people went there to work, but we just went for entertainment, because there was nothing to do here in Neah Bay. So, we'd go to the hop fields, and we'd pick just so much a day, and then the rest of the day we'd just be loafing around, running around from one town to the other, just looking for excitement, like any kid, you know.

Come weekends they'd have these modern dances at a place called Adoma Park in Tacoma. All the Indians used to gather there. Lavern and I used to make it a point to go there every Saturday night to dance. We used to be able to get into any of the dances because my friend was a spunky girl. She'd tell Mr. Applegate, the man who ran the place, that we'd sing one or two numbers if he'd let us in for free. So he would, and we'd sing a couple of numbers. He got to knowing us and liking us, so he always let us in like this. Lavern was a goofy girl, always doing crazy things. We used to get into those dances free because she knew how to talk and I didn't. I'd never say much. But she was always a mischievous one and knew how to talk. So we'd get in without having to have an escort. We didn't want to have any boyfriends because we didn't really want to go steady. Since we were more or less alone when we got in there, we could choose to dance with anybody we wanted. That was kind of fun. It was mostly Indians at those dances, only a few white people.

The band was all white; I never did ask who they were, but the same ones were there every week. Lavern and I used to sing some of the popular songs that came out about then. We sang "Sweet Leilani," "White Christmas," "Rosetta," and lots of others, but I can't think of them anymore. I don't think we ever sang more than two songs. Mr. Applegate used to be satisfied with two each week. Then Indian people who were there kind of liked our songs, looked forward to hearing us every week.

We never practiced before we'd go there, but we used to sing every day. No matter where we were, we'd be singing. Just kept singing every day—white songs, not Indian songs. We used to sing in the hop fields; some of the guys would come over and visit us and pick hops while they were listening to us. We'd get a full day's picking done like that.

We used to have our own band in Neah Bay, too, and they'd go and play for dances after ball games. Sometimes we'd go along. At that time the Makahs were kind of baseball-minded. They weren't like they are today. They're all basketball now. We had pretty good baseball teams then, so wherever they went, we went right along. Then they'd have dances. We'd go to La Push or down to Rialto Beach or to Forks. One time we went clear to White Swan (near Yakima) with them. And we used to do the same thing over there—sing to get in, cause we didn't want to go in with any special boyfriend. We used to like to get around. So it was easier not to have one when you got around like that. You could just pick anybody you wanted.

We had a good band in those days, made up of Neah Bay fellows. They're all gone now. There was Buster Wanderhart, used to play the trumpet; Oliver Hunter, played saxophone and banjo. Then Bill DePoe or Leo Hunter used to play the piano; Bill also played the clarinet. Reg DePoe played sax; so did Pat Wilkie Sr. Charles DePoe played both sax and trumpet. Then Lyle Hunter used to play banjo or guitar, and Oliver Ward Sr. played the drums. They were a real good jazz band. There's nothing like that in Neah Bay now. They all learned to play when they were in school. They were pretty good guys, really played pretty good jazz in all the towns in the area. They played for the dance every weekend in Neah Bay unless they were playing somewhere else. Then when they went out of town, we used to follow them.

So we used to enjoy doing the singing with those bands. It was a lot of fun for us. We didn't really think of going into it for a career or anything, but we thought it was fun, and did it just to get into the dance. That way we didn't have to spend any money.

We sang those popular songs a lot, but we never did sing Indian songs. My dad never did try to teach us. He used to make us listen, though. We listened! I sang white songs when I was a teenager, but I never sang Indian songs until I was in my forties. Now it's really the Indian songs that I love to sing.

CHAPTER 8

THE TIME
THEY MADE
MY FATHER
A CHIEF

I n 1930 when I was about twelve years old, my grandaunt Annie Williams from Clayoquot, B.C., made my dad, Charlie Swan, a chief. I was there for the whole thing, at least as much as they would let a twelve-year-old see.

PREPARATIONS AND ARRIVAL IN CLAYOQUOT, B.C.

One time when Annie was in Neah Bay, she talked to my dad and told him that she wanted him to come across[1] with the family and to bring some chiefs or other prominent people to witness the puberty party she was giving for Clothilda Frank, another grandniece. My father first asked Jim Hunter, who was one of the prominent men around here, because he was a full-blooded Clayoquot Indian. He was not a Makah, but he was adopted Makah. Because he was well-known in Canada, my father wanted to bring him there with us, but he couldn't go at that time. He was our mailman here and had to run his boat, called the *Uncle Jim*, and he couldn't get anyone to take his place, so he had to stay. Then my father asked Joe Pullen and his wife, who were Quileutes from La Push. He was the Number One chief of the Quileutes at that time.

My dad didn't know what Annie was going to do when he got to Clayoquot. He didn't know that he was going to be made a chief during this time. However, before we went over there, Annie came to Neah Bay and said she was giving a party, and asked him to bring a lot of groceries with him when he came. She gave him a list. He had to help out his first cousin Francis Frank, who was Clothilda's father. My dad bought just enough to feed the whole tribe one meal. He was under obligation to do this—Annie relied on him like a son and asked for his help in feeding the tribe this meal. He got the food from the store in Neah Bay—that was Washburn's store by then. It was Harry Washburn's; this was the second generation down. Dad bought a whole case of canned corned beef (these were large cans, twice the size they are today); two hundred pounds of potatoes, ten cases of oranges, ten cases of apples, as well as one hundred pounds of sugar and fifty pounds of flour. There wasn't so much trouble with the customs then, like there is now. You'd just take it in the boat and go. So my dad furnished this food for the first meal because Francis Frank was his relative and Annie asked him to do this.

We went on the *Princess Moqúinna,* a big ocean liner, Canadian. It took us two days to get there from Victoria, B.C., where we had stopped and picked up even more groceries. We spent the night in Port Alberni—tied up there overnight taking off freight. Next day we ended up over in Tofino. Then we had to catch a little fishing boat to go over to Clayoquot Island. When we got there, we couldn't get off the boat for an hour and a half.

We couldn't touch the beach because it belonged to a woman named Mary Jackson, and she wasn't home when we got there. This beach was hers, and everybody had to respect her and not get off the boat until she came home. Whoever came to visit Clayoquot Island had to come to her house first and visit with her. Since she owned the beach, she had to give permission for everyone to come ashore, and then she had to welcome us. This was her *tupáat.* We sat in the boat and waited for her till she came. So those that felt like singing sat together and sang. They told stories, sang a little, told stories again, sang some more until she finally came. After she got home, we finally got off the boat. She hadn't been home because she didn't have anything to feed us, and she had to row over to Tofino to get what she needed from the store there.

Mary Jackson didn't have to throw a big party, but what she did was go across and get boxes and boxes of apples, enough for all the visitors plus the chiefs. We thought she was going to feed us when we got there, because we were hungry. She rolled out her mats on the floor, cattail mats, about six feet long and three or four feet wide. She had chairs, but we didn't sit on them; they'd been removed. We sat on mats on the floor like they did a long time ago. Then after we sat down, she unrolled another mat which was about eighteen inches wide, purposely for eating on. It was kept clean and like a tablecloth—that was all it was used for. Then she came in with her men relatives who were carrying boxes of apples. They poured a half a box of apples in front of each one of us. We had to at least take a bite of one apple and swallow it before we could leave the house, and the rest we could take with us. Apples meant a lot to the Canadians because they were something sweet. This was the first fruit the whites brought, and the Indians enjoyed it because it was sweet and it was something great to them. Then, apples were given to honored guests at potlatches. Even today apples are still given as gifts.

She watched us very carefully to make sure we all had taken one bite, and then she said, "You're free to go now." Those apples were all she had, and that was all she had to do. That was her *tupáat.* After we left there, we were free to go to our relatives' houses or wherever we wanted to go. We went to my aunt Annie's home, and we stayed there.

THE FIRST FEAST IN CLAYOQUOT

Joe Pullen, the Quileute chief, didn't know their ways of inviting up there. When we got to Annie's house, she said, "I'm not going to feed you; I didn't cook anything because now you are invited to go to a home here." We were invited to Mú·chi·nik's house.[2] Joe Pullen, the Quileute chief, not knowing their ways, said, "I'm going to eat before I go; I'm not sitting down just to apples. I'm hungry!" By this time he was really getting hungry. I was hungry too, but my momma wouldn't let me eat. My grandaunt wouldn't let me eat either. She said, "Just go ahead and be hungry." Joe ate. My aunt told him, "Don't eat!" but he did anyway. Annie didn't explain why he shouldn't eat; I guess she just took it for granted that he would know. I didn't know why, either. Well, we got there, and this was Mú·chi·nik's *tupáat*—to be the first one to feed the visitors. He had everything you could think of on the table—the main course, vegetables, the drink, the cakes, the pies. The tables were loaded! And Joe sat there, and he just *looked* . . . you could just see his face drop, because this was really a meal! There was meat and fish there, just everything you could think of.

HOW A CHIEF WAS PROPERLY INVITED TO A CEREMONY

Before we went to Mú·chi·nik's, they sent a man with a staff to my grandaunt's house. He came in with this staff, and he was holding it with both hands. He kept talking. He was saying in Indian, "I came *here* to *invite* you," and he'd hit the floor quite a bit. "You are invited to go to this man's house, whose name is Mú·chi·nik, and you are to come over there and spend the evening doing what you want to do, but you're invited to go *right now*," and he'd hit the floor with his staff. He was going around and around the stick. He never cracked a smile, and he talked very loud, almost hollered at the top of his voice, saying the same thing over and over. That was his *tupáat*. His name was Yášxen. We used to call him Yášxen Jack. When he left, my dad said to my mother, "Well, we better go." My aunt Annie told him, "No, you're not going! You sit down!" Then he came a second time, a third time, a fourth time. This time my dad looked at Annie, then he'd look at my mother, then he'd look at Joe and Joe's wife, Cecil. The speaker came back the fifth time and the sixth time, and my father said, "We'd better go." My dad didn't know anything about this either, but this is what they had to go through, showing him what he was going to have to do, how he was going to have to rule the Indians. I guess he didn't pay attention when he was across there before, even though he'd spent a lot of time there. Annie never told him, either. Finally the speaker came the ninth time, and he was getting louder each time he came in. Finally my father asked, "How long is he going to have to keep coming?"

Then Annie said, "You sit down here while I talk to you! Now, I've got some more things to say to you that you haven't learned. Evidently you haven't been trying to learn since you've been here. Now this is what we call *tupáats,* everything that you've seen so far. You haven't seen half of it. That's what you're going to have to learn; this is what you're going to have to do, how you're going to have to organize your tribe after you get back. This is what's expected of you. All chiefs do *not* go when they're called the first time. His subjects are already there, they should be prompt and on time, and they should be there at the first call. But that gives you nine more calls because you're a chief. You cannot go on the first call because you're not a subject. You go on the tenth call because you are now a chief!" This is what she told him. And my dad was very surprised when he heard this, because he didn't expect anything like this to happen to him.

And Joe Pullen sat there; being a Quileute chief he didn't quite know what to think about it. But he sat there and listened very carefully because he could understand Makah and so could his wife.

Then Annie said, "After this, I want you to notice what everybody is doing, how they're doing it, because this is the way you will organize your people. A *tupáat* is something that you are given to do, and it is supposed to be handed down from generation to generation. That is what they're given to do, so that's what they'll do all of their lives.

After that, my dad carefully watched everything that was going on. As for me, sometimes I watched and sometimes I didn't. Annie knew that sometimes I didn't, so she would set me down and say, "Did you see this, did you see that?" I had to sit and listen, whether I wanted to or not. That's what I was required to do. She knew that my dad didn't have any older sons. There were three of us kids that went across then—myself, my younger sister Dolores, and my brother Emil, who was a baby. There were just the three of us at that time. I think my older sister, Katherine, was already married and gone.

VISITING OTHER CANADIAN TRIBES
BEFORE THE BIG POTLATCH

We were there for thirty days. Two weeks of that time they were teaching my dad what he had to learn, and then the other two weeks we spent mostly visiting. In between times different people would talk to him. While we were going around to different houses, being invited, he was being told what he should do. They didn't tell him what was going on; they just told him he should learn to do this, he should learn to do that. There were no big parties during that time, but there were some feasts, and if some of the women wanted to be extra friendly, they'd give us some dishes before we'd leave. The men never got anything; just the women got all kinds of cups and saucers and dishes when we went visiting. By the time we got back I had a great big box full of their dishes. They were a kind of cut glass, some almost an orange color, some a real pretty blue. You don't see those things around here anymore, or even in Canada. They were all made in England. When I think of all those pretty dishes and cut glass, oh, I wish I had some now. After we got back my mom took them from her box, first, and then when they were all broken, she started in on mine. When she needed cups she'd just go up and take them out of my pile, and I never thought anything of it. So all of mine got broken, too.

I remember when we went visiting down to Ahouset; that was the first time I ever went there. Billy August and his wife were living there, and my dad's other relatives, Alice and Ernest Curley, were there, who came from Sitkeenum's line too. So we had to go visit them because we were invited. We stayed over there a couple of days, and then they brought us back in a boat. When we returned, Annie took us around Clayoquot Island herself, and if we didn't go with her we went with Effie, Francis Frank's wife. There were quite a few living on that island at that time. We also went to Caldonia, old Port Alberni, Bamfield, and other villages in that area. We didn't go too far because it was wintertime and the water was rough. This was in December, and you couldn't have made it very far in small boats then. We didn't get home to Neah Bay until the first or second of January.

"INDIAN SCHOOL" FOR A NEW CHIEF: TALKING, SINGING, AND DANCING

During all that time we were at Clayoquot, my dad had to go to what you might call an "Indian school." It started at eight o'clock each day and went until five in the evening. He had to sit there and listen. Nineteen chiefs were there. Each chief had to get up and speak his piece and tell my dad what he had to do and what he couldn't do. Nineteen of them had to take turns, and they all spoke. It's just like teaching in school—they teach you what you're supposed to do and what you're not supposed to do, what to expect *from* the people and what to do *for* the people. They kept telling him the same thing, and some would think of something else, and they'd add a little bit to it. Then after that, they took turns coming, day after day. Every morning at eight o'clock, dad had to go over to the longhouse, and except for lunch, he'd stay there all day until five o'clock. Different ones would teach him things to do, what to say. Then there were times that they had song sessions, just enough to break the tension of teaching him what to do. They would switch to singing and teach him how to sing the songs. I don't know how many days it took them; being twelve, I didn't pay that much attention, but it must have been for about a week straight, maybe more.

Then there were times when even *I* had to listen; Annie made me go. Captain Jack, the chief from Nootka, came over to the house in the evening one time because he wasn't satisfied with what he said earlier.[3] So Annie made me come in and sit down and listen to him. He said the same thing over and over and repeated, "You have to do this, you have to do that, you can't do this, and you can't do that." My dad was listening so hard that when he wanted to ask him a question, he started talking Nootka.

That just tickled my funny bone because I'd never heard him talk Canadian before. Dad said, "Now you listen to me for a while!" he said that in Nootka. I couldn't understand too much, but I could understand him in spots, like when he said, "Now you listen to me for a while." Being twelve, it just tickled me to hear my dad say that, and I laughed and I laughed, and my aunt sat up and she looked at me so mean, and I didn't pay any attention to her. I looked away, and I looked at my mom, and I hee-hawed there, "Oh, Pop," I said, "Oh, Pop, you're talking Canadian!" And my mother looked at me, and I looked at my aunt again, and I had to straighten up because she was much older than my mom anyway, and I had to respect her, so I quit. I sat there, and I snickered. But Dad looked at me, and he looked kind of mean, so I had to straighten up there and quit laughing. But the old man, he kind of smiled a bit, kind of laughed, but then he got stern. And he stopped talking, and I had to quit. Then my dad talked to him in his own language. So Dad started asking him a few questions, and he finally answered. After that, Captain Jack kind of liked me, I guess, and that's when he decided that the last day of the party he was going to give me a song.

Captain Jack talked to us at Annie's house, but most of the teaching was done in the "Indian school" at the longhouse. All the chiefs and my dad would go to this one longhouse that Francis Frank had, and they'd sit around and either start talking to him, or they'd start singing. And my dad would just have to listen, like he made me do when we were at home. And when they had to teach him a new song, they would sing it over and over till he learned it. They even taught him how to do the dances that went with his new songs. Francis Frank taught him how to do the Wolf Dances he inherited, and Michael Brown taught him the dance to his new Hamatsa song.

THE SINGING OF LITTLE JOE FRANK

While we were up there, there was one person that I'll never forget. One little fellow just fascinated me; his name was Joe Frank, and he was Francis Frank's youngest boy. I imagine he was only about four years old then. He sure knew how to chant! Every day he'd pick the west part of the longhouse, and he'd stand there, lean against a post there, and close his eyes and sing. He had a little rattle, I don't know who made it for him. I never did ask. But it just fascinated me; I had to get up in the morning just to watch him. He'd get up at five o'clock, maybe, and by six o'clock he'd be in that corner singing—every morning. Every evening about five o'clock, he'd do the same thing, and he was only about four years old. He never sang the same one more than two or three times. He did a lot of different ones. That little guy knew how to sing one right after another. He'd stand there and just close his eyes and work that rattle round and round, and he'd just sing to his heart's content. He really meant it, you know! He'd close his eyes and away his rattle would go, around and around, and he'd be singing and singing. And I'd sit there and watch him, and I'd never leave that spot until he got through. Then he'd bring his rattle and put it away, and then he'd go out and play just like any little kid. But while he was there singing, he really enjoyed himself. He looked like he really meant everything he said.

WHY THE BIG POTLATCHES AND SECRET SOCIETY CEREMONIES WERE HELD

Part of this whole celebration was for little Joe's older sister Clothilda Frank. They gave her what we call a *q'its'é·yit* party, a "coming out" party.[4] It was in honor of this young lady who just turned into her womanhood. The other part of the celebration was for my father, who Annie was making a chief. As part of this, we had two whole weeks of Klúkwali and Hámatsa ceremony first. Of course, we didn't have huge feasts every day, just every so often. If there were enough people, they'd gather in the morning and talk or sing all different types of songs; some of them were just plain singing, like what we call *T'abáa.*[5] They sang other songs, too, whatever they felt like. There was dancing every day, there was singing every day, and when it was chanting time, it was chanting time. People went off to do this by themselves. Prayed in secret.

They put on a big Klukwali for Clothilda and for my dad. There was about a week of ritual singing and dancing every night. The Klukwali was a Wolf Dance, and the Canadians used to tell us that the wolf gets around at the same time the Hamatsa man gets around. Children were never allowed to go to Klukwali's in those days, so I have no idea of what was really happening.[6] We were kept in another room, away from the whole ceremony, but we could hear the singing going on, and we could hear Chief Edward Joe on the roof, running about and shouting, "Haam! Haam!" when he was the Hamatsa. We were only allowed to be there for the last two nights when Annie gave the big potlatches for Clothilda and then for my dad. Annie helped Francis Frank put on a potlatch for Clothilda on the next to the last night; and then Annie put one on for my dad on the very last night. Francis helped her out as much as he could, and my dad brought all that food that she asked him to buy. They both helped her some, but she was really responsible for both of those parties.

THE BIG POTLATCH WHERE ANNIE MADE MY DAD A CHIEF

Proper Seating of the Chiefs and Guests

Even though I was only twelve years old, I'll never forget that night Annie made my dad a chief. First, everyone had to be properly seated. Inside the longhouse there is a pole for every tribe; there were nineteen poles for the nineteen tribes plus a pole for the Neah Bays and maybe a few other poles for unexpected visiting tribes that might come. The pole is called *t'iqú·wił*, which means "a place for sitting." They name each pole for a tribe, and then that's where they sit. They all sat at their poles before the feast began. Because my grandaunt Annie's grandfather, Sitkeenum, was a chief, her chief's seat was next to the Number One chief, Chief Edward Joe. The chiefs sat on both sides of the Head Chief during the party and not with their own tribes, who were sitting by their proper poles. Annie and Francis Frank sat in Sitkeenum's chief's seats, and my dad and our family sat at the Makah pole. This was because my dad hadn't been made a chief yet. Joe Pullen, the Number One chief of the Quileutes, and his wife sat at the Makah pole, too, because he was my father's guest. He was supposed to verify the statement that my father was made a chief in Canada. When he got back home, he was supposed to tell this to the people there. What Annie did for my dad in Canada would be considered valid over here, too, but she needed to hold a party on the American side and go through the same thing again to complete it. She died, though, before she could come over and do it, so then Joe Pullen had to verify the fact that this is what she had done in Canada, on Clayoquot Island among the people they call the Oopídzit tribe.

At a potlatch on Clayoquot Island, the chief always sits at the west end of the longhouse, and to his left, on the north side, at the pole closest to him, were the Nootkas. Then each tribe south of them had the poles on around the room, and many of them had poles on the south side of the longhouse. The Makah pole was closest to the chief on his right side, and we are the tribe that's farthest south. The Quileutes didn't have a pole, so they had to sit with us.

Ceremonial Tupáats and Volunteer Activities

When we came in, we were all ushered to our places by a "doorkeeper."[7] This job is also someone's *tupáat* and was more important long ago than it is now, because he had to watch everyone as they came in to make sure they came as friends and not as enemies who were going to start a war. He would never directly usher you to your post, but he'd stand at the door and point to you and tell you where to sit—point at the place where you were supposed to sit. It was against Indian tradition not to sit at your own post; you were under obligation to sit in your own area. I'm not sure why this was so, but maybe it was so that when they had a potlatch and were giving away, then they could take them section by section, so that one didn't get left out. Today they don't sit in this kind of order, and sometimes maybe two or three will get left out because they're not sitting in the right place—they're mixed up with the other people. For instance, if you were with us and you wandered off and sat some other place, well then they wouldn't know you were with us. I think this was the reason for the posts, so you'd sit with your own tribal group.

Just to the left, next to the Head Chief's seat, at the west end of the longhouse, was a big cedar drum. It was about four feet high and eight feet long—a huge drum. It was made out of cedar boards which were tied together with some kind of sinew or root. It was rectangular in shape. Then they had another wood piece that sat on top of it, where three people sat. The middle man was always the "head drummer," *kutx̌ú·ti?i·*, and the two on the sides were the first and second drummer. Instead of using their hands, they beat on it with their feet. The *tupáat* of the head drummer was to get all his drummers in line and to see that they knew the song, that they knew where the drumming would end and where to begin it. He had to teach all his drummers to drum at the same time, to start and stop at once. If there were any people who wanted to be drummers, they had to take lessons from the head drummer. This was his *tupáat*.

Actually, there were three places the Head Chief could sit, all of them at the west end of the longhouse where the secret escape hatch was located—in case they were attacked and had to get the chief out quickly. He could sit to the right of the big drum, in front of it, or on top of it, if it wasn't being used as a drum. He never sat on the left side of the drum. I don't know why.[8]

Usually a drummer will stay a drummer as long as he can. If he gets too old, he gets too tired; drumming is hard work. He'll stay a drummer until he decides he's going to give it up and just sing with the rest of the singers. Up to that time, he's obligated to teach one of his family; if he's got a son, he'll teach his son. If he doesn't have one, then he's under obligation to teach some other male in his family, like a cousin or a nephew. Most generally, it's the number one son that he teaches, however. No matter what the *tupáat*, it's always handed down to the number one son. Only time it goes to somebody else is when he hasn't got one. The same goes for drummer number two and number three. That's their *tupáat*, and they have to pass it on in the same way.

Even in the old days. they didn't use that great big drum too much, except for an extra big potlatch. They did use it the time Annie made my father a chief. There was another drummer *tupáat* as well. There are these other three drummers that use a little round skin drum. So, there's two different kinds of drummers; three for the wooden drum, and three on the skin drums. The skin drums have round rims, are about ten inches to two feet in diameter, and are about three inches deep. They have a skin only on one side of them. In the back of one of these there's strings or a small skin strung and pulled across as a handle so you could hold it with your left hand. You beat with your right hand. We had these drums, too, for my dad's party.

So, we come to the "lead singer," *dukʷí·qsyak*, "the one that carries the song." We couldn't have a potlatch without him. This is his *tupáat*. He's the lead singer; he's different from the drummer. He has a feather—a tail of an eagle—in his hand at all times during the party, and he keeps time with his feather. He uses his feathers like a symphony man will use his wand to lead his orchestra. His hand is up in the air, keeping time. Always in his right hand. Then when a song is through, the feather falls, quick like. Or, if there's a chorus, he'll move his feathers in a different fashion—sideways.

Then they have two other lead singers, and they have feathers, too. But, the only time they lead is if the head singer gets tired or if the head singer decides he wants them to take over and lead somebody else's song. Sometimes, if a party is too long, then they'll use all three lead singers, but not all at the same time—one at a time. This is the *tupáat* of each one of them.

The "speaker" *tupáat* is another important one. The speaker, *tsíq'tsíq qey yák,* is always a man, and he carries a staff which is carved out like a totem pole. At every party he's under obligation to make a speech—if there's visitors, he thanks them for coming, or whatever he wants to talk about. But he is the speaker for that one chief. There is one for each chief, and each speaks only for his own chief at the potlatch. There were as many speakers as there were chiefs.

There are no set speeches that the chief's speaker has to learn; he just speaks on whatever he wants to. Usually head speakers are pretty good. They don't ever make mistakes, and they most generally have good speeches. There are two other speakers, also, in case the first one gets sick. If he's not sick, he's there at all times. They never use the other speakers unless number one speaker couldn't be there. The speaker was also responsible for watching the people, especially visitors, in the days way back in the 1800s when they were still fighting. The speaker had to stand and study all the rest of the Indians to know whether they were acting like they came for war or to steal women or children, or if they came as friends.

Then there was the "town crier" *tupáat.* This man, *hux̌ʔádibiʔí·syak,* also carries a staff, and he goes around the village inviting people. He's different from the speaker. He doesn't speak in public or at the parties. He is for inviting people just in that one town, in his own tribe. This is what Yášxen Jack was doing when he came and called my father ten times to come to the feast. This *tupáat* was like the others in that there were two extras in case the first one got sick or couldn't be there or was not at home at that time. They were always careful to have their stand-ins, but most generally these Indians were pretty good about it; they tried to be there. It was really serious; it was not something that you could just laugh off and say, "Well, I'm not going to be there." They had to make it a point to be there. Most of the time they were there. When the town crier invited the people of the tribe, they all came at the first call. They were there with the drummers, and they were all singing and warmed up before the chief got there. The town crier always had to call the Head Chief, *ʔuʔiłt,* and the first subchief ten times before they came. This is how it was done properly.

All the subchiefs, number one through nine, either had *tupáats* to keep them busy, or if they weren't doing their *tupáat,* they were helping in some way with the party—helping Number One chief, or maybe it was number two, three, or four chief's party, and they were under obligation to help get everything all situated and see that everything was running right. The only one that really wasn't busy was the Head Chief. He just kind of sat there. But if they needed any advice, they'd still have to go to Number One, the Head Chief.

If Annie had been able to do the same thing in Neah Bay before she died, my dad would have ended up the Number One Head Chief here, because on this side he was a direct descendant of Chief Yelák'ub and Chief Peter Brown, both of whom were Number One Head Chiefs long ago. This never happened, however, and my dad never claimed his Makah chiefship over here on the American side. He was content with what he got from the Canadian side, and from this he was number four subchief in Neah Bay.

The chiefs would have to ask for volunteers to do other jobs which weren't *tupáats* but which had to be done for a party. "Passing-out-sticks" was one of these. At that time, instead of clapping their hands together to keep time like we do now, they used sticks. So they passed out two sticks to a person. While they were sitting there, they'd hit them together and sing.[9] Most of the time they were just split out of fir or cedar, but some people who were ambitious would cut them out real nice, flat. Others who weren't, would just take them from the one that passed them out. The whole family of the man who took on this duty had to pitch in and pass out sticks. At the end, when everything was all finished, the guests just left them where they sat, and then the keeper of the sticks would pick them up and tie them in a bundle again for the next party. The guests wouldn't keep them.

"Passing-out-water" was a duty like passing-out sticks.[10] The whole family or relatives of the volunteer family would help pass out water because there was an awful lot of singing at that time and people would get very thirsty. It was an important job to keep the people full of water. So they'd pass a dipper with water, and everybody drank out of the same dipper. Nobody ever got sick, either. There was one bucket, one dipper. They had metal buckets and dippers with a flat bottom. I can remember those times so clearly.

Then, they had to find somebody to keep the fire going. There were always people available to do that. It seemed like they were more willing to do things then than they are today. They never fought about it. If you asked them, they'd say all right, and they'd go ahead and do it without any fuss, without making any excuses.

The same way with the cooking. There was no *tupáat* for that; they'd just have to ask for volunteers. There'd be people who'd volunteer to cook. The ladies just seemed to get along fine, never any trouble. If people with *tupáats* wanted to volunteer for another job, they could go ahead and do it. They could do it even if they had a *tupáat,* as long as it didn't bother what they had to do. But there were quite a few people who didn't have any *tupáat,* so they would be free to volunteer.[11]

The *tupáat* was more or less the way the Indians organized their tribes—organized the jobs they had to do. Ordinarily something like this was given to people who had a little standing in the community (chiefs). If not, things would be just like they are today—nobody has any particular task to do, and everybody fights about it, and they say, "Well I don't want to," or, "You can't make me," or, "I'm going to town today, I can't do it." But if you have a *tupáat* and the chief says, "This is yours!" then it's *yours* and you've got to do it.

So, when Annie was making my father a chief, everybody knew what their *tupáats* were and did them automatically, and other people volunteered to do other jobs so the potlatch would go smoothly. Every one of the chiefs took part.

The Big Feast

After everyone was properly seated, the Dinner songs were sung. Then a great feast was served. There was lots of all kinds of food, but it was so long ago that I can't remember exactly what foods they served. They fed several hundred guests as much as they could eat. After the feast was over, everything was cleaned up, and then the regular potlatch could start.

The First Big Potlatch Dance: Chief Edward Joe's Hamatsa Dance

I remember very clearly Chief Edward Joe started out by being the Hamatsa that night. About a week before that, he had to go out and get ready for it, so he went out and took his bath, and went into the woods for five or six days. He went around in this skirt and headdress made out of hemlock tree limbs. This went on for a whole week. He was up in the hills in the daytime, but in the night you'd hear him come in. Daytime, you could just barely hear him close to the village, hollering, "HAAHM! HAAHM!" the call of the Hamatsa, but at nighttime he'd come right through the village. You could hear him, but he was never seen. He wasn't supposed to be seen; that's why he came around in the night. I could hear him running around like a wild man, hear him on the top of the house every so often. Then I'd hear him hollering, "HAAHM! HAAHM!" very loud, and it was getting scarier and scarier for me, because we stayed right at the longhouse. The people had a lean-to there, where Francis Frank and his family lived. It was attached to the longhouse, and every now and then, if we didn't want to go home at night, if we got too sleepy, well, we'd stay over at the longhouse and not go home. Then each night for about a week before, I could hear him jump on the roof there, and I was getting more and more scared, listening to him hollering, "HAAHM! HAAHM!" I asked, "What's he doing that for?" They just kept telling me, "Never mind." All this time he was getting ready to come in dancing, like a cannibal on the final night, the night of the potlatch. Then I'd hear the whistles every now and then that sound like the wolf—I'd hear that howl. By the seventh day, when he came into the village, he really had no voice left. You could just barely hear him saying, "Haahm, Haahm!" and going around.

And then that night of the big potlatch, he was the first one to come in dancing. He was first on the program. Because he was the chief, he was in the lead for the evening dances. So, he came in surrounded by twenty men holding hands and making a circle around him. He was in the center, acting like a real wild, crazy man. He was the only one that was acting crazy. He was the "Cannibal-eating man," the

Hámatsa. So he danced in the circle of men, and he made like he wanted to get out of the circle, break out and get away. The men held on and kept him inside there. During all of this he kept hollering, "HAAHM! HAAHM!" and kind of crouched down and with his right hand out and shaking above his head. He was wearing hemlock boughs. Then he'd run up against different men, and he bit two or three of them. I don't know if he really bit them, but he made like he did. One of them did bleed, so he must have really bitten him. And, oh, it was real ferocious to me! I was really scared, of course, being only twelve at that time. There was no singing or drumming at this time, while the cannibal was wild.

This went on for about a half hour, then the singers started singing, and the women came out and started dancing background to calm him down. Then he finally came out of it. He was wearing a cedar bark skirt, cedar bark rings on his ankles (with one tassle), cedar bark tied on his wrists, and a huge cedar bark ring around his neck for this part of the dance—when he became tame. When they started singing, he was supposed to regain his senses and not be wild, and then he started dancing the tame Hamatsa Dance. They sang two songs which were pretty long, regular Hamatsa songs. He must have danced for about fifteen or twenty minutes. Then when he was through, two men grabbed him and sat him down, and that was the end of his dance.

The women who were doing background weren't doing anything special; they were just dancing, sort of going back and forth, turning from side to side in place. They all moved together and looked real nice dancing in unison. They all had black capes on, absolutely no designs at all, just plain black. They all let their hair down and wore headbands woven of cedar bark. Everyone had long hair then. They usually had it tied up in the back, but for this they all just let their hair hang. I don't know why they did that. They didn't wear any face paint either, no black around their eyes. Just the man does that—paints his whole face black.[12]

Chief Edward Joe's face was painted black, but there was no other painting on his body. He had just a pair of shorts on. On his head he had a headpiece made out of cedar bark; it was kind of a dark red, twisted like a rope, about two inches wide, and looked like it was frayed in the back and in the front. He wore no shirt but had a lei around his neck, cedar lei, also twisted like a rope. It would be twisted about three or four inches through [thickness], and just rest on his shoulder. The men who were holding him in the circle just wore their everyday clothes and had black paint on their faces. The singers weren't painted either, but certain ones of them who had the cedar bark headbands wore them. Most generally it would be just the family of the Hamatsa who would wear this headband, and when he was finished, they'd take off their cedar headpieces. When Edward Joe had finished his dance that night, then he started giving away money, presents, whatever he wanted to give away.

My Mistake and My Time in the Limelight

That was the night that I made a mistake, too. I came into the longhouse before my mother and dad; I walked in and sat down in Chief Edward Joe's chair. It wasn't until the next day that they told me that this was the chief's chair. They didn't tell me that we had *t'iqú·wił*, a "pole" where we're supposed to sit, ourselves. So, my mom and dad came in shortly after me, and, *oh!* My mother looked at me, and she said, "You get *out* of there!" She was talking Indian and repeated, *"You get out of there! You get out of that chair as fast as you can! You belong over there at that pole!"* I looked at her and I didn't get up, I just sat there, because I felt like I wanted to pick my own chair that night and I wanted to sit where I could see the dances. My grandaunt was walking behind her. So, Annie looked at my dad and she said, "Let her stay there, tonight is her night. Let her stay there." So he looked at my mother, and my mother said, "Well she should come and sit with us; she's supposed to be still." She shrugged her shoulders. So I just kind of settled back a little further after I heard her; I squirmed and settled back. I was bound and determined I was going to sit there. I was sitting in the chair on the right side of the drum because no one was there. This was where I sat while Chief Edward Joe was dancing the Hamatsa. He came in dancing, and then afterward I found out why she let me stay there.

After he was through giving away what he wanted to give away, then, last but not least, he gave me twenty dollars, and then he gave me a song. So that's why Annie said I could sit there, that this was my day. After he gave me this, then he left and came back in, dancing just the regular Standing Wolf Dance. When he finished this, he gave away some more money to his own tribe and other Canadians. We came before all the others this one time because my dad was being made a chief.[13] Well, while he was doing this giving away, I decided I didn't want to sit in that chair anymore, so I got up and went and sat with my mother, and then when he was finished, Chief Edward Joe came and sat down and took his place then. I was ready to give up the chief's chair.

More Singing, Dancing, and Giving Away of Songs

Then the different chiefs took their turns that night. They danced just like we do in Neah Bay today, different ones taking turns dancing and giving away. There was a lot of singing and dancing that night. I was too young to recall all the dances that were done. And on the same night, I got my song from Captain Jack, the Chief of Nootka. I got two songs the same evening—one from Chief Edward Joe and one from Captain Jack. Captain Jack gave me twenty dollars too, besides the song. Twenty dollars was like one hundred dollars at that time; twenty dollars was quite a bit of money. During our last dance, he had my aunt dance, and then he gave me the song, "Wo hey," the Grizzly Bear song (song 4, chapter 10). He announced that there's always two that go together no matter what. He gave the other song, "Ho yeh," (song 5, chapter 10) to my dad because he knew we danced together. He told my dad, "When she gets old enough, you can give her the other one, whenever you feel like it's time for her to have it." But my dad never did give it to me. However, I did have my own song, and I danced it a lot over the years.

Annie Williams Announces Charlie Swan as a New Chief

So finally it was our turn to sing and dance, and for Annie to announce that she was making my dad a chief, and then for her to give away. She had Captain Jack lead the singers, and they sang many of her songs, and Francis Frank danced. Afterwards she announced that she was giving all this to Charles Swan, and he was to share it with Francis Frank (her relative on the Canadian side), and both of them could use these songs, dances, masks, and costumes. Annie told everyone what she was doing and why she wanted to do it. She felt that she was getting too old, and she wanted everybody to know that she chose my dad to be her successor on the American side[14] because Chief Sitkeenum had had an American wife from Neah Bay. She announced this, and that she was giving everything she had originally inherited from her grandfather, Sitkeenum, and from her father, Atliu, to Charles Swan. So the masks, the whistles, and the family curtain that we have are the originals from Chief Sitkeenum and Atliu. She gave those all to him, publicly, right there.[15] But my dad only took a few of them home with him then, because Annie felt like it wasn't time yet. She was to bring him the rest herself. But she announced that she was giving him the chiefship and everything she owned. This is where we got our dances, our songs, costumes, and masks (see figs. 24, 25, 26, 28). We never got all the things we were supposed to, however, because she died before she could bring the rest of them down.

Probably the most important things my dad got were the Big Man pole and the White-Man mask. The Big Man was a carved wooden man who stood about ten to twelve feet high, and he held both hands up like he was welcoming the people. He stood to the right of the big wood drum in the longhouse. Then at the proper time Edward Matthew from Clayoquot put on that White-Man mask (the one that's in the Denver Art Museum now), and did the dance that went with it. The mask was very big, and he was very small, and I always remember him dancing that dance, because he had a broken back and was very short. There was a song that went with that mask, and though my dad learned it at that time, I never did, and now there's no one left that knows that song.

The Changing Mask Dance Song (song 10, chapter 10), with its five masks, was the most important song we got from Annie that night. That's the one that shows the different face of each season and then the chief who watches over all and has the open and closing eyes. Our family curtain and the whistles go along with the song and the masks. She also gave us a lot of other songs and dances that night: Wolf Dance songs, Hamatsa songs, Dinner songs, the Big Man Song, the chant that goes with the Changing Mask Dance, and others I can't remember anymore. She gave us her Feather Game *tupáat,* which she then performed a few years later for my own wedding, and she gave us a Whale Game *tupáat,* which my dad used.

Annie gave my dad a complete Hamatsa costume. She gave him the cedar bark ring that goes over the shoulders, and it had little carved skulls hanging from it. They were carved from white cedar—about six inches long and three or four inches wide, and they were placed two in the front and two in the back. This is supposed to have represented a cannibal.[16]

The Canadians always said that they used blankets at potlatches a lot, but at the time of my dad's party in 1930, they didn't. I don't know why there weren't many blankets then; there were hardly any. It seems like they would have used them because they're on the Canadian side and they can get the Hudson Bay blankets. At that party, though, the only blankets that were given away were the button blankets that Annie gave to my dad. Annie gave him Sitkeenum's and Atliu's button blankets of the grizzly bear and the double-headed raven. These are the only two button blanket designs that belong to us, and we use them all the time.

After all of these things and more had been given to my dad, then Annie had to pay everyone for witnessing the making of a chief. She had to have gifts and money to pay all the chiefs and the other guests that came. A lot of dishes, pots, pans, shawls, just anything she wanted was given away that night, as well as quite a bit of money.

People from chiefs' families keep track of how much they are given and by whom, so that when there's another party they can return the money given by one person and add five or ten dollars more to it. This is the way we usually do.[17] Then the next time he'll give me a little more—it just keeps on building up this way. Then when he feels like it's time to quit, well, he'll just quit at the point where he figures both of us are even. Then we drop the amount of money back down again, and we start all over. No one feels hurt by this; we understand that we have to do it this way. I have never seen it go to the point where they can't give anymore. All my life I've seen that when either side got to a point where they felt they just couldn't do anymore, they both dropped down and started all over again. It would be foolish to give and give and give until you just couldn't give anymore. That wouldn't really make sense.

So, this is how my grandaunt Annie Williams called łu·t'a⁊uX and Xwinxwánimo, made my father, Charles Swan, called Yelák'ub, a chief. She died before she could do the same thing in Neah Bay, but Joe Pullen verified the fact that this is what she had done. All the masks, the curtain, the button blankets, the whistles, and other dance things, and many of the songs which we have, come from her, handed down from her grandfather Chief Sitkeenum, and his son Atliu. We use these things as Makah, and they call them Makah here, but they originally aren't Makah. They're from the Clayoquot Reservation in Canada. They originally belonged to a Clayoquot chief and now they belong to the descendants of a Makah chief and also the descendants of a Clayoquot chief. Two families, one American and one Canadian, share the ownership of these things, which we still use at potlatches.

CHAPTER 9

THE STRUGGLES OF ADULT LIFE

SECOND MARRIAGE: HUSBAND, JOBS, BABIES, THE END OF INDIAN MUSICAL ACTIVITIES

I was about twenty when I got married the second time. In 1938, I married Lyle Hunter, also from Neah Bay. His parents were Shubert and Flora Hunter. Shubert was a full-blooded Clayoquot and the older brother of Jim Hunter. Both of them had lived in Neah Bay most of their adult lives. We didn't have any party; we just plain got married. Perry Ides was the Presbyterian minister then, and we got married at his house. There was no celebration afterwards or anything. My parents weren't there, his parents weren't there, and I don't even remember who we had for witnesses. Our families knew we were going to get married, but they didn't come. People didn't go to weddings much in those days, so this was normal. Usually they would have a party, but since this was my second marriage, and his second marriage they didn't do it. They only did it for the first one.

We lived with my mom and dad for a couple years. My mom didn't actually say it, but my dad didn't want us to move out. We were going to move into Lyle's folks' house because they had a big home with three bedrooms and just his two brothers were living there. His parents stayed out at Tsooyez mostly, so there was lots of room at the house in town. But being that my mom worked so much, she really didn't want me to move out, cause I was the sitter all the time. I was needed to do the household chores and to stay with the kids, even though I was married. So we decided to stay with mom and dad. It was easier to baby-sit there, rather than running back and forth from the east to the west end of town every day. Then I had to take care of my older sister's three kids, too. When she and her husband separated, she moved into Dad's house with her kids. Since she never stayed home much, I ended up taking care of them, too. I was always talking, talking, talking to her, telling her not to be away so much, but she didn't listen. My mother finally asked me to stay with all the kids.

I think my dad was in agreement with me when I married Lyle, because he never said anything against it. I think he liked Lyle more than my first husband, who used to go to drinking parties on weekends. My dad didn't care too much for that.

Lyle didn't drink. For a while he worked as a logger, but that didn't last very long. He worked out at the dock (Bay Fish Company) taking in fish for a little while. Then all of a sudden he was just doing nothing, and he never worked. My parents supported him all the time he was there. This wasn't considered proper, but still they needed me to help them out. My dad never liked to express his thoughts, so I don't really know how he felt about it. I don't think he wanted us to move out, though. I did little odds and ends of jobs, working off and on here and there. Every so often I'd pinch-hit in the restaurant. So I made a little money that way, and it was enough for our food.

The very first job I had, I didn't get paid for. I started working as a cook for a relative of my husband. She was quite sick. Nobody took care of her. This woman was living with a younger fellow, but he wasn't helping her either. Ever since I could remember, she had this restaurant which belonged to her and her late husband. Then awhile after he died, she ended up getting sick, and no one even brought her food. Lyle said, "Why don't you go over and try cooking, so she can get something to eat." So I said, "Well, how can I do that, because I don't have any experience in cooking in a restaurant at all? I don't know how; I don't know anything about it." I think this was in 1938 or '39.

Lyle talked me into it anyway. I said, "What are we going to start with? There is absolutely nothing in there." We went into the restaurant, and he said, "Well, we have potatoes here, and I can get fish from the dock." So we started in. We opened it. We had our own coffee. We brought everything my family had in our cupboard over there cause there was nothing in there. In the mornings when we got up, we'd go over there to eat because we took everything out of our house and brought it over there. We bought a few pounds of hamburger on our own. So I served hamburger sandwiches, hot dog sandwiches—whatever we could afford. We couldn't afford too much, either. We served fish dinners with potatoes, and a few canned vegetables that I had in my cupboard. I think it took us a week or more before we could buy one of those great big boxes of hot dogs and about ten or fifteen pounds of hamburger, along with a few other things. And just about that time, one of her own nieces came in and stole everything out of there. We had just bought a case of corn and half a case of peas— it wasn't too much, but at least we had a start—when this happened. Then we had to have them go over and search her niece's place, and they found everything right there. We got a little bit of it back. We didn't want too much back because we knew they weren't getting anything to eat, either. So, we started all over again. Pretty soon we were clearing forty dollars an evening, and then we'd bring the matchbox with the money in it and give it to Lyle's sick relative.

I ended up getting kind of sore because her boyfriend used to just take it and go play cards and spend all the rest of that money. So actually we weren't getting anywhere, even though we kept trying. By the time I got through there, she started getting a little better. Her boyfriend fed her two to three times a day; at least she had something to eat every day. When she got a little bit better, I quit, and when she was stronger she took over again. She'd been down for about a whole month. I worked all that time and never got paid. We ate there while I was working there, but we didn't even take our food back when we left. We just left it there for her so she could go ahead and get started, because she wouldn't have had anything, otherwise. So we just went home and let her take over. It didn't do her much good anyway, though. She got sick again and died not too long afterwards. After that, the restaurant just folded.

Then I didn't work for a while until my first baby, Arnie, got a little bigger. Arnie was born in 1940. He was born at home with the help of Mrs. Kalappa, the Indian doctor. She delivered my daughter, Babe, at home about three and a half years later, too. I don't think I saw Mrs. Kalappa the first two months, but the third month she would ask to see me. Then she'd sort of feel my tummy to see how the baby was sitting and how big it was and all. She was very good and knew what she was doing. One day she told me, "Your baby's facing the wrong way. That's why you're having such problems with your ribs." I felt like I was just busting and my ribs were very tired! She said, "Your baby's facing the wrong way—toward you, not away from you like it should be. To make matters worse, the baby's sleeping." She said, "Well, it isn't going to move because the baby's sleeping now." She seemed to know that it was sleeping. She kept conversation going so that I wasn't uncomfortable. Finally she got tired of waiting for this baby to wake up, so she just started rubbing in circles. First she felt around, and said, "Well, here's the little back end." Then she started rubbing where the back end was and just kind of gave it a tap. She kept doing that, rubbing and tapping, but not very hard. Finally she said, "Well, there it is now, it's moving and you can feel it." I could feel the movement of the baby then. She'd do the same thing while the baby continued being active, and then she'd push, push one side of your tummy, and she kept that up till you felt the whole baby turn. Then she'd be satisfied and tell me to come back at such and such a time.

Another time, the baby was just standing—like breech (I can't remember which baby it was). She knew that, and so she did the same thing, just kind of found where the little buttocks was, and then she'd give it a tap and work on putting the baby back in its normal position. I had to see her once a week at that time because the baby wanted to stay in that position. She said, "Well, this baby just insists on being in the same position. And he doesn't want to turn." She didn't say "he," she said "it." She always knew what sex this baby was going to be, but she wouldn't tell. She'd say, "That's the best part of it. You're not supposed to know until the baby comes." So, she would work on me and say, "Well, come back next week," because I would be very uncomfortable. But eventually she would get it to turn. She knew what she was doing.

White doctors didn't always do so well with breech babies. Like my good friend Ramona. A Navy doctor delivered this baby, and it was a breech baby and they couldn't get it out. Ramona died; she bled to death! I was terribly upset when this happened! Now had they called Mrs. Kalappa, she would have worked on that baby and got it out. But Ramona's husband didn't want her to come that day, and neither did another lady who was there. But I know she would have been alive if they had gone after Mrs. Kalappa! Her husband just refused. He said Mrs. Kalappa was too old, and he wanted to use a Navy doctor up here, instead. And Ramona just bled to death! That was about the same time Arnie was born.

But Mrs. Kalappa was always so good. She knew just exactly how the baby was positioned. There was no guessing with her. She had me come back about every two months unless I was having trouble or the baby needed to be turned or something. She'd say, "If you don't feel good the baby may have turned over again, so come back if your ribs feel like they can't stay in there." So, I didn't have to go back again until she told me to come back.

By the time the baby was ready to be born, I felt pretty comfortable with Mrs. Kalappa, but I was still kind of afraid because I didn't know what to expect; I'd never had a baby before. I was in labor for thirteen hours the first time. I was at home, right in my own bed. What they did was put a rubber sheet on the bed, and then they sterilized whatever they put underneath me. Then they would just throw all that away when we were finished. And she and my mom and another lady made sure ahead of time that our scissors or knives or whatever they were going to use were all sterilized. The sheet was tied up to the head of the bedstead, and each time we bore down, we pulled on this sheet. My mother was on one side holding one of my legs, and Mrs. Kalappa was taking care of the other one and waiting for the child to be born. In between contractions she would sort of work on my tummy so that I wouldn't be in that constant pain like I was when I had my third child in the hospital. Then she would carry on a conversation, and I'd forget all about the pain until the next contraction. She never did like the doctors do—look to see how fast you're dilating. She never, ever did that; she would just feel my tummy and under my tummy. The talk and the way she would feel my tummy used to take the suffering off my mind—give me a chance to rest. It was thirteen hours for the first baby and fourteen for the second, and I didn't mind it at all, because of the way they were sitting there holding a conversation. And every once in a while she'd ask me a question and include me in the conversation, and in this way I didn't notice how many hours I had been in labor. She always knew how fast I was dilating by feeling under my tummy, and always relieved it until it was time; then she'd say, "It's time now." Then she'd get busy helping push, and she'd say, "Now you push, and I'll push too." But she never forced it. She would just hold real lightly. Then she'd say, "—Again!— Again!" And then in no time the baby was born.

While the baby was being born, she made us chew these little leaves that grow around here. They look like carrot leaves, but they're really not. They're fuzzy all the way down. We'd chew this all the way through until about an hour before the baby was born. Then she'd quit feeding us this stuff. She always used to know about when it would be born. I don't remember what they called those leaves, but my dad or somebody would go after it. I really didn't see that it did anything for me, but Mrs. Kalappa said that it's supposed to be bitter. It *was* bitter! *Really* bitter! "It's bitter enough to push the baby out," she used to say. "It's bitter enough for the baby to want to get out." So that's all I know of it.[1]

After the baby was born, my mom would wash me and clean me up. Either she or another lady would bathe the baby and then put it in the bed right next to me. I didn't have to ask for it. They just automatically put it in bed with me. I wasn't to get out of bed for ten days. They used to keep me in bed, wait on me and everything.

Right after the baby was born, they gave me real strong tea with a lot of sugar in it, regular tea or Indian tea, whatever they had. Mrs. Kalappa would say, "You need some strength now. You're all done with this now, and you need more strength." So they brought me tea with too much sugar in it. But then she'd just say, "Well, you take that for a couple of days, and you'll have enough strength afterwards." So, that's the way they delivered our babies.

Later on when I had Mike, my third baby, it was much different. I went to the hospital with Mike because I thought I was a little bit too old to have him at home, and Mrs. Kalappa was gone. So I experienced the first two with an Indian doctor and then the last one with a white doctor. Mike was only six hours coming, but I felt like it was twenty-four. When I did it with the midwife, it was much easier, even though I was in labor thirteen and fourteen hours. When I was in the hospital, I was among strangers. They weren't people I knew, and I had the hardest time. The doctor wanted to give me painkiller, and I didn't want any. He named one thing at a time: pentathol, ether, and spinal block. I said I didn't want any of them. Finally he told the nurse, "Well, give her ether." And I said, "No! I don't want it. I don't want anything!" And he looked at me and he was kind of disgusted with me, and he said, "Well, it's you that's giving birth." I said, "I know it is. That's why I don't want anything." So I didn't have anything. It was a natural birth, which is what I've always had.

I never found it so hard in my life as when I delivered in the hospital. They strapped me down with my arms in the front of me, and I was supposed to push and bear down. I could not do that, because I was taught to *pull* and bear down. And I just couldn't seem to do that. I just couldn't stand it! And then I couldn't stand my legs being strapped, either. If they had been loose then I would have been able to keep my own feet in there. But this way I couldn't do it. I just couldn't! So that was the hardest six hours I ever had! Mrs. Kalappa just made it so much more enjoyable and easier than they did.

Shortly after my first son, Arnie, was born we moved into Lyle's parents' home on the other end of town. Lyle's two brothers lived upstairs, and we lived downstairs in the other bedroom. We didn't get in each other's way; in fact, we hardly ever ran into each other. We shared the kitchen, but we never used it at the same times. Both Carl and Leo were bachelors and did their own cooking. We got along just fine with them. Shubert and Flora Hunter, Lyle's parents, were very nice people, and I always got along well with them, too. We lived in their house in Neah Bay for quite a long time while they lived in their house out at Tsooyez.

Lyle was working out at the dock at this time, and after Arnie got a little bigger, I got a job cooking at Parker's Restaurant, which later became the Bayview. I cooked there for many years, working eight hours a day for a dollar an hour. Elvrum's Restaurant opened almost next door, and a lot of people went there, but we still always had a crowd at the Bayview. When I quit Bayview I moved on down to what they called Hunter's Hall. I worked there for I don't know how many years. It was a long time. Martin Hunter eventually sold out to his wife Katie's grandson, Lloyd Colfax, but I just kept on working there.

At the beginning after Lyle and I were married, I continued to go to parties with my dad and to dance for him. Then, after Lyle started going to church, I had to quit. Lyle got saved and he didn't believe in parties, so he made me quit. My dad understood that I was married and was on my own, and he never said anything or tried to make me come with him. He just respected my husband's wishes. Lyle decided all of a sudden that he wanted to be a minister, so I couldn't go anymore, and I kind of missed it. My dad never said that this bothered him because he knew that that would make me very unhappy, so he would never have said anything like that. But he continued to be a song leader and a dancer. By then my younger brother Levi was dancing, and my sisters, too, so that just left me who was not dancing.

Sometime during that time when I wasn't dancing, my dad asked some of the other women in Neah Bay to dance our Grizzly Bear songs, "Ho yeh" and "Hu ya." He asked Lucy Green sometimes, or Lizzy Claplanhoo, and then just a few years before he quit dancing altogether, he used to ask his half sister, Mabel Robertson, to dance with him. Then he got too old and quit dancing altogether, and since I wasn't around to continue to claim our songs, another family claimed them. I don't think those people ever knew that the "Wo hey" Grizzly Bear song was given to me because they weren't there at the time that Captain Jack gave it to me. All they knew was that Charlie Swan used to use it, so probably they thought they could just take it from him. Probably something like this happened with some of our other songs, too, because when I finally started singing and dancing again, I had an awfully hard time getting some of them back.

LIFE WITH PREACHER LYLE: CHURCHES, MONTANA, NEAH BAY

All this happened because Lyle wanted to be a preacher and I, as his wife, went along with what he wanted. He had logged for a while, and then after that he went to work out at the fish dock. Then he quit and wouldn't work anymore. That's when he went into religion—said he couldn't work anymore because he had to work for the Lord. When he started out, we went to the Shaker Church.[2] We went for about a year, and I didn't mind it at all. Lyle first became a minister for the Indian Shaker Church. He didn't really need any training because it was an Indian church. He was pretty good as a preacher.

Things started out okay, but soon this church became just the same as the other Christian churches we went to later on. They had problems here just like in the white churches. Originally, the old-time Shaker church didn't have any Bible. They didn't really believe in the Bible, yet they quoted what was in the Bible. They said that this was given to them through prayer. Even though they didn't know how to read, they quoted the Bible. But then the younger ones wanted to have the Bible in there because they knew that that was where the prophesying was coming from. They said, "Well, we know how to read. We want the Bible in the church." So a split developed between the old-timers and the Bible believers. Lyle and I started out in the Bible-believers group. Eventually it got like any other church. There was a lot of fighting going on in there, a lot of name-calling, and I didn't like that. Finally it came out that because Lyle and I had each been married before, they didn't want us in there, in the Bible believers. Finally I got to a point where I just didn't want to mess around with them anymore, so we quit.

Then from there we moved into the Assembly of God. I think we stayed there for about six or eight years. Because of the way Lyle used to preach, they just accepted him right away into the Assembly. They had a preacher there, but Lyle helped him out and preached sometimes on Sundays. So Lyle ended up being an evangelist, just going wherever they needed him. He really didn't have a church where he would preach all the time. He was kind of like an assistant. Since he'd already been a preacher at the Shaker church, he didn't need any other training. We were going to church all the time in those days.

Sometimes we used to go over to Little Boston,[3] to the All-American United Indian Full Gospel Church. Foster Jones used to be the minister there, and he invited all Indians to come to his meeting. So, Lyle heard about it, and we went over there, and he preached there. We enjoyed ourselves in that church; it was really nice. They used to hold camp meetings all the time, and it was all Indians, so we went over there a lot. And this is where we met Brother Carpenter.

Brother Carpenter was a Crow Indian from Montana, and when he heard Lyle preach over at Little Boston, he invited him to go to Crow to preach. He said he was having a camp meeting and wanted us to come. Lyle was working out at the dock then, and he made up his mind that we'd take just one paycheck and go down there. So this is how we ended up going to Crow.

We went to the Crow Reservation in Montana just for a camp meeting. And while we were there, Brother Carpenter ran short of money and asked if we had any. Lyle said, "All I got is one hundred dollars left that I gotta go home on, and I'm not spending that. I can't touch it because we gotta get back home." And Brother Carpenter said, "Well, just let me borrow that until after camp meeting, because then I'll have some money." So Lyle gave it to him. After the camp meeting there wasn't a penny left! Brother Carpenter was still in debt. We never, ever got that money back!

We ended up staying in Montana for a whole year because we couldn't get any money to come back home on. There was no way! The two kids and I had to stay with Delia Cummins for a while, and she took care of us. She tried her best to pick up money for us. She had meetings at her house. She'd take up a collection for us, and that way we had a little spending money. Lots of times we only got twenty cents. They were afraid of Carpenter because he used to say, "When you tithe, you ain't gonna tithe to Brother Lyle, you're gonna tithe to me, because that money's rightfully mine, not his." So they were afraid to tithe to us at all. So this is how we got stuck in Montana.

And that's a very, very prejudiced place. I never, ever thought I'd run away from the door when I saw a white person coming, but I did. I ran and I actually hid. That's how bad it was there. People just *hated* Indians there. They called them down and everything, and still they had to have contact with the Indians there because they leased property from them: uranium and farming lands, copper, and what have you. They hated Indians so badly there that I couldn't even get a job, and I was an experienced cook. I tried. I walked around Billings and Hardin and Lodge Grass looking for a job, and I couldn't get anything! There was no way I could get a job there. It took me a while to realize exactly what was happening. It wasn't only prejudice, though. A lot of those Indians got lease money, and they didn't want to work much. They held a job down just long enough to earn a few dollars, and then they would leave and get drunk. They'd sit around the streets over in Billings. They sat right down on the pavement, leaned up against the buildings. I never saw anything like that up here in the Northwest. Now you do, but then you didn't. There's places where they're prejudiced up here, but really not as much as down there. Here you generally can go into any cocktail lounge, but over there you can't. They send you down to skid row when you're an Indian. Over here on the coast, we mix a lot with white people and lots of times we don't even think anything of it. They become our friends. I'm not scared of them here like I was over in Montana.

We lived in Lodge Grass, Montana, during that terrible year. We rented from some people by the name of Bird-in-the-Ground, and they were Indians. We had one bedroom in there and no bathroom. We had an outhouse. And there was no running water in the house; I had to walk ten blocks to get my water from a pump. In order to haul my wash water, I went down there and carried two buckets at a time from the well and brought it to the house and washed, and then carried more to rinse my clothes. So, it was very, very different down there from our large comfortable houses with lots of bedrooms, and running water, and a bathroom, up here in Neah Bay. But I just had to get used to it down there because we were stuck there.

The kids weren't around to help me haul water or do the chores because they were in school. The school they went to was way, way up on a hill. They called it a mountain, but to me it was a hill.

Lyle was supposed to have been preaching during this time, but he kind of fell by the wayside. Aside from preaching, he knew how to get around with the women folk that were in the congregation. He had been, and continued to go with a series of women while we were married. The time in Montana was especially bad. For a while he was going with an Indian girl over in Billings. I found out about that because one of the kids got very sick once and I had to find him. . . . After this one ended, he started going with this white woman who was teaching over in Glendive, Montana. Her husband was a sheepherder and was gone anywhere from three to six months out in the hills tending sheep, so that made it easier for her to carry on like this. . . .

After I found out about this one, I made up my mind what I was going to do. I went over to the cop's house and told him, "I want to go home." I explained what Brother Carpenter had done to us and said, "This is how come we're stuck here." It was snowing and was ten degrees below zero, and my boy had shoes with a big hole in the bottom. I told the cop, "My kids are going to school with just little, thin jackets, and it's cold out there! I can't stand it anymore and I'd like to go home." But I didn't tell him what else was going on with Lyle. So, the cop said, "Well, I'll try to do something about it. We'll have a meeting here tonight." He was with the church group also, so that night I think we got about three dollars, was all. And I looked at the cop, and I said, "That just isn't going to bring us home. It isn't going to buy our bus fare." And I said, "But I've got to go! I can't stay here anymore! My boy has holes in his shoes, and he puts cardboard in there. Right now, we're down to oatmeal to eat. We *had* milk and sugar, but they're all gone. We *just* have oatmeal." So he said, "I'll try again. I'll talk to some of the people, see if they won't put in money." And they just didn't do it. When he came back, he only had about five dollars or so. We waited around and waited around. Finally I talked to Lyle. I told him, "I gotta get home. I can't stand seeing the kids going to school like this anymore."

We were supposed to pay for our kids' meals in school if they weren't Crow. Somehow they didn't find out that Arnie wasn't a Crow, so he got his lunch there. But they found out that Babe wasn't a Crow, so they started sending her home for lunch. She'd come home and sit there, and she'd cry a little, and she'd say, "I'm so hungry. I'm so hungry." And there was really nothing I could do, just nothing. I didn't have any food to give her.

Finally, I took Arnie's gun, a twenty-two, and his trumpet that he'd brought with him, and I sold them. I think Lyle had a hunch that I was going to take my kids home to Neah Bay with me and not come back to Montana. So, he said, "Well, you can go home. You can take the girl, but you can't take Son." So I couldn't take Arnie, but I did take Babe and returned home.

We didn't stay with Mom and Dad when we got back; we stayed in the little house in back, next to Martin's Pool Hall. We had a hard time. It was cold in there, and we started out with nothing. That house just had a bedroom and a living room and kitchen combined. So we stayed there, and I went to work for Martin. He had a cafe and a pool hall. He had three pool tables and a small restaurant, so I worked there. And with my first month's paycheck I bought Arnie two pairs of shoes and two jackets. I mailed those back to him. I bought Babe some underclothes and some shoes, too. I didn't have to buy a jacket for her, because my sister gave her one.

I worked until I had enough money to go back to Montana, and I decided to take Babe and go back because she got so lonesome for Arnie. She started crying every day because she wanted her brother. I couldn't take that, either, so I left in February or March, and we went back to Montana. This time I decided I couldn't leave Arnie there, either. I told Lyle that the kids had to go home for summer vacation, and I wanted to take them home. I saved just enough money to get back. Since I had come back once, I guess Lyle felt like I would come back again, so I got to bring the kids home for summer vacation. What little money I had saved from here, he didn't know I had. So we were able to buy a one-way ticket for all three of us, and Lyle stayed there. Before I left he said, "You're not taking anything. You're not taking the silverware, dishes, or anything. And your coat is staying here!" I had a real nice fur coat, and I'm sure he thought that if I left my fur coat that I would have to come back again. But I didn't. We just stayed home after we got here. We were here for about four months, and then I wrote him and told him that I was going to get a divorce and that I wasn't going back again. So that's how we got a divorce.

THE DIVORCE

I filed and got a divorce. But he came home and he contested it. He didn't want a divorce. I don't even remember now why he didn't want one. Then he also put on there that I was drinking excessively and that he was going to take the kids away from me. I hadn't been doing any drinking at all. So we went to court, and he couldn't really prove that I had been drinking. I asked John Barker, on the police force in Neah Bay for many years, to be my witness, and he gave me a written statement. Then Ida Ball, the cook over at Elvrum's, came to me and told me that if the court would subpoena her, she'd be glad to come and tell how Lyle came in with his kids but would never feed them. He'd feed some of Babe's girlfriends and would send Babe to sit in the car with a milkshake while they were eating inside. She said to me, "I wondered and wondered why he would never feed his own children, but would take somebody else's kid and give 'em a full meal." I didn't know about any of this until she talked to me and told me what had been going on. So, when Lyle was on the stand, my lawyer asked him, "How much money do you spend on your children?" Lyle answered, "Maybe about fifty-nine dollars a week. I feed them at the restaurant."

Then when the lawyer called me up there, he asked, "How much do you spend?" I said, "I really don't know. I really don't know how much I spend on them. I take care of my two children. I have to pay the lights and the heat and their clothing. Lyle doesn't give me anything. Nothing! I've never gotten a penny from him. But I work, and all my bills I pay myself. I've been taking care of them for over two years now, ever since we got back." And I explained to them how we had to go without, when we were in Montana, and how sometimes we only ate oatmeal because there was no money for anything else—no sugar, no milk, nothing else. Then the lawyer asked, "Okay, how much do you feed them?" "I can't swear," I said, "because I have my food prepared at home. I can't afford it any other way. I pay my bills. I can't afford to feed them in the restaurant even though I do work there. But I make it a point to feed them there once a week. All of us eat there together once a week. I give them their choice whether they want to eat there on Saturday or Sunday. The rest of the time I prepare food at home for them and leave it for them when I'm working. We cook on an oil stove. When I leave in the morning, I leave them a batter of hotcakes or their eggs and potatoes all ready for them. I boil up potatoes, make hash browns, always have food cooked for them at home. Besides their food, I buy their clothes. Once a year before school they each get two new sets of clothes which I buy on layaway."

I wrote the lawyer a note and told him what Ida Ball said and that we could subpoena her if necessary. The lawyer called Lyle back on the stand and looked at him and said, "You mean to tell me that you're an *evangelist*? And you'd *do* something like that? I want you to listen very carefully. *You're* telling me that *you're* an evangelist. Both my mother and my father are full gospel; my grandparents were; so I know what you stand for. Now tell me the truth. And God help *you. I'm* not on the stand, *you* are. I want the *whole truth* and nothing but the truth from you, because *I'm* not going to answer for it. *You* are. Now, *how much* do you spend on your children?" Lyle sat there for what seemed like about fifteen minutes, changing sides of his legs, crossing and uncrossing them. Finally the judge got mad at him and told him, "Answer the lawyer right now, and I don't want any waiting." So Lyle answered, "Maybe two or three dollars." Then the judge said, "Okay, that's the end. She gets the kids, and you pay her twenty-five dollars a month for each one of them." The judge wanted me to charge him seventy-five, but I said I couldn't do that because I wouldn't be able to get it from him. "Twenty-five dollars for each is fine," I said, "if he'll send it. We'll be lucky to get fifty dollars a month." Lyle only sent that money twice. Never sent it again! I could have gone back to court about it, but I didn't. I just decided that I didn't want anything to do with him anymore! Just absolutely nothing! Well, then I had a hard time after that.

For a long time after the divorce, Arnie blamed me for what had happened. His dad had gotten ahold of him and told him that I just wanted to run around, and that's why I left him. The kids did stay with me, however, and were going to school here in Neah Bay. Finally, one day after we'd been divorced for a year, Arnie went after the mail and somehow or other he got hold of this letter which was addressed to his dad, and he opened it. I got after him for doing that, told him it wasn't his to open. Anyhow, Arnie found a check for thirty-five dollars in there from one of Lyle's women friends and a letter which said, "As long as you're having to pay alimony, here's thirty-five dollars. I'll try to squeeze that much out for you every month, honey, no matter what. As long as you're able to stay with me and be free, you'll get this money from me. Whenever, I can, I'll send it." After Arnie read that letter, he began to change a little bit. Before he read it, he kind of hated me for a while after his dad talked to him, and several times he told me it was my fault that they didn't have a dad anymore. But after he got hold of that letter, he was so mad! He said, "I am going to keep this money, and I'm going to cash it." I said, "Don't you do it. That's not yours. You send it back to him. It's not yours!" But he took off. He was just mad enough to cash it and spend it. Babe told me afterwards that he didn't. He just threw the letter away. It was after this that Arnie started drinking. I had a lot of problems with him. He drank for a while and then he quit and decided he was going to leave. He decided he was going to go into the service, and he did.

And Babe—she never said anything. She kept it all inside. She never let anything out. No matter how upset she was. As long as it concerned her dad, she wouldn't let anything out. She's still like that now.

After this marriage ended and the divorce was final, I felt like my life was already spent. I felt pretty bitter . . . like my life had been wasted. I really felt that life had passed me by because I was in my late thirties, which seemed pretty old, and I had to raise my children alone. It kind of got me down for a while.

I tried going to church for a time, but it ended up they wouldn't accept me in there after I got a divorce. They said that I'd left my husband, and they didn't allow divorcées in church. Well, that kind of took me down, too. This happened about two years after I left Lyle.

THE INFLUENCE OF MY DAD ON MY LIFE

Then I remembered what my dad had said to me earlier, when I was still a member of the Assembly of God. My dad said, "All right, you go ahead and stay with that church if it's going to keep you on the right track, but just remember, first of all, you're an Indian. You'll never be anything but an Indian." Then he told me that after a while I might find that I wasn't accepted in that church either, because that's a borrowed religion. It wasn't something that belonged to us. He said, "But if you decide that you don't want to be there, you still must behave yourself and be respectable. Remember you're an Indian, first of all. And Indians have their own religion. You'll still never be accepted anyway because you can't change your color. You'll never be happy unless you stay with your Indian religion." And that seems to be true. I can't see any other way. So, when anybody asks me now, I say, "I've got

HELMA'S STORY

my own religion. I don't want anybody else's religion." This way I can go ahead and be happy and pray by myself without anybody telling me "You can't do this and you can't do that." That's the way I believe now.

My dad was a very important influence in my life. He was a good man and a very hard worker. For thirty-two years he worked as a carpenter, a plumber, an all-round man for the Bureau of Indian Affairs. But one time he got a smidge of something in his eye. He was grinding something—I don't remember whether it was an axe or what—and a piece of the steel flew in his eye. The next year it happened to his other eye. He had cataracts in his eyes pretty bad, so he finally asked for retirement. Of course, Mr. Bitney, our Indian agent, told him, "No damn *Indian* will ever get on *retirement.* Do you think in your life that you'll ever find an Indian on retirement with the government? No siree!" Well, Dr. Boyd was our doctor here, and he helped him after my dad told him what Bitney had told him. Dr. Boyd said, "Well, we'll just see about that!" Dr. Boyd wrote a letter to the BIA in Seattle and told them that my dad couldn't possibly work anymore and that he should get disability retirement. It took about six months before he finally got it, and Dr. Boyd went in himself and talked to them. So, my dad got disability retirement, and, oh, did that make Bitney mad! Oh! He was mad! Dr. Boyd went over his head, and he didn't like that one bit. Dr. Boyd was pretty well liked by the people here. So, he helped my dad get his disability retirement, and then Dad didn't have to work after that.

Even though he had the cataracts, he still carved, but he couldn't do little things. He made two sets of our family masks. I don't know where one set went; Roger Ernesti, who was a collector, got the other set. He got two blankets and four masks and two headgears from my dad. I went over to his place in Toppenish one time to try to take pictures of my dad's stuff, but he wouldn't let me, so I don't know what happened to them. He may have sold them.

One thing that made me sad was that three years before he died, my dad started drinking quite a bit. This was something I'd never seen him do, although my mother said that he did in the first few years they were married. She used to say he'd be gone all night—never came home till morning. I don't know when he quit, because I'd never seen him drink or smoke all my grown-up days. Never! Only thing I used to see him do that was bad was swear. When he got mad, he'd swear. That's all. But when he started drinking a few years before he died, that really hurt me. I don't know why he started. He never was much of a talker, to air out his problems. He always used to say, "If I got problems, they're not *your* problems. They're *mine.* You'll have your own problems in your day. So, I don't need to put my problems on you." And he never did. My dad was a very kind and good person. He got along with everybody, and he didn't want to be mean to anybody. He wanted to believe in everybody, believe everybody was going to be good. But then there were times when people weren't that way, yet he still believed in them. I was quite sad when he died in 1958.

My third child, Mike, was born seven months before my dad passed away. I remember how my dad used to hold him in his arms and say, "You came too late for me to be able to teach you." So it was up to me to talk to him and teach him. Mike has a habit of asking questions, and I always try to answer them. He doesn't go right into anything, he sits and he asks about it and thinks about it first. He's listened to me a lot over the years.

MARRIAGE TO OLIVER WARD, JR.: GOOD AND BAD TIMES, SCHOOL, JOBS

About two years after Mike was born, I married Oliver Ward, Jr., nicknamed Wimpy because he loved hamburgers as a kid. We were married by a justice of the peace in Seattle in 1960. We never did get married in the church. I was through with churches and church services by then, and Wimpy never went to church, so there was no need. The only time we went to a church was for someone else's wedding or funeral.

When we got back to Neah Bay, Wimpy's mother and father, Irene [Hunter Ward] and Oliver Ward Sr., had a big potlatch party for us. They gave a huge feast followed by singing and dancing, and then they gave away a whole lot of things. My dad was already gone then [in 1960], so my family didn't do anything. At that time I hadn't started singing yet, so there was no one to sing so that my sisters could dance. My dad was gone, and we just didn't feel like doing it. Wimpy's family did pick up his grandmother Odelia Hunter in Seattle, where she lived, and brought her down to sing the Hunter family songs for the party. She was Jim Hunter's widow, so she knew his songs, and since those songs were going to Wimpy, as the oldest grandchild, she had the right to sing them for him at our wedding party. Just the locals were invited for this party: the Quileutes, the Hohs, and the Makahs. We didn't invite the Canadians because both Irene's family and our family hadn't been in touch with them for many years.

After we were first married, we started out real good for a while. Then he started doing a lot of drinking, and he began beating me up. This kept on, and so I took him to court, both inside and outside the reservation. Finally, with the help of Judge Church we got things under control. He told Wimpy, "This has got to stop! You can't go on doing this forever. This had better be the last time. If you do it again, I'll just put you in jail and throw the key away." And that was all it took. We had marriage counseling, and for thirty-five years we've gotten along better.

During the time while we were having trouble, his mother would send him away to stay with relatives in California, but then he'd come back after a while, and we'd get together again for a while until things got bad, and then we'd separate for a while. His mother wasn't real pleased with the marriage in the first place, since I was fourteen years older than Wimpy, so she really was no help to us during these years.

Mike and I stayed in Seattle off and on for about three years. I had to go there in the winter each year because I got laid off my job at Rosie's Restaurant in Neah Bay and didn't have any place to stay or any way to support myself and Mike. In the summers I worked in Neah Bay, but in the winters I couldn't find employment, and the house we lived in was not insulated, so I had to go to Seattle, where we lived on welfare. The first time we stayed in Seattle, Mike must have been about two, and we stayed at the Assembly Hotel. They had apartments upstairs. There was everything in that building, so really there was no need for me to go anywhere, unless I needed to go to a department store. They had a barber shop in there, a beauty shop in the basement, a restaurant, and a cocktail lounge on one side. They had sort of a playroom where we'd go sometimes. They had a pool table and games and books there, so we'd spend some time there. We had just two little hot plates in our room, but if I wanted to bake or roast anything, they had a community kitchen down in the basement. So I really didn't have to go out with Mike much at all. I didn't like going out much, so I was happy to stay in there. I was always kind of afraid whenever I was living in the city like that. We were there maybe about five or six months that time. Then we moved back home again, and I went back to work for the summer.

In the fall a few years later, we moved to High Point in south Seattle. There we lived next door to colored people and that was really scarey for me. Seemed like the men around there were all dirty-mouthed, and they scared me. They were just different and I couldn't feel comfortable with them. I just didn't like being alone there! Mike was in first grade then and I had to walk with him over the hill every morning. Even though he was just a little child, I didn't like being without him. I came to Seattle with him because there was just no place to stay in Neah Bay. My dad was gone, and I didn't want to stay with my mom. She'd already started drinking, and I didn't want to move over there and have to watch her and the boys drink. So we moved to Seattle. High Point was low-income housing, and I think my niece Sadie Johnson told me about it. We took a furnished apartment, and I think we were there for the whole school year that time.

The third time in Seattle we lived over on 34th Street. We were right across from a Catholic school. There were four units there, and we had the upstairs two bedroom apartment. I felt better that time cause I had white people and one Alaskan girl around me. No one scared me and no one talked dirty. Mike was in the second grade then, and we stayed there that whole school year.

Then Wimpy came home, we moved home, and we finally made it as a family. We never separated anymore. I got a job at Elvrum's Restaurant, and Wimpy worked as a mechanic for the ice machine, first for the Bay Fish Company and later for the Co-op in Neah Bay.

Not too long after that, in about 1967, we all moved to Tacoma so Wimpy could go to school there. He went to Tacoma Technical School to study electrical appliance repair. When he was done, he had to put in an extra two years to prove to the school that he could hold a job. So I said to him, "*You're* going to have a job when you finish school, how about *me* going to school now." Wimpy said, "Well, go ahead if you can, but I doubt if the government will let you." I said, "Well, supposing you get sick or something. Then I wouldn't know what to do. I'm not gonna go back to cooking. I don't want to." He said, "Go ahead and try, but I know that the government isn't going to let you." So I did. I tried. The government wouldn't let me go. They said, "No, your husband is the head of the family, and he's already gone to school. So you can't." Well, we argued for a while. I said, "What if he gets sick and I'm left alone?" The government man only said, "No, as long as he's alive, you can't go to school." This is what the government does to you. This was about in 1969. I don't know why they won't just let Mr. and Mrs. go to school, because what will she do if he dies? It did end up many years later that Wimpy got sick and couldn't work, and I was left having to make baskets from six o'clock in the morning till midnight or one o'clock just trying to make a living. I did this for about five or six years until he was better and could work again.

So, after the government man told me this, I decided, "Well, I'm not going to give up. I will *not* give up!" So I went to Manpower, and I went to everyone they suggested in order to try to find a way to get my schooling paid for. I went all over Tacoma, and I finally found out I could go to school through the state. So I finally got to go. Actually all the state did was pay my tuition and give me ten dollars a month for bus fare. And I took it. I went to Bates Vocational School (formerly Tacoma Tech). I didn't have any money for a baby-sitter, but I went to school anyway, because Wimpy would get home a little before I left, so that would leave Mike home with somebody. I decided on cooking school because I figured that was the only thing I knew, and I thought I might have missed something because I was a self-taught cook. What I actually wanted to learn was how to run a restaurant. But this isn't what they taught us. What I actually learned was commercial cooking, not restaurant cooking. The chef soon found out what I knew and that cooking wasn't much effort for me. He asked me, "Did you work before?" and I said, "Yes, that's all I've ever done." So I went through the stations real quick, one at a time, and then I ended up being the boss of the place; I was the sous-chef. That's all I ended up doing afterwards.

I really didn't learn all that much in that school. And I was the only one there that knew how to cut fish. Henry, our chef, didn't think I knew how to cut fish, and one time I wasn't paying attention when he was teaching us how to fillet it. I thought, "I don't need to learn." And so he kind of turned on me because he noticed I wasn't listening. So he says, "All right. Let's see an *Indian* cut it, then!" So I just took it and filleted it real quick, like we always do at home. Was he *surprised!* He didn't know Indians could do *anything* like that. He didn't think we were good for anything, and he called us down a lot. Even though I was the sous-chef, he kept talking about one young Indian fellow who cooked down here, but who didn't last too long.

One day, this nice young fellow, John, was cooking with us, and the chef was chewing him out and kept saying, "You want to be like those dirty Indians? Clean up your damn stove!" He could really cuss. "Clean up your goddamned, son-of-a-bitch stove!" he told John. His back was right to me, and he forgot that I was there.

So I turned around and said, "Yeah, John, why can't you be like us damn dirty Indians. Come on, clean your damn stove off." The chef just *looked* at me and *snapped* his eyes, and he walked into his office. He never came out of there the rest of the day. I was working in the salad bar then, and about every ten minutes I looked at the chef, and I hollered to John, "John, you got your damn grill clean?" I was just rubbing it in to the chef so bad that day, but he never looked up once. John was trying to cook for six busloads of kids from Chemawa, and he just couldn't stop to clean his grill because he had all those orders that kept coming in. If the chef had been there watching to see what was really happening, he would not have talked to John like that. The chef and I never got along after that. However, it was toward the end of school. Even before this incident, he was pretty evenhanded with everybody, except that he was really down on Indians. That always got me *mad*.

I completed cooking school and cooked at the Coach Room Restaurant in Tacoma for a short time. They paid waitress wages for the cook; this was a prejudiced place, so I quit and let Wimpy work.

He worked at Zingler Electric on 38th Street for about three or four years. He did okay with them, but white people in Tacoma wouldn't let Wimpy into their homes to repair their appliances because he was an Indian. This got him down pretty bad. He could only work in the shop and repair things. Finally he decided, "Let's go home! I don't enjoy this job where they won't let me do what I'm supposed to do!"

RETURN TO NEAH BAY: JOBS, INDIAN MUSIC

So we decided to return to Neah Bay. This was in 1971 or 1972, and we've been back ever since. Wimpy worked at a number of different jobs after we returned, but he never got to use his training in electrical appliances; there just weren't any jobs for him on the reservation. He was a member of the tribal council for several years; he worked in the tribal real estate office on land claim business for a while; he worked down at the dock; I bought a boat, and he's been a salmon fisherman; and most recently [since 1994], he's been back on the Makah Tribal Council again.[4]

I went back to Elvrum's Restaurant and worked for a while. Then after I quit, a few years later, Wimpy got sick, so I spent several years making baskets to sell to tourists, and we just barely survived on what I made for those years. Later on, I would pinch-hit as a cook for the Senior Citizens' Center for $2.60 an hour, and sometimes also up at the Head Start Center, where I'd cook breakfast and lunch for sixty to eighty kids every day. There the pay was six dollars an hour, so that wasn't so bad.

Since about 1980, I've been working in the Makah Language Program up at the museum, which was directed by Arlie Flynn until his death in May of 1983. Later, Ann Renker took it over for several years, and now Maria Parker Pascua runs it. I got paid six dollars an hour and have worked on a Makah dictionary, a handbook, several language books, and translations of a number of books and stories into

Makah.[5] For a number of years I also went in three afternoons a week during the school year and was teaching Makah language to some of the grade school kids. Now I'm back there again, telling them Makah stories. In the summers I've worked with the Makah Culture Class, teaching the kids the dances they perform for Makah Day in August. I sing the songs and help them with the proper movements. Maria Pascua has been teaching them the dances, too.

MY RETURN TO MAKAH MUSIC

During my adult life there was quite a span where I didn't have anything to do with Indian music at all. Lyle wasn't at all interested for the twenty years I was married to him, and Wimpy wasn't especially interested for about the first ten years I was married to him. Then I began to notice that he was getting interested. I talked to him a little bit about this, a little bit about that. His mom showed him the pictures of some of the Indian dances that his grandpa must have had. Then all of a sudden he decided that we should go to this party over at Queets, given by Pansy Hudson.

At the party Wimpy said to me, "I wish I could get them to sing my grandpa's song." I said, "We could try. Do you really want to sing?" "Yeah!" he said. So I thought, "Since he's interested, I better keep going with this, right now!" So I went over to where the Makah singers were, and I asked one of them, because I knew that she knew their songs. I said to her, "Wimpy wants to sing. Would you please sing his grandpa Jim Hunter's song for him?" She answered me, "No. I feel sick. I feel sick and I can't do it. I barely got through with this song." So I asked another one of the singers who was there, and she said, "Oh, my throat is sore. My throat is so sore! I just barely got through with this song." So I said, "All right, you guys, never mind." By that time my heart was just *beating* like *anything*, because I knew what I had to do. I was going to try anyway.

I asked one of them, "Can I borrow your drum?" She kind of reluctantly gave it to me. Then I went over to Aunt Edith Simon, from Clayoquot, B.C., and asked her if she'd help me, told her what I was going to do. Then I went over and asked Sam Johnson and Johnnie Williams and their wives, from Gold River, B.C., "Could you folks help me sing? I'm going to sing Jim Hunter's song." So they all got up and came over, and even though they couldn't all sing it, I had their moral support. Just as soon as I started to sing, the Makah singers kind of felt funny because I had this Clayoquot couple and this Nootka couple helping me sing, and Aunt Edith. So I had those five people helping me, and then one by one the Makahs stood up, and their mouths were open as they watched me sing.[6] None of them had ever heard me sing before, never knew I could do it. It must have been all right, though; people seemed to like it, and I've been singing ever since.[7]

From that time on, we've been doing a lot of work trying to get our songs, our masks, and other things back, which belong to each of our families. I kept listening

Fig. 33. Canadians singing with Helma Swan Ward at potlatch party in Neah Bay, Washington, May 1978. Helma is in the center, singing at the microphone. Lending support, to the right is her Canadian cousin, Caroline Frank Mickey, and also Odelia David Hunter, holding a drum. *Photograph by Bill Holm.*

Fig. 34. Oliver Ward, Jr. (Wimpy), husband of Helma Swan, wearing a wolf headgear and dancing one of his family Wolf Dances at a potlatch in Neah Bay, May 1978. At left, Odelia Hunter is drumming. *Photograph by Bill Holm.*

Fig. 35. Teaching a song, September 9, 1994. Helma Swan instructs a group of young male singers at an evening rehearsal for a Ward family potlatch that was held in Neah Bay on the following day. *Photograph by Linda J. Goodman.*

to all the songs they sang at parties, and then sometimes I'd remember some that came from Wimpy's family and some that came from mine. Some I heard on old recordings. I taught Wimpy to dance the same way my father taught me to dance—by listening to the song over and over and then by practicing the steps over and over.

As time went on, my memory kept working and working and then it would bring me another song. And then while I'm thinking of that one, eventually I'll think of another one. Because I've heard them all my life, gradually they come back. There are some, though, that don't come back. As hard as I try, I just can't think of them.

When I first started singing, I would practice all by myself. That's the way the old people used to do a long time ago, too. I remember when I was seven or eight, I used to hear Mrs. Annie Long Tom singing—first thing in the morning, real early. She'd be alone, nobody with her, and she'd be singing up a storm. All the time. And then my dad sang alone every day, except when he wasn't feeling good. We'd know he wasn't feeling good if he didn't sing. When I would practice, I would just take my drum, sit down, and sing—usually in the living room. Usually I would be all alone. Sometimes, if Mike was sleeping in late, he'd hear me. I wasn't singing at all when I had the other two kids, so Mike's really heard me a lot more.

There was one thing that happened, though, that really got me started again working on the Swan family songs. I was working at Elvrum's Restaurant, cooking, after we returned from Tacoma, and one day I started talking to this fellow, Dave Fourlines, who was eating in there. He showed me a leather apron that he had made and was going to take to Colorado when he and Arnie Hunter went there to dance for a powwow. Then he asked me if I knew Arnie Hunter, and I said, "Yeah, I know him." Dave said, "He had a grandfather by the name of Charlie Swan, and now there's nobody left from that family but Arnie," and then he went on to tell me that different people were asking him to make copies of our masks for them because "Charlie Swan was my cousin," or "he was just like a brother to me." Dave described every one of our masks just perfectly and told me who he was going to make them for. I guess these people figured that I wasn't coming back to claim these things (I wasn't singing at that time yet), so that was why they wanted to have copies made and use them. I was pretty upset when I discovered that everything was just going to go helter-skelter to everybody, and Dave was going to do it. Well, Dave changed his mind awful quick after he discovered that I was Arnie's mother. I talked to him and explained why he couldn't do what he was planning to do with the masks. It was after this happened that I sang at the party down at Queets. Then Wimpy and I just started going to the parties regularly, so people could see we were back and we were going to use the things that belonged to us (see figs. 30, 33, 34).

I asked Wimpy if he wanted to go to Canada and look up our relatives that we hadn't seen for a long time. It had been like thirty, thirty-five, maybe even forty years since anybody had gone across there. He asked his mom, but she didn't really know too many people there, and she didn't want to go. But he was curious enough to want to go. He made up his mind that we would go across and see who his relations were, because he knew that his grandfather, Jim Hunter, was full-blood Clayoquot. So we went across there and renewed our acquaintance with his relatives and my relatives and our old friends again, and then after that the people started coming back again. This is how the Canadian people started coming back across here to Neah Bay.

Music in Neah Bay now is getting all mixed up. People are taking each other's songs, and they're saying, "Well, this is my song. I can sing this song anytime I want to because he was my cousin, or he was my nephew," or something like that. It's getting to the point where people are almost hating each other because of this. A party isn't a party where you can just go and enjoy yourself anymore. I doubt if it's ever going to get any better because when one family starts singing, other families look daggers at them. Some will help one bunch but not another bunch. And then you hear speeches like, "This is our song, and nobody will ever get it away from us." And it's just not a real good party anymore. I think it will just keep on being like that for another generation, and then I'm afraid the songs will all belong to one or two families, or if we're lucky, the songs might just kind of belong to everybody. The way it looks, that's what's going to happen, because everybody's claiming everybody's songs. It won't be too much longer before no one will really know what belongs to whom, and then it might just be that the tribe will own them all. Either that, or they'll just keep fighting over them and trying to steal them from each other and not follow tradition—that "the oldest in the direct line of descent becomes the next owner." If the oldest is a woman, she is caretaker till she passes it on to the next one who is the oldest male in line, if she thinks he'll take proper care of it.

I think I feel now just about like my dad used to feel about parties. When I was young I used to wonder about him—why was he so broke all the time? And he was working steady—year after year after year—cause he had a government job. I used to wonder: why did he have to sell all his ten acres and other inherited properties that he got? Why doesn't he have any? Everything was sold, and I used to think, why in the world does he have to do that? Now I know. In order to keep on going to these parties, you have to have money. When you go you have to sing, and you always have to give away money to all the prominent people. And that's paying to keep your name. This is what he liked, and this is what I feel I have to keep up— because that's what he did. We're upholding our tradition. It's our obligation to sing and to dance and to give away in order to keep up our name. If you do this, then people know who you are. It's more or less to keep reminding people who you are, where you came from. Otherwise, nobody would know.

Finally, for myself, things in my life have been a lot different than I thought they were going to be. I like singing for my family, teaching our music to the younger generation, and working on the language. I've gotten into a lot of different areas that I never dreamed of when I was younger. I'm more curious now. Now I find I'm content to be alive. It isn't that I'm really happy, because our life is still full of problems, but I am content, and things are much better than they were in the past.

PART 3

SONGS
OF MY
ANCESTORS

CHAPTER 10

TEN SWAN FAMILY SONGS

The Swan family songs, along with their accompanying dances, masks, and costumes, are Helma's most cherished possessions. They have always played a central role in her life and in the lives of a number of other family members. As the oldest surviving child of Charlie and Ruth Swan, Helma has felt the heavy responsibility of song ownership and has spent much of her adult life protecting, defending, and preserving these family treasures. Following is a selection of ten of the family's favorite songs along with remnants of the stories about them. Varying kinds and amounts of information and translations are available for each song. Musical transcriptions and analyses can be found at the end of this chapter.

1. "Ah yi wáyo" ("Stop Awhile")—a Love Song

This *T'abáa* (entertainment) song first belonged to Charlie Swan. He never told Helma where it came from, and she never heard its history from others. Therefore, little is known about it except that it is a Makah love song, sung for general fun and pleasure. Although family-owned, it is not considered to be one of the family's most important songs. As with other t'abaa songs, no dance is performed with it, nor are there any costumes. It is a song that the Swan family members like very much, however, and enjoy singing.

The song text includes a few meaningful Makah words and also vocables (syllables without specific meaning, such as "Ah yi wáyo"). Helma spoke about this song and translated the text into English:

> The vocables can go on and on and on, and then the first [meaningful] part says: "Stop a while, I want to talk to you." Then it has another verse after this is ended: "Why do you act nasty? Why do you act so nasty to me? Stop a while, I want to talk to you." Then it goes on and on like he or she was carrying on a conversation and then another part comes in which says, "Well, look at Herman, he's dancing, but he's coming out the wrong way. He backs out the wrong way." And it goes on and on again. Then there's another set of words, "Bite my bait, it's

sweet. My bait is over at the store." In other words, your bait is candy. Then, after this, you could put your own words in there, if you felt like it.

The first part of the song consists entirely of vocables. The Makah words of the first verse of the "Chorus," with translation, are as follows:

O yi wo ho yi wo	hadá	ƛ'adi·wiƛ'		yu yu	yi wa
	hey	stop		a	
	you			while	

Ha yi wo ho yi wo	hadá	tsitsíqat čiyiksítsux̌		ya ha yi wa
	hey	talk	(I) will	
	you	together	to you	
		with		

English Translation: Hey, stop a while,
I want to talk to you.

Only the words of the first verse are included in the musical transcription presented here. Words of two other verses are as follows:

Bačiƛuis	tiƛa·sis	i wa ya	iyaxaks	baku·wasiqʔa	hi way
bite my	bait		mine is at	the store it is	

Translation: Bite my bait.
My bait is over at the store.

Dačiƛix̌ač	Hami·n	wikuł	x̌alix̌	kʷakʷiyał	i wa ya
look at (with	Herman	without	poor	his rear end	
pity)		a mask	thing	is coming out	
		(nothing	(pity	(he's backing	
		on his face)	some-	out as he starts	
			one)	the dance)	

Translation: Look at Herman,
Dancing without a mask, poor thing.
He's dancing out backwards. [This is a joke and a cause of great mirth.]

The singer may add as many more verses as he or she wishes.

2. "Limey Kašlá"—Dinner Song

This song was originally a chief's Feast Song, which came from the Kʷákʷakyawakʷ (Kwakiutl) Tribe at Alert Bay to the Nootkan chief Captain Jack through marriage. His wife was Kʷákʷakyawakʷ, and it was given by her family at the time of their marriage. Captain Jack and his wife gave it to Annie Williams, the daughter of Benjamin Cedakanim (also known as Atliú) from Clayoquot. At a pot-latch in 1930, Annie gave this song to her nephew, Charlie Swan, from Neah Bay. It now belongs to Charlie's daughter, Helma Swan, and is frequently sung at feasts preceding potlatches.

Meaningful text is in the Kʷákʷakyawakʷ language, but no translation was possible— Kʷákʷakyawakʷ speakers found they could no longer understand or translate the words. The original words probably have been changed beyond recognition as a result of the transfer of the song to a number of non-Kʷákʷakyawakʷ-speaking owners.[1] Pronunciation often undergoes significant change when words are spoken or sung by people unfamiliar with the language.

Dinner songs are always sung before a feast begins, and Helma told one short anecdote about this song:

> It [the song] can go on and on and on, really. My dad used to do that—just because there'd be visitors—he'd see them pick up their fork and knife and get a mouthful, then he'd start in again—he'd start singing. Then they'd have to put their forks and knives down and start clapping again. He teased them like this. They used to have a lot of fun on this particular song.

Customarily, no one could begin eating until the singers had finished singing the Dinner songs. If the singers saw someone getting ready to eat, this frequently spurred them to redouble their singing efforts and, for fun, they would lengthen the song they were singing. This created great merriment among the singers and also among those who were anxiously waiting to begin eating.

3. "Hya'a hya ley" ("The Song of the Seven Daylights")— Whaling Song

This old Anderson family song is also called "The Spiritual." It belonged to Charlie Anderson's grandfather, then to Charlie Anderson; next it was transferred to his daughter, Ruth Anderson Swan, and now it belongs to her daughter, Helma Swan. This is an important family song which was often danced at potlatches. Helma told several stories connected with it.

> The "Song of the Seven Daylights" was made by my great-great-grandfather on my mother's side. I can't remember his Indian name, but when he came out of this, they called him, *Dashúk*, which means "strong."
>
> A long time ago, they went whaling, and my great-great-grandfather was sup-posed to have been a good whale hunter. Every time he went whale hunting, he always came back with a whale. And in those days they never wasted anything. The whale went for food for the whole tribe. Every time they came in with one, they would distribute it among the whole tribe. Each one of the families came down to the beach and cut off what they wanted in strips. They saved the fat and

made oil out of that. They ate the meat. They never wasted anything. They always had enough from one whale for the whole tribe. Some of them smoked their meat, some of them ate it fresh. My great-great-grandfather never did come back with nothing. He always had a whale.

One time when they went out, he speared a whale and got his leg caught in the rope—the sinew rope that they threw out. When the whale dove under, he went right out with the whale because he couldn't get his ankle all untied. The whale took him around in the ocean for quite a while. When the men in the canoe finally let the rope go, they thought that he had drowned, but they waited around for a while anyway. After he went under, he found enough strength within himself to untie himself even though the whale was pulling him around. He got all untied. When he came up, the guys saw him come up—they saw blood all around him (he had a terrific nose-bleed from surfacing too fast). They couldn't believe that he was alive! He lived through the whole thing!

He said to them, "I got a song when I went under. When I went under I saw seven daylights" (in other words he saw seven changes in the light as he was dragged under—farther and farther down). "I knew I went as far down as a person can possibly go and still live!" So, this is the song that he received after he came up from under the water. That's also where he got his name "Dashúk," "strong," because there hasn't been anybody that they know of that went down under as far as a whale could drag him and then come back up again. So, when he came up, he got this song, which my mother used, and I now use, from my great-great-grandfather on the Anderson side.

We use this song for a potlatch party—a birthday or a wedding. Recently they've been using it for Makah Day, too.

This dance has changed a lot over the years. First, my grandfather Anderson's father used to dance it alone, wearing the mask with the green, wavy lines. They used to talk to me about this when I was young, but I never saw him dance it. He had died before I was born. Somehow or another, they stopped doing it with the mask, and I heard my grandparents talk about how they danced it with one girl and one boy, and the boy acted like a whale. He made certain movements like he was under the water, then every once in a while he would come up and say, "Whhhh. Whhhh," like a whale spouting. Then he went back under. He wore a cedar bark headband and had a harpoon and the rope hanging down his side.

Then the dance changed again. For a while when I was young, I danced it alone. The older people said it should have been one girl and one boy dancing it, but we didn't have any boy in the family who was old enough to dance it, so I did it alone for a while.

Since we were short on boys—we had mostly girls—when my sister Dolores (who is six years younger than me) was big enough, then she and I did it together. We both did the girl's part with the hand and arm motions. A girl could never dance the whale part. As my younger sisters grew up, pretty soon they wanted to dance it, too. So, that's how come it's been four dancers—Dolores and me and Joy and Bessie. We've just kind of kept it at four dancers ever since. Now none of us sisters dance it anymore. My younger sister Joy's daughter Lois Smythe, and occasionally her daughter, Theresa, dance it along with my late sister Katherine's two granddaughters, Yvonne Burkett and Marcy Parker, or sometimes my granddaughter Jill Markishtum dances it with three of the others. Two of my young grandnieces are now learning it.

The girls just wear their Indian painted dresses when they dance this dance. They go through certain hand motions to tell the story: the right hand usually goes first, and then it says, "I came down where the earth and water meet." And then when "the water meets," the fingertips of both hands meet. First the hands go out one at a time, almost like swimming—your hands are out. And then when it says, "I went down as far as they meet," then both hands go up together and then go apart. Then you go down to the floor after this. I could do this when I was young, but I can't dance it anymore.

I remember that when I was little, I saw the mask that first went with this dance. It looked like a human face except the eyes were small. They were only little slits. Most generally the eyes will be round, like they are on Arnie's masks. But this one was different. It fit over your face, and parts of it were painted green, like the water. There's a little up and down swirl across the mask—the water spirit goes right across it. I think there's four layers actually—one wavy green line [horizontal] all the way across the chin, one just above the upper lip to the cheeks on both sides, one all the way across the nose, and one across the forehead. The rest of it was left the natural wood color. This is just what I remember about it because there isn't one in existence right now. [Since that discussion in 1974, Helma's son Mike Hunter has carved a copy of this mask, but it is not painted, and no one has danced with it.]

The song text includes both vocables and meaningful words. The first part of the song consists entirely of vocables. The second part includes the following Makah text:

| Hya | ʔuˑčiy qʼatus | ʔuˑčiy qʼatusiš | |
| | down, I went there | down, I went there, emphatic | |

	quba kiduk	quba kiduksiš ·	hita kuwiˑsiq hya ley ley la ha hey
	where something	where something	from the land on
	ends and	ends and meets	top to the land
	meets	(where the daylight	at the bottom
		meets the dark),	(the horizon)
		emphatic	

Helma's free translation is as follows:

I went down as far as any human possibly can,
To where the earth meets with the water,
From daylight to dark,
And came back up again.

Although only a few words are present in this song, they convey the full flavor and meaning of the story to those who know it. They set one's memory in motion. The song captures an image and allows the listener's imagination to do the rest.

4. "Wo hey"—Grizzly Bear Song

This song was given to twelve year old Helma Swan by the Nootka chief Captain Jack at a potlatch party in Clayoquot, British Columbia, in 1930, when her father, Charlie Swan, was being made a chief. It is not known how old this song is or who made it originally. It is thought that Captain Jack received it from his Kʷákʷakyawakʷ in-laws through marriage. According to Helma, it is an important song, formerly used for Klukwali ceremonies, and now used for potlatch parties. There is a Grizzly Bear Dance that accompanies it, but no meaningful words—only vocables. "Wo hey" is considered a Kʷákʷakyawakʷ (Kwakiutl) song, legally transferred first to a Nuu-cha-nulth (Nootka) chief and later to Helma, a Makah chief's daughter.

> I got this song from Captain Jack, the Nootka Chief. His Indian name was ƛix pi·q, which means sort of, "half red," I can't really explain it. He was from Gold River, from the Nootka Tribe.

As part of the Indian school held for Charlie Swan when he was being trained as a chief at Clayoquot in 1930, Captain Jack came over to Annie's house one evening to talk to Charlie. Helma was asked to come in and listen, and, as described in chapter 8, Captain Jack liked her, observed her interest and attention, and decided she was a person to whom he wished to give one of his songs.

> That night of the party, during our last dance, Captain Jack had my Aunt [Annie] dance, and so he gave me this song, "Wo hey," and he gave "Ho yeh" to my dad. These two songs were given to us by Captain Jack in 1930 during a party that was given for Clothilda Frank when she was first coming to womanhood and during the time my dad was being crowned a chief from her [Annie's] side of the family—from Cedakanim's side.
>
> What we call a Grizzly Bear Dance is what the Indians call ƛ'á·x̌sa·t', which means like "a patch on the head"—wearing a mask that only is in the front, or a mask that looks like a helmet. It was like a cap [that sits on top of the head], and it had a beak on both sides—like a bird. Then there were sticks (small twigs) on the top to hold in the feathers. When you dance, you move your head [from side to side and front to back], and that kind of scatters those feathers—the down. Michael Brown, who was supposed to be part Kwakiutl, and was also one of our relatives, was a real good carver, and he made this ƛ'á·x̌sa·t' [headpiece] for me. This goes with the "Wo hey" [Grizzly Bear] Song. . . .
>
> Just once I could remember dancing it with that headdress on—with the feathers in there. I was little. I don't think I was much more than twelve or thirteen. I danced it, and my dad sang it. . . . It's usually women that dance this one.

I was the only one dancing it that time. There wasn't a group of dancers doing it, and no backup dancers. It was just plain old me. . . . It's been a long time since they've done that with the feathers.

So, Michael Brown made me two of these headgears [the original one and a duplicate], but [later] my dad gave them both away. It was easy to talk him out of things, and he often gave them away. He didn't tell me at the time that he gave them away, so I really didn't know. One he gave to William Shelton's daughter Harriet Dover, from Tulalip. She was a member of the Tulalip tribe. My dad gave the "Wo hey" headgear to her and a wolf headgear to her father. He was a friend of my dad's and was chief of the Tulalip Tribe. I don't know who got the other ["Wo hey"] headgear.

Then [many years later], I had to have Dave Fourlines make me another "Wo hey" headgear. . . . My dad had the original one on in one of the earlier pictures, so that's how Dave knew how to make it. My sister Joy used it three or four times. But then there were no feathers in there. She just wore the headgear. I sang for her, and she danced. No one dances with it anymore.

Now for costumes, since my sisters found out that this song came from the Kwakiutl, they've each made a black headband with a little button headgear and a bear on it in the front, and it's piped in red. They use the copies of our grizzly bear button blanket, knowing that that's where the original came from (fig. 25). Also, they've been wearing plain black dresses with red piping on the bottom, around the neck, and on the sleeves. This is what they wear beneath their red and black button blankets.

Often there's about ten to fifteen people who dance "Wo hey" now—Joy's and Dicie's children, both boys and girls, as well as my granddaughter Jill Markishtum and sometimes her sisters Rhonda and Becky. They just all dance together in the center. There is no background dancing.

When I used to dance it, it was quite different from what they do now. I danced it alone or with my dad. I've noticed that when the Kwakiutls do it, I think they have about five or six dancers in a row. And they just stand there and move their heads and go back and forth. But my dad and I used to dance it in a figure 8. Now our kids and grandkids just do whatever they want to when they dance it—just when it has that double beat they all twirl at the same time. Now there's no special dance steps or formation anymore. It's all changed a lot, just like everything else. The kids want to invent their own ways nowadays.

5. "Ho yeh"—Grizzly Bear Song

This song is the other one of the pair of Grizzly Bear songs given by Captain Jack to the Swan family at the potlatch in 1930. "Wo hey" (Song 4) was given to Helma Swan, and "Ho yeh" was given to her father, who was supposed to keep it for Helma until she was older. Charlie never officially gave her this song, but since she is the caretaker of all his songs now, this one also belongs to her. The same headgear was worn for both Grizzly Bear dances.

Helma and her dad always performed this pair of songs together, as Captain Jack said they should be. They are not always done as a pair any longer, although Helma's sisters and their families still like to perform them this way whenever possible. Dancers, costumes, and types of dance steps are essentially the same for both dances. The song text consists entirely of vocables.

6. "Hu ya"—Grizzly Bear Song

This is an old Makah song, first owned by Helma's great-great-grandfather, Chief Yelák'ub. It came from her father's mother's side of the family. It is thought that the song transferred from Yelák'ub (Flattery Jack) to his son Sikesy Balch and eventually to the latter's grandson Charlie Swan. Now it belongs to Helma Swan. Previously, this important family song was used for the Klukwali; now it is performed during potlatch parties. Nothing else is known about it.

There is no information as to how this dance was performed in earlier times. Helma and her father danced it in a manner similar to the above two Grizzly Bear songs—using the figure-8 dance pattern. As a costume, Helma wore a painted dance cape, which she made herself, over her regular clothes. The dance cape had family-owned crest designs painted on it. She also wore a plain cedar bark headband. Her father wore a white shirt and navy or black pants (the traditional ceremonial dress for Makah men at that time) beneath his painted dance cape. He, too, wore a cedar bark headband.

Today, this song is sometimes performed along with one of the two Grizzly Bear Dances above; at other times it is performed following both of them. All three currently use the same dancers, costumes, and dance formations. "Hu ya" should have been one of a pair of songs, but Helma feels that her dad probably was too young to know about such things when he was given this song. As far as she knows, no paired song presently exists. The text consists entirely of vocables.

7. "Yaqʷáyats'i·k"—Wolf Dance Song

This song was formerly owned by Susie Weberhard, a Makah woman who, late in her life, made a gift of it to three younger Makah women: Ruth Anderson Swan, Matilda Johnson McCarty, and Katy Hunter. They were all part Quileute and were somehow related to each other, but no one remembers how. Helma Swan, one of the current owners, spoke about it:

> Before she died, Susie told my mother, "Don't fight about this song. I want to give it to all three of you. You can all three use it one at a time, or all three of you can use it at the same time—dance together." Where Susie got it, I don't know, but it has Canadian words in it. The word qʷáyáts'i·k is in there and that means "wolf" in the Clayoquot language.

In 1916, Edward Curtis also stated that the word *qai ya tsik* meant "wolf" in the Clayoquot language.[2]

In days past, this song was used in the Klukwali ceremony; now it is performed at potlatch parties. Ideally, it includes one male dancer who performs the lead wolf part, and women from the family who do the background dancing. Ruth Swan usually hired a male to dance the wolf, since formerly a woman was not allowed to do so. Afterward, she publicly paid him and thanked him for dancing her dance. During the actual performance, Ruth never danced. Rather, she stood beside the group of male singers in order to let the audience know that the chorus was singing her song. She was the owner.

Later, as Helma was growing up and there still were no boys in the family old enough to dance this Wolf Dance, she learned to dance it, loved to perform it, and often had the opportunity to do so.

> At that time, Katy Hunter [one of the three owners] wasn't interested in parties. . . . So it just kind of left my mother and Matilda McCarty to use this song. I used to like that song really a lot. . . . My mom used to make me wait until Matilda decided what she was going to do. So, I'd stand there and wait, and those guys [the men in the chorus] would smile. They'd know what I wanted to do, cause they knew I wanted to dance. Then Jack [LaChester] would always say, "You want to dance your *Owl* Dance?" He'd always call it my owl dance even though he knew it was my mom's, but he'd say, "Want to dance your *Owl* Dance?" That's because it starts with the words "Huu, huu, hu, huu." He knew it was really a Wolf Dance, but he was joking with me.
>
> I got to dance the wolf cause my mom didn't have any male dancers to do it. Somehow it was okay for me to dance the lead. Even when my younger brother Levi started dancing, he never cared to do this one. I still did it. I wore my dad's dance cape and his wolf headgear. My mother never had a wolf headgear, so I always used my dad's. . . . Matilda McCarty didn't have any headgear for it either, so she danced it without one. She wore just a plain shawl. So, there was never any squabble about this song, even though three people owned it. We'd always talk it out, or else I'd be the one waiting it out to see if I got to dance it.[3]

Presently, this song is owned by Helma Swan, daughter of Ruth Swan, and by Hildred Ides, daughter of Matilda McCarty. Hildred's daughters and granddaughters sometimes dance it at potlatches. Katy Hunter passed the song on to her grandson Leonard Colfax, who also performs it sometimes using a large, nontraditional wolf headgear with blinking red eyes.

Helma continues to sing this song at potlatches, and every time she uses it, she announces that it is owned by three people. Sometimes her grandsons, Ron Jr. and Daryl Markishtum, or occasionally her grandnephews will dance it, wearing fairly simple boxboard wolf headgears. Two of her young great-grandsons also have been learning to dance it.

The song includes some meaningful text; however, aside from the word for "wolf," *qʷayáts'i·k*, the other words are no longer recognizable or translatable. Again, it is likely that the pronunciation changed as the song transferred from one tribe to another. Helma learned this song as a young girl and described its essence:

> This song is about a wolf, and it states that we're a great people, and that we have the wolf power. . . . I can't remember exactly what it says now . . . that we're able to do things just as good as any wolf, and that we can dance like one, because this is the clan we came from, and we're proud of being the wolf clan![4]

8. "Wo hu·ʔOh yiya"—Wolf Dance Song

This Kʷákʷakyawakʷ song was owned by Annie Williams, who gave it to Charlie Swan during the 1930 potlatch when she made him a chief. No one recalls how Annie or her father, Atliu, came to own this song. Now, however, it belongs to Helma Swan, who stated that her father liked it very much and danced it often, at potlatch parties:

> This song had different dance steps . . . double dance steps, and my dad used it as a warm-up just before he did the Masked Dance. . . . It got him into the dancing mood. . . . I could just see him. He was real springy and then he'd really move his head. . . . I noticed that he would dance exactly like a wolf. I watched his moves, . . . and he'd look around, you know, just like *they* do. My dad was *so* good at it! His movements were just graceful. . . . Then after that it was easy for him to get into the Masked Dance.
>
> But today, the boys don't want to do this Wolf Dance. You can't tell them how he used to do it. Now they don't look at *all* like a wolf. They just don't *think* like one, they don't *move* like one.

When he danced to this song, Charlie Swan wore a wolf headgear (fig. 9) which he made himself, and he also wore his painted dance cape (fig. 28). Helma did not dance backup for him, but she always watched him dance it alone. Today, she occasionally sings this song at potlatch parties; however, no one in her family dances it.

Although there are some meaningful Kʷákʷakyawakʷ words in this Wolf Dance song, no one can understand or translate them. In 1974, Helma had a discussion about one of its key words with Mrs. Odelia Hunter, a Clayoquot elder, now deceased:

> I asked Mrs. Hunter, "Is this Clayoquot, or what is it, because I never heard it used?"—the word *ki·ki·qama·*, which is in that Wolf Dance song. I said, "But every time I hear your songs across there, they're all like this, with this same word in there. Now your songs are the same thing as Dad's now. What does it say? Is it Clayoquot?" She said, "No, it's Alert Bay—a lot of the songs seem to come from there." So that's how I found out that this song was from Alert Bay.

Apparently, in this song the only recognizeable word which has survived is *ki·ki·qama·*, which means "chiefs" in the Kwakiutl language.[5]

9. "Waikašna"—Chant Preceding the Changing Mask Dance

This chant (*ts'i·qa*) belonged to Annie Williams and was given by her to her nephew Charlie Swan, at the potlatch in 1930 when she gave him all her father's belongings. It now belongs to Helma Swan. Formerly it was sung preceding the Changing Mask Dance at potlatch celebrations. Helma learned it, but for many years she has not sung it in public. It is no longer used today. According to Helma, there is a difference between a chant and a song:

> A chant says the same thing over and over; it doesn't really have a melody. It stays mostly on one tone and sometimes slides up or down—close to Indian praying in sound. It is always done with a rattle, never a drum.

The chant had sacred meanings in the past, and the audience would grow quiet and attentive while it was being sung. One person, wearing regular street clothes, would stand and shake a carved, bird-shaped wooden rattle and sing, with a very intense, haunting sound. No one would dance. The chant was performed in this manner when Annie was alive, but such performances had mostly disappeared by the late 1930s.

During his many years of singing and dancing, Charlie Swan used this chant only a few times when he was performing the Changing Mask Dance. Annie Williams, however, liked the "Waikašna" chant a great deal and often sang it herself before the performance of the Changing Mask Dance. She sang it at the 1930 potlatch, and then she gave it, along with the Changing Mask Dance Song, to Charlie Swan.

The syllables, *waikašna,* that open the song, have no meaning, according to Helma. A few Clayoquot words appear in the song text:

U·x̌ú·ksiš	*nani·qs*	*ʔAtliu*	*wa ya' ah' ey*
my	grand-father	Atliu	

The literal translation would be "My grandfather is Atliu." This was, indeed, correct, when Annie sang this chant. Her grandfather Sitkeenum or Cedakanim, was said by some to have been called Atliu in his later life. This was also the name of Annie's own father, who was one of Sitkeenum's sons. Helma stated that there were other meaningful words in this *ts'i·qa* (chant), but she has neither heard them nor sung them for a great many years and cannot remember them. She spoke, however, about the general meaning, which she does remember, and gave a free translation of the Clayoquot words she can no longer specifically recall:

The chant says "I know somebody up there is watching us down here because we're doing what my great grandfather and my grandfather from generations back have done . . . and I'm singing this now because he's watching and he knows what I am doing. My grandfather made these things that I'm claiming now. And I'm telling you now . . . who my great-grandfather is. My great grandfather is Atliu."

That's why I can sing this—because he's watching now, and his name is Atliu. In other words, I want these people [attending the potlatch] to know who my great-grandfather is, and that that was Sitkeenum's name after he gave up "Sitkeenum" and became "Atliu." Since he's my great-grandfather, then this way I can use his song. . . . If I sing this, they [the audience] would know then where I come from, who my great-grandfather was, and automatically they should know how many generations down I am.

10. "Wa'nu· Nukwinai Ka·šu"—The Changing Mask Dance Song

This is the most important song and dance belonging to the Swan family. It was transferred from Annie Williams's grandfather Chief Sikteenum to her own father, Atliu, and finally, to her. She then gave it to her nephew Charlie Swan during the potlatch at Clayoquot in 1930 when she made him a chief. After Charlie's death in 1958, Helma Swan became its caretaker, and at a potlatch in 1987, she gave this masked dance to her oldest son, Arnie Hunter, who continues to perform it often. The descendants of Francis Frank, from Clayoquot, also have the right to use this song and dance, because oral history relates that Francis was another of Annie's nephews and was as closely related to her as Charlie Swan. Both families can use this song, dance, masks, and costumes, but officially Annie gave them to Charlie Swan. The Changing Mask Dance was formerly a part of the Klukwali ceremony; now, however, it is performed at potlatch parties.

According to Helma, there were several different pieces of music connected with the Changing Mask Dance, and there was a correct order in which they should be performed. Ideally, the Chant (Song 9) would be sung first, and would then be followed by another dance (long forgotten) which included four large masks. This Four Mask Dance,[6] which included four dancers, each wearing a large face mask that continually turned 180 degrees from right to left to right throughout the dance, was considered an introduction to the more important Changing Mask Dance. The former let the audience know that a special dance would follow. Finally, the Changing Mask Dance, with its five masks worn sequentially by one dancer, was performed as the most powerful and impressive of the series. This was the manner of presentation in Annie Williams's day. Later, Charlie Swan seldom used the Chant. Instead, he performed the "Wo hu·ʔOh yi ya" Wolf Dance (Song 8) as an introduction, and then, immediately after the whistles were blown, he rose from a crouching position and began the Changing Mask Dance.

Ideally, groups of carved wooden whistles were sounded from behind the family curtain, where they were hidden from view, just before the Masked Dance was performed. These whistles imitated birds and other animals but were also connected with spirits and spirit power. Traditionally, both the curtain and whistles accompanied the Changing Mask Dance; however, neither have been used by the Swan family for about the past fifty years.

The Changing Mask Dance itself is a multifaceted performance, more complex than the others described above. The lead male dancer, wearing either the grizzly bear or double-headed raven button blanket over black shorts and dance kilt, dons five different human-type masks during the course of this dance (see figs. 15, 16, 24). Four of them represent the seasons of the year; the fifth has a different purpose, related by Helma below. The masked dancer moves in a large counterclockwise dance circuit in the center of the room. Two wolf dancers, wearing ceremonial wolf headgears and button blanket dance capes, dance in a narrow, oval-shaped path behind the masked dancer. Female family members, usually wearing plain black dance capes, form a wide U shape, and dance background behind the other figures, while the chorus stands to one side and sings the song. When all parts are present, the performance is quite impressive. Helma spoke about the importance of this dance:

> Songs like the Mask Dance, the Wolf Dance, the Grizzly Bear Dance, they represent my background—they tell who I am, where I come from. But this Changing Mask Dance always seemed to mean something extra special to my father. Annie was always telling him things about it, but he never told me all the things she told him. . . . It was more than entertainment; it was also something sacred. And for that reason, long ago they didn't use it at anybody's party [potlatch] except their own.

Helma has spoken about some of the meanings connected with this song and has also translated a few of the words, which are in the Clayoquot language:

> This is in Clayoquot. It starts out saying "I am singing, I am singing . . . because of the seasons." Apparently it was beginning to be spring when the [original] owner received this or got this song; but anyway to me it sounds like the weather was getting better, and so they started singing. This was the end of the real bad season. . . . That's the general idea that I get when they're singing. Because in the spring it's nice; in the summer it's turning; in the fall it's getting kind of bad; and in the winter it's still bad. That's the general feeling . . . of this song. The seasons have four faces—well, this is what they use—four faces [four different masks] . . . the four seasons changing. And then . . . that last mask . . . it opens and closes its eyes. And that's supposed to mean that this last mask is to oversee the tribe—so that nothing happens to the tribe.
>
> There's another part in there that they don't use now, but I know it's there, because it says, "My great-grandfather up there is watching, and he's helping me." And the dancer comes from one side and makes certain motions, and he

points up in the air, meaning, "My grandfather up there is watching." My dad used to sing those words, but I don't know them and have never sung them.

The few words with known translations are as follows:

Waʔ nuʔnukwinai ka·šu o' yeh yeh	*Waʔ nuʔnukwinai ka·šu* oʔ yeh
I am singing	I am singing

Wa ʔah wai kaʔawax̌š	*nukwa* wo' yeh yeh	
That is why	I am	
	singing	

A free translation conveys the essence of this song:

I am singing, I am singing
Because I am happy.
That is why I am singing.
The seasons are changing
And we are beginning anew.
That is why we are happy.
I am singing, I am singing.

Throughout life there are changing seasons, some happier than others, yet mankind survives the difficult along with the joyful, and continues onward. Among the Makah as well as other Northwest Coast tribes, it was the duty of the chief to make those seasonal changes as easy as possible for his people—to watch over them, protect them, and guide them through the many faces of change. In the present, the changes continue at an even faster pace, and the necessity for someone to watch, guide, and protect is more essential than ever. The Changing Mask Dance and its song provide continual reminders, not only of the Swan family history, but also of the responsibilities of a leader for his or her people. Helma Swan, for many years, has shouldered a significant portion of these responsibilities by becoming a cultural and musical leader—watching, guiding, and teaching younger Makah generations and at the same time, carefully protecting, preserving, and renewing the heritage of her family and her tribe. As she sings, and as her oldest son dances with the Mask-Which-Opens-and-Closes-Its-Eyes, they are continuing a tradition of "watching over their people."

1. "Ah yi wáyo" ("Stop Awhile")—a Love Song

Original starting pitch = C♯

♩ ~ M.M. 176

"Ah yi wáyo," continued

FORM:

A = x   a   b   c

B =   y   d   e   c'

B' =   y'   d'   y"   e'   c"

B" =   y'''   d"   e"   c'''

B''' =   y''''   d'''   e'''   c'   z

2. "Limey Kašlá"—Dinner Song

Original starting pitch = C

♩. ~ 80

"Limey Kašlá," continued

"CHORUS" Q'abá·tš'aX'

e mey tła e mey tła tsu tsu la qwa   qu lu man tsi 'et tła kwa   o ho——— hu wey   yi— ye ka šu wa

BEGINNING

A' a'   *Fine*

o——— hu wey— yi— ye wo——————— ye

FORM:

```
A  =  a   b   c
B  =            d   e   c
A' =  a'  b   c
B  =            d   e   c
A' =  a'  (b   c)
```

3. "Hya'a hya ley" ("The Song of the Seven Daylights")—Whaling Song

Original starting pitch = A

♩ ~ 152

FORM:

A = x a b a'
A' = x' a y
A" = x" a" b' a" b'
A'" = a" y
A"" = x' a'" b"
A""" = a"" y

4. "Wo hey"—Grizzly Bear Song

Original starting pitch = F

♩ ~ 92

FORM:

A = x   a   b

A = x   a   b

5. "Ho yeh"—Grizzly Bear Song

Original starting pitch = B♭
♩ ~ 100

FORM:

A = a b c d

A' = b c

6. "Hu ya"—Grizzly Bear Song

Original starting pitch = A

FORM:

A	=		a	b
A'	=	x	a'	b
A'	=	x	a'	b
A'	=	x	a'	b
A'	=	x	a'	b
A'	=	x	a'	b

7. "Yaqʷáyats'i·k"—Wolf Dance Song

Original starting pitch = E

♩ ~ 168

FORM:

A = a b c d y
A = a b c d y
B = e d' y'
A' = a' b' c' d'' y
B' = e' d''' y''

8. "Wo hu·ʔOh yiyah"—Wolf Dance Song

Original starting pitch = A

♩. ~ 63

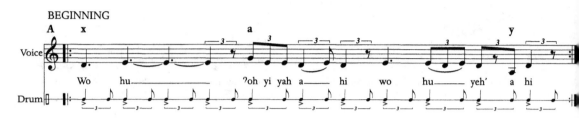

"Wo hu·ʔOh yiyah," continued

wo hu———— hu yi yeh ha—— hi wo hu———— yeh' a hi

wo hu———— hu———— wo yi yeh a—— hi wo hu——— ya a hi

Fine

FORM:

A = x a y x a y
B = b c y
A' = x' a y x' a y x' a y
B = b c y
A" = x a y x' a' y

9. "Waikašna"—Chant Preceding the Changing Mask Dance

Original starting pitch = A

♩ ~ 112

BEGINNING

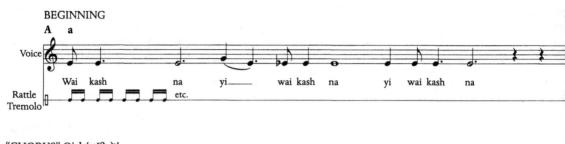

Wai kash na yi— wai kash na yi wai kash na

Rattle Tremolo etc.

"CHORUS" Qʼabá·tšʔaλʼ

o mi x̌uk sish na niqs so wo wa ha ha yi yi yi

o x̌uk sish na niqs sa kyu hu yu ah ya ah wey

BEGINNING

o wai kash na yi— wai kash na— yi wai kash na—

"CHORUS" Qʼabá·tšʔaλʼ

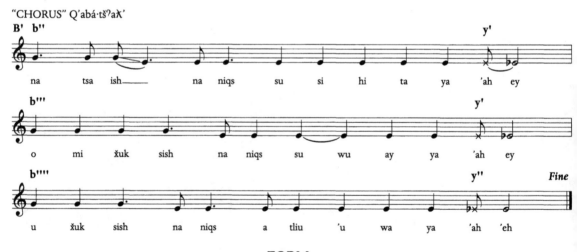

na tsa ish— na niqs su si hi ta ya ʼah ey

o mi x̌uk sish na niqs su wu ay ya ʼah ey

u x̌uk sish na niqs a tliu ʼu wa ya ʼah ʼeh

Fine

FORM:

A = a
B = b b' y
A' = a'
B' = b" y' b'" y' b"" y"

10. "Wa'nu· Nukwinai Ka·šu"—The Changing Mask Dance Song

Original starting pitch = F♯

♪ ~ 160

"Wa'nu· Nukwinai Ka·šu," continued

"CHORUS" Q'abá·tš'aλ'

A''' a'''   q   b   y

wa' a wai ka' a waxš nu kwa wo' ye ye— ye ye'— yo— ho ha wa

BEGINNING

B a'   q'   c   y

wa'— nu' nu kwi nai— ka· šu o' ye ye ye'— yo o ho hi ya— hi ya ha wa

A'''' a''''   q''   Fine

wa'— nu' nu kwi nai ka· šu— o' ye—

FORM:

$$
\begin{array}{llllll}
A & = & a & q & b & y \\
B & = & a' & q' & & c & y \\
A' & = & a & q'' \\
A'' & = & a'' & q & b & y \\
B' & = & a' & q''' & & c' & y \\
A & = & a & q & b & y \\
B'' & = & a' & q' & & c'' & y \\
A''' & = & a''' & q & b & y \\
B & = & a' & q' & & c & y \\
A'''' & = & a'''' & q''
\end{array}
$$

MUSICAL ANALYSES OF TEN SWAN FAMILY SONGS

An ethnomusicological analysis of native songs generally focuses upon specific information such as the overall form of the song, the shape of the melodic lines, significant rhythmic or melodic patterns, the basic meter, scale, range, vocal sound, and interaction of drum and voice. These musical elements will be examined briefly as they are relevant to the Swan family song transcriptions.

First, a few general statements about these songs may be helpful. In the past, important Makah family songs were usually sung in pairs. It was not necessary that the same two songs always be paired; however, only similar kinds of songs could be paired: two Grizzly Bear songs, two Wolf Dance songs, and so forth. Today, this pairing is not always followed.

Concerning the form of these songs, the situation quickly becomes complex. Usually songs of one particular type have underlying structural similarities that can help in their identification. Such structure has not been found in earlier studies of Nootkan and Makah music. In 1955, when Helen Roberts did her examination and analysis of ninety-nine Nootkan songs collected by Edward Sapir between 1910 and 1914, she found that there was little regularity of form in any one type of song, or across song types. The same situation applied to the Makah songs transcribed and analyzed by this author in 1978, and it appears to be true for the songs presented here. Six of these songs consist of two or three phrases while the others have four, five, or six. Three songs have introductory motifs; three have closing motifs; three have both introductory and closing motifs; one has a connecting and a closing motif. However, a different musical construction method (as noted by both Roberts and Goodman) appears to be utilized here. What is apparent in most of these songs is the presence of short musical motifs which vary endlessly and reappear a number of times throughout the course of a particular song, helping to unify it. For example, in Song #10, The Changing Mask Dance Song, the "a" phrase can be considered a musical motif that repeats numerous times throughout the song. Sometimes the repetition is identical to the first statement, sometimes it is varied. This same phenomenon is found in many of the songs transcribed here.

Many, though not all, Makah songs have two main sections: a "Beginning," and a "Q'abá·tšʔaⱡ'"—"the part with the meaningful words," usually the second section of the song, which the Makah call the "Chorus." (The word, "chorus" has a different meaning for the Makah than for musicologists).[7] Sometimes there is meaningful text in both portions of the song, sometimes only in the "Chorus" or Q'abá·tšʔaⱡ'. At least a portion of the text in the "Chorus" is different from that in the "Beginning." Vocables (syllables without meaning) are usually found in both sections of each song. In some songs the melodic and rhythmic patterns are also different in each of these large sections, in others they are not. Often musical motifs presented in the "Beginning" section will reappear in the "Chorus" or Q'abá·tšʔaⱡ'.

Each of these large sections of a song, or portions of them, may be repeated a variable number of times.

Drum beat patterns may or may not be the same for both sections. Strong, steady drumbeats predominate, but short changes in the pattern may occur once or several times over the course of a song, as may some syncopated beats. Voices and drums are synchronized (accenting the same beats at the same time) in some songs or parts of songs, but are purposefully out of synchronization in others.

Melodic lines in these songs are typically undulating (rising and falling one or more times during the course of a single phrase) or descending in countour. Long, extended opening and/or closing notes are typical in many songs. Vocal ornaments such as turns and grace notes can be heard fairly often. Most (though certainly not all) songs are performed by a chorus, which usually sings in a low to medium range. The vocal sound is usually fairly open and relaxed. Accompaniment is normally provided by one or more hand-held drums, or occasionally by rattles.

1. "Ah yi wáyo" ("Stop Awhile")—Love Song

The shape of the melodic lines is undulating with a tendency to descend at the ends of phrases. A few vocal ornaments are apparent as are numerous extended notes. These latter do not often appear at the ends of phrases in this particular song. A six-tone scale is used and the range of the song is an eleventh. The meter is essentially duple, with the appearance of occasional triplet figures. The beat pattern is fairly regular except for the triplets, where sometimes the drumbeat is two-against-three, and sometimes it is absent. The tempo is moderately fast. Concerning the song form, there is a "Beginning," which includes only vocables, and a "Chorus" or Q'abá·tš?aƛ' with meaningful words and vocables. The same melodic material, with small variations, appears in both sections. A traditional musical analysis would state the form as: AB B BB, with motifs from the A section appearing in the B sections. Opening motifs (x and y) and a typical closing pattern (descending slur) are present.

2. "Limey Kašlá"—Dinner Song

The melody is primarily undulating, with rises occurring in a number of phrases, and only a few instances of descending movement. A number of extended notes occur in the central portions of melodic lines but not at the ends. A five tone scale is used and the range is a major sixth. The underlying meter is triple. The most common drum pattern consists of an eighth note followed by an accented quarter note; however this changes at the beginning of each A' section (the a' phrase), then afterwards reverts to the former pattern. Tempo is moderate. At times, the drum and voice are intentionally not synchronized. The song form includes a "Beginning" and a "Chorus" or Q'abá·tš?aƛ' section, each with different Kʷákʷakyawakʷ words but with some of the same vocables. The "Chorus" includes two phrases (d and e) with new melodic and text material, and a "c" phrase which incorporates material from the "Beginning" section. The general form may be stated as: A B A' B A'. No introductory or closing motifs are present.

3. "Hya'a hya ley" ("The Song of the Seven Daylights")— Whaling Song

This song has minimal melodic movement. There is a slight feeling of undulation and a subtle feeling of descent, but neither element is marked. The highest note occurs at the beginning of the phrase, with most of the remaining movement being stepwise within a small range. Extended notes appear frequently at the beginnings and endings of phrases. This song uses a four-tone scale, and the range is a minor sixth. Meter is duple, and drum and voice are generally well synchronized. The drum pattern is steady and unchanging until the final tremolo. Tempo is moderate. Song form includes a "Beginning" and a "Chorus" or Q'abá·tšʔaƛ' section, the latter having the only meaningful text. However, musically, both sections consist of a continuing set of minor variations on the "x," "a," and "b" phrases found in the A section, which is repeated five times. Opening (x) and closing (y) motifs are present.

4. "Wo hey"—Grizzly Bear Song

The melodic movement in this song includes a descending phrase (a), and an undulating phrase (b). A number of extended notes occur, mostly near the beginnings and/or endings of phrases. A six-tone scale is used and the range is an octave. Underlying vocal meter is duple but is accompanied by a triplet drum pattern (a quarter note followed by an eighth). Each "b" phrase has several extra beats added, giving an unexpected accent before returning to the regular pattern. Voice and drum are synchronized. Tempo is moderate. The form of this song consists only of repeats of the "Beginning" or A section, which has no meaningful words. Within it, the melodic lines of the "a" and "b" phrases are quite different, though the text is essentially the same. An introductory motif (x) is present.

5. "Ho yeh"—Grizzly Bear Song

Melodic movement consists of several descending lines which end either on an extended note or a series of repetitions of the same note. A four-tone scale is used and the range is a fifth. The underlying vocal meter is basically duple, accompanied by a drum pattern consisting of a quarter note followed by two eighth notes, or two eighths followed by a quarter. Interspersed in the "b" and "c" phrases are several short segments with straight eighth note drumming, matching the pattern in the vocal line. Voice and drum are synchronized. Tempo is moderate. The form of this song consists only of repetitions of the "Beginning" or A section. Although the music of each phrase is different, the text, consisting entirely of vocables, is essentially the same throughout. No opening or closing motifs are present.

6. "Hu ya"—Grizzly Bear Song

Melodic movement is largely undulating, with a tendency to descend in some phrases. A number of melodic leaps occur throughout. Extended notes appear at the beginnings and endings of most phrases. A six tone scale is used and the range of the song is a minor tenth. The metric pattern appears to alternate between a duple and a triple meter, and is so marked on the transcription. This alternation is evident in the drum and the voice; accent patterns help mark the changes. The tempo begins moderately fast and increases slightly as the song continues. The form of this song consists of five repetitions of the "Beginning" or A section. Although the music of the "a" and "b" phrases is different, "a" flows naturally into "b." The text, consisting entirely of vocables, is essentially the same throughout. An opening motif (x) is present in each A' segment.

7. "Yaqʷáyats'i·k"—Wolf Dance Song

Melodic movement includes both undulating and descending passages, some rises, and repeated notes at the ends of most phrases. Extended notes occur most often at or near the beginnings or middles of phrases. This song can be divided into two melodic sections (A and B), each with its own scale and range. The A section uses a six-tone scale and has a range of a minor seventh. The B section uses a four-tone scale and has a range of a minor sixth. The underlying meter is duple, but the "d" phrases in each section of the song ritard and have a changed accent pattern, giving a different metric feel to this segment. Each "c" phrase includes a triplet figure in the voice part, resulting in a two-against-three pattern with the drum. Drum and voice are generally well synchronized, and the tempo is moderately fast. Song form includes a "Beginning" (A) with vocables, and a "Chorus" or Q'abá·tšʔaƛ' (B) section with meaningful words as well as vocables. The Q'abá·tšʔaƛ', which is short, includes one phrase ("e") with the new melodic and text material, and a "d" phrase which incorporates material from the "Beginning" section. The overall form may be stated as A A B A' B'. A closing motif (y) is also present.

8. "Wo hu· ʔOh yi yah"—Wolf Dance Song

Melodic lines are principally undulating with only a few instances of descending movement. Extended notes appear most commonly near the beginnings or middles of phrases. Rises occur fairly often, especially at the ends of phrases. A four-tone scale is used and the range is a minor seventh. Essentially the meter is compound, approximating 6/8, with numerous triplet figures. The basic drum pattern consists of a triplet in the form of a quarter note followed by an eighth note. Voice and drum are synchronized, and the tempo is moderate. The form of this song includes a "Beginning" (A), with vocables, alternating with a "Chorus," Q'abá·tš'aⴟ' (B), which has the meaningful words. The Q'abá·tš'aⴟ' includes two phrases ("b" and "c") which incorporate new melodic and text material. The overall form would be A B A' B A'. Opening (x) and closing (y) phrases are present.

9. "Waikashna"—Chant Preceding the Changing Mask Dance

As is typical of a chant, the vocal line exhibits much repetition of a single pitch, with a slight tendency, overall, to descend. There really is no definable melody. Extended notes appear mostly at the ends of phrases. A six-tone scale is used and the range is a diminished fifth. Because this is a chant, there is no drum with a regular rhythmic beat. Rather, Northwest Coast chant is usually accompanied by a rattle tremolo (very fast repetitive sound with few accents). The vocal tempo is fairly slow. This chant form consists of a "Beginning" (A) followed by a Q'abá·tš'aⴟ' (B). It is unknown whether the text of the A section includes meaningful words. New musical material as well as new meaningful text appears in the "b" phrases of the Q'abá·tš'aⴟ'. The overall form can be characterized as A B A' B'. A short closing motif (y) is present.

10. "Wa'nu· Nukwinai Ka·šu"—The Changing Mask Dance Song

Melodic movement includes undulating lines with a tendency to descend. Rises occur fairly often, especially near the ends of phrases. Extended notes are found near the beginnings of both "a" and "q" phrases, these latter being either connectives or endings. A six-tone scale is used and the range is an octave. The underlying metric pattern is duple. Voice and drum are slightly out of synchronization during each "a" phrase but are generally synchronized otherwise. Tempo is moderate. Song form includes a "Beginning" and a "Chorus," or Q'abá·tš'aⴟ' section, each with its own meaningful text and essentially the same vocables. The Q'abá·tš'aⴟ', which is very short, contains only one new line of text in the a''' phrase; however, the music is nearly identical with that heard in some of the variations of the "a" phrases from the "Beginning" section. A number of repetitions of each phrase, many with small variations, occur throughout this song. The form may be stated as A B A' A" B'A B" A''' B A''''. Aside from "q," with its final descending slurs, another closing motif (y) is also present.

AFTERWORD

Helma Swan passed away suddenly and unexpectedly on July 9, 2002, as this book was in press. She very much wanted to see it published—wanted others to learn about the Makah people and to read or even hear her tell her stories and sing some of the songs transcribed herein. (Due to Helma's fears of song stealing, a recording does not accompany the book.) Sadly, she will never see the actual publication, although she knew it would be completed before the end of 2002. May Helma now rest in peace, with the comfort that her contribution to her people will live on.

GENEALOGICAL CHARTS

SWAN FAMILY GENEALOGY

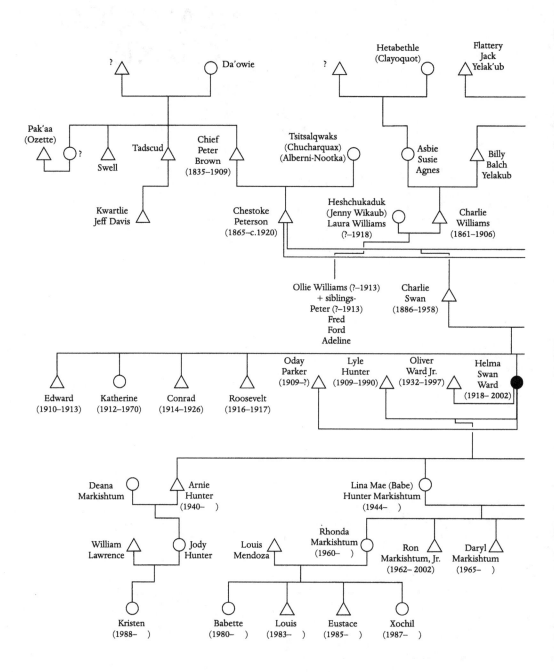

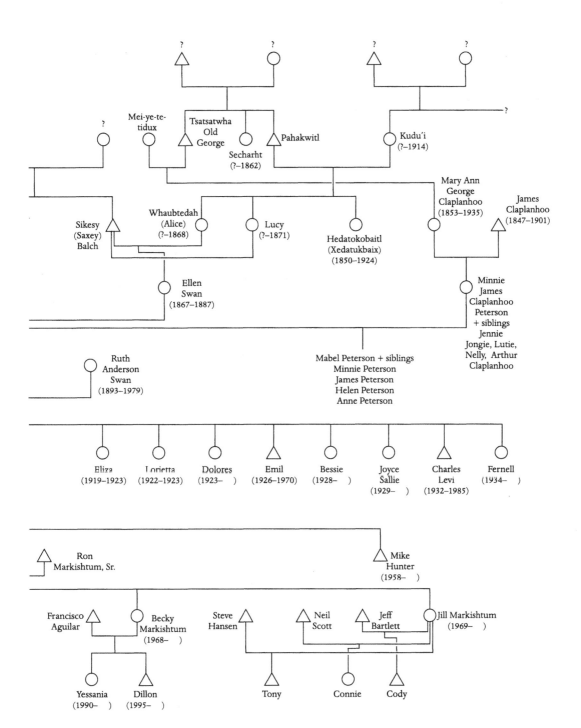

ANDERSON FAMILY GENEALOGY

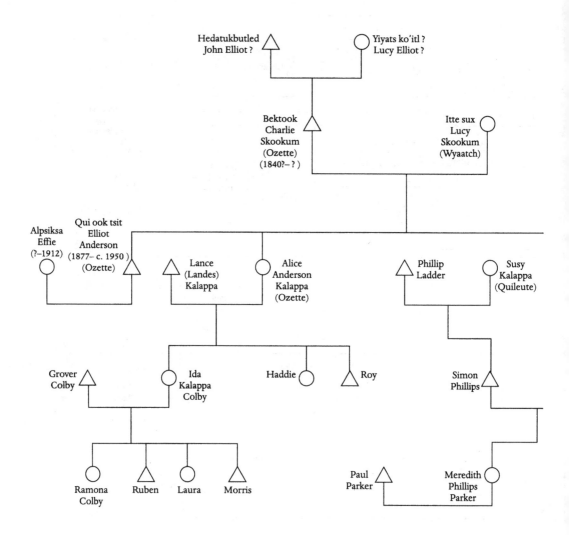

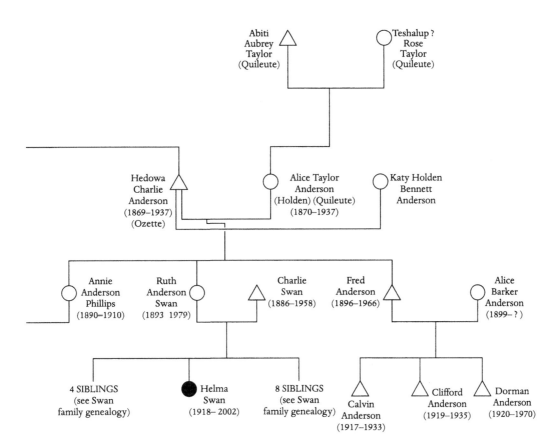

SWAN FAMILY RELATIVES

Stories, Descriptions,
and Documentary Data

Supportive materials such as diary entries, government data and documents, and published stories about ancestral chiefs and other relatives help corroborate the oral history that Helma Swan learned as a child and young adult. The information presented here, she feels, is necessary in order to clarify some of her ancestral family relationships, provide previously unknown additions to some of her stories, and validate her heritage and claims to legitimate ownership of certain ceremonial rights and privileges, including songs. See the Swan Family Genealogical Chart and the Anderson Family Genealogical Chart in Appendix A for an overview of the genealogies discussed here.

THE THREE CHIEFS AND THEIR FAMILIES

1. Chief Peter Brown, How-á-thlub, or As-chad-a-bek (c. 1835–1908)

Little has come down through the oral tradition concerning Peter Brown[1] except for the following: (1) He was the last Makah chief; (2) he was chief of police in Neah Bay for a number of years; and (3) his son, Chestoke Peterson, was Charlie Swan's father. Thus Peter Brown was Helma Swan's great-grandfather (see fig. 1).

Even though scattered and fragmentary, existing written accounts paint a somewhat fuller picture of this forceful personality. Born circa the mid-1830s, probably in the village of Tsooyez,[2] Peter Brown was one of an unreported number of children. Nothing is known of his parents, though mention is made of several siblings: an older brother called Swell in English (Wha-lathl, in Makah), one of the subchiefs of the Makah tribe who was highly regarded by early whites in the area; Tadscud, another brother; and an unnamed sister who married a man named Ah a yah, or Pak'aa, one of the Ozette chiefs.[3]

When Peter was in his seventies, he recounted some of the adventures and stories of his younger life to writer Lucien Lewis, who incorporated them in a *Seattle Post-Intelligencer* newspaper article in 1905. Because Peter had a reputation as an embellisher of tales, it is not known how accurately he may have related these stories which occurred some forty to fifty years earlier. Peter's son, Chestoke Peterson, acted as interpreter.[4]

Stories about Peter Brown

Peter spoke, one time, of a large ship that had wrecked at Waadah Island in the early 1850s. When the Makah went aboard to scavenge the cargo, they discovered a pile of old clothes left there. In a few days, smallpox broke out among the Makah and spread with great rapidity. Having no resistance to this disease, the tribe was devastated. A white man by the name of Hancock,[5] who was living in Neah Bay at that time, took Peter into his house and kept him away from the diseased people. Hancock later wrote that at the height of the tragedy, "The beach [at Neah Bay] for a distance of eight miles was literally strewn with the dead bodies of these people."[6] The Makah Tribe was almost annihilated. Before, there had been hundreds of warriors; afterward, only a handful.

Less than two years after the smallpox epidemic, in January 1855, Governor Isaac I. Stevens and his party appeared in Neah Bay in order to sign The Treaty of Neah Bay with the Makah.[7] Even after signing this treaty, warfare between the Makah and neighboring tribes continued until the early 1870s. (Interestingly, the Makah never mounted hostile campaigns against the whites.) After relating several incidents of successful Makah warfare, Peter recalled an incident where he played the role of peacekeeper. Once, the Ozettes were hosting a large potlatch to which the Quileutes and the Clayoquots from Canada had been invited. During the course of a mock war scene, a Quileute accidently killed a Clayoquot, then quickly fled. The Clayoquots were infuriated and wanted revenge. Peter kept them from attacking and killing the Quileutes by promising to capture the man responsible for the shooting. Peter could not find the killer but did take the man's brother into custody. In order to prevent a war, Peter finally had to turn the brother over to the Clayoquots, who shortly thereafter, killed him.[8]

A highly emotional episode for Peter concerned the death of his own brother Swell, who was a chief of the Makahs at the time. According to the account written by James G. Swan about two weeks after Swell's death, the young Indian chief and his associates were on official business, bringing supplies and mail by canoe from Port Townsend to Neah Bay. On March 1, 1861, near midnight, Swell's party reached Crescent Bay, and seeing firelight on the beach, thought another group of Makahs were camped there for the night and sought to join them. Unfortunately, the group turned out to be Elwhas (a band of Clallam Indians who lived near present-day Port Angeles), and one of them was a long-time enemy of Swell's. As the Makahs departed, this man, Met-so-nack, or Elwha Charlie, shot Swell in the back, and he died immediately. The Makahs pulled him into the canoe and departed, but the Elwhas followed them and shot and wounded another man. Unable to escape by sea, the Makahs headed back to land, and as the canoe broke apart on the rocks, the survivors all ran for the woods, leaving Swell's body on the beach.[9]

James G. Swan, along with Peter and several other Makahs, brought Swell's body back to Neah Bay for burial. Peter Brown asked Swan to help him select and properly prepare a site in which to bury Swell. Peter brought Swell's *tomanawas* boards (tall wooden boards with symbols of Swell's guardian spirit powers), which Swan refurbished and then placed at the burial site.[10]

Upon learning of the murder of their chief, the Makah called for vengeance. James G. Swan, who had been a good friend of Swell's, urged Peter not to take revenge but to let the government catch and mete out punishment to the Elwhas. Peter and the tribe waited patiently for six months. No action was taken. Finally, when it became clear to the Makah that the U.S. government intended to do nothing about the murder, Peter and the others decided it was time to act. Their reasoning, as stated to Swan, was as follows:

> Mr. Simmons [the Indian agent] said he would take the murderers and have them hung. We have waited many moons and he has not come, and lately the Dungeness Indians have killed two more of our people. We think Mr. Simmons has made fools of us, and the Indians on Vancouver's Island, the Nittinats and the Clyoquots, laugh at us and call us old women. . . . Swell went up to Port Townsend for the Bostons, and he was killed; and the Bostons promised to hang his murderers, but they have not done so, and now we will look out for ourselves.[11]

War was declared. The Makahs resolved to burn the Elwha village and kill everyone in the tribe. Twelve canoes of Makah warriors set out for Elwha. They landed first at Crescent Beach to drill and prepare for the conflict. Meanwhile, two Makah canoes, sent out to reconnoitre, unexpectedly came upon several canoes of Elwhas, fishing in the strait. Among the latter was one of the men who had been in the group that killed Swell. A battle ensued; the guilty man and one other were killed. The rest fled.[12]

After this incident, the Makah were aware that the Elwhas would know of their planned attack; thus, there would be no element of surprise. Also, because it was clear that the new Indian agent in Neah Bay, Mr. Webster, did not want them to go to war in the first place, the Makah warriors decided to return home and postpone their attack on the Elwha village until another time.[13]

The murder of Swell had led to two revenge killings—the traditional Makah way of carrying out justice. However, the U.S. government did not find such an approach acceptable. A few weeks later, Indian Agent Webster, in Neah Bay, asked

Peter Brown to talk with several government officials about the recent troubles with the Elwha. It is unclear why Peter was singled out. Perhaps he was considered responsible because he had led the war party, but in any event the government men arrested him for the murder of the two Elwhas. Peter said he would go quietly with them to Olympia, but not in handcuffs. A fight ensued. He tried to dive out the window, was badly cut by glass, and thus the others were able to overpower and handcuff him. Taken aboard a vessel waiting in the bay, Peter was confined to a room and left alone. Immediately, he snapped the chain of the handcuffs and freed himself.[14]

Meanwhile twelve heavily armed Makah men followed the boat in their canoes, boarded it and overpowered the crew. They forced Peter's captors to release him and they took him back to Neah Bay. The Makahs were so angry that they wanted to kill the crew and Agent Webster; but Peter, feeling there had been enough trouble already, requested that they not harm the white men. No one was killed.[15]

A month later, when a steamer anchored in the bay, Peter knew that if he didn't surrender, there would be bloodshed. Shortly thereafter he was imprisoned at Fort Steilacoom (located near present-day Tacoma) for these murders. For a little over a year, he remained in prison, where tales of his great strength quickly spread. Stories about the breaking of his handcuffs circulated widely and led to another handcuff breaking exhibition given by him for the entertainment of the white soldiers. At two other times he was ordered to wrestle with a soldier known to have thrown every man in the fort. To everyone's amazement, Peter handily won these matches, greatly angering the man who lost.[16]

The following year, after being tried for these murders at Port Townsend, Peter was released from prison. The trial judge then had a serious talk with him about what was acceptable behavior, and told him never to engage in this kind of activity again.[17]

When he returned to Neah Bay, a new agent, Mr. Hayes, was in charge. Soon after, Peter was made head chief of the Makahs and Mr. Hayes signed his commission as chief on October 8, 1870. Agent Hayes called a council of the Makahs and told them that henceforth they must live on friendly terms with the whites and with the neighboring Indian tribes. Privately, he told Peter, "I shall look to you, as chief of the Makahs, for the good behavior of your people." Peter promised that he would always use his influence in behalf of peace, and he told Lucien Lewis that he did as he had promised.[18]

James G. Swan, who knew Peter Brown for over forty years, wrote about this colorful Makah chief in his diaries and letters.

James G. Swan's Diary Entries About Peter Brown

[On a boat headed for Port Townsend] We had for passengers . . . 2 Macah Indians and a little Indian boy. One of the Indians . . . was Russian Jim and the other's name is Peter, a smart, intelligent young fellow who has been to California and can talk English pretty well [March 20, 1859].

. . .

Walked with H.B. Webster to Peter's house and there saw old Cedakanim, the Clyoquot chief, with several of his people who were breakfasting with Peter on boiled rice, hard bread, and molasses [March 5, 1862].

. . .

Peter stole a squaw . . . who was part Elwha [Clallam] and . . . took her hostage to enforce pay from the Elwhas for robbing and killing Swell a year and a half ago [August 12, 1862].

. . .

Island Tom . . . brought . . . whiskey from California. . . . Some got drunk and noisy. Peter was also drunk and was round knocking down everyone he could with his fists [August 31, 1862].

. . .

Peter had a potlatch today [September 24, 1862].

. . .

Peter turned off his squaw today and has taken a new one from Waatch [no names given] [March 8, 1863].

. . .

Peter's squaw left him today and went back to Waatch, to her first man. . . . [December 5, 1863].

. . .

Peter, Tahahowtl, and Russian Jim drunk. Peter threatened to shoot Willub and whip Boston Tom. Willub, Pahaquitl, Kyalanhoo and others came in to complain [February 7, 1864].

. . .

On his way back from Port Townsend, Peter killed a Clallam at Crescent Bay, who had killed Dukwitsa's father some years before [February 24, 1866].

. . .

Waatch Tom said the Indians want to meet with Captain Willoughby about his plan. They are willing for Peter to be the policeman, but they want Lighthouse Jim, Billy Balch, and Captain John to be the head men of the tribe. Now there is no chief of the tribe. Captain Willoughby is agent . . . and Peter is his policeman. That is alright but they want head men of their own who can consult on all matters in which Indians are concerned. . . . [November 17, 1878].[19]

. . .

Peter came to me to say he feels bad about his new squaw and wants to get rid of her. [July 16, 1879].

. . .

Peter and Klooch ha putl . . . were married. Captain John, David, and Billy Kalappa were 3 chiefs present. [October 26, 1879].

. . .

Peter paid me $3 for a pair of boots he bought for [his son] Chistoka. . . . [January 19, 1880].

. . .

Peter . . .was one of four men who saved a number of whites from the wreck of the Lizzie Marshall [October 6, 1884].

. . .

. . . you will find that Peter, when you know him as thoroughly as I do, is not the saint he always represents himself to be to all the Indian agents. . . . [Letter to General O. Wood, Indian Agent, January 11, 1885].

. . .

Received letter from Captain Powell giving account of the seals taken by the Indians this year: Schooner James G. Swan, Peter is owner—took 600 seals. . . . [April 28, 1894].

. . .

From these and other entries in Swan's diaries, it is evident that Peter Brown sometimes acted in undesirable ways, yet could be heroic when the situation demanded it. He was married and divorced numerous times.[20] It is not known how many children he may have had; however, Chestoke Peterson was his only surviving offspring. Nothing further is known of his later life. According to the probate file, Peter Brown died in 1908.[21]

2. Chief Sitkéenum, or Cedakánim (?–1897)

Even as a small child, Helma Swan heard stories of the Clayoquot chief Sitkeenum (also known as Cedakanim),[22] who over the course of his life had five wives and many children. According to the oral tradition, Helma is a descendent of Sitkeenum and one of those five wives, who was from Neah Bay. Unfortunately, the specifics of this relationship remain a mystery. James G. Swan never recorded the name of Sitkeenum's Makah wife, and Clayoquot and Makah elders, while stating that she was connected to Charlie Swan's mother's family, no longer recalled either her name or the exact relationship. Census data and church records have thus far not shed any additional light on the issue.[23] James G. Swan did write that the old chief and two of his sons, Frank and Benjamin Cedakanim, spent a great deal of time in Neah Bay in the latter half of the 1800s.[24] Swan never mentioned another, younger, son, Curley (fig. 2).

For a number of years, Frank Cedakanim was married to Makah chief Colchote's daughter, Totatelum; they lived in Neah Bay and had one baby girl, who died as an infant. Totatelum later divorced Frank to marry Peter Brown in 1864. She died of unknown causes less than a year later.[25] Strangely, Swan did not describe the circumstances of her death, though he did for most others.

Swan recorded in his diary that Benjamin Cedakanim, the younger of the two brothers, was half Makah; thus he had a Makah mother.[26] In 1870, Swan wrote the following about father and son:

> The chief of the Clyoquots, named Cedakanim, who frequently comes to Neeah Bay, told me that Cape Flattery was his land, because his mother was a Makah. His wife, who was the daughter of a Makah chief formerly residing at Neeah Bay, lays claim, in behalf of her son, to the land around the bay, as a portion of his grandfather's estate.[27]

Only two other small pieces of oral evidence exist concerning these unnamed Makah women and their connections to the Swan family. Aunt Edith Simon, a knowledgeable elder from Clayoquot, talked to Helma in 1975 and told her that Chief Cedakanim "came across" to Neah Bay and married Helma's great-great-grandmother, whose name has long been forgotten. According to Aunt Edith, this was how Helma's family ended up being related to Chief Cedakanim and his family. Her information thus supports that written by James G. Swan in 1870 more than one hundred years earlier. Odelia Hunter, another Clayoquot elder, told Helma that Benjamin Cedakanim's daughter, Annie Cedakanim Williams, had the right to give all of her father's things to Charlie Swan because she (Annie) and her father were directly related to the Swan family.[28] Odelia Hunter said her husband (Jim Hunter) was related to Sitkeenum through one of the latter's five wives, while Helma and her family were related through a different wife.[29]

Stories of Sitkeenum

Chief Sitkeenum demonstrated an impressive mix of talents and skills. In his younger years, he had a reputation as an outstanding warrior, one who was excellent at planning and executing strategy. Also known for his extreme cruelty and savage attacks on the enemy, he usually gave no quarter. In his day he was responsible for a great many deaths and took many captives as slaves. Due to his skill and wit, and also his considerable oratorical ability, Sitkeenum became one of the most powerful, as well as one of the most feared chiefs on the Northwest Coast.[30]

The Clayoquots, with Chief Sitkeenum as their leader, had a tremendous hatred for the Kyuquots to the north, who at that time were the largest and most powerful Nootkan tribe on the coast (see Map 3). The murder of a half-Kyuquot, half-Clayoquot woman by an unknown assailant, in 1855, allowed Sitkeenum to blame the Kyuquots and plan and launch a major attack against them. As related by Rev. Charles Moser in *Reminiscences of the West Coast of Vancouver Island* (1926), Sitkeenum enlisted the aid of four additional tribes: the Hesquiat, Mo-achat, Ehattisat, and Chiktlisat. On the appointed day, warriors from the various tribes gathered at a prearranged place on the shore several miles south of the Kyuquot village. After planning the attack and making detailed preparations, the party left quietly at nightfall and arrived at their destination after midnight, when the Kyuquot village was asleep.

The battle plan was put into operation: some men had been selected to stand by their canoes, ready at a moment's notice to launch a speedy retreat; others had detailed instructions as to which part of the village to attack, and silently moved to their positions. Each warrior had an assistant whose duty it was to bring the cut off heads of the victims back to the canoe. (In all Northwest Coast Indian warfare, the heads of the slain were taken back to the village of the victors and placed on poles in some highly visible spot, where they often remained for months.) The warriors quietly pushed aside the woven cedarbark mats which covered the doorways of the Kyuquot houses, entered, and began their bloody attack. Many Kyuquots were killed as they slept. As the Kyuquot warriors awoke and began to defend the village, the Clayoquots and their allies beat a hasty retreat, setting fire to the lodges as they left. Only two houses escaped the flames. Seventy people were killed and twenty slaves taken in a short time. The attackers lost twenty-three warriors but felt the price was worth the victory. They returned jubilantly to their villages. When Sitkeenum, leader of the expedition, returned home to Clayoquot, "wild scenes of rejoicing were indulged in by the whole tribe; the heads of the slain Kyuquots were placed on long poles, and these were planted as trophies along the sand spit on Stubb Island."[31]

During his younger years Chief Sitkeenum was involved in many such incidents of warfare up and down the west coast of Vancouver Island. Many of these skirmishes were successful, as in the above account. Occasionally, however, even a great military strategist such as Sitkeenum lost a battle and paid an uncomfortable price. One such attack, probably in the late 1850s or early 1860s, was recounted by Gilbert Sproat in his book *Scenes and Studies of Savage Life* (1868). Again, Sitkeenum had organized several tribes to help him attack the Kyuquots. Sproat described Sitkeenum and the scene where all the tribes were gathered before the attack:

> Twenty-eight canoes arrived in the afternoon at Friendly Cove, Nootka Sound, near the principal village of their allies, the Moouchahts. They [the Clayoquots] arrived singing a war song.
>
> Then Seta-kanim rose in his canoe to address the people on the shore. He was a tall, muscular man, with a broad face, blackened with charred wood, and his hair was tied in a knot on the top of his head so that the ends stood straight up; a scarlet blanket was his only dress, belted lightly round his loins, and so thrown over one shoulder as to leave uncovered his right arm, with which he flourished an old dirk. Such a voice he had! One could almost hear what he said at the distance of a mile. His speech lasted for 40 minutes and was very powerful.[32]

On a nearby beach, the warriors drew the layout of the Kyuquot village in the sand and established a general plan of attack. Everything was properly organized and the attack should have been successful, except for the fact that two Kyuquot fishermen arrived home in the middle of the night, only a few minutes before the enemy canoes came into sight. Immediately the fishermen sounded an alarm, awakening the Kyuquot warriors who were ready for the intruders as soon as their canoes touched the shore. In spite of this, the attackers managed to bring back thirty-five Kyuquot heads and take thirteen slaves. However, eleven of their own warriors died, and seventeen were wounded.[33]

The attack was considered a failure, and soon fear and suspicion arose. The tribe was apprehensive, afraid that the Moouchaahts (whom they had accused of contributing to the failure) and the Kyuquots would unite in warfare against them. "[The Clayoquots] halted all trade to the north in the direction of the Kyuquots. Few Clayoquot canoes ventured more than one-half mile from shore to fish. Sentinels were posted every night and false alarms sounded to practice defending the village."[34]

Soon, the anger of the villagers turned against their chief. If he hadn't been so anxious to go to war, all this would not have happened. Everyone was living in fear of reprisal. Finally, Cedakanim shut himself up in his house so that he would not be shot. He did not venture outside for three months. "He gave away all of his property as presents and thus avoided any further punishment."[35]

Sproat did not state whether the Clayoquots were ever attacked as a result of Cedakanim's miscalculation, nor is there any information on how much longer Cedakanim continued as a leader of war parties. He did write that many wars affected all of the tribes up and down the coast.[36]

Two statements written about the chief by early white traders in the region and presented by Cedakanim as his "credentials" showed very different sides of Cedakanim's character, or at least his attitudes toward different white men:

1. This is Seta Kanim, a villain that would murder his own father for a groat, if we may judge from the lying, deceit, and treachery he has practiced in his dealings with ourselves.[37]
2. This is Seta Kanim, Chief of the Clayoquots, he has been on board our vessel, and we have found him honest and trustworthy.[38]

It is quite possible that Cedakanim liked some white men and chose to deal fairly with them, while others angered him and he responded accordingly.

By 1875, it appears that Cedakanim's warring days were largely behind him, and he had moved on to other activities. In that year, Canadian Indian Commissioner I. W. Powell wrote the following:

Seta-ka-nim has been a great warrior in his day and even now is as strong and athletic as in his palmy days. He is however, to all appearances frank, open, and generous. . . . Seta-ka-nim has promised to control his people and preserve peace and good government among them, and reciprocal assurance of assistance. . . . [His tribe] find no difficulty in procuring all kinds of fish at any time during the proper season, and their trade in large quantities of dog fish oil, sea otter skins, etc., is both constant and extensive.[39]

James G. Swan's diaries and letters document additional information about Chief Sitkeenum, his family, and their presence in Neah Bay:

James G. Swan's Entries about Sitkeenum (Cedakanim)

Cedakanim, chief of the Clyoquots, arrived here [Neah Bay] today on a visit to his son [Frank] who has for a squaw the daughter of old Colchote. Cedakanim reports that the Arhosett are coming over to attack the Makahs [September 2, 1862].

. . .

Totatelum [wife of Frank Cedakanim] had a daughter born today [August 21, 1863].

. . .

Cedakanim came in this afternoon and had a long talk with me. He says that as soon as Frank's little girl gets a few months older that he intends giving a grand potlatch on Frank's behalf and will then give Frank a new name, the name of a famous old chief, Moquilla or Moquinna, mentioned in the narrative of Vancouver and other voyagers [August 29, 1863].

. . .

Russian Jim had a tremendous performance this forenoon and a potlatch during which Totatelum's little baby died, and the assembled crowd set up the most fearful wailing and howling I ever heard. . . .

Previous to the performance, Jim brought in three new masks which he asked permission to have fixed up with locks of human hair and ends of cows tails. . . . The masks were brought over by Frank and Cedakanim who arrived here from Clyoquot this morning. Frank got here just in time to see his child die and he was very much affected, and cried and howled most frantically [October 5, 1863].

. . .

Cedakanim and Frank with their people left this forenoon for Clyoquot. Cedakanim told me that he should not return before next summer, that he had come prepared to make presents to the Makahs on account of Frank's child and intended to have taken Totatelum and her baby back with him and then to have called his tribe together and given a grand feast with many presents. But now that the child was dead he had no heart to remain and should go home and give away his things as a token of his grief.

The child was grandchild to Colchote, who was a lineal descendant of Deeart, the former owner of the land about Neeah Bay. If the child had been a boy there would have been great rejoicing and if it had lived, would have been a chief [October 7, 1863].

. . .

School teachers and children attended the dance at Captain John's house. . . . Clyoquot Frank had his little boy Georgie dance a Clyoquot dance. . . . [December 4, 1878].

. . .

Captain John invited me to a dance at his house tonight. . . . Kolekose, dressed as Raven, was followed by several Indians, one of whom, Russian Jim, held a long bird spear decorated with feathers. Kolekose was preparing to show off his feats of juggling, and Jim, thinking he was going to frighten the Indians, attempted to stick the barbed spear into him. But Frank Cedakanim jumped up and took it [the spear] away from Jim. . . . In a few minutes he [Kolekose] sent a present of 2 blankets to Frank for keeping Jim from punching him with his spear. . . .[December 7, 1878].

. . .

Cedakanim, Chief of the Clayoquot Indians called today to know about oil. They can sell their oil to the trader here, Mr. Gallick, who will pay the duty on it [August 15, 1879].

. . .

Names of some of Cedakanim's family: Nana—grand daughter of Cedakanim; Ha ma sée took—Lucy, grand daughter of Cedakanim, mother of [indecipherable name]; Klu tów it la—Benjamin's daugher; Dát lo quiss—Frank's wife [August 16, 1887].

. . .

A lot of Indians returned from hop picking. I saw Sedakanim, the Clyoquot Chief, who was paralyzed. I had given him some volatile liniment and he was cured, and thinks me a good doctor. . . . [October 6, 1889].

. . .

These as well as other entries in Swan's diaries show various strengths of the old chief. It is clear that Cedakanim undertook the ceremonial responsibilities necessary for a chief in order to uphold his power and position. Once his days of warfare were over, he was concerned with trade and commerce, which allowed his immediate family as well other members of his tribe to earn a living. He was proud as well as supportive of his sons Frank and Benjamin and his grandchildren. He and his family spent a good deal of time in Neah Bay, where they had relatives; some years they all worked in the western Washington hop fields together. Cedakanim shouldered the activities and responsibilities required of a man who was a respected chief as well as the head of an important family. Toward the end of his life, his son Frank took care of him. Cedakanim died in Clayoquot village in 1897.[40]

Other Cedakanim (Sitkeenum) Family Relatives

Helma Swan has spoken of others who were Chief Cedakanim's relatives, as well as hers. Brief bits of information have been handed down orally, often with few accompanying details. Several pieces of written information, recently found, help verify and expand Helma's oral history recollections. Letters and diary entries by James G. Swan also connect various individuals from the Cedakanim and Swan families.

Benjamin Cedakanim, Atliu, or Artlyu, was Chief Cedakanim's half-Makah son.[41] As mentioned previously, Benjamin's mother was one of the unnamed Makah women who was a relative of Helma Swan. In existing written accounts, Sitkeenum himself was not called Atliu or Artlyu. Until the end of his life, outsiders always knew him by the name "Sitkeenum" or "Cedakanim." According to the oral tradition, however, some elders thought his name had been changed to Atliu when he was old and no longer a warrior. No recorded information exists concerning a name change for the old chief. However, it is clear that his son Benjamin Cedakanim was called Atliu or Artlyu, and was well known as an outstanding carver[42] (see fig. 7). Swan collected a number of his pieces over the years, some of which were sent to the Smithsonian Institution in Washington, D.C. A few of Swan's diary entries are especially relevant regarding Benjamin, or Artlyu:

. . .

Benjamin Cedakanim gave carved items to me for a gift. I gave him a certificate stating that he was half Makah and half Clayoquot [August 25, 1879].

. . .

Benjamin Cedakanim brought me a carved club or *tinethl,* which he finished today. . . . Frank and Benjamin Cedakanim related the whole story which the carving represented [September 8, 1880].

. . .

Mailed letter to Prof. Baird [of the Smithsonian] about the seal club. . . . Enclosed in it a photograph of Benjamin or Artlyu, who carved it. [November 8, 1880].

. . .

Gave Benjamin Artlyu a certificate that I have known him 25 years and that he is a skilled carver. Benjamin and Annie, his daughter, left for Dungeness this P.M. . . . [October 6, 1885].

. . .

Ben Sedakanim called and promised to carve me a *Taskea* or cane like the one he made for his father and to bring it to Neeah Bay when it is finished. [October 7, 1889].

. . .

Other than the fact that Benjamin or Atliu exhibited care and concern for his father, brother, wife, and daughter, and that he was a fine carver, little else is known about him or his life.

Annie Cedakanim/Atliu Williams, łuꞏt'aʔux̣, or Xwinxwánimo, the daughter of Benjamin Cedakanim, was, according to the oral tradition, Charlie Swan's aunt and Helma's great-aunt, from Clayoquot, British Columbia.[43] Odelia Hunter and Aunt Edith Simon, the knowledgeable Clayoquot elders mentioned previously, discussed this subject with Helma in 1975 and told her that Annie's maiden name was Cedakanim and that she was Benjamin Cedakanim's daughter[44] (fig. 8). James G. Swan's diaries include three entries supporting the statements of these Clayoquot women:

· · ·

Names of some of Cedakanim's family: . . . *Klu tów it la*—Benjamin's daughter. . . . [August 16, 1887].

· · ·

Annie is Benjamin's daughter, *Klootartl* is her Indian name [October 2, 1887].

· · ·

I saw Sedakanim, The Clyoquot Chief. . . . His son, Benjamin, showed me a beautifully carved cane or staff used by the Old Chief. Annie, Benjamin's daughter, sat down beside me and the whole family were very much pleased with my visit [October 6, 1889].

· · ·

As a young child, Helma knew Annie and her husband, Charlie Williams, from Clayoquot, because they often visited the Swans in Neah Bay, sometimes staying for three or four months at a time. Occasionally the visits were reversed; however, the Swans, as a young working family, usually stayed in Canada for shorter periods of time. Having no children of their own, the Williamses were especially fond of the Swan children, and Helma thought of Annie as another grandmother. Annie had two special talents: she was a first-rate singer and dancer, and she was an excellent basket maker (see fig. 23). Helma not only delighted in the perfection and subtlety of Annie's musical performances, but also enjoyed spending quiet hours beside her great-aunt as she wove fine Nootka baskets.[45]

As Charlie Swan's aunt, Annie felt that part of her family responsibility was to be his lifelong teacher. At appropriate times, she taught him songs and dances, gave him masks, dance robes, and other ceremonial items. She repeatedly told Charlie that he was directly descended from her father's family [Cedakanim/Atliu] and thus was entitled to become a chief and to own her father's chiefly things. In 1930 she made him her heir and declared him a chief at an elaborate potlatch which she hosted, in the village of Oopídzit on Clayoquot Island. Helma attended and was deeply affected by this event (see chap. 8).

Currently, four families—Swan, Frank, Curley, and Sam—claim descent from Chief Cedakanim. The Swans are the only Makah family in this group. The others, all originally from Clayoquot, British Columbia, now live mostly along the west coast of Vancouver Island. Family members know they are related to each other, but the specifics of these relationships are no longer fully recalled.[46]

No other information about Annie Williams has yet come to light. She was, however, a most important influence in Charlie Swan's life. She became his primary cultural guide, and counseled him as long as she lived. Annie was deeply concerned with ensuring the continuation of Clayoquot and Makah traditions. After her grandfather, Chief Cedakanim, and her father, Chief Atliu, passed away, she was left as the caretaker of her father's chiefship and all the belongings that accompanied it. She had to decide which of the young men in the line of descent would make the best chief, and then it was her responsibility to oversee his proper education. Ordinarily this would not have been the duty of a woman, but because there were no males in her family to do it, she accepted this role. Thus Annie preceded Helma as a strong, courageous woman, concerned with passing on the family traditions. Some sixty years later, Helma has followed in Annie's footsteps. It is clear that the survival of the culture is ultimately more important to these women than fitting into the standard, accepted female roles of the society.

Even with the help of a number of Indian elders, as well as existing written records, Helma has not been able to acquire all the necessary information in order to fully understand the precise nature of the Swan family relationship to Chief Sitkeenum, Benjamin Atliu, and Annie Atliu Williams. Charlie Swan's mother and her family will likely remain the missing link in this portion of the family history.

3. Chief Flattery Jack, Yelák'ub, or Yellow-cum (?–c.1853)

Flattery Jack[47] was a well-known and highly respected chief among the Makah.[48] His dates of birth and death are not precisely known; however, according to Chief Kalchote [Colchote] he died before 1855.[49] Charlie Swan and his family are direct lineal descendants of Chief Flattery Jack. Briefly, one of Flattery Jack's sons was known as Sixey, Sikesy, or Saxey Balch. Sikesy's daughter was Ellen Swan, and her son was Charlie Swan. Therefore, Ellen Swan was Flattery Jack's granddaughter; Charlie Swan, a great-grandson, and Helma Swan, a great-great-granddaughter.

Several authors knew Flattery Jack and wrote briefly about this well-liked chief. In 1847, artist Paul Kane met and talked with Flattery Jack, whom he called "Yellow-cum, the head chief of the Macaws."[50] Yellow-cum had arrived in Victoria, where Kane had stopped briefly, and at that time, Kane made a sketch (evidently lost) of Yellow-cum and learned much about this powerful chief's personal history. If Kane recorded this information, it was not published and has not been found in manuscripts; therefore, only a few of Kane's recollections exist. One concerned a revenge raid following the murder of Yellow-cum's brother. The Clallams had slain the brother and another Makah man, according to three Makahs who returned with the news. Thereupon, Yellow-cum, the head chief of the "Macaws" at that time, fitted out twelve large canoes with twenty warriors each and attacked the Clallam village of I-eh-nus. They burned it and took eighteen prisoners, mostly females, who became slaves. Eight Clallams were killed, and their heads were stuck on poles in the bows of the canoes of the victorious Makahs.[51]

Yellow-cum also told Kane an interesting story about his father, the Makah chief who had been "the pilot of the unfortunate 'Tonquin,' the ship sent out by John Jacob Astor to trade with the Indians north of Vancouver Island. The pilot [Yellow-cum's father] was the only survivor who escaped from the vessel, previous to her being blown up."[52] In 1852, Samuel Hancock, living in Neah Bay, related the same story about the *Tonquin*, which was told to him by an "old Makah chief" who had been the "interpreter" on the ship.[53] Unfortunately, the name of this chief was not given in any of the published accounts.

Kane included another noteworthy piece of information concerning Yellow-cum's power and ancestry:

> "Yellow-cum is the wealthiest man of his tribe. . . . He possesses vast influence over all the other tribes and has become head chief from his own personal prowess and ability, and not from any hereditary claim to that dignity."[54]

Makah oral tradition has not maintained the direct connection between the Swan family and Flattery Jack, perhaps because his granddaughter, Ellen Swan, died so young. Family members knew only that they owned one Makah song which had belonged to Yelák'ub, that they had the right to use the Indian names "Willub" and "Yelák'ub" from a past Makah chief, and that these names were tied to Billy Balch, who was somehow related to them.[55] No one recalled how the song or names had been inherited by the Swans.

However, brief statements found in James G. Swan's diaries, when put together, connect the two families. Even though Flattery Jack, or Yelák'ub, had already died when Swan first began keeping his Neah Bay diaries in 1859, he did know two of Flattery Jack's sons: Billy Balch, or Willub, the older son, and Sixey, also known as Sikesy Balch, Captain Balch, or Tsukto, the younger son. Swan's diary entries reveal these family relationships, as well as glimpses of their otherwise unknown lives:

. . .

> "Billy," Old Flattery Jack's son, played, "Oh, Susannah," on an accordion very well [September 22, 1859].

. . .

> Billy Balch came to me for medicine for his baby. [October 31, 1859].

. . .

> Billy Balch, son of Flattery Jack, or Yellicom, showed me a letter signed by James Douglas, Governor of Vancouver Island, Feb. 12, 1852, speaking highly of the services of said Flattery Jack and his people in saving property from the wreck of the H.B. Co. Brigantine Una, wrecked on Waadda. [Waadah is the island just northeast of Neah Bay] [November 8, 1859].

. . .

. . . . I made [a sketch] of the grave of Billy's baby who died a few days since. Billy's uncle and sister are buried in the same grave. His father, Old Flattery Jack, is buried near the brook [November 19, 1859].

. . .

Went to Willub's house, or Billy Balch, where I met Captain John and several other Indians who regaled me with tales of their legends [November 24, 1859].

. . .

This morning Jenny Lind's father [a Clallam chief] bought a slave woman of Billy Balch for which he paid $80. 70 in gold and 10 in silver [January 14, 1860].

. . .

"Captain Balch," the boy, [Sikesy] put a piece of dried venison out to soak and the crows stole it [January 5, 1862].

. . .

Billy Balch had a singing party at his home this evening. It was the commencing of a series of ceremonies given by the mother of a little girl named Duquitsa, who is to give away a lot of presents and have a variety of games. The festivities will last nearly a fortnight [September 24, 1863].

. . .

Billy Balch's party mentioned on the 24th still continues. He and Kyallanhoo are to give presents together [September 29, 1863].

. . .

Hosett, Suez, and Waatch Indians arrive. Dances and songs in Willub's house. Captain Balch and Boatchup dressed in school boys' clothes and looked well. . . . [October 3, 1863].

. . .

Billy Balch and his little boy, Charley, a child about 2 years old . . . present [at the school]. Billy wanted the little boy to pronounce the letters but he would not, whereupon Billy gave him a regular spanking [December 4, 1863].

. . .

Indians drunk in Billy Balch's lodge and all along the beach. . . . [December 5, 1863].

. . .

Billy Balch came in this evening, says that Ah ay yah of Hosett is now the head chief of that village and Sowsom of Tsooes, that Se ah sub is head chief at Waatch, but there is no head chief at Neeah. Says the Indians are anxious for their annuities [December 14, 1863].

. . .

Peter proposed that his slave, Batsie, and Willub's slave, Yahchah, should have a wrestling match which they did, and Yahchah was the winner. This made Peter angry and he took hold of Yahchah, which caused Willub to take his part, but he in turn was opposed by Beershad. Thus they had it until Willub's party proving the strongest, succeeded in throwing down every one of Peter's party. . . . Peter, who was very angry, went after his pistol and as Sixey came out on the beach he fired and the ball passed through his arm, badly breaking the bone, and lodged in his back. This was afterward cut out by the Indians. Peter and

Beershad then jumped on Captain Balch or Sixey, and commenced beating him, but he managed, although his left arm was broken, to give Sam a severe cut across the thigh with a pocket knife.

Capt. Balch is very badly hurt. The ball passed directly through his arm and shattered the bone badly. . . . I advised the Indians . . . to take Sixey to Victoria or Port Angeles to some doctor and have his arm properly set.

Shortly after, Waatchqua came to borrow a shovel and a hoe and for a most remarkable purpose. He went where old Flattery Jack, Sixey's father, had been buried, and dug up one of his arm bones, which was taken and bound on as splints to the arm of Sixey, the Indians believing that the bone from the father's arm would cure [December 18, 1863].

. . .

Billy Balch is repairing his canoe today, intending to start tomorrow for Victoria to carry his brother to have his arm examined by a surgeon [April 5, 1864].

. . .

Willub returned from Victoria this morning leaving his brother in charge of the doctor [April 22, 1864].

. . .

Indians drunk this evening in Willub's lodge. . . . [May 17, 1864].

. . .

Billy Balch and others [who were halibut fishing] returned this forenoon. . . . [June 10, 1864].

. . .

Capt. Balch has so far recovered from the effects of the shot wound in his arm that he went to Mr. Maggs today to cook [July 20, 1864].

. . .

Kyallanhoo, Willub, and others have gone today for whales [July 25, 1864].

. . .

Kichusam . . . said he did not want to be a slave any longer and wanted to know what he should do. . . . [A Nitinat] Indian sold Kichusam for a trifle to a Baadah Indian who sold him to Flattery Jack, Billy Balch's father, who left him at his death, to Billy, who has since sold him to Captain John [February 8, 1865].

. . .

Capt. Balch (Sikesy) commenced working in house as cook today [November 10, 1865].

. . .

Settled with Sikesy for cook to date. From Nov. 13. Nineteen days at 50 cents. $9.50 [December 2, 1865].

. . .

Sikesy and other boys spend much time white-washing school house [July 15, 1866].

. . .

Received letter from Billy Balch's boy Charley. Fifty cents to buy fireworks [October 7, 1877].

. . .

Waatch Tom said the Indians . . . want Lighthouse Jim, Billy Balch, and Captain John to be the head men of the tribe. . . . [November 17, 1878].

. . .

Election of 4 chiefs or headmen in Neeah Bay.

Old Doctor - Youaitl	54 votes
Willub	66 votes
Captain John	66 votes
Kaytub - David	74 votes

This is the first election ever held by the Indians here, and will be followed by similar elections in Waatch, Tsooess, and Hosett [January 23, 1879].

. . .

Kichusan sold his house to Willub who bought it for his son, Charley Williams, who intends to be married to Lechessar's girl, Jenny Wikaub [September 8, 1880].

. . .

Went to Sikesy's house and saw Ellen [Sikesy's daughter] who gave me an order for some things in Port Townsend [June 27, 1881].

. . .

. . . Billy Balch (Yellacoob) told Cheehwin to come to my house and leave her things. . . . [October 24, 1886].

. . .

Billy Balch and wife of Neeah Bay called; everyone going to pick hops [August 18, 1887].

. . .

Billy Balch and Agnes [his wife] came in this evening. . . . [December 16, 1888].

. . .

Went to Neeah Bay. . . . At Sikesy's saw Duqualli things belonging to Billy Balch, which I offered to buy [for the World's Fair]. . . . [June 14, 1892].

. . .

From the foregoing, it is clear that Billy Balch was a chief, that he interacted with the other chiefs in Neah Bay, that he bought and sold slaves, and that at times he did not treat them very well. He was quite knowledgeable about Makah customs, myths, and legends, and talked freely to Swan about some of these things. He participated in the ceremonial life as host, performer, and teacher—all proper roles for a chief. When alcohol was available, he drank it and got drunk along with the other chiefs and their slaves.[56] As a young man his Indian name was Willub. When older, he became Yellacoob.[57]

Willub, or Billy, also took his family responsibilities seriously. In 1859 he called on Swan to give medicine to his sick baby, who afterward died in spite of the treatment. In 1863 he was concerned that his small boy, Charley, learn to read at Swan's school. For most of his life, Willub appears to have been married to one woman, Asbie, who was also called Agnes, and occasionally, Susie. Charley Williams was their one surviving son; Willub was quite proud of him and always concerned about his well-being.[58] Billy also looked out for his own younger brother, Sikesy, whenever the latter became injured or sick.

Billy Balch (Willub) worked at many occupations during his lifetime; a chief did not sit around and expect others to take care of him. He was an excellent hunter—taking whales and seals from the sea, and elk, deer, birds, and other animals from the forest. A talented fisherman, he and his crew often returned with canoe loads of fresh halibut or salmon. For a short time, he even worked in a Clallam Bay coal mine that operated during the 1860s.

It is not clear whether Sikesy, also a son of Chief Flattery Jack and younger brother of Willub, was ever considered a chief. He worked for James G. Swan on a number of projects around the reservation, and the two appeared to be friends. For a period of time, Sikesy even cooked for Swan. Sikesy had a hard life. As a boy, he attended some of the drunken parties held by his older brother Willub, and in December 1863, as mentioned earlier, he was shot and severely wounded by Peter. Then in October 1864, he was injured again when an overloaded gun which he was shooting flew back and hit him between the eyes. Luckily he did not lose an eye, and the wound eventually healed. His luck in marriage was no better. As a young man, he married several times in succession because each of his young wives died after a few years, as did at least one baby. His daughter, Ellen Swan, survived until the age of twenty, even though her mother, Whaubtedah, or Alice, died when Ellen was about one year old.

Swan's diaries indicate that he often interacted with Billy Balch and Sikesy when they were young men. Both brothers could speak English, but probably neither of them learned to read and write. Billy, already married and with a baby in 1859, would not have been a candidate for the new school Swan was creating. It is not clear whether Sikesy ever attended Swan's school in Neah Bay. However, children who were a few years younger than Siksey did attend school and learned to read and write, as did his own daughter, Ellen, in the 1870s and 1880s.

Other Relatives Important in Helma Swan's Life

Ellen Swan, Wa-ái-chitl, or Archillu (1867–1887) lived a short but full life (see fig. 3).[59] Because her mother, Whaubtedah, died when she was about a year old, this granddaughter of Flattery Jack and daughter of Sikesy, lived with her father and at least two stepmothers as a young child, stayed for a time with her uncle, Billy Balch, and his family, then attended boarding school in Neah Bay when she was a little older. She became good friends with James G. Swan, as did several other Makah schoolchildren. From his descriptions, she appears to have had a happy childhood. She and the others did errands and helped Swan with various chores, and he bought them little presents and helped them in a variety of ways. Ellen was a good student who enjoyed school and learned English well. When Swan moved to Port Townsend in 1881, she and her friends wrote to him often, and he always answered their letters.

Ellen fell in love with Chestoke Peterson, the son of Peter Brown, and after an Indian-style marriage, their child, Charlie Swan, was born on April 7, 1886.[60] Unfortunately, Ellen contracted measles in November 1887, and died suddenly. Shortly thereafter, in 1888, Chestoke married Minnie James, and subsequently had little to do with Charlie's upbringing.

In his diaries, Swan speaks often of Ellen and her friends and appears to care about them as if they were his own children. He shared her joy and sent her gifts after the birth of her baby boy, and was quite saddened when she died so unexpectedly. His writings create the only picture we have of her life.[61]

Ellen as a Child

Ellen, Minnie, Jennie and other children put clam shells around my flower beds and improved the appearance very much [May 16, 1879].

. . .

Indian name of Ellen - Wa-ái-chitl [June 1, 1879].

. . .

Martha, Ellen, Fanny, and Mary put up a house back of my house where they have had a fire and cooked some eggs, and made tea, and played with their dolls and have had a very pleasant time [June 12, 1879].

. . .

Minnie, Jennie, Jangi, Ellen, and Mary came to look at pictures. . . . Ellen is a demure, modest little girl, but was ringleader in locking me out of my rooms in the afternoon—all in fun [January 4, 1880].

. . .

Went to Neeah, gave little Ellen a toy wash tub, scrubbing board, clothes wringer as a present to commemorate her *katesae chit1*[62] or her *chee marsh pil,* which commenced on Monday last [February 11, 1880].

. . .

Saw little Ellen at her father's house. Sikesy, her father, and I discussed the question of how old she is. I left here in 1866, and he says she was born one year after I left, that when she was one year old, her mother, Alice, or Whaubtedah died, and he then married her sister Lucy who died in about two years. Ellen is about thirteen years old, but she doesn't look to be over ten [February 24, 1880]

. . .

Ellen was in Captain John's house and I gave her 4 bits. Gave Ellen's little sister, Amelia, 2 bits [January 8, 1881].

. . .

Received letters from Martha and Ellen [August 24, 1881]. [Swan had left his position as Customs Inspector at Neah Bay on August 18, 1881, and had moved to Port Townsend.]

. . .

Wrote letters to Martha, Ellen, and Minnie [August 26, 1881].[63]

. . .

Children all went to Neeah to pass a 10 day vacation, except Martha and Ellen who remained to see me. We had a pleasant evening in the parlor telling stories [March 30, 1883].

. . .

Ellen and Washington were studying arithmetic in Sikesy's house [April 1, 1883].

. . .

Put parcel in post directed to Miss Ellen Swan, Agency School, Neeah Bay. Postage $.56 [December 21, 1883].

. . .

Indian name for Ellen Swan - A'chillu [August 23, 1884].

. . .

Indians returned from the hop fields. This evening Ellen and Billy Balch [her uncle] called [September 27, 1885].

. . .

. . . Wrote Ellen Swan to make me a covered vial like the last and send me a picture if she has one and to color some moss for me [March 28, 1886].

. . .

Ellen as a Young Mother

Received a letter from Martha dated the 8th, that Ellen had a little boy, born April 7, 1886. Wrote a letter of congratulations to Ellen [April 12, 1886].

. . .

Bought a nurse bottle at N. D. Hill's ($.40) and mailed it to Ellen Swan, Neeah. ($.12) [April 28, 1886].

. . .

Called on Mrs. Webster and bought baby clothes for Ellen. $2.00 [April 29, 1886].

. . .

Wrote Ellen Swan and sent her flannel for the baby [May 24, 1886].

. . .

Packed a box of things for Ellen and the baby and sent a book, Echoes From the Valley Parrish [March 23, 1887].

. . .

Received a box with moss, shells, and a basket from Ellen [April 14, 1887].

. . .

Sent candy to Ellen's baby [April 25, 1887].

. . .

Wrote Ellen and sent dress patterns and candy and writing paper [Aug. 11, 1887].

. . .

Wrote Ellen and sent a cape and a cape to Martha [November 3, 1887].

. . .

Ellen's Death

Ellen Swan Archillu died at Neeah Bay today of the measles [November 7, 1887].[64]

. . .

Captain [name indecipherable] who came from Neeah Bay this morning told me that Ellen Achill died of measles at Neeah last Monday the 7th. Wrote to Charley Williams, Minnie James, and Martha Hunter about poor Ellen's death [November 9, 1887].

. . .

. . . I will be a good friend to that little boy [Ellen's son] for his mother's sake. I loved her always, ever since she was a baby, and I am very sorry she is dead. I hope all of my friends will be very kind to her little boy [Letter to Chestoqua Peterson, April 27, 1889].

. . .

Thus ended Ellen's short life. Her son, Charlie Swan, never knew her and never learned much about her life and background.

Ellen Swan is a primary character in the ongoing mystery of the Swan family's relationship to the Canadian Chief Cedakanim and his family. Many questions exist concerning Ellen's ancestry. Her mother, Whaubtedah, or Alice, had one sister named Hedátokobaitl, and another sister named Lucy.[65] The three sisters were apparently all from Neah Bay. Thus far, no information has been found stating what tribe Kudú·ʔi, their mother, was from—whether she was Makah, or perhaps Canadian. In 1868, when Ellen was about one year old, her mother, Whaubtedah [Alice], died. Her father, Sikesy, then married Whaubtedah's sister, Lucy, who died about two years later.[66] It is unknown whether Sikesy had any children with Lucy, and there is no other information concerning either sister. It is not known whether their mother, Kudú·ʔi, was the wife or daughter of a chief; however, Sikesy, the son of Flattery Jack, probably would not have married Whaubtedah, and then Lucy unless both had been chiefs' daughters. Whaubtedah's father was Pahahkwitl, according to James G. Swan, who mentions him but rarely.[67] Swan, however, did state that one time Pahahkwitl was giving a potlatch, which implies that he was a chief.[68] Nothing further is known about this family or their ancestry. Because it has not been possible to trace either Kudú·ʔi's or Pahahkwitl's relatives, a documented connection to the Cedakanim family has not been established. Such a connection presently exists based solely on the oral tradition and several implications in James G. Swan's writings.

Three indirect pieces of evidence in Swan's diaries and letters appear to link Ellen Swan to Chief Cedakanim and his family. The first is a diary entry dated October 12, 1885:

Wrote letter to Ellen Swan, Neah Bay, enclosing a letter from Frank Cedakanim.[69]

It is highly unlikely that Frank would be writing to Ellen unless they were close relatives. Swan, as a white man and a friend to both of them, was in a different category. He could write and receive mail from all these people without being a blood relative.

The second piece of evidence is a letter to Chestoqua Peterson dated April 27, 1889, after Ellen's death:

> I have been to Victoria 3 days ago. I saw Frank Cedakanim from Clyoquot. He said that his father, Cedakanim, is very feeble and he doesn't think he will live long, and as soon as he dies, Frank will go and live at Neah Bay and look after Ellen's aunt and Ellen's little boy.[70]

If Ellen had not been closely related to Frank Cedakanim, he would not have volunteered to take on the responsibility of raising her child.[71] Swan accurately describes the woman who was caring for Ellen's son as Ellen's aunt, although he does not name her or explain any further who she is.

The last piece of evidence is a record Swan made of a new name for Ellen. Included in a list of Indian names for some of the Makah school girls is the following:

> Ellen Swan—"A'chillu" [August 23, 1884].[72]

Swan used this name again when writing of her death: "Ellen Swan Archillu died at Neah Bay today of measles" [November 7, 1887]. He includes a similar statement using this name, on November 9, 1887.[73] It is possible that Archillu may have been the same name as Atliu, or Artlyu, and that she was given this name to connect her with her Canadian relatives. These three pieces of evidence strongly imply a family connection between the two families. Annie Atliu Williams, the daughter of Benjamin Atliu, always stated that she was Charlie Swan's aunt, so it is likely that the two families were related through ancestors who have vanished from memory and who may never have been recorded in the pages of written history.

Chestoke (Chestoqua) Peterson (c. 1865–19?) was the son of Chief Peter Brown and the father of Charlie Swan.[74] Little is known about Chestoke's early life. His mother, Tsitsalqwaks, or Chucharkwax, a Nootkan woman from Port Alberni, Canada, was one of Peter Brown's wives.[75] As a child, Chestoke was adopted by Chief Peter, who always considered the youngster to be his son. Chestoke's real father, perhaps a white man, remains unknown.[76] A number of years later, Chestoke married Ellen Swan in the Indian manner, and they had a son—Charlie Swan.[77] After Ellen's untimely death, Chestoke married Minnie James, with whom he had four daughters and one son.

James G. Swan, who knew Chestoke from childhood on and often mentions him in his diaries, has created the principal written record concerning Charlie Swan's father:

. . . went with some Indians to Sail Rock River to put up a house for Peter. Jeff Davis, Shobid [Hunter], and Chestoka went [April 23, 1879].

. . .

The newly elected chiefs . . . said they would consider who they would have for their clerk, whether Charley Williams or Chestoka [February 14, 1880].

. . .

Chestoqua wants a pair of pants. 26" waist, 34" long on outside seam [April 27, 1880].

. . .

Chestoka wants a book in which to keep an account of the halibut catch of the season [May 11, 1880].

. . .

Peter paid me for one pair pants for Chestoka. $3.50 [May 26, 1880].

. . .

Sent Chestoka to the bay for a canoe to be used by Prof. Jordan for collecting fish during his stay [May 29, 1880].

. . .

Received letters from Martha, Ellen, and Chestoka [November 3, 1882].

. . .

Finished letters to Martha and Ellen, and wrote to Chestoqua Peterson, Neah [November 5, 1882].

. . .

Wrote Chestoqua about Peter's schooner sails which are done [December 3, 1885].

. . .

Received a letter from Minnie James dated Jan. 9, that she was married to Chestoqua on Tues, Jan. 3, 1888 [January 11, 1888].

. . .

Made bill of sale from James Claplanhoo to Chestoqua Peterson for one half of Schooner Lottie for $800 [February 28, 1889].

. . .

Minnie James Peterson, Chestoqua's wife had a little boy born today at Neah Bay [March 24, 1889].

. . .

Chestoqua Peterson bought the Schooner Anna Beck at U.S. Marshal sale yesterday and I told him I would lend him $400 toward paying for her until he can get his money from Neah Bay next week. Schooner cost $907.00 [March 27, 1889].

. . .

Inspector Frank Winslow came from Seattle to check the Schooner Anna Beck which belongs to Chestoqua Peterson and is to be called the James G. Swan [April 11, 1889].

. . .

Went to Seattle with Chestoqua and filed report of appraisers in the case of Schooner James G. Swan [April 14, 1890].

. . .

Went to Hadlock to take a letter to Chestoqua Peterson. Schooner J. G. Swan was on beach with one side of the bottom painted and other side ready to be painted this tide. Chestoqua was mixing paint. . . . [April 23, 1890].

. . .

Wrote Chestoqua to get memo from Ben Butler of the seal skins on the schooner J. G. Swan in Bering Sea last year [May 25, 1890].

. . .

Chestoqua Peterson and wife Minnie, and baby called on me this morning [Feb. 8, 1891].

. . .

Wrote Chestoqua to get a full set of Makah whaling and fishing gear for World's Fair, Chicago [July 19, 1891].

. . .

Wrote Chestoqua—enquiring how the Makah cook sea eggs. . . . [August 24, 1891].

. . .

Received letter—Chestoqua—giving account of seal catch at Neah Bay in 1890–91 [December 12, 1891].

. . .

Wrote Chestoqua to have Schooner Lottie papers renewed, and to invite all the Indians to come to the celebration next Sat.—a huge clambake [May 2, 1892].

. . .

Wrote Chestoqua to send all the things he has ready for Washington World's Fair [August 30, 1892].

. . .

Wrote Chestoqua to hurry up the Indians who are making the articles for Dr. Franz Boas [October 31, 1892].

. . .

Chestoqua made out statement of claim for damages for seizure of Schooner J. G. Swan in Bering Sea, July 30, 1889. $13,670.65. Chestoqua went to Hadlock to see about repairs on his schooner [December 2, 1893].

. . .

Have been at work on the petition to Congress for Chestoqua. I find this a more difficult task than I had anticipated [concerning seizure of Schooner J. G. Swan] [February 1, 1894].

. . .

Chestoqua Peterson and his little girl Mabel came to see me this morning [October 5, 1894].

. . .

Schooner Columbia arrived with 500 seal skins for Chestoqua Peterson. . . . [October 10, 1895].

. . .

Mailed 3 copies of P.I. article, "Makah Indians" to Chestoqua Peterson [November 24, 1895].

. . .

Schooner Columbia arrived from Neah, Chestoqua Peterson, owner, called on me with Mr. Brown. Chestoqua said the Columbia had 404 seal skins. . . . [October 7, 1896].

. . .

Chestoqua Peterson and his daughter Mabel of Neah Bay, called on me this morning. . . . [October 28, 1898].

. . .

Chestoke appeared to be a responsible father and a hard worker. From Swan's diaries and letters it is clear that Chestoke bought and sold a number of sealing schooners and did quite well in the seal hunting business. It was rumored, however, that as time went on, Chestoke was not very happy in Neah Bay. Finally, about 1920 he devised a plan of action. Chestoke came to Charlie Swan and to his other son, James Peterson, and asked them to join him—they would leave Neah Bay, go far away, and start a new life elsewhere. After giving this request serious thought, Charlie finally decided not to join them because he was happily married and had many young children to support. Chestoke and James Peterson left Neah Bay and were never heard from again. Some say they were drowned at sea; others say they made it to Alaska, changed their names, and started anew. No documented evidence has been found to support or refute either story.[78]

Charlie Swan, Tlat-tla-kwokw, or Kitlchissub (1886–1958), the son of Ellen Swan and Chestoke Peterson, was directly descended from the three chiefs discussed earlier: Chief Peter Brown was Charlie's grandfather on his father's side, Yelák'ub or Flattery Jack was his great-grandfather on his mother's father's side, and Chief Sitkeenum, or Cedakanim, was also a direct relative from his mother's side of the family. Flattery Jack had died before he was born, but as a young boy Charlie knew both of the other chiefs.[79]

Little is known about Charlie Swan's early life. Left motherless at the age of one and a half, and having no grandmother to care for him, he was raised by his great-aunt, Hedatokobáitl, his grandmother Whaubtedah's sister.[80] She cared for Charlie as if he were her own son. This woman, whom he later called "grandmother," gave him a deep feeling and love for Makah culture and emphasized the need to uphold it and pass it on to his children. All his life he was most appreciative of her support and guidance, and never forgot what she and the other elders taught him.

Hedatokobáitl was not the only person concerned with Charlie Swan's welfare as a child. According to James G. Swan, Frank Cedakanim intended to provide for both Charlie and his great-aunt,[81] but it is unknown whether he actually did so. As noted earlier, James G. Swan also helped with the care of Ellen's little boy, both before and after her death. His diaries show that he was fond of Charlie Swan as a child, that Hedatokobáitl brought the toddler to see him in Port Townsend, and that Charlie, as he grew older, continued to visit James G. Swan until the latter's death in 1900. Charlie Swan was fourteen at that time.

. . .

Tlat tla kwokw - Ellen's baby's name [back flyleaf of Diary 41, 1887].

. . .

Packed some cakes, figs, whistle, mouth organ, and toy watch in a box directed to Shobid Hunter, Neah Bay, for Ellen Swan's little boy and wrote Mrs. Martha Hunter [Shobid's wife] about it [March 20, 1889].

. . .

Bought a pair of shoes for Ellen's little boy. $1.25. Sent them to Shobid Hunter by Chas. Willoughby [April 22, 1889].

. . .

Ellen's aunt with the little boy came to see me [August 29, 1889].

. . .

Ellen's aunt from Neeah Bay came with Ellen's little boy. Gave the little boy $1.00 and 2 handkerchiefs and a tippet, a suit of clothes, and a new hat [October 28, 1889].

. . .

Ellen's little boy named Kitlchissub [flyleaf, 1892 diary].

. . .

Wrote Chestoqua Peterson, Neeah Bay, and sent a package of toy pistol caps for Ellen's boy, Kitlchissub, and for Horace [a young son of Jimmy Claplanhoo, who was another of Swan's friends] [June 21, 1892].

. . .

Andy Johnson and Charlie Swan, Ellen's boy, arrived from Neeah this morning and called on me. They are bound for the hop fields [August 18, 1897].

. . .

Charley Swan of Neah Bay, Ellen's boy, came to see me this forenoon. He is a bright boy and looks like his mother who died several years ago [October 12, 1897].

. . .

Lots of Makah and Quileutes here [Port Townsend] and many left for Seattle. Charley Swan, Sikesey's Ellen's boy, called on me this morning. He is a fine bright boy and looks like his mother [August 27, 1898].

. . .

Charlie Swan of Neah Bay, Ellen's boy, called on me this evening and I went to the beach and saw his grandmother and a number of the Makah Indians. Gave Charlie a magazine for him to look over the pictures and keep the book [October 3, 1898].

. . .

This was the last entry that the aging James G. Swan made concerning Charlie Swan.[82]

After spending his childhood years with his great-aunt, Charlie, as an older teenager, moved in with his cousin Charley Williams and family.[83] Then, in 1909 at the age of twenty-three, Charlie Swan married Ruth Anderson, the second daughter of Charlie and Alice Anderson from Ozette.[84] Ruth Swan recalled that she was only about fourteen and still playing with dolls at the time she married Charlie Swan. His "grandmother," Hedatokobáitl, being a traditional woman concerned with maintaining the proper order in the society, arranged the marriage. Neither of the young people objected. They grew to love each other, had many children, worked hard all of their lives, and were only parted when Charlie Swan died in 1958.

Although descended from powerful, warring chiefs on both sides, Charlie Swan, was quite different from his colorful ancestors. He loved his family and was concerned primarily with their welfare and happiness. According to his daughter Helma, he was always a peace loving man, not a warrior. Charlie sought harmony and reconciliation; he delighted in bringing people together, not separating them. The days of tribal warfare and killing were over by the time he was growing up, so he was interested in finding and keeping a good job which would allow him to raise his family properly and to fulfill his numerous ceremonial obligations.

Always a responsible and reliable person, Charlie Swan was never without a job. Working most of his adult life as a BIA employee, he held a variety of positions—policeman, handy man, carpenter, plumber, electrician, roofer, and housebuilder. He built two different houses for his family and kept altering them as his family grew. The first house eventually decayed and later burned; he built a second house on the same spot. The persistent rains and storms eventually destroyed the second one as well.

Charlie Swan cherished the Makah arts and cultural traditions, and did his best to instill love, knowledge, and respect for them in his children. He was always busy with some artistic project or another: carving new masks, making rattles or dance capes, refurbishing costumes. His daily routine included singing as well as teaching the songs and dances to his children.

From the time he was very young, Charlie was always drawn to the Indian ceremonies, probably as a result of the training by his great-aunt, Hedatokobáitl, and his Canadian aunt, Annie Atliu Williams. He loved to sing and to dance (see fig. 9). Being a man who was descended from chiefs and a chief himself, he was devoted to maintaining his family's place in the Makah hereditary hierarchy. This meant he had to attend potlatches, perform his own songs and dances, and pay people for witnessing them. An excellent dancer with smooth, graceful movements, Charlie adroitly imitated the bird, animal, or other creatures he was representing. For years he was also one of several song leaders in Neah Bay, responsible for the proper performance of many Makah family ceremonial songs.

Because he received the Canadian chiefship that had formerly belonged to his Clayoquot relatives Sitkeenum and Atliu, Charlie Swan chose not to claim prerogatives formerly belonging to his Makah grandfather, Chief Peter Brown. Charlie felt strongly that he had been given a wonderful gift which brought honor to him and his family, and he needed no more than this. He wanted others in Neah Bay to have an opportunity to inherit their own chiefly privileges.

Charlie Swan "believed the best about everybody, all the time," according to Helma. He understood the value of Makah culture and traditions and worked hard all his life to ensure their continuation. He was respected both in Canada and in the United States as a good person and as a fountain of cultural knowledge.

Ruth Anderson Swan, Bus-sa-dook, or Hi-yesh-hout1 (1893–1979), mother of Helma, remains an enigma.[85] She was a taciturn woman who, throughout her life, seldom talked about her family, her relatives, or her ancestors (see fig. 4). She taught her children little about the inherited Anderson family songs and stories. Ruth Swan never shared much about herself with her children, either, and Helma feels that she never knew or understood her mother.

Throughout her life, Ruth developed many skills, was industrious, and hard-working. In addition to being a good homemaker, she learned the same trades as her husband and worked alongside him for many years. In order to do so, she often took Helma out of school to baby-sit the younger Swan children.[86] Also a fine basket maker, Ruth easily sold all the baskets she made in order to increase the family's income. Aside from these activities, every spring and summer for many years, she planted and tended a vegetable garden with each of her (divorced) parents and also grew a small one of her own on the Swan family land. She often accompanied her father when he went fishing in his canoe. After his death in 1937, she continued to fish by herself because she enjoyed it so much. She was an independent woman who undertook jobs (such as house building and fishing) considered atypical by most Makah women of her day. Since her husband was so devoted to Makah music and ceremonial life, she supported him and their children at the potlatches, where she also sang and danced.

Charlie Anderson, Long Charlie, or He-dów-a[87] (1865–1937), Helma's maternal grandfather, was a chief at Ozette according to oral tradition and was the grandson of another Ozette chief named Háatz.[87] James G. Swan spent little time at Ozette and apparently did not know this family; therefore, he makes no mention of them in his diaries. Aside from Makah census data, no other published accounts elucidate their lives.[88] The Anderson family moved from Ozette to Neah Bay in 1907, seven years after Swan had died. The only personal information about Charlie Anderson comes from Helma, who spent a great deal of time with him and was very close to him as a child.

Charlie Anderson made a living for his family primarily as a fisherman. Secondarily, he grew a vegetable garden. Not an idle man, he never let his grandchildren remain idle. He was always repairing fishing nets, working on his canoe to keep it seaworthy, preparing for ceremonies, hosting singing sessions, baby-sitting his grandchildren, and so forth. He and his younger brother, Elliot Anderson, Qui'ooksit, were excellent basketmakers, an unusual activity for men, but one that they both enjoyed. During the winter months when they couldn't fish, and after their net mending was finished, basket making kept them occupied and allowed them to earn extra money. Because Ruth Swan was too busy to teach Helma, Charlie Anderson enjoyed teaching his granddaughter to make baskets.

When Helma was small, her grandfather had a house at Green Point [now known as Anderson Point] just south of Tsooyez Beach on the Pacific Ocean side of the reservation, and he had a summer house, called a "Warm House," at a place called Midway, or Kiddekabat,[89] located on Cape Flattery. During the spring and summer each year, the family traveled back and forth between the two residences, farming at Green Point and fishing at Midway.

Charlie Anderson, like Charlie Swan, was interested in maintaining Makah customs and was a frequent participant in the ceremonial life (see fig. 10). He owned many Ozette songs and enjoyed singing and dancing them at potlatches. His songs and dances were inherited by his second daughter, Ruth Anderson Swan. This occurred because his oldest daughter, Anna, died about 1910 at the age of twenty.[90] Her only child, Meredith Phillips Parker, was an infant at the time. Therefore, in the traditional Makah manner, the songs and other items were passed to the second child in line, in this case Ruth Swan. Because Ruth did not learn much about the songs she inherited, most of the stories that accompanied them are forgotten. Helma is now the caretaker for these songs, and the Swan family often performs them at potlatch parties.

Charlie Anderson, a generous, patient, and caring person, was dearly loved by the Swan children. He spent many delightful hours with the older children, teaching them tribal lore as well as practical knowledge. He gave them an appreciation for the beauty and wonder of life. Their grandfather always urged them to explore, learn, and be curious.

NOTES

INTRODUCTION

1. Since "Indian" is the term preferred by most of the Makah, as well as many other Indian people, this is the term that will be used most often in this book.

2. Helma Swan was married to Oliver Ward, Jr., (better known as Wimpy) for thirty-eight years. After his death in June 1997, she decided to change her name back to Swan. Therefore, at various times and places in the text, she may be referred to as Helma Swan, Helma Swan Ward, or Helma Ward.

3. In a greatly simplified manner, this discussion deals with aspects of what is currently termed, "reflexive anthropology," as discussed by Prattis (1996:1072–1075), Whitaker (1996:470–473), and Barrett (1996:150–163). Let it suffice to say that dominance, subordination, political agendas, and career advancement were not part of the Swan-Goodman creative process. Rather, exploration, discussion, mutual growth, and understanding were the elements which guided both the relationship and the final product.

4. Some of the knowledgeable elders with whom we spoke during the late 1970s and early 1980s included: Adam and Margaret Shewish, Port Alberni, B.C.; Harry Dick and his daughter, Dora Sanvidge, Campbell River, B.C.; Jimmy John, Nanaimo, B.C.; Margaret Amos, Long Beach, B.C.; Art Peters, Ucluelet, B.C.; Hughie Watts, Port Alberni, B.C.; Johnnie Jacobson, Ahousat, B.C.; Peter Webster, Ahousat, B.C.; Regge Ward, La Push, Wash.; Sarah Woodruff, La Push, Wash., Herb and Lela Fisher, Hoh River, Wash.; Pansy Hudson, La Push, Wash.; Lilly Belle Williams, Hoh River, Wash.; Lillian Pullen, La Push, Wash.

5. Helma has copies of our taped interviews and also of the typed transcripts.

6. Formerly known as Nootka or Nootkans in older publications, these peoples now prefer to be called "Westcoast" or "Nuu-cha-nulth." Depending on the context, all three terms appear from time to time in this book.

7. Several of the principal Makah reference works include: Swan 1870; Curtis 1916; Colson 1953; Gunther 1960; McCurdy 1961; Renker 1994. Information on the Nootkan tribes may be found in Boas 1895; Sproat 1868; Drucker 1951, 1963, 1965; Jewitt 1975; Kenyon 1980; Koppert 1930; Moziño 1970; Sapir 1911, 1913, 1967; Sapir and Swadesh 1939, 1955; Arima and Dewhirst 1990. Discussions of Nootkan and Makah music appear in Densmore 1939, 1943; Ernst 1952; Roberts and Swadesh 1955; Goodman 1977, 1978, 1986, 1991, 1992, 2001; Goodman and Swan 1999.

8. A variety of Makah and Westcoast or Nuu-cha-nulth (Nootka) Indian materials were examined at the Burke Museum, University of Washington; Suzzallo Library, University of Washington; Port Angeles Public Library; Jefferson County Historical Museum, Port Townsend, Washington; Seattle Art Museum; Washington State Historical Society Library, Tacoma; Washington State Library, Olympia; Makah Cultural and Research Center, Neah Bay, Washington; Bureau of Indian Affairs, Portland, Oregon, Area Office; National Anthropological Archives, Smithsonian Institution; Denver Art Museum; Laboratory of Anthropology Library, Santa Fe, New Mexico; Royal British Columbia Museum, Victoria, B.C.; Museum of Anthropology at the University of British Columbia, Vancouver, B.C.;

Union of British Columbia Indian Chiefs, Vancouver, B.C.; Alberni Valley Museum, Port Alberni, B.C.

Helma Swan has her own small personal collection of documents that provided several kinds of family data including allotment numbers; probate records; estate information; parents', grandparents', and children's names; and in some cases dates of birth and death.

The National Archives and Records Administration Center at Sand Point, in Seattle, contains the Makah Census Rolls beginning in 1885. Other useful documents housed there include: Records of the Washington Superintendency of Indian Affairs; Letters Received by the Office of Indian Affairs; various Registers of Vital Statistics; Registers of Indian Families, Marriages, and Annuities Paid; Preliminary Inventory Records of the Taholah Indian Agency; and Neah Bay Agency Letters from Agents and Employees. Some of this material defined and clarified certain family relationships and was even more useful when combined with James G. Swan's material.

The Black Series of materials, housed at the British Columbia Archives, in Victoria, includes Records Relating to Canadian Indian Affairs and also sketchy and incomplete West Coast Indian census information.

9. James G. Swan (1818–1900) was an interesting historical figure who, for much of his adult life, was closely tied to the Makah Tribe and became extremely knowledgeable about their life and culture. In 1855, Swan accompanied Governor Isaac I. Stevens as he made treaties with each of the tribes in Washington Territory. From 1859 on, Swan either lived on the Makah Reservation or in Port Townsend, Washington, approximately eighty miles east of Neah Bay on the Strait of Juan de Fuca. In 1863 Swan became the first school teacher on the newly created Makah Indian Reservation. He left this position in 1866 and moved to Port Townsend, where he held a variety of positions for a number of years. Swan returned to Neah Bay in 1878 and worked as Customs Inspector there until 1882.

He then returned to Port Townsend, where he became a judge and lived for the rest of his life. Over the years Swan assisted many Makah men in various economic endeavors, especially connected with the purchase and sale of sealing schooners. He remained a good friend to many Makah people; he often visited them in Neah Bay, and they in turn came to see him in Port Townsend (Swan Diaries 1859–1898; Swan, *Almost Out of the World* 1971:xviii–xxiii). His forty years of diaries as well as a number of publications include much valuable information on the Makah tribe.

10. For many years James G. Swan was like a father to the young Indian girl Ellen Sikesy, who was Helma Swan's paternal grandmother. Even though no written documentation has been discovered, the oral tradition states that Ellen changed her last name to Swan due to her high regard for this white man who was always available to help her and her family. She was listed as Ellen Swan in the 1885 and 1886 Makah censuses before her untimely death in 1887. After Ellen's "Indian custom marriage" to Chestoqua Peterson (BIA 1926: Miller Letter, Dec. 3), their son, Lewis, was born in 1886. In 1894 the boy changed his name to Charlie Swan (BIA 1973: Makah Census 1886–1894), even though he had no blood ties to James G. Swan. Charlie Swan, along with a number of other Makahs, continued to visit James G. Swan in Port Townsend and maintained a long lasting friendship until the latter's death in 1900.

11. Rosaldo and Lamphere 1974; Rosaldo 1974.

12. Ortner 1974; Ortner and Whitehead 1981.

13. Briggs 1970; Lurie 1973; Jones 1972; Blackman 1982, 1989; Cruikshank 1990; Boyer and Gayton 1992.

14. Klein and Ackerman 1995:14.

15. Gluckman 1968:219–222.

16. Gluckman 1968:220.

17. Gluckman 1968:220–221.

18. Gluckman 1968:221.

19. Klein and Ackerman 1995:14. For other excellent discussions of dominance and values attached to gender roles, and the concept of balanced reciprocity, see Jacobs on Tewa Pueblo culture (1995:178–181, 213), and Klein on Northwest Coast Tlingit culture (1995:30–31, 42–45). See Koskoff (1987) and Keeling (1989) for thoughtful discussions of gender roles in relation to various aspects of music and culture.

20. Colson 1953:237.

21. Gunther 1960:542. In the 1980s, Makah elders reaffirmed that no early Presbyterian church records exist.

22. James G. Swan did take two early Makah censuses in Oct. 1861 and Oct. 1863. He described this work in Diaries #5 and #6, and in an article he wrote for the Olympia, Washington newspaper, *Washington Standard,* Feb. 8, 1862, entitled, "Scenes among the Mackahs: Taking the Census." (The latter is reprinted in Swan 1971:109–116.) This census information, originally collected for the Indian Department, has apparently been lost. Archivists at the National Museum of Natural History, Smithsonian Institution, and at the Smithsonian Institution Archives have searched but been unable to locate either of these censuses (Kathleen Baxter, Museum Specialist, National Museum of Natural History, Smithsonian Institution, Sept. 28, 1984: personal communication).

23. In Canada, in the mid to late 1800s, the Oblate Catholic Order was present in the Clayoquot-Tofino area where some of Helma's relatives lived (specifically, the old Clayoquot Chief Cedakanim and his family). Evidently some Catholic records do exist, but their whereabouts remain unknown. Helma and I wished to see if they perhaps included information on relatives unnamed in either the U.S. or Canadian census material. Numerous phone calls and several visits were made in 1983, 1984, 1994, and 1995 to try to locate the Oblate sacramental records, written in French over one hundred years ago. After talks with priests in British Columbia, Catholic archivists in Seattle and Victoria, B.C. and the head of the Kakowis Family Center in Tofino, B.C., it was not clear where those documents currently reside. Each person with whom we spoke thought someone else had them, and neither Helma nor I were able to find and examine them in the time available to us.

24. Probate File #56085–26, Peter Brown (BIA 1927). The only existing photo of Chestoke Peterson was taken by an unknown photographer in 1877 and is held in a folder with the A. W. Smith Papers, neg. #MSS 172, at the Washington State Library, Olympia. The library would not allow its publication.

25. BIA 1926, Miller Letter, Dec. 3.

CHAPTER 1

1. Efrat and Langlois (1978a:55). According to these two authors, Peter Webster, from the Wescoast village of Ahousat, an elder and resident native historian (now deceased), talked about the name *Nu·tka·* in the 1970s. He said: "They [Cook's ships] were anchored out in the open Pacific and a bunch of Indian people took off with a whaling canoe . . . and they directed these ships that couldn't get in 'cause they didn't know, they were told to come around that point, *nutkši?a.* ("come around" or "go around" over there), where the lighthouses stand today." Mrs. Winifred David, a Clayoquot elder, told a similar story but used the

word, *nuꞏtkaꞏ·ʔičim*, for the same concept (Efrat and Langlois 1978a:54–55). For other discussions of the meaning of the term *Nuꞏtkaꞏ*, as well as various spellings, see Arima and Dewhirst (1990:410) and Gough (1978:15).

2. The number of Nootkan tribal groupings fluctuates over time due to a variety of factors such as warfare, disease, natural disasters, and so forth. Thus, authors list different names (with a variety of spellings) and numbers of tribes at different times. See Guillod 1882–1900; Royal Commission on Indian Affairs, 1916; Curtis 1916:180–182; Drucker 1951:3–6, 220–243; Arima 1983:2–7; Arima and Dewhirst 1990:391–393. Following Arima and Dewhirst 1990, (who took most of the native names from Drucker 1951), these tribes may be listed roughly as follows: "Northern Nootkans": (1) Chickliset, (2) Kyuquot, (3) Ehattesaht, (4) Nutchatlaht, (5) Mowachaht (formerly the Nootka band, proper), (6) Muchalat. "Central Nootkans": (7) Heshquiaht, (8) Manhousat, (9) Otsosat, (10) Ahousaht, (11) Kelsemat, (12) Clayoquot, (13) Ucluelet, (14) Toquaht, (15) Uchucklesaht, (16) Sheshaht, (17) Opetchesaht, (18) Ohiaht. "Southern Nootkans": (19) Nitinat (termed Ditidaht by Arima and Dewhirst), (20) Clo-oose, (21) Carmanah, (22) Pacheenaht, (23) Makah (located in the United States, on the Olympic Peninsula).

3. The interpreter for the Makah treaty signing was a Clallam Indian who used his tribe's word for the Cape Flattery people. Evidently, the Clallam word, *maq'áꞏh*, meant "You never leave here without being full." This was in reference to the fact that Clallam visitors were always invited to eat in four or five Makah houses before they could return home. They would offend their hosts if they did not eat in each house before they departed. (Helma Swan, personal communication, March 25, 1995).

4. Goodman Field Notes 1975. Other authors have recorded the same Indian name, using a number of different spellings but with a similar meaning: "people who live on the cape" (Swan 1870:1; Curtis 1916:182; Densmore 1939:1; Renker and Gunther 1990:429; Renker 1994:326). The cape referred to is Cape Flattery, on the northwest tip of the Olympic Peninsula.

5. Drucker 1951:3.

6. Boas 1891; Sapir 1911; Drucker 1951:3; Arima and Dewhirst 1990:391–393.

7. Highsmith 1973:47–53; Kozloff 1982:3.

8. Tatoosh and Waadah Islands were claimed by the U.S. government in the 1855 treaty, even though, in the Minutes of the Treaty Negotiations, at least one chief begged to be allowed to keep his house and land on Tatoosh (BIA 1960: Makah Treaty Negotiations 1855; Swan 1870:1; U.S. Congress, Senate 1904:685). The tribe did not regain these islands until 1984 (Renker and Gunther 1990:429).

9. James G. Swan wrote that, at the time of the 1855 Treaty, the Makah tribe claimed as theirs the land as far east as the Hoko River (Swan 1870:1). Helma Swan (personal communication, 1995) stated that the Makah claimed the land all the way to the Lyre River, approximately twenty miles east of the Hoko River.

10. Swan, 1870:2–3.

11. There has been some confusion over summer habitation sites located on the northeast portion of Cape Flattery. Kíddekabat (*Q'idiq'ábit*) was the old summer village now called Midway in English. Located approximately three miles west of Neah Bay on Cape Flattery, its houses were situated on one long, sandy beach. A number of the old house poles were still standing as recently as nine to ten years ago. In contrast, Warm House, consisting of only one house built by Helma's grandfather, Charlie Anderson, was situated just west of Midway across a little ridge. It was located on a steep cliff face with only enough room for the one

structure. According to Helma, who lived there as a child, it was never a summer village, only one family's summer residence, but it could be considered part of Midway. Two large rock formations, which the Makah call "Two Rocks Standing," ƛaƛakiš x̌úˑwís, stand in the bay below Warm House.

Samuels and Daugherty (1991:11) considered Midway and Warm House to be the same village. James G. Swan (1870:6, 105; Diary #6, Mar. 22, 1863) stated that only one village was located in this area long ago, and it was called Kíddekabat. Swan's information was supported by Makah elders over the age of seventy-five, who remember one village in this location, which they visited and lived in as children. After the Anderson family abandoned Warm House, it was apparently used by white fishermen for a period of time. Currently, no houses are present and no one occupies this area.

The other Makah summer villages included Tatoosh, on Tatoosh Island, located north and slightly west of Cape Flattery, and Árchawat (Hač'áˑwaʔat), on the western or Pacific Ocean side of Cape Flattery between Tatoosh and Wyaatch (Swan 1870:6; Helma and Oliver Ward, Jr., personal communication, 1994). These summer villages were considerably closer to good fishing areas and thus more convenient for the fishermen. Much of the fishing took place during the summer months when the weather was better and the sea calmer.

12. Drucker 1951:9; Swan 1870:2; Goodman 1977:2.

13. Swan 1870:5; Curtis 1916:15. House sizes, as recorded by a number of observers, varied greatly (Mauger 1991:98, 154).

14. Drucker 1951:99–101; Goodman 1978:33–34.

15. Swan 1870:10, 11, 52; Sapir 1967:30; Drucker 1963:124; Goodman Field Notes 1975.

16. Sapir 1967:39; Drucker 1963:120; Goodman Field Notes 1975.

17. Drucker 1951:247–260; 1963:121; Goodman Field Notes 1975.

18. Drucker 1951:244.

19. According to George C. Shaw, the word *potlatch* originally came from the Nootkan term *pahchitl*, *pachaetl*, or *pachatl*, meaning, "a gift," "to give," or "to pay." It was later adopted into Chinook Jargon and is now termed *potlatch* (Shaw [1909] 1965:20). See also chap. 1, endnote 83.

20. Goodman 1978:38; 2001:397–398.

21. Curtis 1916:64.

22. Goodman 1978:38–39.

23. Drucker 1963:132–133.

24. Helma Swan Ward, personal communication, 1975.

25. Drucker 1951:244–245; Goodman Field Notes 1975.

26. Swan 1870:50–52; Reagan 1934:73–86.

27. The term *tumánuwos* is a Chinook word, later adopted into Chinook Jargon (Bill Holm, personal communication, 1997; Shaw [1909] 1965:24–25). How and when the Makah came to use this term remains unknown. James G. Swan spoke of several types of Makah "Tamanawas" activities which existed in the 1860s but made no reference to the borrowing of the concept or the term (1870:62–63). More than one hundred years later, Helma Swan spoke a number of times about the importance of the *tumánuwos* to the Makah people. She was aware, however, that the term was either Chinook or Chinook Jargon.

28. Swan 1870:63; Drucker 1963:155; Densmore 1939:31; Boas 1891:597; Goodman Field Notes 1975.

29. Curtis 1916:179; Swan 1870:76–78; Drucker 1951:181–185; Densmore 1939:286–294; Goodman Field Notes 1975.

30. Swan 1870:73–75.

31. For further information on the Klukwali see Swan 1870:66–69; Ernst 1952:2–27; Drucker 1940:225; 1951:386–387; Boas 1891:599–601; Sapir 1911:20–28.

32. Holm 1977:15; Goodman 1991:228.

33. Drucker 1951:370–371; Goodman 1991:224.

34. Gough 1978:1.

35. For more information on expeditions to the Northwest Coast, see Henry 1984; Pethick 1976; and Gunther 1972.

36. Hoonan 1964:5,7–9; Gunther 1972:56–57, 63–65.

37. Gunther 1972:67–72; Hoonan 1964:11–14.

38. Gough 1978:20, 24; Archer 1978:36, 41, 50; Cole and Darling 1990:120–122.

39. Hoonan 1964; Gunther 1972; Archer 1978; Dewhirst 1978; Cole and Darling 1990; Renker and Gunther 1990.

40. Dewhirst 1978:22; Archer 1978:53; Renker and Gunther 1990:427; Colson 1953:297–298; Marino 1990:172; Boyd 1990:141, 145; Cole and Darling 1990:130.

41. Dewhirst 1978:22; Cole and Darling 1990:131.

42. Dewhirst 1978:22, 24; Arima and Dewhirst 1990:408.

43. Annual Reports of Commissioners of Indian Affairs 1852–1906; Bancroft 1890:90–92; Boyd 1990:145; Colson 1953:297–298; Cole and Darling 1990:130.

44. Bancroft 1890:6–7,90–91; Hoonan 1964:17.

45. Wilson 1849–1851:53–56.

46. U.S. Congress, Senate 1904;682–685; Swan 1870:1; Hoonan 1964:19–21. Although the original boundaries of the Makah reservation were established in the 1855 treaty, the total land area was increased by executive orders in 1872 and 1873 (Colson 1953:9; Marino 1990:171; Ruby and Brown 1986:126–128; Wight, Mitchell, and Schmidt 1960:44).

47. Colson 1953:9.

48. Colson 1953:11.

49. Swan 1870:11, 51, 76; Colson 1953:8–21; Goodman 1978:229–238; Renker and Gunther 1990:427; BIA 1923.

50. Renker and Gunther 1990:427; Marr 1987:15–16.

51. Hoonan 1964:25. The building of the school in Neah Bay, and the requirement by the Indian agent that all Makah children attend school, led to the demise of the other four Makah villages in the early twentieth century. Families from the villages of Baháda, Wyaatch, Tsooyez, and Ozette moved to Neah Bay so their children could go to school and still live at home (Goodman Field Notes 1975).

52. Annual Report of Commissioner of Indian Affairs 1874:333.

53. Annual Report of Commissioner of Indian Affairs 1875:363.

54. Colson 1953:20–21.

55. Annual Report of the Commissioner of Indian Affairs 1890:224.

56. See Cole and Chaikin 1990 for a description and discussion of the legislation that outlawed the potlatch in Canada in 1885.

57. BIA 1931: Bitney Letter, March 3.

58. Annual Report of the Commissioner of Indian Affairs 1872:351.

59. Annual Report of Commissioner of Indian Affairs 1880:155–156.

60. Annual Report of Commissioner of Indian Affairs 1881:163.

61. Swan Diary #6, Dec. 14, 1863; Swan Diary #23, Nov. 17, 1878.

62. Annual Report of the Commissioner of Indian Affairs 1894:318.

63. Swan 1870:54.

64. Marino 1990:175; Josephy 1969:350; Spicer 1969:200–204.

65. Colson 1953:21–23.

66. Colson 1953:21–22; Josephy 1969:352.

67. Josephy 1969:352; Spicer 1969:212–217.

68. Renker 1994:327.

69. For a description of an old-time longhouse, see Chief Charles Jones 1981:23–24.

70. Ruby and Brown 1986:127; Oliver Ward, Jr., personal communication, 1994.

71. Hoonan 1964:25.

72. Gunther 1960.

73. In western Washington State, gypos are men who find the remains of fallen cedar trees which are not usable for lumber but are good for making shake shingles. Working independently, they cut the remains into shakes and sell them.

74. Oliver Ward, Jr., personal communications, 1984–1994.

75. Oliver Ward, Jr., personal communication, 1994.

76. Swan 1891: letter to Dr. Dawson, Nov. 28, 1891; Swan Diary #60, Oct. 4, 1894.

77. Williams and Dietrich 1994; M. Williams 1994a, 1994b, 1994c; Judd 1994; Dietrich 1994; S. Williams 1994; Ho 1994; Pryne 1994.

78. Andersen 1998; Shukovsky 1998a, 1998b; Mapes 1998.

79. Colson 1953:8.

80. Precise figures and statistics are currently not available. Funding for their publication was eliminated in 1982 due to budget cuts, according to the Department of the Interior (BIA Annuals and Biennials 1982). Employment figures in possession of the Makah Tribal Council for 1990 (U.S. Census 1990) show 315 total employed and 58 unemployed. A number for the total labor force is not given. Not in the labor force are 187 people. According to the census calculations for 1990, the civilian labor force unemployment rate is 15.6 percent. This percentage is undoubtedly low. Renker (1994:327) states that in 1992, there were 1,079 enrolled members on the reservation and that the average unemployment rate of approximately 51 percent fluctuates seasonally.

81. Helma Swan lived off the reservation several different times, the last and longest being when she and her late husband, Oliver Ward, Jr., attended school in Tacoma and then held jobs there for several years after finishing their training. Both were affected by the strong prejudice against Indians in the 1960s. Eventually the family decided to move home to Neah Bay to escape the prejudice and to be among their own people once again. They were away for about seven years, a very long time, according to them. Other families report similar kinds of situations.

82. Unless otherwise noted, the material presented in this music section and also in chapter 10 is drawn from the author's field notes, journals, tape transcripts (1974–1995), dissertation (1978), and additional discussions with Helma Swan.

83. According to Helma Swan, the Makah word *p'a* means "to throw," and *p'ačił* means "to throw gifts." The Makah and other Northwest Coast tribes speak of this activity as the "giving of gifts" at a potlatch (see also chapter 1, endnote 19). According to Bill Holm (personal communication, 1997), the "gifts" are actually payments for services rendered, such as witnessing certain events at a potlatch ceremony and passing on the information.

84. Since the potlatch ceremony was outlawed by the U.S. government in the late 1880s, the word "party" has become the principle term used in place of "potlatch." The newer term is still

in use among the Makah, even though the ban on potlatches was lifted in the 1930s as part of the Indian Reorganization Act. The term "potlatch party" is also sometimes heard now.

85. At the request of tribal members, details of these activities will not be discussed.

86. Swan 1870:11–12; Densmore 1939:247–248.

Helma Swan briefly told the story of her great-aunt Alice Kalappa's courtship and wedding. As a young woman and bride-to-be, Alice, the sister of Helma's grandfather, Charlie Anderson, was brought by canoe from Ozette to Neah Bay. Once there, she had to walk across the backs of Makah men who laid down on the beach (so her feet wouldn't touch the sand) all the way from the canoe to her family's house in Neah Bay. A new, very thick wooden front door had been put in place there, and her husband-to-be, Lance (Landes) Kalappa, had to split it (on the first try) by thrusting a whaling harpoon through it to prove his strength. After this had been successfully accomplished and songs and other rituals performed, he and Alice were allowed to marry. Alice delighted in telling this story to Helma and the other Swan children. These were the inherited courtship privileges that belonged to her family. The rituals of other families might or might not be similar.

87. Swan 1870:14.

88. Densmore 1939;77, 82; Sapir and Swadesh 1939:153; 1955:305.

89. Swan Diary #23, Dec. 31, 1878.

90. The financial commitment for a Kʷákʷakyawakʷ potlatch in the late 1990s is often twice or three times that of a Makah potlatch (Bill Holm, personal communication, 1997).

91. Concerning the outlawing of ceremonies, James G. Swan wrote in a letter to Franz Boas on June 22, 1892: "The present agent prohibits the public performance of any of their dances by order of the . . . Superintendent of Indian Affairs. . . ."

In a letter dated Oct. 23, 1893, Swan again discussed the outlawing of Indian ceremonies and related how neither he nor Boas supported this policy. Then he stated: ". . . . At Neah Bay, Agent McGlynn forbade the Makah Indians from having their Dukwalli, Dothlub, Tsiahk, and other Tomanawos ceremonies. . . . Agent McGlynn told me that the Indian Department had ordered these ceremonies stopped as they believe they were all like the spirit dances, intended for hostile purposes."

92. Among the Nootkans and the Makah, a "copper" is a large, shield-like sheet of hammered copper with a particular shape (approximately eighteen to twenty inches high), owned by a chief. It is a symbol of his great wealth and power, is displayed at important potlatches, and in the past had various meanings and activities connected with it. For example, in earlier days, according to Helma Swan, the host chief at a potlatch might take out his copper, present it to another chief, and ask him to break a piece off of it. As Helma described it: "He couldn't say no, because the copper was something very big in those days. If he broke a piece of the copper off, it meant that he was obligated to the [host] chief's wife and family, to take care of them if anything ever happened to him [the host chief]. . . . In this way it worked like a regular insurance policy. Although there was nothing written, it was known to each one of us that we were under obligation. . . . They carried this down from generation to generation. This was why they had this copper, so that this way they took care of one another. . . . That's the way the families were held together—by responsibility" (Goodman Field Notes 1974). Coppers only appear on rare occasions today, and they are no longer broken.

93. Hoonan 1964:23; Goodman 1977:19; 1991:230–231.

CHAPTER 2

1. Snow may fall once or twice during the winter along the Washington coast; many years there is none. The snow is usually washed away by rain shortly after it falls.

2. The record is not totally clear, but Ruth Swan may have never been officially hired by the BIA. However, she did do all the jobs that her husband did.

3. Owls are symbols of death among the Makah, and many people are frightened by them.

4. The BIA introduced farming to the Makah in the 1870s, and for a period of about seventy years many people grew vegetable gardens. The raising of crops was not a traditional occupation in this area—fishing, whaling, hunting, and gathering of wild vegetables and berries had always sustained the people more than adequately. Today there are very few gardens in Neah Bay. As the old people who had them have passed away, the gardens have been abandoned, and the younger people have not exhibited much interest in continuing this activity.

5. Helma's grandparents on her mother's side were divorced and each had remarried. Her grandfather, Charlie Anderson, lived at Green Point on the Pacific Ocean. Her grandmother, Alice Holden, lived first at the east end of Neah Bay, at a place called Baháda, and later she and her family moved to a house in the middle of Neah Bay.

6. Helma first spoke about Bertha Smith in 1975, saying that she had died twelve or thirteen years before. She probably did not plant a garden after the late 1950s.

7. Cedar bark is stripped only at certain times of the year (late spring). The outer bark must be peeled from the inner bark, which is used for making baskets and mats and, formerly, for clothes and blankets. A cedar tree was never stripped of all its bark. Only one-third of the bark was taken from any one tree. The people were careful not to kill the trees for the bark.

8. Some summers, especially when Helma was very young, were spent at Midway. As she grew a little older, there were frequent trips back and forth between Midway and Green Point during the summer, depending on tasks her grandfather was doing.

9. Glass balls were used as floats on Japanese fishing nets. When separated from the nets, often during storms, the balls crossed the ocean and ended up on beaches along the west coast of the U.S. Some of them are now collectors' items.

10. Helma's grandfather never told her the Indian name for this plant. He called it Indian candy. It was sweet and at the same time salty, from the salt water. It grew only in deep tide pools. He and the children gathered it in the summertime.

11. Kwaatie is the trickster character who causes all kinds of trouble. Ishkus is the evil woman in Makah tales. Snot Boy is the young hero who saved the Makah children from being killed by Ishkus.

12. Gilbert Holden had a large house, but it was divided into a number of rooms. His son Tom's house wasn't divided into as many rooms and had a large open area in which many people could gather to play the bone games. Most often the games were held at Tom Holden's house.

13. Stories say that Tatoosh Island was off limits for the government agents; no one seems to know exactly why this was so. No government documentation has been found relating to this issue.

14. According to Helma, *hupáčakt* means "something round, floating in the ocean." The other Makah word, *čá·di·*, also is a name for Tatoosh Island, but she did not know what it meant. Tatoosh was called by either of these names.

15. *Ba?ás* was the term for a longhouse where several families lived. Fires in the center of the earthen floor made the interior smoky, so sometimes this structure was referred to as a

smokehouse, though it was never considered a real smokehouse (where fish were smoked). Helma's grandfather's longhouse or *baʔás* on Tatoosh Island had four partitioned sections or stalls, so four families could stay in it.

16. See chapter 5, endnote 8 for more information concerning the first Makah Day.

17. Here Helma is speaking of family knowledge. Her father taught her about his Canadian family and their songs, whereas her mother didn't teach her much about her Ozette and Quileute relatives.

18. Basket making was traditionally women's work, so the three Anderson men were somewhat unusual in being excellent basket weavers as well as fishermen.

19. Undersea cables connected the mainland at the edge of Cape Flattery to Tatoosh Island where there was a lighthouse.

20. Makah Census Rolls list him as being married only once, in 1907. He is listed as a widower in 1912 and every year thereafter.

21. It was common for a single adult to informally adopt a child, usually from the same extended family.

22. No complete written records exist concerning Makah burial customs in early contact days. James G. Swan (1870:83) stated that the body of a dead person would be wrapped in a blanket, placed in the fetal position, firmly bound with ropes, then placed in a box that was tied with ropes. The box would either be placed in a tree or buried in the ground. Burial in the ground was becoming more common during Swan's time at Neah Bay. Drucker (1951:147) indicated that the burial box might be taken by canoe to a burial island. When this occurred, the box was put in a canoe of its own and was towed by men in another canoe. No one rode in the canoe with the dead person. Neither Swan nor Drucker mentions hoisting the canoes to the tops of the highest trees, as Helma speaks of here. However, Goddard (1934:98) states that the Salish tribes of Washington often placed their dead in canoes and elevated them either on scaffolds or in trees beyond the reach of animals. It is possible that the Makah also had this custom or that they borrowed it from some of their Salish neighbors.

23. The Clayoquot are a central Nootkan band living on Meares Island, which is a short distance north of the town of Tofino off the west coast of Vancouver Island.

24. According to the BIA Register of Vital Statistics, 1901–1933, Conrad Swan died of lobular pneumonia at the age of twelve in 1926. Helma was eight years old at the time.

25. Charlie Swan's "grandmother" was actually his grandmother's sister, He-da-to-ko-baitl, who lived with Charlie and his family from 1921 until her death in 1924 (BIA 1973: Makah Census Rolls, 1885–1940). See Appendix B for additional information on this woman who raised Charlie after his mother died.

26. The Makah word for this process is *ʔux̌wí·duk*—"chewing food for the baby and putting it in the baby's mouth."

27. The great-grandmother also did this for a little friend of Helma's, Lillian Tucker, Virginia Holden's daughter, whenever she was over at the Swan's house.

28. The word "pack" has the same meaning as "carry." Makah women "pack" cedar bark, firewood, a pot of food, a cedar mat, the baby, and so forth.

CHAPTER 3

1. According to Helma, *p'áp'ʔés* means "things that were spilled on the ground." This is the word used for cranberries.

2. Helma stated that the men used to burn off the underbrush every ten years. (They all

stayed while the fire was burning to make sure it didn't get out of control.) Burning the area kept the cranberry marsh open so it wouldn't get overgrown with trees and shrubs. Now, no one burns it off, only a small area is left in the open, and no one gathers cranberries anymore. A few people gather Indian tea, also known as swamp tea or Labrador tea (Turner 1975:143), which grows in this area.

3. See chapter 1 for the story concerning Spanish Fort.

4. Frances Densmore (1939:plate 8) includes a picture of several houses in Neah Bay taken either in 1923 or 1926 when she made trips to the reservation to record Makah music. On the upper right-hand side of the Densmore photo is Charlie Swan's tool shed. Before it became a shed it had been the house where his aged "grandmother" (actually his grandmother's sister, He-da-to-ko-baitl) lived out the last years of her life. The house where Helma grew up was in front of this structure and can't be seen in the picture.

5. This was the name of the company that put up the breakwater and turned the bay into a protected harbor. After the job was completed, the company sold the houses their workers had lived in. According to Helma, her father bought two houses from Mr. Gum, of Metheny and Bacon, and then combined them into one house.

6. During the 1920s, when the large boat *Comanche* was coming from Seattle and Port Angeles once a week, Jim Hunter ran a smaller boat, called the *Uncle Jim,* daily from Neah Bay to Clallam Bay and back. Clallam Bay (nineteen miles away) was where he picked up the mail for Neah Bay, along with any passengers and needed groceries.

7. According to Helma, *qeʔiꞏks* means, "hooking one's fingers in the fish's gills." When she was a child, this was the way people used to carry their fish home from the beach.

8. According to Helma, clear red snapper broth was used to cure a fever or a cold. "You stayed in bed and they gave you this to drink." They called it *ƛ'ubúꞏxsit,* "something you sip on." Eaten very hot, it was used for chills. It also could be used to help an upset stomach.

9. Helma's mother, Ruth Swan, was quite unusual in that she went fishing every summer. She was the only woman that Helma knew who did this. Ruth fished with her father, Charlie Anderson, because she didn't want him to go out in his boat alone. Then she discovered that she really enjoyed fishing and would go out in the boat by herself sometimes. Often, though, her father would go with her, because he didn't want her to be out there alone. She fished for black bass, which sold for five cents a pound, or for salmon, which sold for seventy-five cents to a dollar a pound, when Helma was a child. Ruth had a small flywheel motorboat that made a funny noise and was called *ƛ'uƛ'ubuq'ad,* "the sound of something hitting." Helma's dad would fix up and paint this boat every winter so her mother could take it out fishing every summer.

10. The Makah say that the harpooner, the man who actually killed the whale, was the one who got the dorsal fin—the most prized part of the whale. James G. Swan stated that the dorsal fin was always the property of the man who first struck the whale with his harpoon. Other portions of the whale were distributed according to an accepted rule, and each man knew what he was to receive (Swan 1870:21).

CHAPTER 4

1. Makah men in boats would tow big logs home that they found drifting at sea. Helma's mother did this too. If she were out fishing and saw a big log, she'd stop fishing, attach a rope to it, and tow it back home for firewood.

2. The men who had big barns in Neah Bay at that time were Edwin Hayte, Jim Hunter, Shubert Hunter, Horace Claplanhoo, Bill Penn, Charlie Smith, Frank Smith, and Charlie Swan. Today, no one in Neah Bay has a big barn.

3. The Government Field was tribal land which the government was supposed to have leased from the tribe. Because Charlie Swan was a government employee, he was allowed to grow hay on the government land. Other men in the village, who did not work for the government, had to rent their plots in order to grow hay.

4. The Prairie was a flat clearing, good for growing hay, just east of the Wyaatch River. The surrounding area was heavily wooded.

5. According to a letter dated Mar. 19, 1932, from Dr. H. J. Warner, Medical Director, District 2, and received by the Neah Bay Indian Agency, Neah Bay still had two public schools, one for whites and one for Indians. The letter goes on to say that Clallam County appropriated $20,000 to build a consolidated school, but the Indians refused to donate sufficient land on which to place the school (BIA 1932a).

6. The Taholah Indian Agency School Census of Indian Children lists Helma Swan, age 10, as a student in the fourth grade at Tulalip Boarding School in 1928 (BIA 1928). Helma stated that she went to fifth grade at Tulalip, not fourth grade.

7. The Tulalip Boarding School closed on June 30, 1932, according to a letter from Commissioner C. M. Rhoads to Mr. Nels O. Nicholson, Superintendent of the Taholah Indian Agency (BIA 1932b).

8. The Taholah Indian Agency School Census of Indian Children lists Helma Swan as a seventh grade student at Tulalip Boarding School in 1931, and then as a sixth grade student back at the Neah Bay Day School in 1932 (BIA 1928–32), information which Helma says is incorrect. Rather, she states that she was at Tulalip for fifth and sixth grades, then had to return to Neah Bay for the seventh grade when Tulalip closed in 1932.

9. According to Helma, Nellie Sam Williams, Nina Bright, Rebecca Cole, and Flora Shale Logan were some of the old Indian ladies who entered the beauty contest and brought their baskets with them.

10. Later, at a Lake Quinault celebration, Helma decided not to enter the beauty contest because others had said nasty things about her after she entered the first one. Her father felt she needn't expose herself to their criticism anymore, so she never entered another beauty contest.

11. Helma felt very uncomfortable talking about this marriage and asked that the name of her first husband not be stated.

12. In this case the *tupáats* were family-owned games which were played at weddings.

13. See chapter 5 for more description of the Swan family whale games played at weddings.

14. This was the first time Helma saw Annie do this dance.

15. These are the names of the two Grizzly Bear songs which Helma and her father got from Captain Jack, the Nootka Chief, at the 1930 potlatch where Charlie Swan was made a chief.

CHAPTER 5

1. Jim Hunter married Odelia David in 1928 (BIA 1901–1933: Record of Marriage Licenses, Makah). Both were from Clayoquot, B.C., but Jim had settled in Neah Bay. He was following the proper Indian courting procedures by bringing with him a group of prominent people who sang, danced, and gave speeches in order to properly ask for Odelia's hand in marriage. They travelled in Jim's motorboat (named Hunter Number 4). Formerly the trip would have been made in several canoes.

2. See chapter 4 for a description of this game as it was played at Helma's wedding. According to Bill Holm (1978), this game and other similar ones were played at the wedding of a chief's daughter.

3. Often, guessing games included the placing of bets on the outcome. This did not occur during games connected with a wedding ceremony.

4. Charlie Swan, Jim Hunter, and several other Neah Bay men—Jongie Claplanhoo, Edwin Hayte, and Dan Quadessa—were members of the Hamatsa Society and were entitled to own particular Hamatsa songs which had been passed on in their families. Helma Swan was taught this as a child.

5. According to Edward S. Curtis, whaling rituals in the past were performed only by the individual whaler who was assisted by his wife (1916:38). Helma agreed with Curtis's statement.

6. The dance that Helma calls the "Black Face Dance," of the Coast Salish tribes is more commonly called the "Spirit Dance," in English. For more information on this dance and related activities see Altman 1947; Amoss 1978; Duff 1952; Suttles 1987b.

7. There were two types of "real" smokehouses in the past, according to Helma. One was a large, rectangular wooden building used exclusively for secret society gatherings and other ceremonial activities. No living quarters were present. This structure had a dirt floor and three very large fires (six to eight feet in diameter) built in a row down the center. Helma attended a ceremony in the last of these smokehouses at Taholah on the Quinault Reservation in the 1930s. It is possible that this large smokehouse was a Quinault rather than Makah structure, because James G. Swan stated in 1870 that there were no large Makah buildings set aside for public purposes (Swan 1870:6). Or perhaps the large structures developed later in time. No Makah term has so far been recalled for them.

The other kind of smokehouse, called qʷišóˑwas, was a small wooden structure where fish were smoked. No one lived in these small houses.

By way of comparison, a longhouse (or big house), baʔás, consisted of a rectangular wooden structure partitioned into living quarters for several related families. A small fire was built near each end. The central floor was earthen. According to Helma, no ceremonies were held in a longhouse, only in a smokehouse or a potlatch house. This evidently had changed from the time of Swan's writings. He said that the largest lodges in the village were thrown open and used when an unusually large number of people were expected for a major event (1870:6).

Potlatch houses, according to Helma, were different from all of the above structures. Aside from their dirt floors with fires in the middle, their huge interiors were supported by many big log posts. Each post was named for a tribe and this was where the chiefs of that tribe, as well as other tribal members, always sat. The Westcoast tribes in Canada used these potlatch houses; it is not known whether the Makah ever had one.

Suttles (1991:219) speaks of special, large potlatch houses, used only for this purpose. Drucker (1951:71–72; 1963:68–71; 1965:26) and Suttles (1991:212–222) described various longhouse types in the central and southern Nootkan areas as well as the Salish areas, some of which bear similarities to the house types described by Helma. Swan (1870:5–6) describes Makah wood plank houses similar to those discussed by Helma. For more complete coverage concerning longhouses and their structures, see Mauger (1991). He includes descriptions of the large plank houses uncovered at Ozette and compares them to others in the region.

8. Conflicting dates and reasons are given for the occasion of the first Makah Day. According to Hoonan (1964:23), the first Makah Day was held on August 26, 1926, in order to officially celebrate the Makahs' newly acquired status as American citizens. (Citizenship was granted in 1924.) However, correspondence between the Neah Bay Indian agent and the Commissioner of Indian Affairs for 1923 indicated there was already a Makah Day and the Indians were *not* free to perform any dances they wished. The policy was still clearly to try to

eliminate the old Indian ceremonies and substitute activities which were acceptable to white society (BIA 1923). Elizabeth Colson (1953: 221) stated that Makah Day was inaugurated about 1920 and that she had received a number of different accounts of its origin. She did not include these accounts in her publication, however. Helma felt that Makah Day began in 1926, was held to help preserve Makah culture, and always included traditional singing and dancing.

9. Helma was always told by her elders that there were nineteen Nootkan tribes on the west coast of Vancouver Island. (See chapter 1 for discussion of complexity surrounding the number of Nootkan tribes.)

10. A Makah sealing canoe, *yašá·baqats,* normally held six men.

11. A Makah fishing canoe, *ʔu·ʔu·št'i·łyak,* carried one or two men. It normally ranged in length from twelve to twenty feet and was smaller than a sealing canoe.

12. The Plains Indian Dance, now also called the War Dance, was formerly called the Yakima Dance. The Makah word for this dance has always been *łaqáta·tx̌.* Long ago, several Makahs had seen the Yakimas dancing, liked what they saw, so created a new dance that imitated some of what the Yakimas had done. It was never an actual Yakima dance, but it was similar in some ways. In recent years, a Yakima man heard that the Makahs had a Yakima Dance and became upset, not understanding the circumstances surrounding this dance. He thought the Makahs were performing an actual Yakima dance and felt that they had no right to do so. Therefore, the Makahs have changed the English name of this dance to avoid similar problems and confusion in the future. In reality, tribes throughout the region often visited each other and borrowed ideas for songs and dances which they saw, heard, and liked. This was standard practice and was considered a compliment—the visiting tribe had liked the songs of the host tribe so much that they created an imitation and named it after the host tribe. In the past, everyone understood that this was what was happening, and no one was upset by it.

13. It is no longer clear where and how the Pentl'achee Dance developed. These songs are considered "marching in" songs (Group Dance songs) sung at the beginnings of old-time potlatches. Anyone could take part in Pentl'achee performances. Helma recalled that different families from Tsooyez, Wyaatch, and Ozette owned these songs when she was a child, and she never questioned this. She remembers that a man named James Guy owned some of these songs. Frances Densmore (1939:152–153) states that this dance was originated by a man at Wyaatch about fifty years prior to her study (approximately in the 1870s or 1880s), and it came to him in a dream because his people needed some new entertainment dances. The men carried bows and arrows when they danced it, and the women danced with their hands on their hips. Another opinion was offered by John Thomas, a trained linguist from Nitinat, who stated that there was a tribe in Canada called the Pentl'atch, and the Makah picked up this dance from them (John Thomas and Helma Swan, personal communication, late 1980s). The Pentl'atch area is on the east coast of Vancouver Island, slightly south of the center of the island (Suttles 1987a:map, inside front cover).

14. Young Doctor was well known as a carver and as a person who communictated with supernatural spirits and often had visions and dreams in which he acquired new songs. His father had been called Old Doctor and had the same special powers and abilities. Young Doctor had a small store in Neah Bay and also a hall for the performance of native ceremonies (Goodman Field Notes:1975, 1994; Densmore 1939:xxv).

15. In a letter dated May 20, 1936, from Rudy's Radio Shop, Port Angeles, to Mr. N. O. Nicholson, Superintendent, Taholah Indian Agency (BIA 1936), Mr. Rudy Lauckner stated that he had signed an agreement with Henry St. Clair (Young Doctor's son) to run motion

pictures for Mr. St. Clair at his hall, called Makah Hall. This agreement, signed Jan. 15, 1934, would last for two years, with both men sharing the profits equally.

According to Helma, the Makahs later learned that Rudy was a German spy. During the World War II blackouts, he supposedly poured gasoline on a huge arrow and lit it on the ground near Joyce, pointing toward Bremerton, where there was a large navy base and naval shipyard. Helma recalled seeing a photograph of this big arrow in the Port Angeles newspaper at the time. Then, "the authorities got him and that was the last anyone ever saw of him. The Makahs heard they picked him up because he was a spy." (No documentary evidence has been found to either confirm or deny this statement.)

CHAPTER 6

1. Makah dancers usually wear a long dance cape over street clothes or over a costume when performing. (There are a few exceptions.) For the girls to practice the dances properly, however, they had to find something that approximated a dance cape which they could place over their regular clothes.

2. The ƛaʔiɫ ceremony renewed supernatural power given by a guardian spirit (see Chapter 5). Tsáyak was a curing ceremony performed by a secret society of the same name (see Chapter 1). The Indian Shaker Church on the Northwest Coast included a blend of native and Christian beliefs and practices (Winick 1961:481). Singing, ringing of hand bells, going into trance, and shaking were all parts of the Shaker ceremonies.

3. As a Quileute, Alice Anderson Holden, Helma's maternal grandmother, sang in her native language rather than in Makah. The shaking referred to is one of the religious activities of the Indian Shaker Church, of which she was a member.

4. Buckskin bread is made as follows: mix a batter of flour, water, shortening, and a little molasses (or a little brown sugar or, later in time, white sugar). Flatten the dough. Then cook under the sand (in the old days). Scrape out ashes from fire in hot sand, put batter on the sand, cover it over with hot sand, and let it bake. Take it out when cooked (about forty-five minutes), and shake off the sand. It will be smooth and ready to eat and have no sand on it. Or, after the introduction of ovens, it could be baked in an oven.

To make boiled bread, the same dough would be wrapped in a flour sack, dropped in boiling water, and cooked. For fry bread, the women again made the same dough as for buckskin bread but then broke off small pieces and fried it in seal oil. Later, when commercial shortening became available, they fried it in lard and dipped it in seal oil before eating.

5. Some of the Canadian and American Indian elders who either attended or knew about the potlatch where Charlie Swan was made a chief included: Aunt Edith Simon, Peter Webster, Hyacinth (Hyson) David, Odelia David Hunter, Harry Dick, Jimmy John, Sarah Woodruff, Reggie Ward, and Helen Peterson. All of these people have passed away since we talked with them in the 1970s and 1980s.

6. All things, and especially masks, have spirits in them. These spirits know when things are not working properly, and the Indians say, "It turned into nothing." In other words, what formerly existed, is no longer. Helma could say no more than this.

7. Charlie Swan was paid for witnessing other people's songs and dances. Helma, as his daughter, was also paid for witnessing.

8. Background dancing consists of a group of women, standing in a semicircle or U-shaped formation, doing a quiet, supportive dance, in unison. The lead male dancer performs a flashier dance in front of them. Therefore, the women provide "background." This is

the normal arrangement for the performance of important family-owned dances. Women are not normally the lead dancers.

9. Helma did not know of any Makah word for the lead male dancer. Rather, they would say that a certain man was going to dance a particular dance, such as the Changing Mask Dance, and it was understood that he would be the lead dancer.

10. The dancers proceed in a counterclockwise circuit beginning in the southeast area of the dance space, moving to the northeast, then the northwest, the southwest, and finally back to the southeast. They turn as they reach each directional corner, and they flap their wings when they turn and face each other in the middle of the dance area. They blow their small whistles (held in their mouths) when their right arms are up and their left arms are down.

11. Currently, there is no data which specifically supports the past existence of Makah or Nootkan clans (Curtis 1916:62; Colson 1953:4; Drucker 1963:120), so their existence and function remain a question. It is possible that the dances of which Helma speaks were hereditary privileges that only certain people or families had the right to use, or perhaps they may have been parts of earlier secret society ceremonies. Often, Westcoast peoples use the terms "clan" and "society" interchangeably; thus an eagle clan may be essentially the same as an eagle society. All the "clans" or "societies" to which Helma's family belonged disappeared long ago.

12. This chief was actually Benjamin Cedakanim, also known as Atliu, the son of old Chief Cedakánim, or Sitkéenum.

13. In the past, many of the chiefly families had a family curtain. It consisted of a large piece of white cloth (often canvas) with painted designs that represented various mythological creatures and family names, all connected through family stories. Each family's curtain was different from the others. When used at a party, a curtain provided a visual picture of the history of the host chief's family, and also served as a backdrop for all the dances performed.

A few of these curtains still exist and are used by the families that own them. Ideally, the curtain should undergo changes in succeeding generations as new family members are born, marry, and so forth. It should not remain a static piece of art used for ceremonial gatherings. Seldom are these curtains changed or updated anymore. Knowledge of how to do this is fast disappearing, as is the number of remaining curtains.

14. This photograph of the Swan family curtain appears in *Nootka and Quileute Music* by Frances Densmore (1939:Plate 19a). Densmore does not discuss it other than to mention that a large painting on a cloth was placed in front of one of the walls of the community hall where dances were performed for Makah Day on Aug. 26, 1926. She witnessed these activities (p. 135). The first time Helma saw this photo in Densmore's book, she was quite excited, saying that this was her dad's family curtain. She then began talking about some of the figures represented and what they meant.

15. The family names and objects continue to be inherited within the family, but the lines of the chiefs and the objects inherited get crossed. Yelák'ub was a Makah chief, and Arnie Hunter now has his name. However, Arnie received the songs, masks, costumes, and other items that belonged to Chief Sitkeenum from the Clayoquot tribe, in Canada. It is not known what happened to Yelák'ub's songs, dances, and masks. Most of them have been lost. Only his name and a very few of his privileges (song 6 in chapter 10) have been passed on.

16. According to Odelia Hunter, last wife of Jim Hunter, Annie Sitkeenum Williams was a direct descendant of old Chief Sitkeenum and one of his wives, while Shubert Hunter and his brother, Jim, were descendants of Sitkeenum and a different wife. If this information is correct, then Annie was a cousin to both of the Hunter brothers (Goodman Field Notes 1975).

17. The curtains of the Swan and Frank families are similar, but not identical. The same

basic characters appear in each, but with slight variations. In recent years several articles have been written about the Frank family curtain, which, according to Helma Swan, display either confusion or lack of knowledge concerning the ownership of two slightly different curtains which belonged to two and perhaps three separate families. Since these publications (Hoover and Inglis, 1990:276–280; Black 1999:78; Black 2001:50, 52) present one point of view, it is equally important that Helma Swan's somewhat different version also be related. Chief Sitkeenum's original curtain was officially given by his granddaughter Annie Atliu Williams to Charlie Swan at the 1930 potlatch when she made him a chief. The whale on this curtain is painted completely black. There are no other figures or designs in its body. Also, a sea serpent is wound around a plain wooden pole on the left side of the curtain, with only the head of a bear at the top—representing Annie's other relative and good friend, Shubert Hunter, who was originally from Clayoquot but also lived in Neah Bay (see fig. 26). Annie Williams had another copy of this same curtain made for Shubert, and she gave him permission to use it, but he did not own it. So, Charlie Swan and Shubert Hunter each had a copy of the same curtain described above, and one or both curtains were already in use in Neah Bay when Frances Densmore visited in 1923 and 1926 and took the photo which appears in her 1939 book, *Nootka and Quileute Music* (plate 19a). (Helma was five to eight years old when Densmore visited and does not know whose curtain appeared in the photo.)

Annie Williams had a slightly different version of Sitkeenum's curtain made for Francis Frank and his family. Helma was not sure of the time frame but thought this curtain was also created before 1930. (A picture of a portion of this curtain may be seen in the background of a 1928 photograph of the Frank family wearing some of their masks [Black 1999:81].) According to Odelia David Hunter and Edith Simon, Clayoquot elders, Annie was as closely related to Charlie Swan as to Francis Frank. They were cousins, and Annie Williams wanted each to have his own copy of Sitkeenum's curtain, so that the same songs, dances, and ceremonies could be performed by both her Canadian and American relatives. Her precise family relationship (cousin?) to Shubert Hunter remains unknown. However, she wanted him to have the right to use, though not own, the same curtain she had given to Charlie Swan.

The curtain that was given to Francis Frank and passed down to Alex Frank, burned in a house fire in 1966. Therefore, Alex's sister, Marie Frank (Precious) made a new curtain and painted the characters on it herself. Her copy is supposed to be a re-creation of the old curtain which belonged to Francis Frank, according to Helma. The whale on this curtain has ribs and other figures drawn inside its body. The pole on the left side includes a number of painted figures, one of them being a small circular rainbow similar to the large one on the right side of the curtain. The sea serpent winds around only the upper half of this pole (see fig. 27).

Helma's sister Joy sold Charlie Swan's curtain many years ago. Shubert Hunter loaned his copy of the curtain to his brother, Jim Hunter, who never returned it. After Jim's death, his wife, Odelia Hunter, sold it. Therefore, both of these curtains left the Makah reservation. As stated above, after the Frank family curtain burned, a new copy of their curtain was made. The curtain which eventually came to be in Andy Warhol's collection (Hoover and Inglis 1990:275–80) was either the one that had been given to Charlie Swan or the one given to Shubert Hunter. According to Helma Swan this particular curtain never belonged to the Frank family.

18. According to Helma, the scallop shell rattles were used only before the ceremony began. Her father would run back and forth in front of the singers shaking that rattle and calling, "Tsú! Tsú! Tsú!" And everyone else would respond by calling out "Huuuuiiiii!" There

would be lots of noise. Then he would stop, run behind the singers, and leave the shell rattles there. Soon after, the dance would begin.

19. Many years ago, several different songs and dances directly preceded the Changing Mask Dance. The specific songs used depended on who was responsible for the Mask Dance at the time. Helma's aunt Annie Williams used one particular song; later, Helma's father, Charlie Swan, used another.

Annie Williams almost always began with the Chant, which was followed by the Four Mask Dance. The Changing Mask Dance (with its five masks) was then the third in this series. The Chant (see chapter 10, song 9) prepared the audience for what was to come, and Helma said that it had formerly belonged to Annie's father, Atliú.

Helma described the Four Mask Dance, which she saw performed several times at Clayoquot: "There was another song that went with the Changing Mask one, because two songs always go together. But we never got to use this other one. It included four masked dancers wearing larger masks than the changing ones that Arnie wears. The markings on these masks were different, though the shapes were the same. These four stood in front of the curtain and just the heads turned in unison from right to left to right. Annie gave the song and these masks to my dad, Charlie Swan, but they were never sent over to him in Neah Bay, and he never used them.

"The dancers for this Four Mask Dance wore plain gray wool dance capes, and they wore them backwards—pinned in back. The whistles were sounded before this dance started. This was a long dance, and it let the audience know that there was an important masked dance coming. Nothing else was in between. When these dancers left, then the Changing Mask Dance started."

Because this Four Mask Dance never came to Charlie Swan, he used another dance instead. He performed the Alert Bay Wolf Dance Song, *Wo hu·ʔOh yi yah*, which he had received from Annie and Captain Jack in 1930 (see chapter 10, song 8). He called this his warm-up dance and almost always used it preceding the Changing Mask Dance. He loved this song, and dancing it put him in the proper mood to do the Changing Mask Dance.

20. The whistles were sold a number of years ago (not by Helma) and are no longer available for the family to use in their performances.

CHAPTER 7

1. This was true in 1975. By 1990 or 1991, the situation was beginning to change again. A group of young men were starting to learn the songs and sing, but they were not yet expert singers. They did not speak the Makah language and therefore didn't always pronounce the words correctly. Musically, they didn't always pause in the proper places or get the more complex beat patterns right, even though the elders tried to teach them. Since then, this group has improved considerably. The hope is that they will remain interested and continue to learn and improve even more. In 1994–1995, this group of young male singers included Greig Arnold, Spencer McCarty, Gregg Colfax, Joe McGimpsey, John McGimpsey (now deceased), John Goodwin, and Champ McCarty (now deceased). Others who sometimes sang with them were Pat Hammond, Thomas Parker, and Lester Green.

2. After Nora Barker died, different members of various families began to lead their own family's songs. Until very recently most of the song leaders were women. The song leader situation in Neah Bay in 1990 was as follows: Laura Perry, Minerva Wheeler's daughter led the Claplanhoo family songs for a short time until she left Neah Bay. Kibby Lawrence (now deceased) and Marianne Martin sang with Muzzie Claplanhoo's daughters, Jeannie Johnson,

Pattie Crittenden, and Linda Moss. They started their own family's songs and did this for a few other people, too, such as Helen Peterson, Ed Claplanhoo, and Pete Ward. Melissa Peterson sometimes led Helen Peterson's songs, and then more recently, her son, Micah Vogel, did this until Helen passed away in 1996. Helma Swan always started and sang the Swan family and the Anderson family songs, and often led the Hunter family songs as well. Eleanor (Sissy) McCarty started the McCarty family songs. Patty Smiley and her mother, Alice Arnold (now deceased), and niece, Maria Parker Pascua started songs for the Wilson Parker family. Sometimes Greig Arnold led the songs for them and Joe McGimpsey would be *súʔap*—the one who "caught" the song when the first song leader got tired and couldn't carry it anymore. Since 1990, a few of these people have continued to lead songs, several have moved away, some have died, and several new family song leaders have emerged. There is still not one song leader for the whole tribe; the situation is complex and continually in flux. By 1994, the group of young men mentioned in the previous endnote were leading and singing a number of the songs at Makah potlatches.

3. In the 1970s, when Helma decided to teach herself to sing, none of the Makah men were making drums. Since then, in the 1980s and 1990s, a number of the young men have become carvers and drum makers and it is now easy to acquire a fine, handmade Makah drum.

4. See chapter 6, endnote 15, for the relationship of chiefs' names and items given.

5. As part of the preparation activities for several of Helma's potlatches in the 1980s, I bought some items she needed to give as gifts.

6. In Makah, a Group Dance song is called either *bačidiƛyak dukú·* or *hu·ƚeyíƛyak dukú·*— "a song for dancing in." Both terms, which originally meant that "anyone could join in as they danced into the smokehouse at the start of a ceremony," more recently have come to mean a Group Dance song (see chapter 1). Helma recalled twenty-nine different Group Dances, many of which are no longer performed.

7. The Makah did not keep other people out after they closed the door and the dancing started. People could still come and go as they wished, even though the dancing was in progress.

8. For further information on the Plains Indian Dance or War Dance, see chapter 5, endnote 12.

9. Helma is describing a type of hemlock costume used for a particular group entrance dance she saw when she was very small. Everyone in the group dressed in this manner. This costume should not be confused with the hemlock branch costume worn by the Hamatsa dancer when he is in his wild state.

10. This was the correct order for singing and giving away in the mid-1990s. However, since then, Helen Peterson, Wilbur Claplanhoo, Oliver Ward, Jr., and Hildred McCarty Ides have died, so the situation is once more in flux.

11. According to Helma, the students at the Tulalip Boarding School were divided up into five companies: A, B, C, D, and E. Each had a company officer who was in charge of that group of children, gave them commands, and when appropriate, marched them to places where they needed to be.

CHAPTER 8

1. "Coming across" means to go by boat from Neah Bay across the Strait of Juan de Fuca to Canada. Standard terminology for traveling from the American to the Canadian side, or vice versa, is to "come across" or to "go across."

2. Mú·chi·nik was the name of an important man on Clayoquot Island. *Muu* means

"four" in their language, and his name means "going with four people." According to Helma, this name may have referred to a *tupáat* that he owned in which he had to go somewhere or do something with four people—perhaps for ceremonial reasons.

3. Captain Jack, the chief of Nootka, was not the same person as Yašxen Jack, who was the Clayoquot town crier. The two men were not related, as far as is known.

4. A *q'its'é·yit* party was a type of potlatch given for a girl at the time she was becoming a woman (after her first menses). Normally held for daughters of upper-class families in the past, this celebration rarely occurs now.

5. *T'abáa* songs are considered entertainment songs, sung "just for fun."

6. Formerly, children were initiated into the Klúkwali, but by 1930 they were no longer allowed even to attend, let alone be initiated. It is not clear what kinds of changes were occurring in the performance of this ceremony at that time because initiated members did not share their knowledge with the uninitiated.

7. Helma could not recall the Makah term for " doorkeeper."

8. Many years ago, this very old Clayoquot longhouse burned down along with the drums and everything else in it. The big box drum, formerly located inside, hid the escape door behind it, which was for the use of the chief and his family. The escape door dated back to the time when warfare was a common part of life.

9. In conjunction with the beating sticks, a hollowed-out log would sometimes be used for an especially important party. According to Helma, four to six people would beat on this log with their sticks, thus creating a different percussive sound.

10. Neither Helma nor the other elders could recall the Makah terms for "passing-out-water," and "passing-out-sticks."

11. People who were not chiefs (or members of their families) did not have *tupáats*. They usually volunteered to help with some part of a potlatch.

12. Neither Charlie Swan nor the other elders ever told Helma why the men paint their faces black. Black face paint has a connection with the Klúkwali ceremony of the past, but this is all that is known.

13. In general, the order for giving away at a potlatch went from north to south. The tribes from farthest north received their gifts and money first, those from the south were last. The Makah, being the farthest south were usually the last to receive gifts and money. In this particular case, because Charlie Swan was being made a chief, he "came before all the others."

14. Helma stated that Annie Williams chose one of her descendants from each side of the border to be a chief. (More specifically, Helma thought that Francis Frank had been made a chief at Clayoquot earlier than her father, but she did not know who did this, whether it was Annie or someone else.) According to Clayoquot elders Odelia Hunter and Edith Simon, Helma Swan's father, Charlie Swan, was a direct descendant of Chief Sitkeenum (Cedakanim) and one of his five wives who was a Makah woman from Neah Bay. Francis Frank was also descended from Sitkeenum and another of his five wives, a Clayoquot woman. Stories relate that because both were direct descendants of Sitkeenum, each was entitled to ownership of the old chief's things. Helma felt that perhaps Annie tried to ensure the continuation of the line of chiefship and descent on both the Canadian and American sides of the border by giving the same items to each man and asking that they share their use. (As stated earlier, documented evidence for these family relationships has not been discovered.) See appendix B, endnote 46 for additional information.

15. According to Helma, Francis Frank had earlier been given copies of these same ceremonial items and a separate (but similar) curtain, which showed his specific family history.

16. Many years ago, a nonfamily member who had been drinking had access to this Hamatsa costume, cut off the little skulls, and sold them.

17. Helma is describing the rationale behind the concept of "giving away" at a potlatch. Payment is made by the family showing their privileges (family-owned songs, dances, masks, and so forth) to members of other chiefly families who are witnessing this reaffirmation of ownership. When the situation is reversed, at a different potlatch, the chief who formerly received, displays his privileges and then gives away a little more. The increases continue until an upper limit is reached, after which both sides reduce the payments.

CHAPTER 9

1. James G. Swan wrote that *la ul uch siouk* was the name of an herb given to females to assist in giving birth (Diary #5, 1862, note at end of diary). No description of the plant or other information was included.

2. As stated previously, the Indian Shaker Church on the Northwest Coast included a blend of Christian and Native religious elements. Healing the sick was a major part of Shaker religion and ceremonies.

3. Little Boston is the familiar name for the Port Gamble Indian Community, a small Clallam reservation located across a small inlet from the town of Port Gamble on the northern Kitsap Peninsula in northwestern Washington State (Ruby and Brown 1986:164–165). It is approximately a three-hour drive east of Neah Bay.

4. Wimpy (Oliver Ward, Jr.) remained on the Makah Tribal Council until he died of cancer, June 26, 1997. One of his major accomplishments before his death was acquiring the funding and seeing to completion the new Makah Marina, which he had dreamed about and planned since the early 1970s and which opened a few months before his passing.

5. At the Makah Culture and Research Center (the Makah Museum) in Neah Bay, Helma has enjoyed working over the years on a variety of projects with the following individuals: Hildred Ides; John Thomas (from Nitinat), who passed away about 1991; Maria Pascua; Greig Arnold; Anne Renker; Kirk Wachendorf; Yvonne Burkett; Cora Buttram; Bobbie Rose; Keely Parker, Jeff Mauger; and the current director, Janine Bowechop.

6. Prominent members of Canadian Nootkan tribes often help validate the song ownership of their Makah neighbors to the south. In this case, all these Canadian people had known Jim Hunter, knew that he formerly owned this song, and knew that Wimpy, his oldest grandson, was the current owner. Therefore they were happy to assist Helma in singing this song. Those who are singing always stand to perform. The Makahs who were not singing, however, stood up in order to show respect for the Canadians, who were standing in support of Helma, who was singing her husband's song.

7. For another piece of the story of how Helma began to sing her family-owned songs, see chapter 7.

CHAPTER 10

1. Bill Holm, personal communication, 1978.

2. Curtis 1916:199.

3. For more information concerning Helma's performance of this dance see chapter 6.

4. For a discussion of clans see chapter 6, endnote 11.

5. According to Roberts and Swadesh (1955:313), the word *ki·ki·qama* means "chief, wealthy." Bill Holm (personal communication, 1997) refined the definition given by the above authors. He stated that the word *ki·ki·qama·* means "chiefs" (plural) in Kʷákʷakyawakʷ.

Ki·qama means "chief" (singular). He felt that there was no connotation of wealth in regard to this word.

6. See chapter 6, endnote 19 for more details about the Four Mask Dance.

7. For musicologists, a chorus usually means a "refrain," and includes a text and melody which repeat several times during the course of a song. For the Makah, the term "chorus" simply means "the portion of the song with the meaningful words," or "Q'abá·tš?aƛ'," which is usually the second section of the song.

APPENDIX B

1. Peter Brown was known by the following Indian names: Ta-date-sup-she-chate, How-a-thlub, As-cha-e-kek, As-cha-a-beck, As-chad-a-bek, or As-chad-a-back (Swan Diary 1: Mar. 21, 1859; Lewis 1905; Miller 1972a and 1972b; BIA 1973: Makah Census Rolls, 1885–1909).

2. Lewis 1905.

3. Lewis 1905; Swan Diary #2, Oct. 14, Oct. 20, Oct. 27, 1859; Diary #4, Mar. 12, 1861; Diary #8, Aug. 10, 1964; Diary #25, Mar. 4, 1879.

4. Lewis 1905. In this instance, Chestoke acted as interpreter for Peter; however, it is interesting to note that James G. Swan spoke of Peter in 1859 as "a smart, intelligent young fellow who has been to California and can talk English pretty well" (Swan Diary #1, March 20, 1859). Either Peter had lost his facility in English by the early 1900s, or else he did not want Lucien Lewis to know how well he could actually speak and understand English.

5. Samuel Hancock, who opened a trading post at Neah Bay in October 1852, was buying furs, oil, and salmon, and selling goods to the Indians (Hancock 1927:159). His version of the smallpox story is somewhat different from Peter Brown's. According to Hancock, in 1853 a ship from San Francisco, commanded by Captain Fouber, arrived at Neah Bay. A white man on board had smallpox, which was soon contracted by two Indians who were also on board. In a few days smallpox began to ravage Neah Bay. According to Hancock, vast numbers died daily. Those who escaped were frantic with grief and fear. Some went to the Canadian village of Nitinat to escape, but spread the infection there. After about six weeks, the disease abated; many lost most of their relatives and friends. The survivors tried to blame Hancock for the sickness, but he eventually convinced them that he had nothing to do with it. Therefore they did not kill him, and he was allowed to stay (182–183). He never mentioned whether or not he kept Peter Brown in his house to save him from the ravages of smallpox. For a third version of the smallpox epidemic, see Bancroft (1890:90–92).

6. Hancock 1927:182.

7. U.S. Congress, Senate 1904.

8. Lewis 1905.

9. Swan 1971:100–101; Diary #4, Mar. 9, 1861.

10. Swan 1971:100–104; Doig 1980:8–9. Several other versions of this story have been recorded by Lewis 1905; Swan Diary #4, March 1861; Miller 1972a and 1972b.

11. Swan 1971:107.

12. Lewis 1905.

13. Swan 1971:104–109; Lewis 1905; Miller 1972b:14; Doig 1980:38–40.

14. Lewis, 1905.

15. Lewis 1905.

16. Lewis 1905; Miller 1972b:15.

17. Lewis 1905; Miller 1972b:14–15. Interestingly, James G. Swan never wrote about this significant event in his diaries of 1861–62. Rather, he describes many of these events as occurring

in 1866 (Swan Diary #9, Feb. 24, 25, 28, Apr. 10–21, 1866) after Peter killed a Clallam man who some years earlier had killed the father of a Neah Bay girl named Dukwitsa. Peter was infatuated with this girl, and one time, when drunk, did as she requested and killed the Clallam who killed her father. This then set into motion the series of events where Peter was arrested, broke his handcuffs, was imprisoned in Ft. Steilacoom for a period of time, and so forth.

18. Lewis 1905; Miller 1972b:15.

19. Swan's statement indicates that Peter was no longer considered to be head chief by 1878, even though he had been so commissioned in 1870. It is unknown what transpired in the interim. As a younger brother of Swell, Peter would have been eligible to succeed him as chief, but there is no information regarding this subject.

By 1878, or earlier, the system of hereditary chiefs obviously had changed. With the guidance of Captain Willoughby (the Indian agent), and James G. Swan, the first tribal elections were held to select four chiefs or head men for Neeah village, on Jan. 23, 1879, according to Swan's diary for this date. Elected were Captain John, David, Willub (Billy Balch), and Old Doctor. It is probable that the first three were hereditary chiefs; it is unclear whether or not the fourth was a chief. The lengths of their terms in office also are not known. No other documentation has been found relating to this subject.

Swan also noted that the Indian agent allowed the women to vote in this 1879 election, and several of them did so. Thus, women's suffrage was established early.

20. Peter was married many times and little is known about his wives or his relationships with them. Here is a brief accounting of some of his wives. A woman named Secharht, the sister of Pahaquitl, perhaps a Makah chief, was his earliest known wife. She died Mar. 12, 1862, of dysentery and in childbirth (Swan Diary #5, Mar. 13, 1862, and back flyleaf). He married another woman who was not named and divorced her on March 8, 1863, when he took another wife, from Wyaatch. She left him on Dec. 5, 1863, and returned to her former husband at Wyaatch. Peter married a young girl named Totatelum, on Oct. 18, 1864, according to Swan. The daughter of Chief Colchote, Totatelum formerly had been the wife of Frank Cedakanim, from Clayoquot, until she left him for Peter. She died less than a year later, on June 20, 1865, and Swan gave no explanation for her death (Swan Diary #6, Mar. 30, 1863; Diary #8, Aug. 10, Oct. 18, 1864; Diary #9, June 20, 1865). Only two weeks after Totatelum's death, Peter married a young girl named Dukwitsa (Swan Diary #9, July 4, 1865).

Chu-char-kwax, a Canadian woman from Pt. Alberni, was perhaps Peter's next wife. Swan did not record their marriage. She was the mother of Chestoke Peterson, who was born sometime between 1865 and 1869. Chu-char-kwax, also known as Tsi-tsal-qwaks, died sometime between 1869 and 1878 (Swan Diary #23, Nov. 16, 1878; BIA, n.d.: Genealogy Sheets for Helma Swan and C. Levi Swan). Peter married another unnamed woman in 1878 or 1879 and divorced her by early fall of 1879 (Swan Diary #10, 1879; Diary #26, 1879). On Oct. 25, 1879, he married a woman known as Klooch-ha-putl, or Chloat-a-pootl or Ota-potl, who was the older half sister of Molly Claplanhoo (same mother). Klooch-ha-putl had formerly been the wife of another Makah man, Boatchup, before she married Peter Brown. This marriage lasted almost twenty years, until 1898, when it is likely that Klooch-ha-putl, also known as Lucy Brown, died. For a while, Peter lived alone with their nine-year-old daughter, Winnie. In 1900, Peter married a woman named Lillie, but she probably died in 1904 or 1905 because she is no longer listed in the census. From that time, until his death, the Makah census lists Peter Brown as a widower (Swan Diary #10, July 16, 1879; Diary #26, Oct. 26, 1879; Gunther 1934a; BIA 1973: Makah Census Rolls 1885–1909).

21. Peter Brown appears in the Makah Census between 1885 and 1908, but not in 1909 or

any year thereafter. Probate File #56085–26, for Peter Brown (BIA 1927), states that he died on Sept. 6 or 7, 1908, and that Chestoqua Peterson, his only surviving son, was his heir.

22. Chief Sitkeenum's, or Cedakanim's, name was spelled many different ways by various authors. Some of the more common spellings are as follows: Cedakanim, Cetakanim, Sitkeenum, Sitakanim, Seta Kanim, Setta Canim, Cee-Ta-Ka-Nim, Cedar-Kanim (Anonymous 1864; Barrett-Lennard 1862; Jacobsen 1977; Moser 1926; Powell 1875; Sproat 1868; Swan 1870; Swan Diaries 1862–1889).

23. The name of Sitkeenum's Neah Bay wife has not been located in any historic documents and records to date. Various Nootkan tribal historians with whom this issue was discussed have not been able to recall this woman's name, but knew that she was from Neah Bay, as was the chief's own mother.

James G. Swan's diaries confirm that Sitkeenum had a Makah wife (Diary #10, Aug. 25, 1879). Also, a rough, handwritten genealogical chart sketched by anthropologist Philip Drucker (who worked with the Nootkan tribes in the 1930s and 1940s), included one Neah Bay woman as Sitkeenum's mother, and another as one of his wives. Drucker did not include the names of either of these women, however (Drucker, n.d.: Field Notes, File #32, housed in the British Columbia Archives).

24. James G. Swan documents the presence in Neah Bay of Frank and Benjamin Cedakanim and their father numerous times in his journals (Diary #5, Mar. 5, June 11, Sept. 2, 1862; Diary #6, Sept. 2, 1862, Mar. 6, Mar. 22–30, May 31, Aug. 29, Sept 5, Oct. 5–7, 1863; Diary #8, June 18, Aug. 10, Aug. 18; Sept. 29, 1864; Diary #13, Sept. 13, 1869; Diary #23, Dec. 4, Dec. 7, 1878; Diary #32, Mar. 29, 1883; Diary #48, Oct. 6–8, 1889).

Aside from Frank and Benjamin, it is likely that the old chief had many more children by his five wives. Canadian census material is incomplete and includes minimal information on this family. Since they were not American, they do not appear at all in the U.S. censuses. James G. Swan's diary entries, however, clearly state that Chief Cedakanim is the father of Frank and Benjamin Cedakanim, although he names no other children (Swan Diary #29, Aug. 30, 1880; Diary #48, Aug. 23, and Oct. 6, 1889). Swan does mention Frank Cedakanim's son Georgie (Diary #30, Oct. 15, 1881); Benjamin's daughter Annie (Diary #41, Aug. 16 and Oct. 2, 1887); and several of Cedakanim's other grandchildren (Diary #41, Aug. 16 and Oct. 2, 1887).

25. Swan Diary #6, Sept. 2, 1862; Diary #6, Aug. 21, Oct. 5, Oct. 9, 1863; Diary #8, Aug. 10, Oct. 18, 1864; Diary #9, June 20, 1865.

26. Swan Diary #10, Aug. 25, 1879.

27. Swan 1870:59.

28. Goodman Field Notes 1975. Aunt Edith Simon and Odelia Hunter both passed away in the mid-1980s.

29. These statements are most likely correct because other Canadian elders in the 1970s and early 1980s (now deceased) knew of the marriages and family connections between the Swan and Sitkeenum or Cedakanim families. Written documentation to either support or refute these relationships has not been discovered, however.

30. Moser 1926; Barrett-Lennard 1862; Jacobsen 1977; Sproat 1868; Anonymous 1864; Powell 1875.

31. Moser 1926:188–189.

32. Sproat 1868:189–190.

33. Sproat 1868:191–195.

34. Sproat 1868:195–196.

35. Sproat 1868:196.

36. Sproat 1868:196.

37. Barrett-Lennard 1862:131.

38. Barrett-Lennard 1862:130.

39. Powell 1875:52.

40. Moser 1926:174.

41. Atliu is also spelled Atliyu, Atlyou, Atleu, Artlyu, or Artlu (Swan Diaries and Letters 1862–1889; Newcombe Family Papers 1905–6; Canadian Census 1881; Drucker Field Notes, n.d.).

42. One of several written sources clearly shows that Atliu was the son of Cedakanim. In correspondence between Atliu and collector Charles F. Newcombe, the former wrote, on Dec. 28, 1905, that he was finishing a large house in memory of his father and brother, who died long ago. Newcombe responded, on Jan. 6, 1906, that he was glad that Atliu had put up a house in memory of his father, Cedakanim, who was a famous orator and politician (Newcombe Family Papers 1905–1906: Atliu Letters).

43. Annie and her father, Benjamin, are sometimes called Cedakanim and sometimes Atliu. Both surnames are correct and can be used interchangeably. The same is true in this publication. After her marriage, she was known as Annie Williams.

44. Supporting this statement by the two Clayoquot elders are the Canadian Census Returns for 1881. Annie is listed as the sixteen-year-old daughter of Atlyou (Census Office, Canada, 1881 Census Returns, B.C. Portion).

45. Goodman Field Notes 1975–1990.

46. Even though specific genealogical or census data has not been found, it seems likely that Francis Frank and his family are descended from Frank Cedakanim, whom James G. Swan mentioned numerous times in his diaries. Annie Williams, the daughter of Benjamin Cedakanim, or Atliu, selected her nephew, Charlie Swan, to inherit her father's belongings, because she had no son of her own. Alice and Ernest Curley were probably descended from one of Cedakanim's younger sons, named Curley Ishkab (fig. 2). Dixon, Stanley, Alice, Sidney, Evelyn, and Katy Sam are the children of Alice Curley Sam, and perhaps direct descendants from this son. The same is true of Ernest Curley's twelve children.

Each of the sons of Cedakanim may have had a different mother since the old chief is said to have had five wives. This then could account for the fact that the Swans, Franks, Curleys, and Sams know they are related to each other but are not quite certain how. They all know they are descended from Chief Cedakanim or Sitkeenum, and they all have ownership rights to certain objects and names which belonged either to the old chief or to his sons.

47. Flattery Jack's Indian name was spelled a number of ways by different authors, and often it was spelled differently even by the same author. Some of the more common spellings are as follows: Yelacob, Yelák'ub, Yalák'ub, Yellácub, Yellacum, Yall-a-coom, Yellúkub, Yellacoob, Yellicom, Yellow-cum, Yellowcub, Yasacum, Yulacuum, Yelak! ob (Kane 1925; Hancock 1927; Swan 1859; BIA 1960: Treaty Negotiations of 1855; BIA 1973: Makah Census Rolls, 1885–99; Gunther 1934b Census Notes).

48. Wilson 1850:53–56.

49. Included in the Minutes of the Makah Treaty Negotiations of January 30, 1855, was a statement by the Makah Chief Kalchote [Colchote], that Yall-a-coom, or Flattery Jack, had already died (BIA 1960). James G. Swan, when he first began keeping a Neah Bay Diary (Diary #2, Sept 22, Nov. 19, 1859), also stated that Flattery Jack had passed away but did not state the year. His Nov. 8, 1859, diary entry spoke of a letter signed by Governor Douglas of Vancouver

Island, dated Feb. 12, 1852, referring to help obtained from Flattery Jack. Since Paul Kane talked with this chief in 1847, and he was in good health then (Kane 1925:160–166), it is possible that Flattery Jack died in the smallpox epidemic of 1853. No census data exists and no other written records have been found to either confirm or refute this possibility.

50. Kane 1925:160–166.

51. Kane 1925:160–161.

52. Kane 1925:164–165. According to the official historical account of this tragedy, in 1811, the ship *Tonquin*, under the command of Captain Jonathan Thorn, who was greatly disliked by his crew, sailed north up the coast from the mouth of the Columbia River to trade with the Indians for sea otter skins and then to visit and trade with the Russians in Alaska. Along the way, trouble ensued. Since no whites lived to tell the tale, all details of the events which occurred on the west coast of Vancouver Island were later conveyed by the Indians, especially the one who escaped from the ship.

The *Tonquin* had probably stopped at Clayoquot Sound to trade with the natives. Captain Thorn wanted to conclude the arrangements quickly and move on; the Indians wanted to spend time bargaining. Thorn became impatient, surly, and disregarded the advice of crew members to let only a few Indians come on board the ship at one time. Finally, he struck one of the Indians—a terrible insult. As others of the crew feared, the next day the Indians returned to the ship to exact revenge; they killed all the white men on the deck, including Thorn. Five men who had been in the hold escaped notice, and four of them fled that night in a rowboat. The Indians soon found them, however, and killed them also. The fifth man evidently stayed on the ship until the Indians returned to loot it; then, either accidently or on purpose, he blew it up, killing approximately one hundred natives.

An Indian interpreter who had been on board and who did escape, eventually returned to Astoria and related the events he had seen (Avery 1961:107–109). According to Paul Kane (cited above), the Indian who escaped and told the story was Flattery Jack's father.

53. Hancock 1927:172–178.

54. Kane 1925:166.

55. Billy Balch was Sikesy's older brother. Willub was Billy Balch's Indian name as a young man; Yelák'ub was the name he received when he was older—the name that had formerly belonged to his father, Flattery Jack (Swan Diary #2: Nov. 8, Nov. 24, 1859; Diary #6, Dec. 18, 1863; Diary #8, Apr. 5, 1864; Diary #40, Oct. 24, 1886; Kane 1925:160–166).

56. Swan describes numerous incidents of Makah drinking and sharing behavior in his diaries, and over a number of years the following picture emerges. It appears that when one Makah chief acquired some alcohol he almost always shared it, traded it, or sold a portion of it to the other chiefs. There was no hoarding. When the chiefs had drinking parties, they also usually included their slaves. Most participants were men; only occasionally did one or more women join them. None of the chiefs were aware of the deleterious effects alcohol would have on them or their descendants in the future. Addiction was a concept entirely unknown to them. They just thought that drinking alcohol was a way to have some rowdy fun, and they all apparently enjoyed it. Sometimes the drinking got out of hand and fights, knifings and shootings resulted. Such incidents did not appear to quench the desire for alcohol more than temporarily, however. Statements by Swan and others regarding the dangers of alcohol were ignored by the Indians.

57. Swan Diary #2, Nov. 24, 1859; Swan Diary #40, Oct. 24, 1886.

58. Charley Williams, the son of Billy Balch, or Willub, was a different person from the Clayoquot Charlie Williams who was married to Annie Atliu and lived in Canada. Willub's

son lived in Neah Bay his whole life. Charley Williams of Neah Bay, died in 1905; two of his sons died in 1913; his wife, Laura, died in 1918; and their daughter died in 1931 (Swan Diary #6, Dec. 4, 1863; Diary #22, Oct. 7, Nov. 12, Dec. 3, 1877; BIA 1973: Makah Censuses 1885–1918; BIA 1901–33: Register of Vital Statistics).

59. Ellen was called by the following names: Ellen Sikesy, Ellen Swan, Ellen S. Balch, Wa-ái-chitl, Wo-ech-etl, We-ech-etl, Archillu, Achilloo, or A'chillu (Swan Diary #26, June 1, 1879; Diary #10, Feb. 24, 1880; Diary #30, Sept. 12, 1881; Diary #36, Aug. 23, 1884; Diary #41 Nov. 7, 1887; Diary #64, Aug. 27, 1898; BIA 1973: Makah Census Rolls 1885–1887).

60. According to James G. Swan, Ellen's baby was born on April 7, 1886 (Diary #39, Apr. 12, 1886). The 1886 and 1887 Makah Census Rolls show Ellen Swan living with her aunt, Mrs. Simmons, Dat-quia-bui, and the latter's husband. In 1886, Ellen has a four-month old baby called Lewis. No Indian name is given for him. Because Ellen and Chestoke were only married in the Indian fashion (BIA 1926, Miller Letter, Dec. 3), no husband is listed for Ellen in either year (BIA 1973: Makah Census Rolls 1885–1887). Lewis later became Charlie Swan, and documentation for his parentage does exist. According to the BIA 1935 Makah Basic Membership Roll, his mother is Ellen Swan and his father is Chestoqua Peterson.

61. No documents exist stating when or exactly why Ellen Sikesy changed her name to Swan. Perhaps it was because James G. Swan was like a father to her. Swan made no mention of her name change in his diaries and existing letters.

62. Swan describes these Makah words as meaning a girl's "monthly courses." Diary #28, Feb. 4, Feb. 11, 1880; Diary #10, Feb. 11, 1880.

63. And thus commenced a number of years of frequent letter writing between Swan, in Port Townsend, and several of the Makah children and teenagers in Neah Bay. Some continued to write to him even after becoming married adults with families of their own. These letters have not been found in existing archives and libraries. Unfortunately many were destroyed when a fire burned down the building in which Swan had his office (Diary #48, Oct. 14, 1889); and he, himself, burned some memorabilia on Dec. 4, 1894 (Diary #60), when he was feeling sad because most of the people from whom he had received them had died.

64. According to letters written by Sarah Willoughby, wife of the Indian agent in Neah Bay at that time, a measles epidemic broke out in September 1887. Many of the children became quite sick with it, and she nursed a number of them back to health. Some children and adults, however, did not survive. (Sarah Willoughby Letters, Sept. 27, Oct. 15, Oct. 31, 1887). Ellen Swan was among the latter.

65. In 1934, anthropologist Erna Gunther compiled a variety of types of information on the Makah for the U.S. Census Bureau. Evidently, at that time she talked with some of the old people in Neah Bay about their family histories and relationships. Thus, in her notes she included pieces of information not available elsewhere. A few of these notes expand the knowledge of Ellen Swan's ancestry.

According to Gunther, a woman by the name of Kudú·ʔi, a widow, lived with her daughter, named Xedatúk! baix (Hedátokobaitl) in Neah Bay. The latter had no descendants. However, Kudú·ʔi had another daughter who had died previously and left a child known as Ellen Swan. The family thought that Judge Swan [James G. Swan] gave Ellen the name "Swan." Ellen's child, Charlie Swan, used his mother's name (Gunther 1934b).

U.S. Census data supports some of the above information. The Makah Census Rolls of 1886–1913 show the older woman, Kudú·ʔi, living with her daughter, Xedatúk! baix, and the daughter's current husband. The names of each of them are spelled in a variety of ways over the years, but by checking the same family groups for each succeeding year, it is evident that these are the same individuals.

Kudú·ʔi, the older woman's name, may appear as Quidahe, Quidahu, Quedowe, or Codowie, and sometimes she is also listed as Ya-te-ba-sux, Ya-ha-ha-sux, or Ya-de-ba-sux, with Codowie written in parentheses. She died in 1914 (BIA 1973: Makah Census Rolls 1885–1939; BIA 1903: Register of Indian Families, 1903).

The names written for the daughter, Xedatúk! baix [Hedátokobaitl] vary even more than those for her mother. The younger woman may appear as Dat-quia-bui, Da-took-bi, He-dat-bi, He-da-to-ko-bailth, Ha-da-to-baik, He-da-took-ba-yitl, and He-da-ta-baik. In English she was listed as Mrs. Simmons (who became a widow in 1889), and as Mrs. Weassum, or Mrs. Weassub beginning in 1895. She again became a widow in 1917. Mrs. Weassum, He-da-ta-baik, died in 1924 (BIA 1973: Makah Census Rolls 1885–1939; BIA 1903: Register of Indian Families; BIA 1901–1933: Register of Vital Statistics. This woman, who was actually Charlie Swan's great-aunt, was Ellen Swan's mother's sister. She was the one who raised Charlie, and he called her "grandmother." Charlie Swan's real grandmother, named Whaubtedah, or Alice, had died in 1868 (Swan Diary #10, Feb. 24, 1880).

66. Swan Diary #10, Feb. 24, 1880. Since the U.S. Census was not officially begun in Neah Bay until 1885, it cannot be used to varify Swan's information.

67. Swan Diary #8, Nov. 22, 1864.

68. Swan Diary #11, August 13, 1867.

69. Swan Diary #38, Oct. 12, 1885.

70. Letter from Swan to Chestoqua Peterson, April 27, 1889. (Letters of J. G. Swan, 1887–1890).

71. Even though Chestoke Peterson was Charlie Swan's father, neither Chestoke nor Peter Brown took on the responsibility of caring for Ellen's child. It appears that initially her Canadian relatives were the principal people who tried to help Ellen's aunt and the child. As a teenager, Charlie Swan did live, for a few years, with his cousin Charley Williams, who was Billy Balch's son (BIA 1973: Makah Census Rolls 1903–1906). In this case, Ellen's father's brother's son was caring for her son.

72. Swan Diary #36, 1884.

73. Swan Diary #41, 1887.

74. Chestoke Peterson was listed as Peter Brown's son (BIA n.d.: Genealogy Sheet for Helma Swan; BIA 1927: Probate File #56085–26, Peter Brown) and as a member of the old chief's household from 1885 through 1899 (BIA 1973: Makah Census 1885–1899). Chestoke is listed as Charlie Swan's father on the 1935 Makah Basic Membership Roll, on the BIA n.d., Genealogy Sheet for Helma Swan, and in the Dec. 3, 1926, letter from James H. Miller, Examiner of Inheritance, to the Commissioner of Indian Affairs (BIA 1926).

75. Swan Diary #23, Nov. 16, 1878; BIA n.d.: Genealogy Sheet for Helma Swan.

76. The information about Chestoke's father has been passed down through the oral tradition and was the story Helma had heard about Chestoke Peterson. This bit of oral history is confirmed by James G. Swan, who spoke of Chestoke as a half-breed in a letter written Dec. 27, 1884, to Gen. Oliver Wood, Indian agent in Neah Bay (Letters of J. G. Swan, 1883–1885).

77. Letter dated Dec. 3, 1926, from James H. Miller, Examiner of Inheritance, to the Commissioner of Indian Affairs (BIA 1926).

78. Both Chestoke and James Peterson are listed in the Makah Census Roles through 1919. In 1920, both of their wives—Minnie Peterson and Nora Peterson—were listed as widows (BIA 1973: Makah Census Rolls 1885–1939). The father and son were considered drowned at

sea (BIA 1926), but their bodies were never found, and no other evidence of their whereabouts has been discovered.

79. Charlie Swan's first Indian name is recorded as Tlat-tla-kwokw by James G. Swan (back flap of Diary #41, 1887). Later, he was called Kitlchissub (Swan Diary #56, June 21, 1892). In BIA 1973: Makah Census Rolls, 1900–1902, he was noted as Kee-yak-to-do.

80. Documented statements and information on Charlie Swan are as follows:

James G. Swan noted that Ellen Swan's baby was born on April 7, 1886 (Diary #39, Apr. 12, 1886). No name was stated at that time.

BIA 1973: The Makah Census Rolls, 1885–1939 show the following sequence of events and name changes:

1886   The four-month-old baby of Ellen Swan, Wo-ech-etl, is listed as Lewis (with no last name). Ellen and baby are living with her aunt, Mrs. Simmons, Dat-quia-bui, and the latter's husband, Kakmal, or Simmons.

1888   Ellen Swan is no longer listed (she died on Nov. 7, 1887). Lewis Simmons is listed as "nephew" living with Mrs. Simmons, Dat-qua-bui, who in 1889 is listed as a widow. Mrs. Simmons's mother, Quid-a-hui, is living with them.

1892   Lewis Simmons, "son," is living with Mrs. Simmons, Dat-took-bi, widow, and the latter's mother, Que-do-we.

1894   Lewis Simmons becomes Charles Swan, "son" of Mrs. Simmons, Da-took-bi, widow. Que-do-we is living with them.

1896   Charles Swan is called "grandson" of Dat-took-bi, who has remarried and is now also called Mrs. We-as-sub.

1899   Charley Swan, "grandson," is living with Weasum and Mrs. Weasum.

1900   Charley Swan, Kee-yak-to-do, is living with Weasub and his wife, He-da-to-ko-baith. The old couple are no longer given English names but are known only by these Indian names in all of the subsequent censuses.

1912   We-ah-sum and He-da-te-ba-ik are still together and Ko-do-ie, also called Ya-ha-ha- sux, is living with them and is called the mother of He-da-te-ba-ik.

1917   Weasub has died and He-da-to-ba-ik is listed as a widow. Her mother has also died.

1918   He-da-ta-ba-ik is listed as "Charlie Swan's grandmother," a widow.

1921   He-da-ta-ba-ik is living with Charlie Swan's family. She continues to live with them until her death in 1924.

81. J. G. Swan Letter to Chestoqua Peterson, Apr. 27, 1889 (Letters of J. G. Swan, 1887–1890).

82. James G. Swan's health was deteriorating by 1898. No diaries have been found for 1899 or 1900, so it is possible that he was too ill to keep them. It is not known whether he had any further contact with Charlie Swan. The elder Swan died in May 1900.

83. Charley Williams was the son of Billy Balch (also known as Willub or Yelák'ub). Billy was the brother of Sikesy or Saxey Balch, Ellen Swan's father. Since their fathers were brothers, Charley Williams and Ellen Swan were cousins. Therefore Charley Williams and Charlie Swan, were also cousins (BIA 1973: Makah Census Rolls, 1885, 1903–1906; James G. Swan Diary #6, Dec. 19, 1863; Diary #23, Dec. 19, 1878; Diary #10, Oct. 4, 1879; Diary #31, Oct. 22, 1882; Diary #40, Oct. 24, 1886; Diary #58, back flyleaf, 1892).

84. BIA 1973: Makah Census Rolls, 1885–1939; BIA 1903: Register of Indian Families, 1903; BIA 1901–1933: Register of Vital Statistics, 1901–1933.

85. In the Makah Census Rolls of 1897–99 (BIA 1973), under the subcategory of Ozette,

Ruth Anderson is called Boos-sa-dook or Bus-sa-dook, the second daughter of Long Charley and Alice, from Ozette. From 1900–1901 she is called Hyas-walk, and from 1905–1907 she is called Hi-yesh-houtl.

86. According to Helma, her older sister, Katherine, married and left home as soon as possible so she would not have to care for her younger siblings. This left Helma, who, as the oldest remaining child, had to take on these responsibilities at age seven or eight.

87. Charlie Anderson was also called Ha-dow-a, Hi-dow-ey, or Long Charlie (BIA 1973: Makah Census Rolls, 1895–1937).

88. Only sketchy information concerning the Anderson family exists in published Makah census material. According to the Makah Census Rolls, 1885–1939, and the 1935 Makah Basic Membership Roll, the father of Charlie Anderson was called Charlie Skookum, Bek-took or Hek-took, and his mother was listed as Lucy or Lucy Skookum, It-te-sux, He-tue-e-sux, He-tue-e-sax, or E-tuts-te-e-sux. They all lived at Ozette.

Charlie Anderson's grandfather, also from Ozette, was called He-da-tuk-butled, or John Elliot in English. Charlie's grandmother may have been called Lucy Elliott, or Yi-yats-ko-itl. The census is not clear on the names and relationships of these two people. Since neither of them is listed in 1909 or thereafter, it is likely that they have passed away.

Charlie Anderson's first wife was Alice Taylor Anderson (1870–1937), from Quileute. She is listed in the Makah Census Rolls as We-le-shos-tub, or Alice Charlie, the wife of Long Charlie, until 1905; thereafter, she becomes Alice Anderson. Her father was Aubrey Taylor, perhaps called Abiti, and her mother was Rosie Taylor (perhaps known as Teshalup or Tesallup) (1935 BIA Makah Basic Membership Roll; BIA 1937b: Alice Anderson Holden Probate File #14753–40). According to BIA Swan Family Genealogy Sheets, Alice is listed as Alice Wellish Anderson; however, Helma states that this may have been a short form for her Indian name, Wileshóstub. Both the 1935 BIA Makah Basic Membership Roll and her probate record list her as Alice Taylor Anderson Holden.

In the Makah Census Rolls, 1885–1939, the Anderson family members were listed as residents of Ozette until 1907. Thereafter, they were listed as residents of Neah Bay. The U.S. government had ordered them, as well as other families with children, to move to Neah Bay so the children could attend school.

Charlie and Alice Anderson had three children. In the Makah Census Rolls, Anna Anderson Phillips (1890–1910) was listed as Soos-ue, Soos-ul, Wy-at-ta, Wy-uc-ti, or Wy-we- ti. Ruth Anderson Swan (1893–1979) was called Boos-sa-dook, Hy-as-walk, or Hi-yesh-houthl. Fred Anderson (1896–1966), the only son, was listed as Cha-la-a-lubs, Cha-la-a-luks, Qaulth-see-witch-it, or Koo-uth-a-we-chut.

Charlie and Alice Anderson divorced and each remarried in 1920. Charlie married Katie Holden Bennett, and Alice married Gilbert Holden (BIA 1937b: Alice Anderson Holden Probate File #14753–40; BIA 1937a: Charlie Anderson Probate File #14735–40). Katie and Gilbert were sister and brother. These second marriages lasted until the partners' deaths.

89. During the 1860s, James G. Swan noted in his diaries that the Makah moved to their "warm houses" about mid-March each year and moved back to Neah Bay or the other Makah winter villages, usually in August. The three summer villages that he mentions most frequently are Kíddekabat (where Helma's grandfather had a "warm house"), on Cape Flattery a few miles west of Neah Bay; Tatoosh Island, northwest of Cape Flattery; and Árchawat, on the west side of Cape Flattery (Swan Diary #3, Mar. 11, 1860; Diary #5, Mar. 23, 1862; Diary #6, Mar. 22, Aug. 6, 1863).

90. On her father Charlie Anderson's, Probate Record #14735–40 (BIA 1937a), Anna Anderson is listed as the first child, who died about 1910.

GLOSSARY

Words from the Makah song texts do not appear in this glossary due to a variety of linguistic changes necessary in order to accomodate the music. The words when sung are sometimes quite different from the spoken words.

Aab   Grandmother.

á·čpab   Stink eggs. King salmon eggs prepared in a special way to make a kind of caviar (very smelly).

Anderson Point   *See* Green Point.

Árchawat   Common spelling for one of three former Makah summer villages, this one located on the Pacific Ocean side of Cape Flattery between Tatoosh Island and Wyaatch (linguistic spelling: *Hač'á·wa?at*).

Báadah   A common spelling for one of the five former Makah winter villages, this one located just east of Neah Bay proper (linguistic spelling: *Bi?id?a*).

Baháda   Another common spelling for one of the five former Makah winter villages, located just east of Neah Bay proper (linguistic spelling: *Bi?id?a*).

ba?ás   A Makah longhouse where several related families lived, each in its own partitioned section.

bačidíx̣yak dukú·   "A song for dancing in." Originally this term meant that anyone could join the group that was getting ready to dance into the big house at the start of a ceremony. It has come to mean a Group Dance song. *See also hu·łeyíx̣yak dukú·.*

background dancing   Also known as backup dancing, it is performed by the women of one family as support for the male lead dancer. The women create a "U-shaped" formation, then dance, rotating, in place behind the lead male dancer. *See hu·łsáts'i?i.*

backup dancing   *See* background dancing.

ba·dápax̣   A singing session. A pleasant musical as well as social event held at an individual home, in the past, for the purpose of reviewing and practicing the family-owned songs of those attending. Singing sessions no longer occur.

Bi?id?a   Linguistic spelling of Bahádah or Báadah, one of the five former Makah winter villages.

bone game   A traditional Indian gambling game involving the hiding of bones and the singing of special bone game songs to insure winning power and to confuse the other side trying to guess in which hand the bones are hidden.

Cape Flattery   The point of land at the far northwest tip of the Olympic Peninsula in Washington State.

Cape Flattery People   Another name for the Makah tribe. *See also Kʷidič'če?at.*

čá·di·   One of two words for Tatoosh Island. *See also hupáčakt.*

chee marsh pil   According to James G. Swan, this is a term for a girl's "monthly courses."

čidí·qakt   A long string of seal ribs (prepared for eating).

čití·duk   A dentalium breastplate formerly worn by Makah women as a sign of wealth and high standing.

copper   *See λ'á·qʷa·.*

crest figure.   Either an animal or other supernatural creature with special characteristics that mark it as belonging to the particular family that owns it.

Dashúk   "strong." A name given to an Anderson family ancestor who escaped drowning in a whaling accident.

Díia   The former name for the town that is now called Neah Bay; more specifically, the western end of present-day Neah Bay.

Dinner Songs   Family-owned songs sung before the meal at a feast as a way of offering thanks and also showing appreciation to all those who helped make the event a success. No one begins eating until this singing is finished.

dudú·k   Sing.

dukú·   Song.

dukʷí·qsyak   "The one that is for leading the song," the lead singer, sometimes called the song leader.

Green Point   A wooded area just south of Tsooyez Beach on the Pacific Ocean side of the Makah reservation. Charlie Anderson built a house and lived there with his family for many years.

Group Dance   An entertainment dance in which anyone may participate, often performed for Makah Day and sometimes as a break between serious parts of a potlatch. Some are family-owned but none are strongly connected with power and status. *See also bačidíλyak dukú·.*

Haahm! Haahm!   The call of the Hámatsa or Cannibal Man when he is wild and untamed.

Hač'á·waʔat   Linguistic spelling of Archawat, one of the Makah summer villages.

hahá·wakts'ub   An activity that involves "sitting at the feet" of those who know and are giving a song—in other words, learning it from them; then, hosting a meal for the teachers as well as the witnesses.

Hámatsa   A secret initiation ceremony, known as the "Cannibal Dance," which first belonged to the Kwakiutl (Kʷákʷakyawakʷ) people and later was acquired through marriage by some of the Nootkan and Makah families.

he·tá·x̌   Daughter.

headgear   A family-owned, carved and painted, wooden headpiece that sits on top of the head and often represents a wolf, thunderbird, eagle, or sea serpent. It is worn by a lead dancer when performing at a potlatch.

hisí·ʔa·d   Red huckleberries.

hití·d   A dance cape.

hu·łeyíx̌yak dukú·   "A song for dancing in," at the beginning of a ceremony. The dance is already under way. More recently, this term has come to mean a Group Dance song. *See also bačidíx̌yak dukú·.* The two words have similar meanings.

hu·ɫsáts'iʔi Background dancing: "The one who is dancing in the back, in place." *See also* background dancing.

hú·ɫuk Dance.

hupáčakt Tatoosh Island—literally "something round, floating in the ocean." *See čá·di·.*

hux̌ʔádibiʔí·syak Town crier. The man who invites people to potlatches.

húx̌šiƛ Holler. This refers to particular hollered sounds made at the beginning of a potlatch just before the singing and dancing begin.

k'akyí·tsapix̌ Salal berries.

k'a·š č'uʔu· Harbor seal.

katesae chitl According to James G. Swan, this is a term for a girl's "monthly courses."

Kíddekabat Common spelling for one of three former Makah summer villages. Also called Midway, it is located on a Cape Flattery beach approximately three miles north and west of Neah Bay (linguistic spelling: *Q'idiq'ábit*).

k'idi·ɫ tubáts Sea anemones (or sea roses, as the Makah term them) found on the rocks in the tidal pools around Cape Flattery.

ki·kí·qama· Chiefs, in the Kwakiutl (Kʷákʷakyawakʷ) language ("chief" is ki·qama·).

Klúkwali Common spelling for the Makah Wolf ceremony in which young people were initiated into the secret society of the same name. Later in time, children were no longer allowed to attend these ceremonies. Now extinct (linguistic spelling: *ƛú·kʷali*).

kutx̌ú·tiʔi· Drummer. This term is used for the head drummer and for his assistants, no matter what type of drum is being played.

Kʷágiulth· A name currently used by some bands of the people formerly called Kwakiutl.

Kwakiutl· The former name for the tribe that lives directly north and east of the Westcoast (Nuu-cha-nulth) peoples on Vancouver Island and the adjacent mainland in British Columbia. *See also* Kʷákʷakyawakʷ, Kʷágiulth, and Kʷákʷala.

Kʷákʷakyawakʷ· A name currently used by many of the people formerly called Kwakiutl. *See also* Kwakiutl, Kʷágiulth, and Kʷákʷala.

Kʷákʷala· A name currently used by some bands of the people formerly called Kwakiutl.

kw'ičká·pix̌· Sea urchins (or sea eggs, as the Makah call them), found on beaches around Cape Flattery and eaten by the Makah.

Kʷidíč'čeʔat (also spelled **Kʷidich'cheʔat**) A common older spelling of the word the Makah people use when speaking of themselves: "People who live on the Rocky Point," or "the Cape People." *See also Maq'á·h and Qʷidičča'a·tx̌.*

ɫaqáta·tx̌ The Plains Indian Dance, now also called the War Dance; originally a partial imitation of a Yakima Dance.

la ul uch siouk The name of an herb given to females to assist in childbirth, according to James G. Swan in 1862.

lead dancing Traditionally performed by a male as the central character in a Makah family-owned potlatch dance. According to Helma, there is no special Makah term for this or for the lead dancer.

lí·šal The black shawl worn by a woman when dancing.

longhouse   A large cedar log and plank abode which housed several related families. *See also baʔás.*

ƛ'ačá·pł   Small black rocks used when weaving baskets, softening fish, making wood carvings shiny, and so forth.

ƛ'a·čqʷa·l   Small black-shelled limpets found on the beaches around Neah Bay.

ƛaʔíił   Literally, "a post standing up inside." Actually, a ceremony (perhaps borrowed from the Quileutes) that utilized personal guardian spirit songs for renewing supernatural power. It is now extinct.

ƛ'á·qʷa·   A "copper." A large, shieldlike sheet of hammered copper, owned by a chief. It symbolized his wealth and power and was often shown at potlatches. In the past, breaking a copper and giving a piece of it to another Westcoast chief obligated the receiver in certain ways to the giver.

ƛaƛakiš x̌ú·wís   "Two Rocks Standing." Two large rocks which stand like people in the water, offshore, near the old summer village of Midway on Cape Flattery.

ƛ'á·x̌sa·t'   "A patch on the head." A mask that consists either of a carved piece that sits in front on the forehead; or a helmet-type headgear which sits on top of the head, has a bird or bird beak carved on front and back, and has small vertical twigs stuck in the top to hold duck down.

ƛ'ix̌ p'í·q   "Half red." Used as a name for the Chief of Nootka, Captain Jack. This word means more than just half red, but Helma could not explain it further.

ƛ'ubú·xsit   "Something you sip on." Red snapper broth. Used for an upset stomach or for fever, a cold, or chills.

x̌ú·kʷali   Linguistic spelling of Klúkwali, the Makah Wolf Ceremony.

ƛ'uƛ'ubuq'ad   "The sound of something hitting," said in reference to a certain kind of noise, and used as the name of Ruth Swan's small flywheel motorboat.

Makáh   The current name of the Cape Flattery People, the Indian tribe inhabiting the northwest tip of the Olympic Peninsula in Washington State. *See also Kʷidič'čeʔat.*

Maq'á·h   A Clallam term for the Cape Flattery People, which, according to Helma, means "you never leave here without being full." It is the basis for the current Makah tribal name.

Midway   The English name for *Kíddekabat,* one of the former Makah summer villages located on Cape Flattery.

Neah Bay   The only surviving Makah village on the reservation.

Neeah   Name of a former Makah winter village that was located in the western portion of the present village of Neah Bay.

Nootka   The name given by Captain Cook to the Westcoast peoples in 1778 and commonly used until about the 1980s. The term refers to tribes along the west coast of Vancouver Island. *See also* Nuu-cha-nulth, *nutkší ʔa,* and Westcoast.

nu·tka·ʔičim   *See nutkší ʔa.*

nutkší ʔa or **nu·tka·ʔičim**   "Go around over there!" Said, perhaps, to guide European ships to a safe harbor. Later, this became the basis for the word *Nootka,* the name given by Captain Cook to the Westcoast peoples.

Nuu-cha-nulth   Literally, "mountains along a length." A name currently used by the former Nootkan tribes when referring to themselves. *See also* Westcoast.

oral tradition   A primary method for teaching the music and other elements of culture based on oral repetition and memorization.

Ozette   Common spelling for one of the five former Makah winter villages, this one located about fifteen miles down the west coast, at Cape Alava (linguistic spelling: *ʔuseʔił*).

p'a   To throw.

pachaetl   *See p'ačił.*

pachatl   *See p'ačił.*

p'ačił or **p'achił**   "To throw gifts." This term is used when speaking of giving gifts to those attending a potlatch who witness the use of family privileges, the transfer of names, songs, and other property. This word (sometimes spelled *pahchitl, pachaetl,* or *pachatl*) was later adopted into Chinook Jargon, becoming the word now known as "potlatch."

pahchitl   *See p'ačił.*

p'áp'ʔés   Cranberries.

"party"   The English word often used by the Makah when speaking of a potlatch ceremony.

Pentl'achee   Name of a Makah Group Dance, formerly performed at the beginning of a potlatch or for Makah Day but seldom performed today. This dance might have been borrowed from the Pentl'ach tribe of eastern Vancouver Island; however, specific knowledge of its origin remains obscure.

potlatch   A ceremonial display of inherited privileges, including songs and dances, where witnesses are paid to validate the proper ownership of these privileges. *See also p'ačił.*

qaʔáwats   Burden basket, used by the women when they picked berries.

q'abá·tšʔaƛ'   "The part with the Indian words!" Usually the second section of a song.

qákwey   Salmonberries.

qaqá·waš k'uk   Blackberries.

qeʔí·ks   Hooking one's fingers in the fish's gills. This was how a fish was picked up and brought home to be cooked in the old days.

Q'idiq'ábit   Linguistic spelling of Kiddekabat, one of the Makah summer villages.

q'íniq'ču   Indian dumplings.

q'its'é·yit   A "coming out," or womanhood potlatch, given in the past, for daughters of upper-class families.

quʔáyč'id   A person's spirit or shadow. Without it, one dies.

q'uq'u·dá·bats   A type of limpet shell with a sharp, pointed top found on beaches around Neah Bay.

qʷayáts'i·k   "Wolf," in the Clayoquot language.

Qʷidičča ʔa·tx̌   A recent linguistic spelling of the word for the Makah tribe. *See also Kʷidič'čeʔat.*

qʷi·qʷi·diččaq   Speaking the Makah language.

qʷišó·was   A small wooden structure, called a "smokehouse" in English, used only for smoking fish. No one lived in this structure.

Shakers   Members of the Indian Shaker Church, which includes a blend of Native and Christian religious elements.

sidúʔu· A small limpet found on the beaches around Neah Bay, smaller than those known as ƛ'a·čqʷa·l. Both were eaten by the Makah.

singing sessions *See ba·dápaƛ.*

song leader An individual who knows many family-owned songs and starts each song at a potlatch or other ceremony. In the past, this person often used a feather fan to keep time and to signal the chorus and the dancers. *See also dukʷi·qsyak.*

smokehouse A large rectangular wooden building with a dirt floor, three large fires down the center, and no interior wooden partitions. It was used for secret society gatherings and other ceremonies in the past. According to Helma Swan, no one lived in this type of smoke-house, which was different in structure and function from either a qʷišó·was or baʔás.

šuʔ "I'm ready now!"

súʔap "You catch the song!" At a ceremony, when the first song leader tires, he calls out this word, and the second song leader steps in and continues.

t'abáa Makah social or entertainment songs. Although some are family-owned, they are not considered among a family's important prestige songs. They are sung "just for fun."

Tapláa Eyes closed.

Ta·qʷáʔat "Poling out," a term used to refer to Green Point beach, on the Pacific Ocean.

taskea According to a James G. Swan, this is a carved, wooden cane.

Tatoosh The name of the island located north and slightly west of Cape Flattery. Also the name of a former Makah summer village which was located on this island. *See also čá·di·* and *hupáčakt.*

t'ič'ú·p Salmonberry sprouts cooked under the sand (on the beach).

tinethl. According to James G. Swan, this is a carved wooden club.

t'iqú·wił A pole inside the longhouse. Literally, "a place for sitting." Each tribe had a desig-nated pole where its members sat during potlatches.

t'í·tsqeyaƛ A straight, very fast drumbeat, sometimes called a drum tremolo.

Tsáyak Common spelling for a Makah curing ceremony performed by a secret society of the same name. Both are extinct (linguistic spelling: *Ts'á·yiq*).

ts'í·daxtup Small black chitons, eaten by the Makah, who also call them China Slippers.

tsíkyey. Elderberries.

Ts'í·qa A chant, formerly with sacred meanings. It is always accompanied by a rattle, never by a drum.

tsíq'tsíq qey yák A term for "speaker" at a potlatch. Each chief had his own speaker.

Tsóoyez Common spelling for one of the five former Makah winter villages; this one located on Tsooyez beach facing the Pacific Ocean (linguistic spelling: *Ts'ú·yas*).

Ts'ú·yas Linguistic spelling of Tsooyez, one of the former Makah winter villages.

tumánuwos A personal spirit helper which an individual seeks and acquires in private. It often bestows special powers, including songs, on its owner. It is a Chinook Jargon word, originally from the Chinook language, borrowed by the Makah.

tupáat A hereditary privilege, duty, or responsibility belonging to one person (formerly a chief), who was obligated to perform it or show it on particular ceremonial occasions. Aside from specific ceremonial duties, tupáats also included personal possessions such as songs, games, carvings, territorial rights, and so forth.

Two Rocks Standing *See ƛaƛakiš x̌ú·wis.*

ʔuʔiłt "First to be Called." The number one Head Chief of the Makah.

ʔu·ʔu·št'í·ɫyak A Makah fishing canoe.

ʔux̌wí·duk The process of chewing hard food for a baby, then putting it in the baby's mouth, so he or she won't choke. Old people used to do this for Makah infants and small children.

Waʔač' Linguistic spelling of Wyaatch, one of the former Makah winter villages.

Wáadah The small island in Neah Bay harbor, returned by the U.S. government to the Makah tribe in 1984 (linguistic spelling: *Waʔádʔa*).

Waʔádʔa Linguistic spelling of Wáadah, the island in Neah Bay harbor.

wá·bit Linguistic spelling of wahbit, meaning "extra food."

wáhbit Extra food. A wahbit potlatch is held when one person gives a large quantity of food to another (formerly a chief), who then hosts this ceremony to distribute the food. Or, this term can refer to extra food taken home by each family upon completion of any potlatch where excess food has been prepared.

Wakashan A language family that includes the Nootkan and Kwakiutl languages.

Warm House A general term meaning a summer house, formerly in one of the three Makah summer villages. More specifically, the name of Charlie Anderson's summer house, which was located just west of the village of Kíddekabat on Cape Flattery.

warm-up party A one-evening practice session occurring about a week before a potlatch.

Westcoast A name currently used by the former Nootkan tribes when referring to themselves. *See also* Nootka, *Nuu-cha-nulth,* and *nutkší?a.*

Wyaatch One of the five former Makah winter villages, this one located at the mouth of the Wyaatch River, on the north side (linguistic spelling: *Waʔač'*).

x̌ux̌ú·yaqƛ Black huckleberries.

Yaqʷáyats'i·k Wolf Dance Song that belonged to three Makah women. Ruth Anderson Swan was one of these women. *See also qʷayáts'i·k.*

yašá·baqats A Makah sealing canoe.

BIBLIOGRAPHY

Altman, George J.
1947   "Guardian Spirit Dances of the Salish." *Masterkey* 21(4):155–160.

Amoss, Pamela T.
1978   *Coast Salish Spirit Dancing: The Survival of an Ancestral Religion.* Seattle: University of Washington Press.

Andersen, Peggy
1998   "Whaling Takes Center Stage for Indian Tribe." *The New Mexican,* Oct. 1:C4.

Anonymous
1864   "Conflict with the Indians of Vancouver Island." *Illustrated London News,* Dec. 31.

Archer, Christon I.
1978   "Spanish Exploration and Settlement of the Northwest Coast in the 18th Century." In *Nu·tka· Captain Cook and the Spanish Explorers on the Coast.* Sound Heritage VII(1):33–53. Victoria, B.C.: Provincial Archives of British Columbia.

Arima, E. Y.
1983   *The West Coast (Nootka) People.* Special Publication no. 6. Victoria, B.C.: British Columbia Provincial Museum.

Arima, Eugene, and John Dewhirst
1990   "Nootkans of Vancouver Island." In *Handbook of North American Indians.* Vol. 7, *Northwest Coast,* ed. Wayne Suttles, 391–411. Washington, D.C.: Smithsonian Institution, GPO.

Avery, Mary W.
1961   *Washington, a History of the Evergreen State.* Seattle: University of Washington Press.

Bancroft, Hubert H.
1890   *History of Washington, Idaho, Montana, 1845–1889.* San Francisco: The History Company.

Barrett, Stanley R.
1996   *Anthropology: A Student's Guide to Theory and Method.* Toronto: University of Toronto Press.

Barrett-Lennard, Capt. C. E.
1862   *Travels in British Columbia.* London: Hurst and Blackett.

Black, Martha
1999   *Out of the Mist: Treasures of the Nuu-chah-nulth Chiefs.* Victoria, B.C.: Royal British Columbia Museum.
2001   "Out of the Mist: HuupuKwanum—Tupáat: Treasures of the Nuu-chah-nulth Chiefs." *American Indian Art Magazine* 26(2):44–53, 92–94.

Blackman, Margaret B.
1982   *During My Time: Florence Edenshaw Davidson, a Haida Woman.* Seattle: University of Washington Press.
1989   *Sadie Brower Neakok, an Inupiaq Woman.* Seattle: University of Washington Press.

Blinman, Eric, Elizabeth Colson, and Robert Heizer

  1977   "A Makah Epic Journey: Oral History and Documentary Sources." *Pacific Northwest Quarterly* 68(4):153–163.

Boas, Franz

  1891   "The Nootka." Sixth Report of the North-Western Tribes of Canada, 1890. In *Report of the British Association for the Advancement of Science* 60:582–604, 668–679.

  1895   "The Nootka." In *The Social Organization and the Secret Societies of the Kwakiutl Indians*, 632–644. Washington, D.C.: Annual Report of the U.S. National Museum.

Boyd, Robert T.

  1990   "Demographic History, 1774–1874." In *Handbook of North American Indians*, Vol. 7. *Northwest Coast*, ed. Wayne Suttles, 135–148. Washington, D.C.: Smithsonian Institution, GPO.

Boyer, Ruth M., and Narcissus D. Gayton

  1992   *Apache Mothers and Daughters: Four Generations of a Family.* Norman: University of Oklahoma Press.

Briggs, Jean L.

  1970   *Never in Anger: Portrait of an Eskimo Family.* Cambridge, Mass.: Harvard University Press.

Bureau of Indian Affairs (BIA)

  n.d.   Individual Genealogy Sheets (unpublished) for Swan Family Members: Helma Swan, C. Levi Swan, Michael J. Hunter. Included in Helma Swan family papers.

  1901–1933   Register of Vital Statistics, 1901–1933, including Record of Marriage Licenses, Makah, Births and Deaths 1910–1931. Preliminary Inventory Records of the Taholah Indian Agency: Roll Number 572. National Archives and Records Service, Washington, D.C.

  1903   Register of Indian Families, 1903. Preliminary Inventory Records of the Taholah Indian Agency: Roll Number 570. National Archives and Records Service, Washington, D.C.

  1923   Commissioner of Indian Affairs Correspondence: Feb. 24, Aug. 20, and Aug. 27, 1923. Record Group 75. Taholah Indian Agency, Decimal File 153: Proselytizing and Religious Controversies (Neah Bay, 1916–1933). National Archives and Records Service, Washington, D.C.

  1926   Letter from James H. Miller, Examiner of Inheritance, Dec. 3, 1926, to Commissioner of Indian Affairs. Record Group 75, Taholah Indian Agency, Decimal File 150, Inspections, Investigations, Reports, Etc., Neah Bay Agency. National Archives and Records Service, Washington, D.C.

  1927   Probate File, #56085–26, Peter Brown. Titles and Records Section, Branch of Realty, BIA Area Office, Portland, Oregon.

  1928–32   Taholah Indian Agency School Census of Indian Children. Record Group 75. Taholah Indian Agency, Decimal File 054: School Census of Indian Children. National Archives and Records Service, Washington, D.C.

  1931   Letter from Raymond H. Bitney, Indian Agent, to the Commissioner of Indian Affairs, March 3, 1931. Record Group 75, Preliminary Inventory Records of the Taholah Indian Agency, Decimal File 150: Inspection and Investigation Reports of Neah Bay, 1920–1933: Shaker Religion, Potlatches, etc. National Archives and Records Service, Washington, D.C.

  1932a   Letter from Dr. H. J. Warner, Medical Director, District 2, March 19, 1932. Record Group 75, Preliminary Inventory Records of the Taholah Indian Agency, Decimal

File 150: Inspection and Investigation Reports of Neah Bay, 1920–1933: Shaker Religion, Potlatches, etc. National Archives and Records Service, Washington, D.C.

1932b Letter from Commissioner of Indian Affairs, C. M. Rhoads to Mr. Nels O. Nicholson, Superintendent of the Taholah Indian Agency, April 18. Record Group 75, Taholah Indian Agency, Decimal File 806: Schools—Reservation, Boarding—Tulalip. National Archives and Records Service, Washington, D.C.

1935 Makah Basic Membership Roll, 4-1-35. Tribal Government Services Division, BIA Area Office, Portland, Oregon.

1936 Letter from Rudy's Radio Shop to Mr. N. O. Nicholson, Superintendent, Taholah Indian Agency, May 20. Record Group 75, Taholah Indian Agency, Decimal File 751: Moving Pictures, Etc., 1933–1940s. National Archives and Records Service, Washington, D.C.

1937a Probate File, #14735–40, Charlie Anderson. Titles and Records Section, Branch of Realty, BIA Area Office, Portland, Oregon.

1937b Probate File, #14753–40, Alice Anderson Holden. Titles and Records Section, Branch of Realty, BIA Area Office, Portland, Oregon.

1960 Documents Relating to the Negotiation of the Treaty of January 31, 1855, with the Makah Indians. Ratified Treaty No. 286. Treaty of Neah Bay, George Gibbs, Secretary. Record Group 75, Roll 5, Ratified Treaties 1854–1855. National Archives and Records Service, Washington, D.C.

1973 Indian Census Rolls (Makah), 1885–1940. Record Group 75, Rolls 283–286, Neah Bay Jurisdiction (Makah, Ozette, Quileute, and Hoh). National Archives and Records Service, Washington, D.C.

1976–1982 Annuals and Biennials, 7504. G.S.A., Washington, D.C.

Census Office, Canada.
1881 Census Returns. British Columbia Portion. Black Series - Canada, B-390. On microfilm, British Columbia Archives, Victoria.

Cole, Douglas and Ira Chaikin
1990 *An Iron Hand upon the People: The Law against the Potlatch on the Northwest Coast.* Vancouver, B.C.: Douglas and McIntyre.

Cole, Douglas, and David Darling
1990 "History of the Early Period." In *Handbook of North American Indians.* Vol. 7, *Northwest Coast,* ed. Wayne Suttles, 119–34. Washington, D.C.: Smithsonian Institution, GPO.

Colson, Elizabeth
1953 *The Makah Indians.* Minneapolis: University of Minnesota Press.

Commissioner of Indian Affairs
1852–1910 *Annual Reports of the Commissioner of Indian Affairs to the Secretary of the Interior.* Washington, D.C.: U.S. Government Printing Office.

Cruikshank, Julie
1990 *Life Lived Like a Story.* Lincoln: University of Nebraska Press.

Curtis, Edward S.
1916 "The Nootka." In *The North American Indian.* Vol. 11: 3–112, Norwood, Mass.: Plimpton Press.

Densmore, Frances
1939 *Nootka and Quileute Music.* Bureau of American Ethnology Bulletin 124. Washington, D.C.: Smithsonian Institution.

1943   *Music of the Indians of British Columbia.* Bureau of American Ethnology Bulletin 136. Washington, D.C.: Smithsonian Institution.

Dewhirst, John

1978   "Nootka Sound: A 4,000 Year Perspective." In *Nu.tka. The History and Survival of Nootkan Culture.* Sound Heritage VII(2):1–29. Victoria: Provincial Archives of British Columbia.

Dietrich, Bill.

1994   "Current Crisis 'Is No Surprise' to Scientists." *Seattle Times,* Apr. 6:A6–7.

Doig, Ivan

1980   *Winter Brothers.* New York: Harcourt, Brace and Co.

Drucker, Philip

1940   "Kwakiutl Dancing Societies." *Anthropology Records* 2:201–30. Berkeley: University of California Press.

n.d.   Field Notes. Chiefs, Family Histories, Other Ethnological Notes. Box 5, File 29. British Columbia Archives, Victoria.

n.d.   Field Notes. Hesquiat Seats, Clayoquot Genealogy. Box 5, File 32. British Columbia Archives, Victoria.

1951   *The Northern and Central Nootkan Tribes.* Bureau of American Ethnology Bulletin 144. Washington, D.C.: Smithsonian Institution.

1963   *Indians of the Northwest Coast.* Garden City, New York: The Natural History Press.

1965   *Cultures of the North Pacific Coast.* Scranton, Penn.: Chandler Publishing Company.

Duff, Wilson

1952   "The Upper Stalo Indians of the Fraser River, British Columbia." *Anthropology in British Columbia, Memoir No. 1.* Victoria, B.C.: British Columbia Provincial Museum.

Efrat, Barbara S., and W. J. Langlois

1978a   "The Contact Period as Recorded by Indian Oral Traditions." In *Nu·tka· Captain Cook and the Spanish Explorers on the Coast.* Sound Heritage VII(1):54–62. Victoria: Provincial Archives of British Columbia.

1978b   "Contemporary Accounts of Nootkan Culture; Potlatches and Music." In *Nu·tka· The History and Survival of Nootkan Culture.* Sound Heritage VII(2):34–44. Victoria: Provincial Archives of British Columbia.

Ernst, Alice

1952   *The Wolf Ritual of the Northwest Coast.* Eugene: University of Oregon Press.

Gluckman, Max

1968   "The Utility of the Equililbrium Model in the Study of Social Change." *American Anthropologist* 70:219–37.

Goddard, Earl Pliny

1934   *Indians of the Northwest Coast.* 2nd ed. Handbook Series No. 10, New York: American Museum of Natural History.

Goodman, Linda J.

1974–1995   Field Notes, Makah.

1977   *Music and Dance in Northwest Coast Indian Life.* Occasional Papers, Vol. 3, Music and Dance Series No. 3. Tsaile, Ariz.: Navajo Community College Press.

1978   This is My Song: The Role of Song as Symbol in Makah Life. Ph.D. Dissertation, Washington State University.

1986   "Nootka Music." In *The New Grove Dictionary of American Music,* ed. Stanley Sadie and H. Wiley Hitchcock, 3: 380–82. London: Macmillan Press.

1991   "Traditional Music in Makah Life." In *A Time of Gathering: Native Heritage in Washington State,* ed. Robin Wright, 223–233. Seattle: Burke Museum and University of Washington Press.

1992   "Aspects of Spiritual and Political Power in Chief's Songs of the Makah Indians." *The World of Music: Journal of the International Institute for Traditional Music* 34(2):23–42.

2001   "Northwest Coast." In *The Garland Encyclopedia of World Music,* Vol. 3, *The United States and Canada,* ed. Ellen Koskoff, 394–403. New York: Garland Publishing.

Goodman, Linda, and Helma Swan
1999   "Makah Music: Preserving the Traditions." In *Spirit of the First People: Native American Music Traditions of Washington State,* ed. Willie Smyth and Esmé Ryan, 81–105. Seattle: University of Washington Press.

Gough, Barry M.
1978   "Nootka Sound in James Cook's Pacific World." In *Nu·tka. Captain Cook and the Spanish Explorers on the Coast.* Sound Heritage VII(1):1–31. Victoria: Provincial Archives of British Columbia.

Guillod, Harry
1882–1900   Annual Reports for the West Coast Indian Agency. In *Annual Reports of the Department of Indian Affairs.* Ottawa: Dominion of Canada.

Gunther, Erna
1934a   Facts Derived from 1888 and 1903 Makah Censuses, Allotment Records, and Agency Records. Accession 614–70–20, Folder 1–29. MSCUA, University of Washington Libraries, Seattle.

1934b   Information relating to Map of Neah Bay, 1934, and Census by House, 15 and 48, Neah Bay, 1934. Accession 614–70–20, Folder 1–27. MSCUA, University of Washington Libraries, Seattle.

1960   "Makah Marriage Patterns and Population Stability." *Proceedings of the International Congress of Americanists* 34:538–45.

1972   *Indian Life on the Northwest Coast of North America as Seen by the Early Explorers and Fur Traders.* Chicago: University of Chicago Press.

1974   *Ethnobotany of Western Washington.* Revised ed. Seattle: University of Washington Press.

Hancock, Samuel
1927   *The Narrative of Samuel Hancock, 1845–1860.* New York: Robert M. McBride.

Henry, John F.
1984   *Early Maritime Artists of the Pacific Northwest Coast, 1741–1841.* Seattle: University of Washington Press.

Highsmith, Richard M., Jr.
1973   *Atlas of the Pacific Northwest.* 5th ed. Corvallis: Oregon State University Press.

Ho, Vanessa
1994   "Native Americans Mourn the Devastation of a Cultural Mainstay." *Seattle Times,* Apr. 6: A8.

Holm, Bill
1977   "Traditional and Contemporary Southern Kwakiutl Winter Dance." *Arctic Anthropology* 14(1):5–24.

1978   Class lecture notes for a course entitled Drama and Dance of the Northwest Coast Indians. University of Washington, Seattle.

Hoonan, Charles E.

1964 *Neah Bay, Washington: A Brief Historical Sketch.* Seattle: Crown-Zellerbach Corporation.

Hoover, Alan, and Richard Inglis

1990 "Acquiring and Exhibiting a Nuu-Chah-Nulth Ceremonial Curtain." *Curator* 33(4):272–88.

Jacobs, Sue-Ellen

1995 "Continuity and Change in Gender Roles at San Juan Pueblo." In *Women and Power in Native North America*, ed. Laura F. Klein and Lillian A. Ackerman, 177–213. Norman: University of Oklahoma Press.

Jacobsen, Johan Adrian

1977 *Alaskan Voyage 1881–1883*, trans. Erna Gunther. Chicago: University of Chicago Press.

Jewitt, John R.

1975 *Narrative of the Adventures and Sufferings of John R. Jewitt While Held as a Captive of the Nootka Indians of Vancouver Island, 1803–1805*, ed. Robert F. Heizer. Ramona, Calif.: Ballena Press.

Jones, Chief Charles with Stephen Bosustow

1981 *Queesto, Pacheenaht Chief by Birthright.* Nanaimo, B.C.: Theytus Books.

Jones David E.

1972 *Sanapia, Comanche Medicine Woman.* New York: Holt, Rinehart and Winston.

Josephy, Alvin M.

1969 *The Indian Heritage of America.* New York: Bantam Books.

Judd, Ron

1994 "At Every Step, Politics Took Precedence Over Salmon." *Seattle Times*, Apr. 6:A5, 8.

Kane, Paul

1925 *Wanderings of an Artist among the Indians of North America.* Toronto: The Radisson Society of Canada.

Keeling, Richard

1989 *Women in North American Music: Six Essays.* The Society for Ethnomusicology, Inc. Special Series No. 6, Bloomington, Indiana.

Kenyon, Susan

1980 *The Kyuquot Way: A Study of a West Coast (Nootkan) Community.* Mercury Series, No. 61. Ottawa: The National Museum of Man.

Klein, Laura F.

1995 "Mother as Clanswoman: Rank and Gender in Tlingit Society." In *Women and Power in Native North America*, ed. Laura F. Klein and Lillian A. Ackerman, 28–45. Norman: University of Oklahoma Press.

Klein, Laura F., and Lillian A. Ackerman.

1995 "Introduction." In *Women and Power in Native North America*, ed. Laura F. Klein and Lillian A. Ackerman, 3–16. Norman: University of Oklahoma Press.

Koppert, Vincent

1930 *Contributions to Clayoquot Ethnography.* Washington, D.C.: Catholic University.

Koskoff, Ellen

1987 "An Introduction to Women, Music, and Culture." In *Women and Music in Cross Cultural Pespective*, ed. Ellen Koskoff. Contributions in Women's Studies, no. 79. New York: Greenwood Press.

Kozloff, Eugene
    1982   *Plants and Animals of the Pacific Northwest.* Seattle: University of Washington Press.

Lewis, Lucien M.
    1905   "The Last of the Makah Chiefs, Chief Peter (How-a-thlub)." *Seattle Post-Intelligencer,* Nov. 26.

Lurie, Nancy Oestreich, editor
    1973   *Mountain Wolf Woman, Sister of Crashing Thunder.* Ann Arbor: The University of Michigan Press.

Makah Language Program
    n.d.   Qʷiˑqʷiˑdiččaq, Makah Alphabet Pronunciation Key. Unpublished guide housed at the Makah Cultural and Research Center, Neah Bay, Washington.

Mapes, Lynda V.
    1998   "Feds Have Whale of Conflict." *Seattle Times,* Oct. 15: A1, 18.

Marino, Cesare
    1990   "History of Western Washington Since 1846." In *Handbook of North American Indians.* Vol. 7, *Northwest Coast,* ed. Wayne Suttles, 169–79. Washington, D.C.: Smithsonian Institution, GPO.

Marr, Carolyn
    1987   *Portrait in Time: Photographs of the Makah by Samuel G. Morse, 1896–1903.* Neah Bay, Washington: The Makah Cultural and Research Center in cooperation with the Washington State Historical Society.

Mauger, Jeffrey E.
    1991   "Shed-Roof Houses at Ozette and in a Regional Perspective." In *Ozette Archaeological Project Research Reports.* Vol. I, *House Structure and Floor Midden,* ed. Stephan R. Samuels. Washington State University Department of Anthroplogy Reports of Investigations 63:31–173. Seattle: National Park Service, Pacific Northwest Regional Office.

McCurdy, James G.
    1961   *Indian Days at Neah Bay.* Seattle: Superior Publishing Co.

Miller, Genevieve H.
    1972a   "Our Northwest Heritage: Peter, Chief of the Makahs (Part 1)." *Age of Achievement* 3(2):1, 10.
    1972b   "Our Northwest Heritage: Peter, Chief of the Makahs (Part 2)." *Age of Achievement* 3(3):14–15.

Moser, Reverend Charles
    1926   *Reminiscences of the West Coast of Vancouver Island.* Victoria, British Columbia: Acme Press.

Moziño, Jose Mariano
    1970   *Noticias de Nutka,* ed. and trans. I. H. Wilson. American Ethnological Society Monograph 50. Seattle: University of Washington Press.

Newcombe, Charles F.
    1905–1906   Family Papers: Atliu Letters. Vol. 1, Folder 9. British Columbia Archives, Victoria.

Ortner, Sherry B.
    1974   "Is Female to Male as Nature Is to Culture?" In *Woman, Culture, and Society,* ed. Michelle Z. Rosaldo and Louise Lamphere, 67–88. Stanford, Calif.: Stanford University Press.

Ortner, Sherry, and Harriet Whitehead

    1981   "Introduction: Accounting for Sexual Meanings." In *Sexual Meanings: The Cultural Construction of Gender and Sexuality,* ed. Sherry B. Ortner and Harriet Whitehead, 1–27. Cambridge: Cambridge University Press.

Pethick, Derek

    1976   *First Approaches to the Northwest Coast.* Vancouver, B.C.: Douglas and McIntyre.

Powell, I. W., Indian Commissioner

    1875   Report of the Deputy Superintendent General of Indian Affairs, Canada. *Annual Report for the Province of British Columbia,* No. 28:44–53.

Prattis, Ian

    1996   "Reflexive Anthropology." In *Encyclopedia of Cultural Anthropology,* ed. David Levinson and Melvin Ember. Vol. 3:1072–1076. New York: Henry Holt and Company.

Pryne, Eric

    1994   "Many Fish Species on Decline in Northwest." *Seattle Times,* Mar. 18:A16.

Reagan, Albert B.

    1934   "Some Traditions of the West Coast Indians." Proceedings of Utah Academy of Sciences, Arts, and Letters 11:73–93.

Renker, Ann

    1994   "Makah." In *Native America in the Twentieth Century: An Encyclopedia,* ed. Mary B. Davis. Garland Reference Library of Social Science, 452:326–327. New York: Garland Publishing.

Renker, Ann M. and Erna Gunther

    1990   "Makah." In *Handbook of North American Indians.* Vol. 7, *Northwest Coast.* 422–30. Washington, D.C.: Smithsonian Institution, GPO.

Roberts, Helen H., and Morris Swadesh

    1955   *Songs of the Nootka Indians of Western Vancouver Island.* Transactions of the American Philosophical Society, New Series Vol. 45, Part 3. Philadelphia, Penn.: American Philosophical Society.

Rosaldo, Michelle Zimbalist

    1974   "Woman, Culture, and Society: A Theoretical Overview." In *Woman, Culture, and Society, ed.* Michelle Z. Rosaldo and Louise Lamphere, 17–42. Stanford, Calif.: Stanford University Press.

Rosaldo, Michelle, and Louise Lamphere

    1974   "Introduction." In *Woman, Culture, and Society,* ed. Michelle Z. Rosaldo and Louise Lamphere, 1–15. Stanford, Calif.: Stanford University Press.

Royal Commission on Indian Affairs

    1916   *Report of the Royal Commission on Indian Affairs for the Province of British Columbia.* Vol. 4, *Minutes,* 849–908.

Ruby, Robert H., and John A. Brown

    1986   *A Guide to the Indian Tribes of the Pacific Northwest.* Norman: University of Oklahoma Press.

Samuels, Stephan R., and Richard D. Daugherty

    1991   "Introduction to the Ozette Archaeological Project." In *Ozette Archaeology Project Research Reports,* Vol. 1, *House Structure and Floor Midden,* ed. Stephen R. Samuels, 1–27. Washington State University Department of Anthropology Reports of

Investigations 63:31–173. Seattle: National Park Service, Pacific Northwest Regional Office.

Sapir, Edward

1911　"Some Aspects of Nootka Language and Culture." *American Anthropologist,* New Series 13:15–28.

1913　"A Girl's Puberty Ceremony among the Nootka." *Transactions of the Royal Society of Canada,* 3rd ser., 7(2):67–80.

1967　"The Social Organization of the West Coast Tribes." In *Indians of the North Pacific Coast,* ed. Tom McFeat, 28–48. Seattle: University of Washington Press.

Sapir, Edward, and Morris Swadesh

1939　*Nootka Texts: Tales and Ethnological Narratives.* Philadelphia: University of Pennsylvania, Linguistic Society of America. (Reprinted: New York: AMS Press 1978).

1955　*Native Accounts of Nootka Ethnography.* International Journal of American Linguistics 21, Part 2: 1–452. (Reprinted New York: AMS Press 1978).

Shaw, George C.

1965　*The Chinook Jargon and How to Use It.* Facsimile reproduction of 1909 edition, Seattle: Shorey Bookstore.

Shukovsky, Paul

1998a　"The Makah Hunt: Tribe Women Working to Revive Spirit of 'Old Ones.'" *Seattle Post-Intelligencer.* Oct. 7:A1, 4.

1998b　"Makah Postpone Whale Hunt—And Danger at Sea Grows." *Seattle Post-Intelligencer,* Oct. 15:A1, 13.

Spicer, Edward H.

1969　*A Short History of the Indians of the United States.* New York: Van Nostrand.

Sproat, Gilbert Malcolm

1868　*Scenes and Studies of Savage Life.* London: Smith, Elder, and Co.

Suttles, Wayne

1987a　*Coast Salish Essays.* Seattle: University of Washington Press.

1987b　"Spirit Dancing and the Persistence of Native Culture Among the Coast Salish." In *Coast Salish Essays.* Seattle: University of Washington Press.

1991　"The Shed-Roof House." In *A Time of Gathering: Native Heritage in Washington State,* ed. Robin Wright, 212–222. Seattle: Burke Museum and University of Washington Press.

Swan, James G.

1859–1898　Diaries. MSCUA, University of Washington Libraries, Seattle.

1862　"Scenes among the Mackahs: Taking the Census." *Washington Standard,* II(13):1. (Feb. 8).

1870　*The Indians of Cape Flattery.* Smithsonian Contributions to Knowledge 16(8):1–106. Washington, D.C.: Smithsonian Institution, GPO.

1883–1885　Letters of J. G. Swan, Sept. 29, 1883–Jan. 14, 1885. Bound volume, copies. Seattle Historical Society Library.

1887–1890　Letters of J. G. Swan, Jan. 30, 1887–Jan. 18, 1890. Bound volume, copies. Seattle Historical Society Library.

1891–1893　Letters of J. G. Swan, Oct. 1, 1891–June 27, 1893. Bound volume, copies. Seattle Historical Society Library.

1893–1896　Letters of J. G. Swan, June 27, 1893–Nov. 1, 1896. Bound volume, copies. Seattle Historical Society Library.

1892   Letter to Franz Boas, June 22, 1892. Seattle Historical Society Library.

1893   Letter to Franz Boas, October 23, 1893. Seattle Historical Society Library.

1971   *Almost Out of the World.* Tacoma: Washington State Historical Society.

Turner, Nancy J.

1975   *Foodplants of British Columbia Indians, Part 1—Coastal Peoples.* Handbook No. 34. Victoria: British Columbia Provincial Museum.

U.S. Census

1990   Census Labor Force, Education and Income Data for Makah Reservation, Washington. 1990 Census, Sample Data from STF 3A, compiled by Indian & Native American Employment and Training Coalition, photocopies.

U.S. Congress. Senate. Committee on Indian Affairs.

1904   "Treaty with the Makah, 1855." In *Indian Affairs. Laws and Treaties,* Vol II, *(Treaties).* 58th Cong., 2nd sess., S. Doc. 319:682–685. ed. and comp. Charles J. Kappler. Washington, D.C.: G.P.O.

Webster, Peter S.

1983   *As Far As I Know: Reminiscences of an Ahousat Elder.* Campbell River, B.C.: Campbell River Museum and Archives Society.

Whitaker, Mark P.

1996   "Reflexivity." In *Encyclopedia of Social and Cultural Anthropology,* ed. Alan Barnard and Jonathan Spencer, 470–475. New York: Routledge.

Wight, E.L., Mary Mitchell, and Marie Schmidt, compilers and editors

1960   *Indian Reservations of Idaho, Oregon, and Washington.* U.S. Department of the Interior, Bureau of Indian Affairs, Portland Area Office.

Williams, Marla

1994a   "Anger, Blame Dominate as Season Closure Looms." *Seattle Times,* Apr. 6: A1, 9.

1994b   "Running Out of Time." *Seattle Times,* Apr. 6:A5.

1994c   "Salmon Fishing Off Coast Hit Hard." *Seattle Times,* Apr. 9:A1, 12.

Williams, Marla, and Bill Dietrich

1994   "Coastal Fishing Areas Begin Bracing for the Worst, Start Looking for Relief." *Seattle Times,* Mar. 18:A1, 16.

Williams, Scott

1994   "Coastal Towns Stand to Take Tremendous Hit in Fishing Closure." *Seattle Times,* Apr. 6:A8.

Willoughby, Sarah

1887   Letters dated Sept. 27, Oct. 15, Oct. 31, 1887. Correspondence Outgoing. Box 2, Folder 2–15. Charles and Sarah Willoughby Papers. Manuscripts, Special Collections, University Archives Division, University of Washington Libraries, Seattle.

Wilson, George O.

1849–51 Journal of a Voyage from East Machias, State of Maine, to San Francisco, California [1849–1850] on board of the Brig Oriental, [and . . . from San Francisco to Puget Sound, Oregon on board the Brig Geo. Emory, 1850–1851]. Photostat of unpublished manuscript. MSCUA, University of Washington Libraries, Seattle.

Winick, Charles

1961   *Dictionary of Anthropology.* Patterson, N.J.: Littlefield, Adams.

INDEX

Aab (grandmother), 74, 77, 89, 303. *See also* Hedatokobaitl

A'chillu, 265. *See also* Swan, Ellen

Ackerman, Lillian, 11–12, 13–14

Ah a yah, 243, 258

Ahouset, B.C., 169, 252

Alcohol (drinking), 39, 190, 192, 193, 194, 195, 247, 258, 260, 298n.56

American Council of Learned Societies, 5

Amos, Margaret, 273n.4

Anderson, Alice Taylor. *See* Holden, Alice Taylor (Anderson)

Anderson, Anna (Phillips), 17, 272, 302n.90

Anderson, Charlie (Chief), 56–65, 271–72; basket making, 69, 129, 272; caring for grandchildren, 58–66, 81; ceremonial property of, 130–31, 149, 205, 272; family history, 17, 270, 302n.88; fishing, 60, 79, 272, 283n.9; gardening, 56–58, 59, 272; names, 302n.87; peeling cedar bark, 59; singing and dancing, 130–31, 145, 272; teaching Swan children, 21, 67, 69, 272

Anderson, Elliot, 69–73, 79, 282n.20; adopts Bessie Swan (Bain), 72, 282n.21; basket making, 69; cobbler, 72; seal hunting, 70–71, 93; song composing, 71–72; work on telephone lines, 70

Anderson, Fred (Freddie), 17, 79, 117–18, 145; basket making, 69; family history, 302n.88; fishing, 17, 91; singing ƛaʔiiɬ songs, 118

Anderson, Katy, 60–62, 131; family history, 302n.88; storytelling, 65

Anderson, Ruth. *See* Swan, Ruth Anderson

Animal designs, 88, 142–43, 144, 288–89n.17

Anthropological field methods, 8–9

Anthropological theories: balanced reciprocity, 11–12, 13–14, 275n.19; feminist anthropology, 10–11; Max Gluckman's equilibrium model, 12–13; reflexive anthropology, 273n.3

Apples, distributed as food gifts, 165–67

Árchawat, 28, 277n.11, 302n.89, 303

Archillu, 263, 264, 265. *See also* Swan, Ellen

Arnold, Alice, 290–91n.2

Arnold, Greig, 150, 290n.1, 290–91n.2, 293n.5(ch.9)

Arts and crafts, 28, 41. *See also* Basket making

Asbie, 260

As-chad-a-bek, 15. *See also* Brown, Peter (Chief)

Assembly of God Church, 187

Assimilation, government policy, 35–38

Atleo, Mr. and Mrs., 155

Átliu, 17, 297nn.42, 43. *See also* Cedakanim, Benjamin (Chief)

August, Billy, 169

Babysitting, 77–78, 82–86, 98, 110–111. *See also* Child-care

Background dancing, 120, 138–39, 145, 287n.8, 303

Baháda, 26, 278n.51, 303

Bain, Bessie Swan, 17, 86; helping with potlatch, 47; living with uncle, Elliot Anderson, 72, 282n.21; performing at potlatches, 157, 186, 206

Balanced reciprocity, 11–12, 13–14, 275n.19

Balch, Billy (Chief), 16, 247, 257–61, 295n.19; family history, 16, 258–59, 298n.55, 301n.83; James G. Swan's writings about, 257–60, 263; names, 260

Balch, Sikesy (or Saxey), 16, 210, 256–61; family history, 16, 256, 259, 262, 264, 269, 298n.55, 301n.83; James G. Swan's writings about, 258–60, 262–63

Ball, Ida, 190–91

Bamfield, B.C., 169

Barker, Nora, 149, 153, 155, 159. *See also* Peterson, Nora

Baseball games, 125, 163–64

Baskets/basket making, 41, 68, 69, 76–77,

"Getting under power," 117–18

Ghost Dance, 125

"Giving away" (gifts) at potlatches, 30, 43, 45, 47, 49–50, 156–57, 161, 177, 178, 180, 200, 291n.10, 292n.13, 293n.17

Gluckman, Max, 12–13

Gold River, B.C., 49, 141, 198, 208

Goldstein, Mr. (Tulalip teacher), 105

Goodman, Linda J., 3–5; helping with potlatch preparations, 9, 46–50, 291n.5; life history research, 4–5, 8–10; relationship with Helma, 3–5; research funding, 5

Goodwin, John, 290n.1

Green, Alec, 145, 148, 158, 159

Green, Francis, 158, 159

Green, Ham, 159

Green, Lester, 290n.1

Green, Lucy, 186

Green, Walter, 159

Green Point, Wash., 56–60, 64–65, 272, 304

Grizzly Bear Dance, 49, 152, 156

Grizzly Bear Dance headdress and costumes, 112, 142, 208–10

Grizzly Bear Dance songs, 112, 130, 141–42, 143, 178, 208–10; musical analysis, 233–34; ownership, 186; transcription, 222–24

Group Dances, 45, 48, 51, 153, 159–61, 286n.13, 291n.6, 304; costumes for, 160–61; types of, 125

Group Dance songs, 45, 48, 51, 160, 286n.13

Guardian spirit. See Tumánuwos

Gunther, Erna, 299–300n.65

Guy, James, 286n.13

Gypos, 40, 279n.73

Haatz (Chief), 271

Halibut, 28, 29, 60, 67, 88, 92, 266

Halls, for dances and ceremonies, 88, 112, 117, 126, 159

Ha ma sée took, 253

Hámatsa (Cannibal Dance), 32, 44, 49, 171, 176–77, 304; costume, 176–77, 180, 291n.9, 293n.16; songs, 44, 49, 151, 170, 179, 285n.4; tame, 177; wild, 176–77

Hamatsa Society, 117, 285n.4

Hammond, Pat, 290n.1

Hancock, Samuel, 34, 244, 257, 294n.5

Harmonica band, 107, 162–63

Hayes, Mr. (Indian agent), 246

Haying, 59, 100–102, 284n.3

Hayte, Edwin, 283n.2, 285n.4

Headgears, 112, 139–40, 141–42, 147, 208–209, 211–12, 304

Head Start Center, 197

Healing and curing. See Curing practices

Hedatokobaitl (Mrs. Weassub), 16, 282n.25, 283n.4; arranged marriage of Charlie and Ruth Swan, 270; basket making, 76–77; caring for grandchildren, 74–78; family history, 16–17, 264, 299–300n.65; names, 299–300n.65, 301n.80; raising Charlie Swan, 268–69, 301n.80

He-dow-a. See Anderson, Charlie (Chief)

Hi-yesh-houtl. See Swan, Ruth Anderson

Hobucket, Harry, 148

Hoh, 7, 47, 49–50, 110, 112, 156, 194

Hoko River, 26, 276n.9

Holden, Alice Taylor (Anderson), 17, 79, 270; caring for grandchildren, 56, 68, 81–83; family history, 56, 281n.5, 302n.88; food gathering and preparation, 81–83; gardening, 58; Indian Shaker Church, 131, 287n.3; names, 302n.88; singing lullabies, 68; singing X̣aʔlil songs, 117–18; speaking Quileute, 69

Holden, Gilbert, 66, 79; house at Tsooyez, 281n.12; marriage, 56

Holden, Tom, 66, 281n.12

Holm, Bill, 279n.83, 284n.2, 293n.5(ch.10)

Hoonan, Charles, 285n.8

Horse Dance, 125, 159

Horses and races, 56, 100, 124

Houses, 38–39, 88, 181, 185–86, 188, 281n.12, 283nn.4, 5, 285n.7; built by Charlie Swan, 89, 102–103, 270; Charlie Anderson's, 62; longhouses, 28, 38, 277n.13, 281–82n.15, 285n.7; smokehouses, 121, 281–82 n.15

Housing and Urban Development (HUD) housing, 39

How-á-thlub. See Brown, Peter (Chief)

Huckleberries, 81, 83, 101

Hudson, David, 147

CPSIA information can be obtained
at www.ICGtesting.com
Printed in the USA
LVHW101619160421
684727LV00014B/521